About the Authors

Robert Oliver is the head network administrator of the Columbus State University software engineering project in Columbus, Georgia. A Microsoft Certified Professional in Windows NT, and a Visual C++ software engineer, he is part of the special projects group which received Microsoft's "Innovators in Higher Education Award," one of five worldwide awards for the most innovative uses of Microsoft's new technology. He is part of the New Technology Group; a software design team founded by Dr. James Leonard, whose program won the Microsoft award for the University. Robert also has worked as a solution designer for Thomas Optical Measurements Inc., a scientific camera measurement company, specializing in Windows-based medical and astronomical imaging systems using high-powered medical cameras. When not delving into Windows NT APIs and devoting long hours to every corner of the Internet, Robert enjoys obscure literary and historical pursuits, which invariably give him more excuses to log back on the Net. He also admits an abiding interest in handmade electric guitars, which he professes to play rather badly, too often, and never loud enough.

Christian Plazas spent his childhood years in Bogota, Columbia; Albuquerque, New Mexico; and Mannheim, Germany. He graduated summa cum laude from Columbus State University with a BS in Computer Science. In addition to writing, Christian also is the TCP/IP Network Manager, as well as Webmaster and Host Master, for Columbus State University, and is working on his Master's degree in Computer Science.

John Desborough was born in Toronto, Ontario and graduated in 1984 with an MBA from York University, Toronto, Ontario. For the past five years, John worked with the Federal Government of Canada in the Department of Industry as Manager of the Electronic and Internet Publishing in the Strategic Information Branch, and left in May of 1996 to pursue consulting and authoring full time. His most recent work is the bestseller *Intranet Web Development* (New Riders Publishing). John is married and has two children.

David Gulbransen (dgulbran@bluemarble.net) is the Director of MIS at Dimension X, a Java tools development company. He has been working with the Internet for more than six years, and is currently exploring new Internet technologies such as Java and ActiveX. His other titles include *Creating Web Applets with Java* and the *Netscape Server Survival Guide*. In his spare time, he likes to experiment with the art of cinematography and digital videography.

Joel Millecan has been involved in the growth of the computer industry since learning basic programming, in 1971. He currently specializes in Network and Telecommunication Systems, with a strong focus on Windows NT, Novell Netware, and various Unix Operating Systems. Joel considers the task of keeping pace with the rapid growth of technology, both hardware and software, an enjoyable responsibility.

George Eckel has written manuals for a wide variety of audiences, including software engineers, end users, software project managers, and system administrators. He has researched and designed a GUI interface design course for software engineers and project managers. George also has worked as a collaborative author on other books published by Macmillan Publishing, including John Goodman's best seller, *Memory Management for All of Us*. George lives with his wife, Shirlee, and his three children, Madeline, Nathalie, and Genevieve.

Trademark Acknowledgments

All terms mentioned in this book that are known to be trademarks or service marks have been appropriately capitalized. New Riders Publishing cannot attest to the accuracy of this information. Use of a term in this book should not be regarded as affecting the validity of any trademark or service mark. Windows NT is a registered trademark of Microsoft Corporation.

Dedication

Robert Oliver: I dedicate my portion of this book to Mr. Lewis Kimber.

Christian Plazas: This book is dedicated to Lavonda, my wonderful wife.

John Desborough: I would like to dedicate my efforts in this work to my wife, Andrea, and my children, Zoë and Evan. They make it all worthwhile.

Acknowledgments

Robert Oliver: I foremost would like to acknowledge and thank the two best friends I still can't manage to get rid of: Doug Herron, who knows the true meaning of NT; and Priscilla Gonzalez, who claims to give my life meaning and purpose—she's probably right. Thanks to Dr. Jim Leonard, director of the software engineering project here at CSU, without whom I would have a dull finance degree, a boring job, and probably a 21-inch monitor. Thanks to Professor David Johnson, who always believed in the quality and importance of my work. And a big thanks to everyone who helped make this book possible, especially Christian Plazas. I couldn't write an acknowledgment section without mentioning the people who have in some way helped out in writing this book. Thanks go to my parents; my family at Rucker's; all the people at Vineyard for putting up with late-night rants; Michelle Bechtel for constant interest and encouragement (and then some), Anthony Roberts for trying to show me the light; Craig Boyko for providing Canada with a version of me; Liz Hoff for cheering me on; Douglas Taylor for constant inspiration and dedication to the cause; John Lutz, Paul Bogans, Shannon Dew, Jeff Balaz, Chris Feyrer, Tom Jackson, and Hans Peterson for

Building a Windows NT 4 Internet Server

Robert Oliver

Christian Plazas

Desborough

David Gulbransen

Joel Millecan

Contributions from

George Eckel

Rick Segal

New Riders Publishing, Indianapolis, Indiana

Building a Windows NT 4 Internet Server

By Robert Oliver, Christian Plazas, John Desborough
David Gulbransen, Joel Millecan, George Eckel, and
Rick Segal

Published by:
New Riders Publishing
201 West 103rd Street
Indianapolis, IN 46290 USA

Copyright © 1996 by New Riders Publishing

Printed in the United States of America 1 2 3 4 5 6 7 8 9 0

Library of Congress Cataloging-in-Publication Data

CIP data available upon request

Warning and Disclaimer

This book is designed to provide information about the
Windows NT computer program. Every effort has been
made to make this book as complete and as accurate as
possible, but no warranty or fitness is implied.

The information is provided on an "as is" basis. The
author(s) and New Riders Publishing shall have neither
liability nor responsibility to any person or entity with
respect to any loss or damages arising from the information contained in this book or from the use of the disks
or programs that may accompany it.

Publisher	Don Fowley
Publishing Manager	Julie Fairweather
Marketing Manager	Mary Foote
Managing Editor	Carla Hall

Product Development Specialist
Linda Barron

Acquisitions Editor
Nancy Maragioglio

Software Specialist
Steve Flatt

Senior Editor
Sarah Kearns

Development Editors
Ami Frank, Naomi Goldman

Project Editor
Jill D. Bond

Copy Editors
Gina Brown, Jennifer
Eberhardt, Keith Cline,
Greg Pearson, Cliff Shubs,
Karen Walsh

Technical Editors
Jack Britton, Joel Millecan

Acquisitions Coordinator
Tracy Turgeson

Administrative Coordinator
Karen Opal

Cover Designer
Sandra Schroeder

Cover Production
Aren Howell

Book Designer
Gary Adair

Production Manager
Kelly D. Dobbs

Production Team Supervisors
Laurie Casey, Gina
Rexrode, Joe Millay

Graphics Image Specialists
Daniel Harris, Oliver
Jackson, Marvin Van Tiem

Production Analysts
Jason Hand, Erich Richter

Production Team
Lori Cliburn, Tricia
Flodder, Linda Knose,
Daniela Raderstorf,
Pamela Woolf

Indexer
Christopher Cleveland

providing ideas, information, and advice; everyone in the program, present and past: Justin, Mark, Kevin, Lynn, Duane, Junior, everybody named Mike, Robert, Jeff, Noah, Brian, and anyone else I've forgotten; Carla Hubbard, who knew she'd be mentioned here; Laura Wilson, Laura Hester, Mani White; all my editors, especially Nancy Maragioglio who got me the job in the first place; Becky Campbell for the unmentionable pleasures of tech editing; everyone at Norton's; Jim Morrison for all things; and finally, the entire cast of the 70s comedy *Good Times*.

Christian Plazas: I'd like to thank Nancy Maragioglio, who first contacted me regarding this project. Ami Frank, for all her help and patience. Robert Oliver, whose collaboration was invaluable. Thanks to my parents, Luis and Eva Calderon, for always believing in me. Special thanks to all the staff at Computer Information and Networking Services at Columbus State University, for their support. I'd also like to thank all the people involved with the production of this book—you've all done a great job.

David Gulbransen: Special thanks to Ken Rawlings, Stephanie Boys, Kate Jenkins, and Mike Clark. Thanks to Ami Frank and Linda Barron, and to and everyone at Dimension X.

Joel Millecan: One of the more pleasurable aspects of being an author is having the opportunity to thank others involved with the evolution and culmination of the project. I want to thank Ami Frank and Linda Barron of New Riders, for their exemplary support, and Pete Bitar for initially bringing me aboard the project. Special thanks to Marc Teitler, for providing Internet access and hosting the development systems. I also want to acknowledge the technical excellence and creativity of Jill Bond and the production staff, and the programmers and developers of Microsoft. Without them, this book would not have been possible.

Contents at a Glance

Table of Contents

Part II: Requirements and Planning   57

3 Windows NT as Your Internet Server Platform   59

Part III: Site Construction   223

8 Getting Windows NT Up and Running   225

Introduction

If you could imagine an organism so fantastic that it could embody the thoughts, ingenuity, and humanity of the entire world, the Internet might well be that entity. Over the quarter century of its lifetime, the Internet has grown from a Spartan research tool, to a rich tapestry of culture, innovation, and communication. It's no surprise that millions of people from all over the planet are becoming Internet "residents." An even lesser wonder is that companies are realizing the tremendous potential for an Internet presence. The Internet's power as a marketing and information tool for companies is finally beginning to be realized, as indicated by your interest in this book.

If you are engaged in providing an Internet presence for your corporation, or extending an existing one, read on. This book will help get you started providing that expertise using Microsoft's Windows NT operating system. If you have to justify your Internet connectivity with strong examples of how it can benefit your company's profits and potential, you will find suggestions and examples throughout this volume; notably in the first chapter, "Internet Basics" as well as in Chapter 2, "Business Opportunities with Internet Technologies."

Whether your company is interested in providing a simple Internet service for information exchange and e-mail, or desires a full Internet presence for advertising, multimedia, and cutting edge technology, there are key factors you should understand. It is essential to understand the nature of the Net and its expansion, as well as the server options with which you will be faced. While your company may not require an elaborate Internet presence, it is important to provide the most cost-effective and attractive solution possible. Although not everyone in your organization may understand the magnitude of the Internet, this new medium is one that cannot be ignored.

NOTE

MICROSOFT Info While this book aims to take a nonexclusive approach to Internet servers, any important technologies and innovations by Microsoft which may help the reader in planning for the Internet server, will be designated by this icon.

The Aim of This Book

This book is designed to take the reader through the standard process of configuring a computer running the Windows NT operating system as an Internet server platform. Because of the increasing number of powerful and specialized servers on the market today, the aim of this book isn't focused on a particular server, with the exception of a chapter on Microsoft Internet Information Server, an unignorable server solution from the designers of the operating system. The reader will benefit not only from hands-on walk-throughs of installing the necessary protocols and services for NT, but also from administrative tips, security standards, and advice on justifying the Internet presence to a corporation.

What You Will Need To Use This Book Effectively

To properly use this book, you will need a system capable of running either Windows NT Server or Workstation. NT Server is usually recommended for use as an Internet server, because it maintains many more connections and has better support software for maintaining various servers. This book pays special attention to Windows NT 4, but stays faithful to the NT 3.51 environment as well. Another useful addition to your arsenal of Windows NT support tools is the Windows NT 3.51 Resource Kit, commercially available from Microsoft. If you are interested in professional network administration with NT, you won't want to be without the NT Resource Kit.

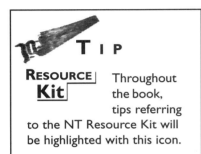

TIP

RESOURCE Kit Throughout the book, tips referring to the NT Resource Kit will be highlighted with this icon.

Who Is This Book Written For?

This book, while obviously written for the network administrator with the project of setting up a successful Internet server, will prove beneficial to anyone in the corporation who is involved in decision making for such a project. The staff in charge of determining the best network operating system and Internet server software will benefit from the information on Windows NT. Administration and optimization chapters will allow the network administrator to gain a functional understanding of the abilities and limitations of NT Server and Workstation. Those in the decision making echelons of the following job functions will also benefit from reading:

NOTE

WINDOWS NT4.0 Throughout the book, information specific to Windows NT 4 will be highlighted and designated by this icon.

❏ Network Managers
❏ Administrators

- ❏ MIS Managers
- ❏ Network Planners
- ❏ Systems Engineers
- ❏ Anyone interested in establishing a Windows NT Internet server

How is This Book Structured?

This book is arranged in five sections that logically outline the planning, construction, and administration of a Windows NT Internet server. The chapters in each section cover basic information about Windows NT networking and the Internet, and then delve into the specifics of how to configure Internet services and provide content and professional management. Following are the five parts of the book:

- ❏ **Part I: The Big Picture.** This section provides an overview of the Internet and its phenomenal impact on business and technology. This initial section offers a view of the history of the Internet, and what its present form can accomplish for business and the corporation.

- ❏ **Part II: Requirements and Planning.** This section is the first introduction to the Windows NT operating system, and the NT 4 release. Communications fundamentals and TCP/IP protocols are introduced here. Recommendations and requirements for both software and hardware are presented, with close attention to the capabilities of the Windows NT operating system.

- ❏ **Part III: Site Construction.** After an introduction to setting up Windows NT to run on the Internet server, this section explains the various services an Internet server can offer, and how to install and configure them. World Wide Web, FTP file transfer, e-mail, news, and other services are all discussed here.

- ❏ **Part IV: System Administration.** After the Internet server is up and running, there are certain administration issues that should be addressed. While individual server service (FTP, mail, and so on) administration will be discussed in each server's corresponding chapter, security and maintenance concerns are covered here. Windows NT and general server security are covered, with an added emphasis on NT's advanced security capabilities. Performance tuning and site maintenance are discussed along with server management concepts.

- ❏ **Part V: Appendices.** This resource guide includes a command, reference, list of security resources, CD-Rom contents and an overview of Microsoft's new suite of Internet servers, formerly referred to as Normandy.

The Chapters in This Book

Each chapter of the book is arranged to give the reader a progressive understanding of the uses of Internet servers, and how to use them to create an effective Internet presence. Introductions to concepts lead to more in-depth instruction on how to set up and configure Windows NT and Internet server services. Following is a brief synopsis of what each chapter has to offer.

Chapter 1: Internet Basics

This chapter is divided into three sections that bring the reader up-to-date in the modern Internet uses. The first section is a brief recap of the history of the Internet. The second section is a justification for a corporate presence on the Internet, and the third section discusses Windows NT as a choice for Internet connectivity. *By Robert Oliver.*

Chapter 2: Business Opportunities with Internet Technologies

This chapter makes a first attempt at outlining the business opportunities that exist in the Internet environment. The rules of the game in this electronic marketplace are radically different from traditional commerce. Marketing and advertising budgets no longer determine market share. Small companies can compete with multinationals, and local vendors with international vendors. Building a presence can be technically complex and intimidating. This book will help to mitigate the intimidation factor by helping you setup and operate an Internet server to allow you to participate in this exciting new environment. *By John Desborough.*

Chapter 3: Windows NT as Your Internet Server Platform

This chapter introduces the Windows NT operating system, Microsoft's premier 32-bit multitasking, secure network operating system. The use of Windows NT as an Internet server is evaluated with focus on the latest release, NT 4. An analysis of the differences between Windows NT Server and Workstation is provided, along with information on the Internet benefits new to NT 4. *By Robert Oliver.*

Chapter 4: Basic Communication Fundamentals

This chapter covers the basics of Local Area Networks. It includes a sample network configuration. Options for connecting to the Internet make up the bulk of the rest of the chapter. A general overview of the most popular high bandwidth Internet access methods is given. The overview includes a description of the required hardware under each method. Example configurations for many of these methods are also shown. *By Christian Plazas.*

Chapter 5: Understanding the Transport Layer: TCP/IP

The TCP/IP, or Transmission Control Protocol/Internet Protocol, is the data communications protocol of the Internet and is used to coordinate the exchange of information between two network devices. TCP/IP is so important to the Internet that Microsoft has included TCP/IP support in the base Windows NT system. Before setting up the Internet server, it is a good idea to understand the basic fundamentals of the protocol and how it is used. *By John Desborough.*

Chapter 6:   Hardware Requirements

This chapter discusses the hardware requirements involved in creating an Internet server. The architectures supported by Windows NT Server are discussed in detail. The chapter includes in-depth discussions on the different hardware components that go into an Internet server. Topics covered include memory, storage options, and processor types. *By Christian Plazas.*

Chapter 7:   Software Requirements

This chapter provides a detailed run-down of the software capacity of Windows NT. Not only does it cover the components that come with Windows NT, it also provides a strong discussion of diagnostics, policy editors, the Windows Directory Service, Internet Information Server, RAS, and some of the new communication features such as Multilink PPP. *By Rick Segal.*

Chapter 8:   Getting Windows NT Up and Running

From running setup to configuring network connections to customized adjustments, this chapter brings you all the information you need to start actually building your server with Windows NT. The details of setting up the file system, setting up computer accounts, selecting a directory, and creating an emergency disk are all covered. The section on network connections will help you with network adapted cords, protocols, source bindings, and domains. Finally, the chapter winds up with a section on trouble-shooting. From the basic to the nitty gritty, this chapter will get you started. *By George Eckel.*

Chapter 9:   Getting Web Services Up and Running

Since the advent and acceptance of the Internet as a global publishing medium, knowledge is now distributed to millions of people in a matter of seconds. The WWW server on your NT server will be your tool to publish information to the global Internet community. This chapter will guide you through the steps necessary to install and configure the Internet Information Server from Microsoft that ships with the Windows NT Server. *Repurposed by John Desborough.*

Chapter 10:   Getting FTP Services Up and Running

The File Transfer Protocol (FTP) service provides a means for you to collect your files together, put them into an "archive" and make them available for retrieval. File access using FTP can offer files for the world to download, or for providing a secure archive for receiving files. This chapter discusses how to set up the FTP Publishing Service within the Internet Information Server. *Repurposed by John Desborough.*

Chapter 11: Getting E-mail and List Services Up and Running

At the heart of Internet communications is electronic mail. The capability to quickly exchange written messages has become commonplace in the Internet world, and e-mail continues to evolve, allowing users to integrate files, graphics, audio, and multimedia into their messages. Chapter 11 covers the basics of Internet e-mail functionality, including an overview of the most common protocols used for Internet e-mail today. The chapter continues on to provide an overview of Windows NT mail servers and their features, including a step-by-step installation guide, and a guide to configuring and maintaining Internet mailing lists. Even if you choose a mail server not covered in this chapter, you should gain all of the knowledge necessary for make decisions related to e-mail, and gain the experience necessary to install and configure your own mail server. *By David Gulbransen.*

Chapter 12: Getting News Services Up and Running: NNTP and INS

Internet newsgroups have become a mainstream transport for information exchange. Individuals can participate in discussions, and share views with others interested in the same topics. Many companies and organizations have discovered that newsgroups can be used for various applications, for example, communications and technical support. The Microsoft Normandy NNTP News Server can handle high traffic loads and host thousands of connections. It also shares setup, administration, and operation tools with other Microsoft Internet Services. This chapter will guide you through the steps necessary to install and configure the Internet News Service, and get the service up and running. Features, installation guidelines, installation, and configuration will be discussed. *By Joel Millecan.*

Chapter 13: Other Services for Your Users

What if your corporate Internet presence demands even more user-oriented Internet server services? This chapter covers Microsoft's Internet technology innovations, from Microsoft FrontPage Web site authoring and administration tools, to Microsoft's high-end Commercial Internet Servers system family for large scale providers. Web site development and Web browser innovations with Microsoft Internet Explorer are also covered. In addition to these services, Chapter 13 walks you through setting up Windows NT 4 Server's DNS Server. *By Robert Oliver and Christian Plazas.*

Chapter 14: Security Practices

The security of both the operating system and the Internet server are primary considerations for a professionally administered sever. The integrity and operability of crucial data or services should always be ensured with proper security measures. This chapter discusses Windows NT operating system security, concentrating on basic file permissions and auditing. Using network firewalls for Internet server security is another capital issue discussed in this chapter. More in-depth information about NT's security architecture, and NT's capability to comply with government specified "C2 security" is also provided for those interested in advanced security practices. *By Robert Oliver and Christian Plazas.*

Chapter 15:   Site Management

The installation and configuration of an Internet server is only the first step to creating an Internet presence. Once your server is installed, there are still issues of maintenance and administration. Chapter 15 deals with the common maintenance issues confronted by Internet site administrators, such as preventative maintenance, emergency repairs, upgrades, and backups. Beyond the physical upkeep of your server are the administrative areas associated with any multi-user service. The chapter discusses several issues that confront administrators daily, such as personal use policies and users right to privacy. A skilled administrator needs to manage people as often as hardware, and the chapter sets out to help develop the well-rounded skills needed for successful Internet server administration. *By David Gulbransen.*

part

The Big Picture

Internet Basics

f you already have a working (or expert) knowledge of the Internet and how to provide Internet connectivity, you may be inclined to skip over this chapter and jump right into setting up NT Internet server. If you have a strong understanding of Windows NT and have already justified Internet connectivity to your company, this chapter might not be of great assistance. For those new to Windows NT, or those interested in how an Internet presence can improve a company's overall corporate well-being, this chapter familiarizes you with the environment in which you will be working. The chapter is divided into the following three sections, each an introduction to the concepts covered in this book:

❑ Introduction to the Internet
❑ Justifying a Corporate Internet Presence
❑ The Windows NT Choice for Internet Connectivity

Section I: Introduction to the Internet

This section seeks to familiarize readers with the basics of how the Internet works, the history of its beginnings, and what it has become. Examples of new technologies give the reader a good grasp of what to expect and what to look for. Consider these examples and your own ideas when justifying Internet connectivity for your company. For those interested in the origins of the Net, and where this giant communications medium got its initial momentum, this section contains much of that information.

Note

The term Internet connectivity is used throughout this book to represent a company's capability to use Internet resources, as well as provide its own resources and information in a total Internet presence.

What is the Internet?

A simple explanation, which does little justice to the grand social and technological accomplishment of our age, is that the Internet is the largest global wide area network (WAN). The Internet is a world-wide collective of internetworks communicating with each other through standard protocols and packets. The hardware necessary to maintain these connections (such as bridges and routers) determines which internetwork packets are sent within the network, and which are sent out to the Internet for remote hosts to receive. Figure 1.1 illustrates how networks on the Internet communicate.

Internet Usage

What is the world using the Internet for? Just about anything you (or the several billion other inhabitants of this planet) can imagine. To best discover what people are doing on the Net, explore it. Because this can be an addicting (yet enlightening!) habit, look at some of the major tools for making residency in the Internet community enjoyable: namely, client software.

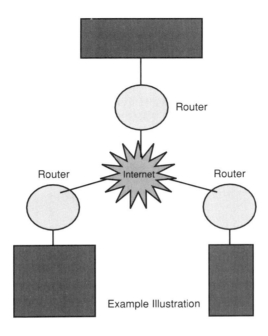

Example Illustration

World Wide Web Browsers

Web browsers such as Netscape Navigator, Mosaic, and Microsoft Internet Explorer enable users to search through content-rich multimedia Web sites for information and entertainment. In the last year, the technology present for authoring dynamic, full-featured Web pages has enabled companies and individuals to provide impressive multimedia support. Features such as inline AVI movie files, Java applets, and database access to a company's information systems have enriched the Web browsing experience. The Web offers everything from research and business information to the ridiculously enjoyable pursuits every enthusiast eventually encounters. Web browsers are popularly considered *the* necessary Internet information tool. Different aspects of the Internet make receiving information easier. These include the following:

❑ E-mail

❑ Newsreaders

❑ FTP clients

A more in-depth explanation of each follows.

Electronic Mail

E-mail is one of the most popular forms of information transfer on the Internet today. Millions of messages are sent each day from all over the world. Corporations use e-mail to contact customers and often to make deals. Friends and colleagues around the globe (or across the street) keep in touch with this virtually free communication. One strong indicator of e-mail's importance to the Internet community is the recent improvements in e-mail client software. Innovations that prove a growing desire for sophisticated and friendly electronic mail transfer include spelling checkers, filters to route specific mail to certain *mailboxes*, and new standards for including multimedia.

Newsreaders

The Internet UseNET newsgroups are perhaps the greatest indicator of the variety of interests and information on the Internet. Discussions range from optical physics to networking on any platform imaginable—even to favorite television shows. The Internet newsgroups provide information and discussion on almost any subject imaginable—from the inhumanly dull to the frighteningly bizarre. As a result, the software used to access these newsgroups, newsreader software, has improved greatly in recent years. A good newsreader enables the user to subscribe and unsubscribe to newsgroups, to view messages, to reply to the newsgroup or to individual posters, to filter out common phrases in undesirable posts (such as ignoring all messages with subjects that contain foul language), and to download files and pictures from posts.

Companies are benefiting from newsgroups in several ways. Many companies simply use the idea and information exchange of newsgroups to benefit their work and development. Others are using in-house news servers to host their own newsgroups to handle customer and technical support.

FTP Client

For those who frequently transfer documents, images, programs, and any other files across the Internet, an easy-to-use ftp (file transfer protocol) program is a must. These applications enable users to download and upload files between a remote host and their own computers. Some people prefer to use the older command-line ftp programs; these are often much quicker to use. Those unfamiliar with ftp commands and preferring a graphical user interface often use ftp programs that offer drag-and-drop, multiple site connections, and graphical display of the file's progress.

A History of the Internet

From its inception over a quarter of a century ago, the global wide area network that expanded into the Internet has changed the way governments, scientists, companies, and now the general populace interact with the world. Although the origins and history of this network organism may not interest everyone, an understanding of the Internet as a whole may foster a greater respect for what it has become today, and where users may lead it.

This brief history of the Internet involves a timeline of important deciding events and factors in the evolution of the Internet.

- ❏ ARPAnet
- ❏ Independent Networks
- ❏ The National Science Foundation Network
- ❏ Information Everywhere
- ❏ Today's Problems

ARPAnet

In the 1960s, the initial stirrings of the Internet derived from the United States government and research universities. Scientists wanted a way to share data with each other through one central terminal rather than one computer for every connection to every remote network. The U.S. military wanted to develop a network that could withstand partial destruction and still be able to route information to its hosts.

The United States Advanced Research Projects Agency (ARPA) was the first to commission a wide area network between research university campuses in California and Utah. At first, four sites were established in this network; the network eventually grew to dozens of nodes or sites. These sites routed information based on network addresses with *packets* of data in the first incarnation of the Internet Protocol (IP). This network became known as ARPAnet, and is considered the first ancestor of today's Internet.

This far-reaching network was used initially for sharing information among scientists, often through transfer of files, accessing remote computers through remote login, and accessing remote hardware. In 1973, the government publicly demonstrated the potential of the ARPAnet to scientists and researchers throughout the country; the demand for inclusion on this revolutionary new internetwork exploded. Hundreds of sites joined the ARPAnet. The concept of a network spanning the world, not just the

United States, became a much closer reality. This immediate acceptance of the ARPAnet eventually lead to repercussions; because of the heavy public network traffic, the U.S. military eventually decided to close the ARPAnet to the public.

The U.S. military was a prime contributor to ARPAnet traffic by now, and decided to step in before it became too gargantuan a task. After the Department of Defense took control of the ARPAnet in 1975, many universities and private research centers no longer qualified for network access according to the new guidelines. Although some stayed with the ARPAnet, many who did not qualify (and quite a few who did) decided on an important step in the evolution of the Internet: they would create their own nation-wide networks for research, education, and eventually business.

Independent Networks

In time, the independent networks such as CSNET (Computer Science Network) and BITNET (Because It's There Network) began to interact, and users realized more social purposes for the Internet. Researchers and students formed some of the first virtual communities to discuss science fiction and speculation. Soon, special-interest groups began to crop up, covering everything from nontechnical interests to better ways to improve networking performance. No longer was the Internet a domain of only professional researchers routing packets of hard data back and forth. By the mid-1980s, students, professors, administrators, and scientists alike were all becoming part of an online community of regional networks all across the country connected through high-speed phone lines. Although the growing need for network support and information exchange was demonstrated and improved by this initiative to create other internetworks, it was yet another government agency that launched nation-wide, high-speed Internet access into the present.

The National Science Foundation Network

When ARPAnet fell under the jurisdiction of the military, a U.S. governmental agency called the National Science Foundation (NSF) created what would be the progenitor of the current Internet. NSFnet was originally a network of six supercomputers around the country that used ARPAnet's IP addressing system and the (then) high-speed 56 kilobits per second (Kbps) special phone lines. Following is a list of the original supercomputers linked in NSFnet:

- ❏ Cornell National Supercomputer Facility, Cornell University
- ❏ The Scientific Computing Division of the National Center for Atmospheric Research in Boulder, Colorado

- ❏ San Diego Supercomputer Center, University of California
- ❏ National Center for Supercomputing Applications, University of Illinois
- ❏ John von Neumann National Supercomputer Center in Princeton, New Jersey
- ❏ Pittsburgh Supercomputer Center, operated jointly by Westinghouse Electric Corp., Carnegie Mellon University, and the University of Pittsburgh

Soon after its inception, the NSFnet grew into a larger network of hundreds of colleges and universities linking to their nearest supercomputer facility. NSF upgraded its network backbone to a high-speed T1 connection (1.54 megabits per second or Mbps) to accommodate the growing sites. In 1992, a T3 line (45 Mbps) was adopted. By now, the government had stopped funding NSFnet. Commercial providers, phone companies, and advertisers picked up the load. This ended any controversy that had arisen about all the commercial use of the new Internet, as opposed to research and educational purposes. Coinciding with this, the U.S. Department of Defense phased out ARPAnet and began using its own MILnet for all military internetworking. ARPAnet was shut down and all left-over traffic migrated to NSFnet, which, along with other world-wide internetworks, became collectively known as the Internet.

Information Everywhere

The early 1990s witnessed a burgeoning information system that greatly needed standardized protocols to facilitate easier searches for information. The Internet became a massive commercial explosion, with millions more users each year. Many long-time users of the Internet cringe at the phrase *Information Superhighway*. Much like a large highway, however, the Internet was a busy virtual world with poor road maps and as many potholes as gas stations. To attempt to bring some order to this situation, several types of servers and clients were written to search and organize information. Gopher servers, which listed information in menus, lead users to information ranging from newsgroups to chat programs to online government information systems.

The next major information breakthrough was the (now all- encompassing) World Wide Web, created for a simple standard method of publishing information and accessing resources through hyperlinks. The first major Web browser, Mosaic, led to other popular browsers from companies like Netscape and Microsoft. Soon, most of a user's Internet needs could be accomplished with one application.

The result has been the information, advertising, multimedia, and entertainment standard-bearer for the Internet.

The Internet Today

The Internet refers to the current, but by no means final, culmination of over 20 years of the global networking expansion. Although any definition today will be insufficient in a year, it is vitally important to both server administrators and users alike to understand today's standards and technologies (and the importance of such in the corporate world). Luckily, the Internet has changed the image and direction of many avenues of business and technology, and has thereby made the corporate world considerably more enjoyable to interact with.

Today's Internet offers a wealth of corporate and personal information resources, and a variety of methods to access this information. The following Internet achievements and corporate benefits of today are outlined in this section.

- ❏ Multimedia
- ❏ Information Systems
- ❏ Software Design
- ❏ Today's Problems
- ❏ Case Studies

Multimedia

Browsing the Web for content-rich information about a company has grown from a neat trick into an advertising standard. The marriage of multimedia presentations and higher speed connections has proven a leading factor in Internet-based technological advances. Advertisers use moving graphics and interactive scripting languages such as Java and VBScript to provide application-like functionality to their once lifeless screens full of hyperlinks.

Video clips are another multimedia attraction that incorporate sound and sometimes user interaction. Apple's QuickTime has reached the Web in interactive videos such as walk-through houses and offices. Microsoft's ActiveMovie enhancements enable users to preview the interiors of popular sports cars in a user navigable *video* advertisement embedded seamlessly in a Web page. Real motion video is also an emerging feature that will enable viewers with higher speed connections to see movie-like video images at approximately real time. Along with real-motion video comes the necessity of full-duplex sound over the Net. Simply put, this means people all over the world can communicate as if over the phone, on the Internet. This is rapidly becoming an attractive feature, with software that turns your sound card and a microphone into a virtual telephone, minus the long-distance charges.

Imagine a medical-based business performing a demonstration with a microscope that has a video camera attached (not an especially uncommon practice). Imagine further, however, that the company transmits the video image over the Internet to clients or researchers in other states or countries. The scientists communicate charts, facts, and figures over a simple *white-board* conferencing program, and speak to each other with little more than a sound card and a microphone. The foundation for multimedia exchange over the Internet is just beginning to solidify. The possibilities for learning and corporate growth will continue to be realized long after a set of standards has been defined and accepted by both businesses and end users.

Information Systems

The bottom line is information. Timely and accurate information is central to a business's overall capability to perform optimally and to satisfy its customers. The Internet is rapidly becoming an information systems tool to leverage this potential. Companies are standardizing the use of online transaction processing, credit card sales over secured Web transmissions, and database querying or updating. Although much of the information technologies on the Net today are variations on older themes, the Internet has placed a new importance and accessibility on them.

Database querying servers (such as Microsoft SQL Server or Oracle SQL Server) that store large amounts of customer data could be used over the Web in a secure transaction system that enables users to update their customer information, for example. Before, this would have been difficult to accomplish without a phone call or written letter (with little way to benefit from instant transaction). The capability to further automate information systems is one of today's greatest reasons for investment in the Internet.

Today, security is becoming an increasingly important factor in Internet commerce. In earlier days, very little business was conducted over the Net; few would not have cringed at the notion of transmitting credit card or social security numbers over a form in a Web browser. Although many still cringe, Internet security has improved to such a level that a host of businesses are conducting complete sales of products and dissemination of customer records over secure transactions. Through encoding, encryption of file transfers (such as Web browser security), protocol level security (such as Secured Socket Layers [SSL] and Point-to-Point Tunneling Protocol [PPTP]), the Internet is leaving its infancy in the realm of reliable secure transactions.

Software Design

Yet another major impact of the Internet (in the last year or so) has been the rapidly changing software development environments. Internet-aware software has become a major design goal; software developers seldom write an application now without some thought to the Internet. Microsoft's Windows NT 4 operating system is a primary example. Windows NT 4 is a powerful contender in the Internet-ready OS platform market. Its features include Internet Information Server and the shell interface that enables Microsoft's Internet Explorer 3 Web browser to work so tightly with the operating system.

Interactive Web-based applications are being written in languages such as Java, or with entire platforms such as Microsoft's ActiveX controls and documents, and legions of specialized languages and tools for virtually anything that needs to be accomplished. Although many of today's "standards" will be history in the next few years, it is important to isolate the leading edge of software design that will enable Internet content providers, Web site designers, and software developers to write the information and idea exchange of a nebulous future. Although many readers may have little interest or experience in writing software for Internet sites, it is important to be conversant in today's emerging tools and options for developing a professional Internet presence.

Today's Problems

Over 25 years after the birth of what is now known as the Internet, growing pains persist. The 32-bit numbering address system (IP addressing) will soon no longer be able to supply unique numbers for every host in the world. New schemes may eventually have to be used. Internet censorship is a huge controversy now—the U.S. government is attempting to grapple with that through legislation. Corporate dominance of the Internet, and problems with standardizing communications and protocols, are only a sample of the challenges facing the Internet as it evolves from its adolescence.

Case Studies

The goal of this section is to inspire and inform, not to impart technical knowledge or advise the reader in establishing a corporate Internet presence. In keeping with this concept, several brief case studies of companies taking full advantage of today's Internet technologies follow:

❏ An Atlanta, Georgia based business-solutions company is designing custom Internet-based decision support systems for businesses with large databases. The applications will be contained on a central Windows NT Internet Server, and downloaded via a Web browser, and thereby enable the user to access information from either a workstation in the office complex, a computer at home, or from a laptop and modem anywhere on the road. This enables a business to incorporate its internal network with the Internet, without any major restructuring. Primary technologies used will be Microsoft ActiveX controls and Java applets.

❏ One consulting company manages software-design projects across the world by teaching project leaders how to organize and administrate a remote project team. This is enabling companies to recruit engineers from all over the world to work from home, and be managed in a consistent and professional manner. This is also ensuring in-house development advantages, without the overhead of staffing and relocating.

❏ A university in Europe is using a Java language-based interface that enables Web surfers to access its mainframe library cataloging program. This not only puts an easy-to-use interface on the command-line mainframe program, but also enables remote use via any Web browser that supports Java. Another advantage is that the university is using a legacy system application with a modern look and feel, possibly extending its useful lifetime.

Internet Regulation and Standards

So who makes up the rules for the greatest collaborative networking effort in the history of our planet? In a sense, you do. Although companies and government agencies have a fair amount of say-so over what standards and policies are implemented, most of the organizations that regulate the technologies of the Internet are nonprofit volunteer entities, open to any qualified person interested in the direction of the Internet.

The InterNIC

The Internet Network Information Center (*InterNIC*) is the body responsible for issuing IP address and domain names to all Internet hosts in the United States. The InterNIC makes certain that IP addresses and domain names remain unique and regulated. If you don't obtain your domain registration and IP addresses from a service provider or institution, you will probably obtain them directly from the InterNIC. The InterNIC also maintains a large repository of information about Internet standards, protocols, and policies, including Requests for Comments (RFCs)—explained in the following paragraphs.

NOTE

The InterNIC Web site is located at http:// www.internic.net

The ftp site is ftp.internic.net

Development of Internet Standards

With all the emerging technologies, new applications, and a small army of different operating systems out there, it's often hard to believe that the Internet exists in its arguably harmonious state because of set standards. Although companies often battle to make their products standard on the Net, the standardization of protocols and procedures is governed by nonprofit organizations and volunteer members. The two major leaders in Internet standardization and growth are The Internet Society (ISOC) and the Internet Engineering Task Force (IETF).

The Internet Society assembles groups of invited volunteers to promote the interest and technologies of the Internet. The ISOC appoints these volunteers to an Internet Architecture Board (IAB) that reviews ways of steering the direction of the Internet (through evaluating standards and ideas).

The Internet Engineering Task Force exists to help develop solutions to Internet technology problems and concerns. The IETF is a voluntary organization that invites anyone to attend its meetings and conferences. The efforts of the IETF have made it possible for the internetworking world to interoperate smoothly (thanks to published specifications and adoption of standards). Working groups of volunteer professionals assemble for the IETF to research problems and solutions that usually result in a published white paper known as a Request for Comment (RFC). RFCs are published for networking request specifications, protocols such as TCP, IP, SMTP, and many other Internet technology standards. Request for Comment specifications can be obtained from the InterNIC via e-mail, ftp, or for the adventurous, postal mail.

Where the Internet is Going

When contemplating the future of the Internet, you will find yourself somewhere between the realms of speculative fiction and the imagination and needs of Internet users. What many Internet-savvy individuals laugh at in movies and on television as impossible and misrepresented technologies, may well be the future rewards of our dreams and good-old-fashioned research and development. Although it is difficult (if not impossible) to enumerate all the future uses and technologies of the Internet, you can speculate as to what the Internet world may see in the future of Internet develop-ment. That speculation usually derives from the current needs and wants of the corporation and the single user. Companies such as AT&T promote a futuristic view of communications technology in their commercials, with full knowledge that the foundation exists to make such visions a standard.

Section II: Justifying Your Corporate Internet Presence

Convincing an established and profitable company of the benefits of a new information tool like the Internet is often difficult. In the last year, however, thousands of companies have made the move to the Net. Common sense and the desire to keep up with competition often provide all the incentive necessary. Although buying Web space from an Internet service provider is often the extent of many companies' Internet existences, your interest in this book probably means that you are interested in providing an in-house Internet server—often a more challenging investment to justify. This section provides the facts that readers can use to help plan a successful strategy for justifying the need for a Windows NT Internet server.

Business Uses of Internet Servers

Some readers may have a clear idea of what they want out of their Internet server, but may not be aware of the many possibilities that exist in hosting Internet services. A seasoned Internet server administrator or active user may know exactly what applications are available and needed. For those unsure or just beginning Internet administration, the different uses of a Net server may be elusive.

Following are the most common commercial Internet servers:

- ❑ World Wide Web Servers
- ❑ FTP Servers
- ❑ Electronic (e-mail) Servers
- ❑ News Servers
- ❑ Gopher Servers
- ❑ Remote Login Servers

World Wide Web Servers

World Wide Web servers are becoming increasingly popular, and often are what companies mean when they say *Internet server*. Although the Web is a remarkably inclusive tool, several other considerations for a functional Internet server exist.

FTP Server

An FTP server, combined with a WWW server, often are all a company has use for. Storage of files for public and private download is a stepping stone to several advertising and customer support benefits.

Electronic Mail (E-Mail) Servers

If your company wants its own e-mail server to route mail throughout the office and out to the Internet, you should be aware of the various mail transfer protocols, the software available for Windows NT, and have a strong understanding of how Internet mail protocols and procedures work.

News Servers

Will you want your company to have access to UseNET newsgroups, while restricting exactly what groups are available? A news server could also enable your company to host its own newsgroups on the Internet or within your own corporation.

Gopher Servers

Although the Web is quickly overshadowing the usefulness of gopher servers, many of them are still firmly in place. A company that wants a menu-oriented information catalog for access to numerous Internet resources should consider a gopher server.

Remote Login Servers

Some networks may still need remote login (such as Telnet) to enable access to resources on the server. Although Microsoft seems to downplay the usefulness of a Telnet server on Windows NT (there is no shipping NT Telnet server; they are currently all third-party software), you may have a specific need or preference for a remote command-line login option.

Your Internet Server Needs

Before evaluating reasons why your Internet presence could be beneficial, you should ask a few important questions; then relate each major point to your needs. First determine your goal for the Internet server; what will be its primary function as your point of Internet presence? Following are some of the questions you should be asking yourself:

❑ *What type of Internet connection do I need?* Will your company require a high-speed T1 connection for heavy bandwidth? Will you need to run your own server for dial-in connections? Your Internet connection is governed by price, availability of services, and the specific needs of the company. Internet connectivity issues will be discussed later in the book.

❑ *What do I want out of the Internet?* Does your company need e-mail services for communication with clients and employees? Are you interested in your own high-speed connection for a dynamic Web site to advertise your wares? Understand your needs and the priority of each.

❑ *What other benefits can the Internet provide?* Besides your primary networking needs, are there other benefits such as easy access to research materials or variety in vendors that may increase the desire for an Internet connection?

❑ *What tangible benefits can be realized?* How might your profits increase with an Internet presence? Through advertising, marketing, or improved customer support, will you be able to realize higher profits? Will it save money in any way?

❑ *What intangible benefits might be realized?* Could your Internet presence improve customer relations? Your corporate image, or your credibility? Intangible benefits may be hard to list and even harder for some to fathom, but such benefits could eventually pay for your Internet connection several times over.

Reasons for Establishing a Corporate Internet Presence

The arguments for establishing a corporate Internet presence are limited only by the imagination and needs of the company and the server administrator. There are so many excellent examples of creative use of the Internet for profit and exposure that this entire book could preface the topic. To compose a strong proposal for an Internet presence in your organization, you will probably need to brainstorm for several unique ideas tailored to your product or services. The expanded ideas that follow are only a few to get you thinking on the right track.

Now that you have some guidelines and are asking the right questions, look at specific ways the Internet can improve your company's standing in the information technology world.

Communication with Employees

If your Internet server goals include providing e-mail for your employees, you will soon realize the tremendous opportunity in instant written communication. The savings in paper and interoffice memos alone will be evident. Imagine getting precise written information instantly across to anyone (or a certain group of employees) in your company. This could include file attachments, forwarded messages from outside the organization, or weekly company newsletters. Your company's Web pages could contain employee information such as meeting times, manager of the month, or anything else to communicate effectively and constantly to the entire enterprise.

Communicating with Customers and Contacts

Staying in contact with your customers does not have to remain as impersonal as a brochure and a form letter. Keep your customers and contacts satisfied with the fastest response time possible by using e-mail, Web pages of important information, and ftp sites for any updates or necessary files a customer might need. One of the key reasons why e-mail is such an effective tool for reaching current and prospective business is that it enables the reader to respond at his or her convenience—no bothersome phone call in the middle of a meeting—very seldom do companies have receptionists screen private e-mail.

Marketing

If your company has considered an Internet presence, it must have some idea of how that presence can improve business. It probably has a product or service that could reach some target audience on the Internet. What better way to market these products and services than with a world-wide tool that can reach a vast potential market almost instantly? There are a myriad of ways to get your company noticed and frequented including promotional Web sites, mass mailings, and write-ups in online magazines and trade publications. Most of the expenses in such marketing plans lie in research and information gathering, not in the traditional trappings of marketing sales.

Advertising and Business Promotionals

Your Web site can advertise your company for basically no charge at all; the savvy Internet site administrator can have a company's site listed in hundreds of search engines, business newsgroups, online advertising magazines, and other Web pages. Many of today's popular Web search engine services will advertise a company's product (with a link to their Web site, of course) on the search page. This enables thousands (often millions) of viewers to see the advertisement while searching for whatever topics interest them.

Mailing lists can be maintained for interested businesses to keep up with the latest changes or best buys in your company, and demonstration software can be placed on your ftp site for any interested party to evaluate. Creativity is the primary ingredient in a successful Internet advertising strategy. After your site is up and running, ideas will start solidifying into solutions.

Virtual Storefronts for Internet Sales

One growing trend in business today is the virtual storefront. This enables Web surfers to view a company's major products, and then order those products via the Net by using a credit card. Although those new to the Net may think twice about transmitting such information, it is actually becoming much safer thanks to encrypted security and better site administration. Many companies still stick with phone or fax sales, and have their major product line featured with pictures, specifications, and prices on their Web pages. This can dramatically increase sales because of the huge audience the Internet reaches.

When shopping, consumers want to know precisely what they are getting and the exact price for a particular product. A virtual storefront enables customers to experience just that. Do not think this is limited to computer hardware and software; everything from flowers to RISC processors can be found for sale on the Internet.

File and Information Distribution

Companies use ftp sites to store files and documents for disseminating information and files to the public and to customers. Whether you want to provide anyone on the Internet access to software demos, or only certain customers access to upgrades or documents (or both), an ftp site can be an ideal method of enabling file access to the world at-large.

Customer Support

Customer and technical support can be a costly necessity to your organization. Typical customer technical support involves costly telephone and staffing liabilities. With some skillful planning, you could create a support center on your Web and ftp sites to handle your most common situations and frequently asked questions: software bug fixes, documents and instructions, links to pertinent newsgroups and help pages, for example—anything that might provide the viewer with enough information to make a costly technical support call unnecessary. Some companies publish Web *bulletin boards* of technical information on their products. These bulletin boards have pages for questions, problems, and solutions. Some also save not only their organization money by cutting down support time, but also pass on the savings to the organization's customers. Information on the Web or ftp site is available 24 hours a day, at the customer's convenience. An accurate expense report on support services could be used as justification for an Internet *help desk*.

Technical Information Exchange and Research

The Internet can help you find others out there who have had the same technical or business problems your corporation has experienced. The Internet offers thousands of newsgroups and mailing lists where professionals and beginners alike turn for exchanging information. Network administrators, software developers, scientists, even CEOs turn to newsgroups and professional mailing lists every day to posts questions and answers. Imagine saving thousands of dollars each year on trivial technical support and research because someone has already experienced and corrected the same problem.

These vast informational coffers are not limited to newsgroups and e-mail, however. What if you needed to do more in-depth research on a problem? Assume for example that you have been assigned the job of evaluating Web server software for your company's Internet server (not too inconceivable a situation, is it?). A simple Web search could turn up not only the company's Web site for finding specifications and prices of the software, but also independent reviews on the benefits and disadvantages of the Web servers. In only a few hours, you can assemble enough information for an informed appraisal, and possibly download trial versions of the software for your own hands-on evaluation.

Instant Growth of Smaller Businesses

What if you run a small business? Your worries will likely lie in sales, not routing newsletters to an entire office complex or staffing full-time technical support. With an Internet presence, a small business can appear as professional and as high-tech as any major corporation. The Internet essentially enables small businesses an equal share of a vast advertising and information medium. Professionalism of advertising is only a matter of creativity, taste, and a knowledge of your product or service. Many small businesses utilizing a Net presence contend effectively with much larger corporations; an Internet presence and an ability to quickly adapt to the growing trends on the Net keeps them in contention.

Long Distance Contracting

An emerging trend in the work environment today is long-distance consulting—contracting out work to qualified professionals in other parts of the country or world via the Internet (for example, the copy editor of this book, which was compiled in Indiana, is in Australia). Because of the capability of sending and receiving information almost instantly, the former barriers of geographic location are no longer a major concern to many companies. This is a particular advantage to those seeking skill sets often unavailable in the immediate location. Software engineering companies often begin recruiting prospective engineers through long distance consulting over the Net. Many publishing companies allow writers and technical editors to work remotely and send in the works via e-mail. This type of distanced work has several advantages to both company and employee. Companies save thousands of dollars per long distance employee because most are hired on contract basis and do not require benefits; there are no office space or relocation expenses (smaller companies greatly benefit from reducing these costs). The contracted employee can work from home, often on more consulting jobs. This has proven an effective way for both company and employee to determine the possibilities of future on-site positions.

Long distance consulting over the Internet also provides a huge selection of qualified professionals, students, and researchers from which to choose. Even if your company handles all of its work in-house, it may eventually be able to save money by contracting out smaller jobs such as proofreading manuals, distributing mailing lists, custom software components, or necessary work unrelated to the expertise of your business.

Keeping Up and Staying Ahead

Can you afford *not* to have an Internet presence? Companies are gaining a foothold on the Net every day, and are reaching customers across the country and the world. It's as easy to find a company on the Net as it is to look in the local phone book. Is your business concerned with large-scale competition like this? An Internet presence of some kind (whether simple Web pages on a provider's site or an in-house server) is almost a necessity to keep up with the competition around you.

The Corporate Intranet

A year ago, the term intranet might have easily been mistaken for a slip of the tongue while pronouncing *Internet*, or possibly mistaken as a nonstandard generic term for a LAN. Recently, the term intranet has become one of the biggest buzzwords in the corporate information systems world. But what exactly is an intranet?

Intranets are a merging of Internet technologies, standards, and applications with a company's internal network. Whether this is integrating with an existing network or established as the initial model for the entire network, the term still applies. Examples of what intranets are accomplishing today include integrating Web browsing and e-mail inside companies, and providing discussion forums and newsgroups for enterprise-wide information sharing. Distributed applications are being designed to take advantage of the client-server architecture available on an Internet-like internal network.

Several directions are being taken to develop corporate intranet standards and solutions; the ones discussed here are mainly those of Microsoft because of the integration with Windows NT. There are, however, server and application tools from many other companies with clear definitions of intranet solutions. Before committing to any package, evaluate your intranet needs and the solutions provided by several alternatives to find the most suitable.

NOTE

For an in-depth discussion of intranet implementation and architecture, see *Intranet Web Development*, by John Desborough (New Riders, 1996).

Although this book is mainly concerned with Windows NT as an Internet server, it is important to understand that most of the information presented here can apply just as easily to a company's intranet server.

Section III: The Windows NT Choice for Internet Connectivity

For years, the Internet community was maintained primarily by Unix servers. Unix is a powerful network operating system originally developed by AT&T Labs in the late 1960s and early 1970s. Because its architecture is open and its source code is readily available, Unix has evolved into a variety of *flavors* (versions developed by various institutions and companies). Although some argue that this openness is a benefit to networking and software development, others believe that the lack of a standard, steadily evolving operating system is a major problem in the advancement of corporate computing. Microsoft Windows NT addresses the concern of a standard operating system that historically was unable to be changed by any other organization or entity except through the pressure or influence of the users. This debate over an open system versus a specific evolving standard will probably continue for some time, regardless of which OS becomes the leader in internetworking computing. The important thing to recognize and remember for now, especially for the administrator and MIS professionals, is that Microsoft has created a powerful and effective network OS.

The Windows NT Choice

For many years, variations of Unix dominated the network operating systems (NOS) market; PCs were predominantly the domain of MS-DOS and Microsoft Windows. As the importance of mission-critical stable operating systems increased, Microsoft developed its own high-security, stable networking platform: Windows NT Server and NT Workstation. This completely redesigned version of Windows (absolutely no dependency on DOS or 16-bit technology) has quickly become one of the leading network operating systems of the business world.

Although NT still lacks the widespread acceptance of Unix as a network operating system, it is quickly becoming an operating system of choice in business and research. An independent research firm recently reported that in 1995, licenses for Windows NT Workstation surpassed the combined workstation shipments of the two largest competitors, Sun Microsystems Inc. and Silicon Graphics Incorporated. NT's estimated growth in the next few years is expected to increase even more.

Microsoft is apparently very serious about steering the development of NT toward Internet-centric design goals. The latest evidence of this is the upcoming new release, NT 4. Before delving into the enhancements of 4, take a look at a few of the underlying concepts behind Windows NT, both design- and business-wise. These are a few of several considerations for choosing NT as your Internet server.

Client-Server Design

Windows NT networks are typically based on central servers containing (among other things) accounts, data, and applications. These contents are being accessed across the network by client computers, not dummy terminals. Client-server computing enables distributed processing load and a much more efficient design. NT is also designed in this way at the software level. This is covered more in-depth later in the book.

Multiple Protocols

Windows NT enables multiple protocols on the same system and bound to the same network adapters. TCP/IP is the protocol most important to the Internet server. A site can isolate its server from the rest of the network, however, by running a different protocol on the other computers and TCP/IP on the Internet server only. This is often used as a security measure to prevent external threats such as hacking.

Multi-Threaded Design

Windows NT goes beyond the multiple process barrier and implements multiple threads of execution. Threads are the smallest portion of executable code, and are allotted CPU time just as processes are. Multiple threads can exist for one application, however, and can run on multiple processors. A multi-threaded graphics program, for example, can have several threads running on multiple processors. One thread can render the image, the other can continue accepting user input, while threads for other processes are still active in the background. The operating system assigns threads priority levels. Threads are synchronized to prevent simultaneous changes to one critical resource, such as a file. NT's multi-threaded architecture dramatically increases the overall speed and stability of the operating system, and is utilized in all high-quality NT software including Internet servers.

File-Level Security

Windows NT enables file level security assignable to individual user accounts or groups of users. The NTFS file system is a secure and self-maintaining file system exclusive to Windows NT. This is a particular advantage to the Internet server administrator because permissions can be assigned and removed for any file, directory, or resource.

Additional Security

Windows NT has all the auditing and security features professional network administrators demand: security, application, and system event logging; customizable auditing of access to resources; ownership of files and other resources; and a kernel-mode protected login sequence at the physical computer to prevent *password grabbing* or *packet sniffing* programs.

NT has the capability to act as a C2 secure stand-alone system with minimal upgrades. C2 is the Department of Defense rating for a secure computer system. Although NT has not been evaluated for this as a network component, Microsoft is addressing this concern and is working with the National Computer Security Administration to evaluate NT as a C2 secure network operating system.

Scalability

Windows NT addresses the concern of the scalable network architecture with not only multiple domain options, but also with enhanced features and excellent third-party support. Multi-threaded advantages were reviewed previously. Because threads can execute on multiple processors, this is yet another key advantage NT has for improved scalability. Microsoft is currently planning a 64-bit version of NT that would launch the OS into the heavy-weight realm of massive data warehousing and increased bandwidth networking.

Ease of Configuration

Before NT entered the Internet server market, most Internet sites were maintained with Unix servers that required a fair amount of command-line and troubleshooting knowledge (often more trouble than it was worth). Installing and maintaining protocols and severs was the domain of a networking professional or a long-time user. With NT, you can easily configure all protocols and servers with a graphical user interface that abstracts all the complicated and often trivial command-line operations of Unix. Don't be fooled, however; NT enables very low-level administration of servers and protocols. The administrator can dig as deeply as required, or only skim the surface, to rapidly publish information on the Internet.

Compatibility

Windows NT will run programs written for 32-bit Windows NT, many Windows 95 programs and 16-bit Windows apps, DOS applications up to DOS 5 (later versions of DOS make direct calls to hardware, which NT will not allow), POSIX-1 compliant programs, and some OS/2 text based programs. Windows NT 3.51 has file system support for OS/2's HPFS file system; Microsoft has discontinued this in NT 4, however, because the demand for OS/2 has dropped considerably.

Reliability

Windows NT has several features for disk reliability including fault tolerance and self-maintaining file systems. NT Server enables RAID (Redundant Array of Inexpensive Disks) fault tolerance levels 0, 1, and 5 by using software implemented fault tolerance. (NT, of course, can utilize RAID hardware.) Tremendously important benefits to an Internet or file server include disk mirroring, disk duplexing, striping with parity, sector-sparing, transaction-based disk access, and a self-defragmenting file system.

Business Solutions

Windows NT networks benefit from the expansive set of network servers called Microsoft BackOffice. These include MS SQL Server for database query and administration, MS Exchange Server for mail and Internet mail, MS SNA Server (which bridges the gap between desktop and mainframe), Internet Information Server, and several other mission-critical enterprise-wide servers. Because of the interoperability among these packages, the artful Internet server administrator can give a secure and dynamic view of any part of the corporation's Information System to the outside world.

Windows NT 4

All the above points are valid for the last release of Windows NT 3.51. Improved Internet functionality, overall optimization, and a much better look and feel (the

Windows 95 interface) have been added to the upcoming release of NT 4 Server and Workstation, however.

What does NT 4 offer that previous versions of NT did not? Microsoft has realized the inability of an operating systems company to survive without serious attention to the Internet. Although they were once lacking in this area, the release NT 4 and the recent major Microsoft releases of browsing software has given them a clear advantage in the Internet server and application market. Several of the new innovations in Windows NT 4 Server follow:

❏ **The Windows 95 *shell* interface.** The old Windows 3.11 interface has finally been replaced with the easier to use graphical user interface. This includes greater support for drag-and-drop, right mouse button menus, and tighter integration with the new line of Microsoft Internet client software.

❏ **Internet Information Server 2.** This ships with Windows NT. This is one of the fastest NT Internet servers available because it is integrated with the operating system and NT security. Windows NT 4 actually comes with everything needed to have an Internet server up and running within an hour.

❏ **Improved DNS Server.** NT 4 comes with an improved Domain Name Resolution (DNS) server with easy to use graphical administration tools. This can be installed and configured as an internal NT service and stopped and restarted easily.

❏ **Improved Internet Security.** Microsoft and third parties have developed a new CryptoAPI (applications programming interface) that enables software developers to take advantage of various cryptographic methods of securing data. Windows NT 4 includes the CryptoAPI for developers to incorporate into their own network based applications. Another security advantage to NT 4 is the Point-to-Point Tunneling Protocol (PPTP), a secure protocol for network transmissions. These are discussed in detail later in the book.

❏ **The New Task Manager.** Windows NT 4 comes with an impressive new utility for at-a-glance performance monitoring of your overall system. The Task Manager, available by right clicking on the task bar (the *Start* bar on the new interface) has not only an improved view of all applications running (with the ability to close and switch to), but also has enhanced features for more control over the tasks of your system. You can now view each process running on your computer, including 13 process specific attributes (such as CPU usage, page faults, and thread count) of each. Processes can be killed or given different priorities. A quick-glance performance monitor shows real-time graphs and meters of CPU usage and memory, as well as the number of threads and handles open.

❑ **Distributed Component Object Model (DCOM).** This is a network version of COM, Microsoft's modular software design standard.

Windows NT Server versus NT Workstation

Windows NT Server is the high-end OS that drives Microsoft's NT networking architecture (including Microsoft BackOffice servers, and Internet Information Server). NT Server and NT Workstation have fundamental differences. Although they share the same operating systems architecture and applications, some server software runs on NT Server only. Internet Information Server is a primary example. Some software, such as Microsoft SQL Server, can be purchased for either platform. It is important to remember that most server software for NT Server is designed to fit an enterprise-wide corporate network, or will be accessed in great volume over the network or Internet.

NT Server still runs any Internet server software designed for NT Workstation. Although Microsoft has tightened its grip on the NT Server Internet server market with the introduction of the free MS-IIS, there are still several excellent Web and FTP servers from third-party companies that offer extended or different features from Microsoft's. One major complaint about IIS is that it only runs on the more expensive NT Server. This has enabled third-party vendors to develop Internet servers for both Server and Workstation. Companies such as Netscape and O'Riley and Associates provide full-featured Web servers, and often FTP, news, and mail servers for Windows NT Server *and* NT Workstation.

For heavier Internet traffic, NT Server is the obvious choice between the two. It is not only optimized to handle a heavy workload, but can host SQL database servers and other company information systems that can be used to enhance the capabilities of a site. NT Server is the only platform that supports the Microsoft BackOffice suite of server products.

For smaller sites, NT Workstation (running one of the many free or commercial Internet server packages today) is a very cost-effective and easy to maintain solution. All the networking tools inherent to NT are present in the Workstation version of the OS; little is fundamentally different from Server in this area. Here are a few differences to consider when choosing a Windows NT platform for an Internet server.

Feature	Windows NT Server	Windows NT Workstation
TCP/IP protocols and tools	Yes	Yes
MS Internet Information Server	Yes	No
Maximum Remote Access Dial-Ins	256	1
MS BackOffice Support	Full BackOffice Support	Only client-side applications. No Servers.
Maximum Number of In-Bound Network Connections	Unlimited	10
Maximum Number of Processors out of the box	4	2

The choice of NT Server or Workstation should depend on your needs as an Internet site, and the expected network load on your server. Although NT Server is the recommended Internet server platform, Workstation may suit the requirements of a smaller company. Before making your decision, you should have a clear idea of how your server will be used, and what role in your company's Information System it will play.

You've read how Windows NT can provide an effective Internet network operating system. The next chapter will familiarize you with the various types of Internet connectivity. This will help you to determine the best type of connection and networking hardware for your Internet server.

Summary

This chapter discusses the environment in which you might be working. It addressed introductory material about the Internet, justification for a corporate Internet presence, and the best Windows NT choice for Internet connectivity.

2

Business Opportunities with Internet Technologies

Companies now operate in a global market. This global market is competitive, one in which businesses are being forced to change the way they think about and undertake business. New business models are being developed and implemented by companies that seek to exploit their core competencies. New markets are being sought for existing and new products.

The Internet has become "*the* new marketplace" for business. To help companies take advantage of this new marketplace, there are countless seminars and conferences across the country that deal with getting your business onto the Internet and marketing your products on the Internet.

The Internet enables businesses to contact customers directly, eliminating the middleman, without expensive information channels, without delays. For some industries, the software industry for example, the Internet eliminates distribution costs by providing uniform access to customers around the globe and by redefining business boundaries. The Internet is not just a means for undertaking commerce, but also a tool that can be utilized to securely and inexpensively share critical data across an organization, linking geographically dispersed facilities, telecommuters, and mobile employees.

NOTE

"The Internet will almost certainly have a stronger impact than the PC...a reasonable guess might put it ahead of the telephone and television but behind the printing press." *The Economist*, July 1, 1995

Not surprisingly, everyone is jumping on the Internet bandwagon. From four supercomputers connected together in 1971, the Internet has grown to over 6 million computers and over 50 million users (source presentation by net. Genesis at Internet World, Fall 95).

The Internet has consistently doubled every year for the past decade. The Internet's growth and capabilities will further expand as media and telephone companies invest heavily, as seen in the popular press, in the next decade to build the infrastructure for high capacity communications into the home.

Along with the advantages of the Internet come an entirely new set of hurdles. It is imperative that companies move beyond the obvious capabilities of the medium and take advantage of its full potential. Companies must work to expand their relationships with their customers and their suppliers into a transaction-oriented environment; they must go beyond pushing old products down a new distribution channel. There is a need to create fresh, innovative products, taking advantage not only of the global, mass-market audience, but also of the capability to develop customized offerings marketed to a narrow or niche audience.

NOTE

"If you're not an active Internet citizen by the mid-1990s, you're likely to be out of business by the year 2000." Industry Analyst Patricia Seybold

The rules of the game in this electronic marketplace are radically different from traditional commerce. Marketing and advertising budgets no longer determine market share. Small companies can compete with multinationals and local vendors with international vendors. Building a presence can be technically complex and intimidating. This book will mitigate the intimidation factor by helping you set up and operate an Internet server to enable you to participate in this exciting new environment.

Who Uses the Internet (and Why You Should Care)

The Internet is a large potential audience for your company's offerings. Today the Internet spans over 150 countries and is estimated to be used by over 50 million users.

Individuals normally connect to the Internet through the companies for whom they work or through an Internet Service Provider (ISP) who provides them with an individual account. ISPs provide the following several levels of service:

- ❑ Connection to the Internet
- ❑ E-mail services
- ❑ Hosting of Web sites
- ❑ Writing customized scripts and programs for a company's site
- ❑ Managing a domain name service (DNS) for companies

To understand the user demographics of the Internet, review the following numbers in terms of a quick look at the types of organizations that have established a *presence* on the Internet. The data is based on registered domain names and is from *The Internet Business Companion*, by David Angell and Brent Heslop.

Table 2.1 Business Presence on the Internet	Organization Type	Percentage of Total
	Commercial	51%
	Research	29%
	Government (including Defense)	16%
	Education	4%

This indicates that over half the users of the Internet access the Internet from a commercial entity, including the ISPs.

Although there are several Internet services available to undertake business on the Internet, the current growth in corporate Internet *presence* is in the World Wide Web (Web) site. The following table shows the growth figures of Web sites on the Internet and demonstrates the rapid growth of commercial sites (as indicated by *.com* domain names) (source net.Genesis).

Table 2.2	Date	Number of Web Sites	Percent .com
Growth of Commercial Web Sites	June 1993	130	1.5
	June 1994	2,738	13.5
	June 1995	23,500	31.5
	Jan. 1996	90,000	50.2

NOTE

A home page produced for an individual person will be referred to as a "personal home page" while a home page that is produced by a business, regardless of its size, will be referred to as a "corporate home page."

From the preceding figures, approximately 45,000 of the Web sites that existed as of January, 1996 were corporate *presences* sites (including ISPs) in the .com domain.

This does not mean that only 45,000 businesses had Web sites in January, 1996. Many, many more corporate Web-based *home pages* can be found on ISP computers. Figure 2.1 shows a typical small business' home page, hosted by an ISP (as indicated by the /~rhuber/ in the address).

Figure 2.1

Corporate home page hosted on a .com ISP.

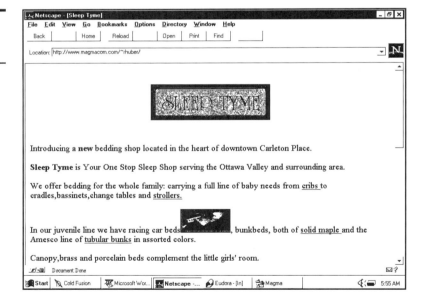

In addition to having ISPs host their Web sites, many businesses use one of the *Internet malls* to host their pages. These electronic malls are similar to shopping malls that can be found in almost every town and city. These electronic malls and their virtual storefronts run the gamut of narrowly focused to an industry sector to a general purpose shopping mall. Two examples are Industry Net (`http://www.industry.net`), which focuses on manufacturing companies, and Aerolink (`http://www.aerolink.com`), which focuses on the aerospace and aviation sectors. Figure 2.2 shows the Company Index page of AeroLink's mall.

Figure 2.2
An Internet Mall: on AeroLink MarketPlace.

When considering the Internet for business opportunities, it is a good idea to keep the typical user in mind. *The Internet Business Companion*, by David Angell and Brent Heslop, lists the following demographics of the Internet user:

❑ 60 percent of users are male

❑ Greater than 66 percent of the users are between 18 and 44 years of age

❑ Greater than 90 percent earn more than $25,000

❑ Greater than 90 percent have some college education, a college degree, or an advanced degree

CommerceNet and Nielsen have recently released a follow-up to their study of Internet usage and have provided the following summary points regarding user demographics:

N O T E

This book cannot warrant the suitability of these Internet malls for any particular business nor should this book be considered as an endorsement for any Internet mall. The concept is raised here to demonstrate what is happening in the world of the Internet.

❑ Among long-time users (more than 6 months), approximately 67 percent are male, versus 60 percent among newcomers.

❑ Among long-time users, 88 percent own a home computer; among newcomers, 72 percent own a home computer.

❑ 55 percent of long-time users have at least a college degree, and 39 percent of newcomers have at least a college degree.

❑ 27 percent of long-time users live in households with incomes of $80,000 or greater, and 17 percent of newcomers live in households with $80,000+ incomes.

What could these statistics mean for your business? These figures suggest that, as individuals, the Internet user community is relatively affluent and well-educated. If your company's product offerings are targeted at the individuals who fit into this category, you may well wish to find the appropriate Internet business model to reach these people.

To summarize the demographics of the Internet relative to the business opportunities that may be available for your company, the individual users of the Internet are educated and have relatively high incomes. They are a potential marketplace you cannot afford to ignore. The rapid growth in the number of commercial Web sites probably includes your competitors—don't let them get the edge on you in tapping the Internet marketplace.

The Benefits of Doing Business on the Internet

The Internet is revolutionizing modern commerce. In addition to using the Internet for advertising their wares, companies that have been using online technology like Electronic Data Interchange (EDI) for years are now combining this technology with the power of the Internet. By using the full potential of the Internet, your company will realize the following benefits:

❏ Broaden the reach of the business

❏ Rapid information dissemination

❏ Integrate your "partners"

The following sections explore these benefits in more detail.

Broaden the Reach of the Business

To grow your business, you must reach and sell to new clients. You must expand your relationships with existing customers as well as new ones.

You can develop a competitive advantage by learning how to effectively do business in this new paradigm. Figure 2.3, for example, shows the home page for Hawaii's Best Espresso Company. The company moved from the storefront espresso business to selling Hawaiian coffee over the Internet full time. This company changed its business completely from a coffee shop to a cyberstore, and ships its products around the world. With an estimated user-base of 50 million, the Internet offers a very large market for (in this example) coffee sales.

Figure 2.3
Extend Your Reach: selling coffee worldwide.

Another example in this same vein is Lobster Direct in Nova Scotia. Lobster Direct provides fresh Atlantic lobster and lox to the world from its Web site. Figure 2.3 displays its home page.

Figure 2.4

Extend Your Reach: lobsters for sale.

By opening themselves up to the Internet market, with over 50 million users in 160-odd countries in the world, Lobster Direct and Hawaii's Best Espresso Company have indeed broadened their reach. Rather than the walk-in customers, primarily tourists, both companies now service markets well beyond their initial markets.

To facilitate these operations, you have to provide security for a business environment. Ensuring all aspects of security is the paramount concern when doing business on the Internet. These security aspects include privacy, authentication of buyer and seller, message integrity (no digits were removed from the price), non-repudiation (parties in the transaction cannot deny that they authorized it), and robustness (the capability to deal with network failures). For information on security measures with NT 4 Server, see Chapter 14, "Security Practices."

Rapid Information Dissemination

To be successful, you often have to collapse your information and product distribution time frames. This will result in customers, suppliers, and vendors getting information they require more effectively, 24 hours a day, 7 days a week. This also permits your staff to respond to client/supplier queries more efficiently and effectively and to ship products, if applicable, on a more effective basis.

Figure 2.5 shows the On-Line Reservations capability of the Hampton Inn hotel chain. This use of Internet technology enables the user to check whether rooms are available in a desired location and to make reservations immediately. Instant gratification! For the hotel chain, it has cut out the person on the phone handling the call and has instant access to the information at the hotel desk.

Figure 2.5

Rapid Information Dissemination: book your own hotel rooms.

Generate compelling content that attracts traffic. Online *stores* with descriptions of product offerings need to be created in such a way that they can be viewed on the Web quickly and effectively. The more compelling the content and products offered, the more likely you'll hook buyers into the store.

Allow online order taking and payment processing. To encourage spontaneous commerce, offerings need to be connected to a transaction processing system that both authorizes and settles the transaction online and in real time. For more information, please refer to *Internet Commerce*, by Andrew Dahl and Leslie Lesnick (New Riders Publishing, 1995).

A successful Internet business must be able to handle the delivery of whatever the customer wants to purchase, whether the products are soft goods (things delivered immediately over the network, such as information) or hard goods (things physically delivered to the customer's home). By automating as much of the order-to-delivery process as possible, businesses can dramatically reduce distribution costs and provide immediate delivery of goods.

Integrating Your "Partners"

Connect your *partners* (suppliers, vendors, distributors, and customers) and focus on establishing a strategic foothold in the Internet business model by focusing on long-term growth for the entire *value chain*. The key is to start gaining experience and building strong relationships now; the cost of *catching up* later may prove insurmountable. This integration of partners reduces customer support costs across the board. This reduction should, in turn, produce greater profitability downstream.

To encourage your partners to participate in this exercise, start with something simple. *NewsPage Direct*, from Individual, Inc., is an example of a commercial offering wherein you can build a personalized news profile for yourself and have articles matching your profile appear as an e-mail every weekday morning. By offering a similar service to your customers and providing them with new information on your products and services that match their profiles/interests, you can keep them interested in your firm. By establishing a means for the individuals to update and modify their profiles, you develop a feedback loop. Figure 2.6 shows the NewsPage Direct information page.

Figure 2.6
Integrate Your Partners: NewsPage Direct personal news profile.

The next step is to facilitate customer service. Every time a customer picks up the phone to dispute a purchase, it costs the merchant at least $25–50. An effective Internet-based electronic commerce environment must take advantage of online methods of information distribution, such as account activity and account statements to facilitate customer service. When customers have online access to the full record of their transactions, their questions are minimized, disputes can be efficiently resolved online, and the goods available on the Web site can be reacquired easily.

The feedback loop enables you to build customer relationships and generate reports. Because the Internet is a transaction-based environment, buyers don't physically walk into your storefront. Comment forms, special offers, reward programs for repeat customers, or any other techniques you might use in a traditional store to build relationships with your customers are also necessary for online stores. In addition, businesses need to track the traffic through the store: where people went, how long they were there, how many people did what to effectively hone the offerings for each individual buyer.

The Changing Face of Business on the Internet

The Internet has become more than just a place to make your documents available to other interested parties. Three or even two years ago, businesses were trying to figure out how to use the Internet for *fun and profit*. The most common complaint from the business community was that there just wasn't enough easily accessible, business-related content.

Given the growth in the number of computers connected and the number of users of the Internet, it is safe to assume that the amount of information on the Internet has increased dramatically. Now it seems that the problem is to get the right information into the right hands at the right time—you can extend that metaphor to include the right product into the right hands.

A Brief Review of the Business Uses of the Internet

Over the past several years, organizations have used various functions of the Internet server to operate within the Internet. This book covers how to implement many of these functions throughout the remaining chapters. This section introduces the various functions (in the following list) to help develop an understanding of how they have been employed within a business framework:

- ❏ File Transfer Protocol (ftp)
- ❏ Gopher
- ❏ Wide Area Information Server (WAIS)
- ❏ Usenet newsgroups
- ❏ Telnet
- ❏ Electronic mail (e-mail)
- ❏ World Wide Web (Web) sites

File Transfer Protocol (ftp)

The File Transfer Protocol (ftp) service provides a means to collect files, put them into an archive (a storage space for the documents), and make them available for retrieval.

This was, and still is, the primary method for digital product distribution—software programs, for example. Figure 2.7 shows the Netscape Home Page; you will note on the right-hand side of the image the capability to *Download or Purchase the Latest Netscape Software*. The download capability is handled by ftp software. This is one of the means that Netscape employs to get its product into your hands. Any company that is distributing product in electronic format, be it software or competitive intelligence reports, ftp can be used to satisfy the business needs of the organization.

New products and updates are made available to customers immediately for them to download at their convenience. This is one method of making information files and products available on the Internet.

Gopher

Gopher was the first *easy-to-navigate* information service. Gopher clients display a menu of text-labeled choices, and the user selects one. This selection may result in the display of another menu or a text document. The architecture is easy to administer if well organized. The file and subdirectory names become menu items to the Gopher client. The user has only to click on the appropriate item, and it will be delivered to the screen. Figure 2.8 shows the Gopher menu of the ASCII Art Gopher.

Figure 2.7

Netscape Home Page: ftp service to download software.

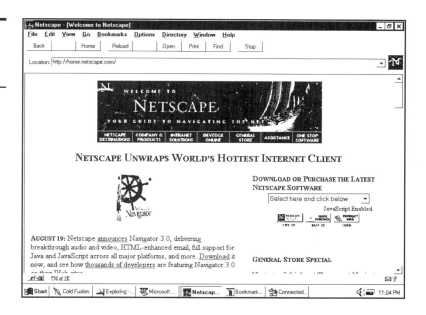

Figure 2.8

Gopher menu example.

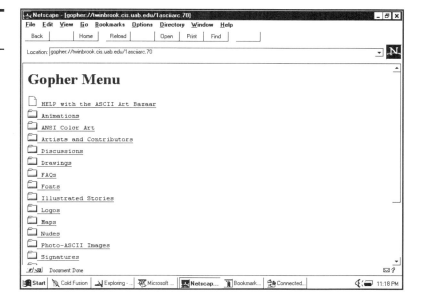

The service is essentially text-oriented; it currently only displays ASCII text data. You can transfer binary data from a Gopher menu and display it with other software at the user's workstation. When searching a Gopher site for information, only the menu headings can be searched. This means that the critical information about the content of the file has to be captured succinctly within the title or the searcher will not find the document.

Before the Web came in to being, Gopher was the primary mechanism for distribution of text-based materials, such as annual reports of a company. Combined with password access, Gopher distribution services are still used (but not often) to distribute information products to clients.

Wide Area Information Server (WAIS)

The Wide Area Information Server (WAIS) is used for searching data and has minimal support for browsing. Often used in conjunction with a Gopher or World Wide Web server, WAIS enables a user to search the documents in a list of servers to find the documents that contain the information the user seeks. WAIS is often used on Web sites to allow users to search through the HTML pages of the site, seeking the information they desire. Without some form of search capability, a large Web site must be explored page-by-page to find the information needed. This is time consuming and not conducive to generating repeat business.

WAIS works through the creation of an index by the system administrator beforehand that enables users to search. A large variety of file types are supported. One drawback is the size of the index file(s) created to run WAIS. Figure 2.9 shows the input screen used to search a WAIS database, and figure 2.10 shows the output of a search of the WAIS document collection.

UseNet Newsgroups

UseNet is the name of a newsgroup format that has developed into a good source of up-to-date news in specific areas. If a newsgroup does not already exist on a topic, you can create one—you can provide product support and obtain feedback in a self-managed newsgroup. Thousands of newsgroups exist, and monitoring the ones that could impact the affairs of your business can give you a leg up on the competition.

Establishing a newsgroup enables you to feed your customers or potential customers with information and to provide a forum for input and feedback. UseNET newsgroups are generally seen as a form of goodwill by the companies who implement and manage them.

Figure 2.9
WAIS input screen.

Figure 2.10
WAIS search output: list of available documents.

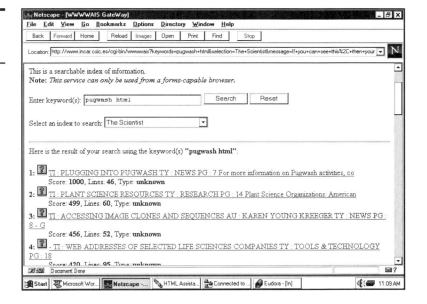

Telnet

Telnet enables the user to log on to a remote computer and take advantage of the services offered by the remote site. Traveling users used to have to dial long distance back to the office through modems, log on to the local network, and then enter information into the data application. As Internet usage grows within companies, travelers (wherever they are) connect to the Internet through a local service provider, and use Telnet to obtain the same access to the data application. This, for example, enables a salesperson on the road to connect to and enter orders into an existing Order Entry application—the same application that is used by telemarketing staff at headquarters. There is no need to create another data entry application for the road reps.

Most users tend to feel that Telnet is using a dumb terminal to enter information into the application—even if the Internet is used to access the application. They are probably right in most cases.

Electronic Mail (E-Mail)

Electronic mail (e-mail) is fast becoming the dominant form of business communications. It is replacing the phone tag that many people play, even if voice mail is available. Anyone in the world can communicate with you at his or her convenience, 24 hours a day, 7 days a week.

E-mail is less expensive than fax or overnight couriers, and most e-mail programs support the attachment of a variety of file types. International messages can be delivered in minutes and can incorporate all the questions that need to be answered. Many companies have implemented e-mail as their only Internet application.

Combining regular e-mail with a mailing list application enables you to reach multiple recipients with no printing or mailing costs. If you allow people to join/subscribe to your mailing list, you can keep them informed of the latest updates and developments. You don't even have to worry about them being no longer interested —the recipient can *unsubscribe* if no longer interested in receiving the information from you.

World Wide Web (Web)

The advent of the graphic user interface of the Web, and its subsequent discovery by the marketing departments of many companies, has led to the phenomenal growth in the use of the Web by companies.

Initially started as a sort of cyberspace advertisement, Web sites have grown in size, scope, and functionality over the last three years. Because this is the mainstay of business on the Internet, you will read more about this in the following sections. From a Web site, companies distribute information, market their wares, and sell products and services. Figure 2.11 shows the typical home page of a company within an Internet mall. This is one of the easiest ways to develop a presence on the Internet. As the next section shows, however, the business opportunities on the Internet are now more than this form of *advertorial*.

Figure 2.11
Typical internet mall home page.

More Than Just Advertising

Today's business uses of the Internet are more than just advertising. They have to be! To compete, companies have to be faster, more innovative, and continually breaking new ground to survive and thrive.

The Internet can be used to cut costs. As the previous section discussed, e-mail has become one of the most widely used Internet applications by companies—it is cheaper than faxing or using couriers to get information across town or around the world. But how can you reduce costs elsewhere in your business through the use of Internet technologies? The following two short sections discuss how to use Internet technologies internally as well as externally to reduce costs.

External Services

Earlier in the chapter, you were introduced to Hawaii's Best Espresso Company. This company has cut the middleman out of the ordering process by enabling you to place your order for coffee directly online. By putting you in charge of preparing and verifying your order, the company can put its efforts into getting the product out the door to you faster.

Lobster Direct enables you to place your orders directly into its Web site, and ships via courier to your door—cutting out the middleman. You no longer have to go to the fish market or supermarket to place your order.

Figure 2.12 shows a sample of an order for coffee from Hawaii's Best Espresso Company. You can see contact information in the bottom half of the image. The form goes on to ask for shipping information and for payment information—Visa and Mastercard are accepted. For those who claim to be faint of heart about giving their credit card information out over the Internet, how many of you think twice about booking tickets over the phone (including cell phones) and giving your credit card number? How many of you think twice about giving your credit card to a waiter or waitress you have never seen before to pay a tab at a restaurant? Electronic commerce on the Internet is not that scary or insecure.

Figure 2.12

Ordering coffee on the Internet.

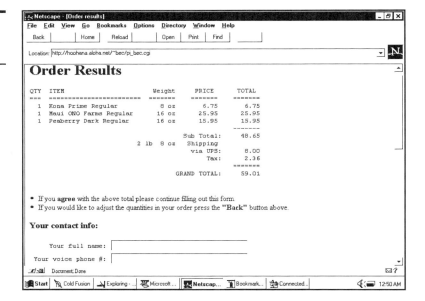

Assuming that you are planning on basing your Internet offerings around the Web, a list of services that could be put in place to service your customers' needs via the Internet follows. You could do the following:

N O T E

For more information on establishing active Internet Commerce, see *Inside JavaScript*, by Bill Bercik and Jill Bond (New Riders Publishing, 1996). It includes in-depth coverage of LiveConnect and LivePayment, new technologies from Netscape that make credit card payments over the Web a reality. You may also want to review the CommerceNet Web site (`http://www.commerce.net`) for information and products that can assist you in this discipline.

❏ Publish your marketing literature and product specification documents on your Web site.

Clients and sales people can obtain the required documents from the Web site and print them on their own printers. This should reduce your printing and associated distribution costs. The costs associated with design and layout will still be incurred but printing costs can be substantial.

❏ Create searchable product manuals and FAQ (frequently asked question) lists for customer support purposes.

Many products ship with user manuals and not technical reference manuals. By creating searchable (using WAIS or some other search engine) documents, you can reduce the time spent looking for information as well as reducing the demands on your technical support staff. In many cases, customers will attempt to find the solutions to their problems on their own before contacting your support staff.

❏ Establish an ftp site to enable customers to obtain manuals, updates, software patches, and so forth.

Distribution costs of products that can be encapsulated in electronic "packages" can be drastically reduced by using an ftp site. Only one copy of the "package" needs to be loaded onto the ftp site where it can be downloaded to (hopefully) several million computers.

❏ Establish a feedback system to enable customers to enter comments and questions.

Put a hyperlink or a button on your Internet page(s) that enables users to provide comments—bouquets or bricks—to the people in your organization who are best positioned to deal with the feedback. The method used can be either an e-mail message or a form that accepts user input. A separate "feedback survey questionnaire" page can be created and included in the site to obtain and record visitor comments and opinions. This enables your organization to respond to customer queries more quickly by having them routed to the person responsible, as well as allowing the user to make the comments while the "thought is still fresh in his or her mind."

❏ Create a mailing list of customers and potential customers for distribution of corporate newsletters or product announcements.

Use the e-mail functionality of the Internet to quickly notify your clients and prospects of information. The cost of stamps has been eliminated, and the opportunity costs associated with the time delay between posting the letter in the mail and its receipt can be minimized by using e-mail. By allowing users to subscribe and unsubscribe, the list can become "self-managing" (within limits). Be sure to follow the etiquette of the Internet and only send mail to those who have requested information.

❏ Enable customers to review the information you hold about them, including invoices and profiles—the more information they know about themselves, the more information they may provide you.

You can reduce the costs associated with the amount of time that your staff have to spend preparing reports for prime customers regarding their activities with your company. By providing them with password-protected access, or using similar security measures, you can enable customers to review the status of their current orders and possibly help customers create new business opportunities. Being able to look at your inventory levels and commitments, customers may be better able to bid on projects, creating a win-win scenario for both of you.

Internal Services

Many companies are now starting to use Internet technologies internally to create intranets. In addition to making internal documents available to all the employees, Internet technology now enables users to access the wide variety of information resources within the organization through the browser at the user's desk.

One example of cost reduction that can be achieved through the implementation of Internet technologies in an intranet is as follows:

Traditionally, all employees are issued manuals covering financial and human resource policies, including benefit entitlements. These cost approximately $20 each (in this real organization) to print and distribute. As changes are made to the policies, copies are printed and mailed to all individuals.

By publishing the manuals and the changes on the intranet, the users can access the documents whenever they may need them. Notices about changes can be posted in the *What's New* section, instructing the staff to review the changes as necessary.

The savings realized include the printing and distribution costs for new manuals and the ensuing changes. Assume, for this example, that approximately 400 of an organization's 4500 staff turn over annually. The estimated annual savings of using an intranet equals $8,000 in new manuals. An estimated six changes per year are made to the policy manual. At $2 per employee per change for printing and distribution, the estimated annual savings equals $54,000.

Intranets can be a valuable tool in helping to achieve competitive advantages.

More Than Just Shuffling Paper Between Companies

As more and more people become willing to shop online, their concerns about the security of the transaction information need to be addressed. The technologies of the Internet enable users to place orders for goods and services, and most users are comfortable with this aspect of the transaction. Unless the transaction is completed electronically and the payment for the transaction is negotiated and settled in the same online transaction, the Internet marketplace will be stuck in a paper-shuffling paradigm—moving purchase orders and invoices between both ends of the transaction.

The technologies required for secure electronic commerce are very close to being iron-clad as you read this book. Organizations like CommerceNet (`http://www. commerce.net`) are working very hard to develop an understanding of electronic commerce on the Internet. CommerceNet is a nonprofit consortium of companies and financial institutions working together to create the electronic marketplace.

Even if the technologies are in place, the users of the systems that you can put in place need to be assured that their transactions are secure. A recent study by FIND/SVP revealed that only 19 percent of Internet users had shopped online. Of those surveyed, 59 percent were interested in making online purchases. The security seemed to be less of an issue than familiarity—after the users are familiar with the technology, online shopping is poised for an explosion. The study indicated that 64 percent of online shoppers used credit cards online, representing a trend toward acceptance. For more information, contact FIND/SVP at 516-671-7748 or at their Web site `http:// www.findsvp.com`.

In an article in the April 8, 1996 issue of *Internet Week*, by Phillips Business Information, Inc., the online shopping sites of three catalog stores were discussed (L.L. Bean, Spiegel, and The Sharper Image). As well, the different philosophies of taking credit card information were reviewed. The article indicated that the firms felt that the Internet would not replace their printed catalogs, but would help to expand their reach while attracting a new customer base. In the aforementioned article, Joy Villalino, public relations manager for Spiegel, is quoted as saying "It's obviously cheaper to put a catalog on the Web than to make a printed catalog. But we don't think that it will in any way take the place of the traditional catalog. In many ways, the Web catalog supplements our printed catalog, but it also attracts a new customer base who will only shop that way."

Creating a Competitive Weapon

Internet technologies can enable organizations to create competitive advantages. By offering products and services for online purchase rather than passive advertising, you can reduce the time it takes to deliver the product. You can also reduce the cost of the transaction by extending your company's capabilities to handle electronic commerce, moving funds from the buyer's bank right into your accounts.

After deciding on the appropriate type of Internet technology or technologies that you will put in place, you need to determine how to make your business known throughout the potential marketplace. The following section discusses acceptable advertising practices on the Internet and provides a list of sites where you can find information about marketing on the Internet.

Acceptable Internet Advertising Practices

The basic principles, regardless of the medium used to advertise your wares, include:

❏ Choosing a specific target audience
❏ Adding value to the information
❏ Keeping the information up-to-date

When advertising on the Internet, do not send unsolicited information out via e-mail, especially via a mailing list. The culture of the Internet frowns on this sort of behavior and will probably retaliate—at the very least, you will be flamed (Internet hate mail). In fact, some people have gone as far as putting notices up regarding this sort of unsolicited behavior. Figure 2.13 is offered as an example of one such notice.

Figure 2.13

Notice regarding unsolicited E-mail traffic.

Netscape - [User Agreement]

File Edit View Go Bookmarks Options Directory Window Help

Back   Home   Reload   Open Print Find

Location: http://www.afn.org/~afn09444/agreement.html

Copyright Laws and is punishable by fine AND/OR imprisonment.

4. Any unwanted 'advertisements' sent to me shall be considered to be harrassment and do greatly injure Todd L. Sherman, as well as being considered to be a violation of Copyright Laws, punishable by fine and/or imprisonment.

5. Prior accepted approval from me to receive your 'advertisement' negates this USER AGREEMENT and you shall then not be billed for my reading or mulling over your 'advertisement.' [See #2 - 'Permission' under DEFINITIONS below, for a description of how to obtain such 'prior accepted approval.']

6. From this moment on (18:54 ET, June 7th, 1996), for each 'advertisement' that I recieve at my Internet user account here at Alachua County Freenet (AFN) - said 'advertisement' having been sent without any previous permission asked of me to have that ad sent to me - you (being the individual as a civilian, or as an employee of a business or organization or, yes, even the business or organization that you are employed with itself if it seems to occur just a little bit too often from that site yet seems to come from varying and different individuals within said business or organization - depends on how often it is occuring and upon how angry and annoyed it is making me) shall be billed $250.00 (US) per ten minutes of time taken to read the "advertisement" and mull over it, with a minimum charge of $250.00 (US) billed no matter how much time is actually spent reading the ad or mulling over it - even if less than ten minutes.

7. If you use an anonymous address which takes extra effort and time for me to track you down, I SHALL INDEED track you down, and when I find you, you shall be billed first per Item number (6) above, and then, an additional $500.00 (US) per ten minutes spent tracking down your actual address - with a minimum $1000.00 (US) billed to you no matter how much time is actually spent hunting down your actual address - even if less than 10 minutes.

8. As well, a MINIMUM of $1000.00 (US) shall be also asked for in compensation for 'pain and suffering', 'damages', and any lost time spent on you. (So, get this straight: I'll be asking for a MINIMUM of $1250.00 to $2500.00 dollars (US funds) from you, depending upon whether your return e-mail address is legit or not, respectively, PLUS court costs and other incurred expenses.) However, per Item number (9), below, I reserve the right to adjust 'damages' to a higher amount at any time.

Document: Done

Start   Cold Fusion   Exploring -   Microsoft ...   Netscap...   Bookmark...   Connected...   2:05 AM

Passive advertising is more acceptable. This includes your corporate Web site address appearing on all paper documentation and as the signature file of all e-mail messages. In a newsgroup posting, it is acceptable to respond with product information if it has been requested. One should not get out the straw boater and cane to hawk one's wares in newsgroups.

The most important thing is to make certain to submit your Web site address to the major Internet search engines. Table 2.3 lists these major search engines.

Table 2.3

Search Engine Address List

Site Name	Address
Yahoo!	http://www.yahoo.com
AltaVista	http://www.altavista.digital.com
Open Text	http://search.opentext.com
Webcrawler	http://www.webcrawler.com
HotBot	http://www.hotbot.com
Lycos	http://www.lycos.com
excite	http://www.excite.com

Someone searching the Internet for information contained in your Web site may use one or all of these search engines; it is a good idea, therefore, to have your Web pages indexed within all these search services. In some cases, you may even consider advertising your company's wares within one of the search engines' pages. Most of these organizations sell common space on pages and in some cases, space on context-specific results pages. For example, your ad may show up if someone searches for "bioremediation of septic fields" and you have associated your ad with the context of "septic" and associated terms. Consult with the search engine organizations for more details.

Marketing Indexes Available for the Internet

The following is a list of marketing indexes available on the Internet that can provide information about getting your products and services into the hands of customers. In addition to the information discussed in the previous section regarding the search engines, these marketing indexes will provide you with much more concrete information on how to incorporate your Internet marketing efforts into your traditional media marketing. For example, put your Web address (your URL) on all printed materials. For this type of tip, please refer to the following information sources:

High Tech Marketing Communications: `http://www.bayne.com/wolfBayne/htmarcom`

The Alliance of Global Business Exchange: `http://www.globalbiz.com`

MouseTracks: `http://nsns.com/MouseTracks/`

InterNetWork Marketing: `http://www.he.net/~image/nwm/`

The Internet Advertising Guide: `http://pilot.msu.edu/unit/adv/internet-advertising-guide.htm`

Internet Marketing Index: `http://www.xs4all.nl/~malens/index2.htm`

Can the Internet Be a Business?

Take a look at the types of businesses that currently exist on the Internet, and review the information presented in the previous pages. You should realize that it is entirely possible to create a business unit or a separate organization that uses the Internet and its technologies as the basis for a business.

Is there something that you can do with Internet technologies that would enable you to earn a living from the Internet? The remaining sections of this chapter provide a few examples to whet your appetite.

Within the previous pages, several business opportunities were discussed but may not have been overly apparent to you. In finding the right Internet business to pursue, you must match a personal interest with an opportunity. The personal interest is a must because you will be doing the work initially, and you should enjoy what you are doing.

Remembering the basic principles of specific target audience, value-added information, and continuous updates, the following are some simple Internet businesses that can be started and operated fairly easily. The Internet technologies on which they are based are discussed in detail later in this book.

Hosting of Other Home Pages

Become a small Internet Service Provider, after a fashion. You need to establish your own Internet server (this book helps you do just that) with a connection to the Internet—a 56 KB line should cost you about $400/month for continuous service. This enables you to have your own Web site up and running at all times. After this is done, you can canvass the small businesses in your area who are not yet *on the Internet* to create a home page for them on your server.

The typical address that would be used would be similar to the following:

```
http://www.yourhomeserver.com/~otherpeoplesbusiness/
```

In the April 1, 1996, issue of *Internet Week*, MCI announced its MCI WebSite Services offering. This is a Web Hosting service that it hopes to use to expand the Internet services it offers clients. MCI's client base is relatively large, and the investment required is substantial. Your technology investment is probably in the range of a 150 MHz Pentium, 32 MB RAM, 2 GB of storage and associated software to create and maintain 25–50 small business Web sites of the advertising type.

Document Distribution Services

In many towns and small cities, not-for-profit agencies have information and reports that they make available to the community. In an effort to reduce their costs of operations, obtain an electronic copy of the documents and put them on an ftp site, perhaps with a WAIS search engine to assist users in locating the correct documents online. Your local tourism bureau would be most happy to provide you with information that can be used or given away online.

You could even set up a billing system (not an EDI system for this crowd) that enables the user to search for, find, and download the required document but not before agreeing to pay a small fee, or the price of the document, upon receipt of the invoice.

These are just a couple of examples of how you can put in place a document distribution business by using FTP services.

Management of Distribution Lists

Obtain a copy of the Majordomo mailing list software or something similar and install the software. Approach the businesses in your community to see whether they have a supplier, customer, or lead e-mail list that you could manage on their behalf. Whenever the company has a requirement to send an item to the members of a list, it would be sent to your list server and then re-distributed to all the subscribers.

Maintenance of a News Feed

Many companies obtain printed newspapers along with magazines, journals, and newsletters. A large number of these publications have electronic copies available. One of the problems for most business people is information overload. By receiving only the critical information they request to see, a business person can reduce the amount of time spent sifting through the content to find the nuggets.

A number of news feeds can be obtained and accessed free of charge. Subscribe to these and learn how to build a *personal profile* to extract only the information that matches the profile. After doing this, you can canvass the business community in your area and *sell* them the service of creating a personal profile that meets their information needs.

By picking the appropriate niche market, you can become the focal point to obtain information, not only from the news feeds but also from any other source on the topics selected. This enables you to become the expert in the field.

Summary

The Internet provides many business opportunities—both as a means to augment or innovate current business activities and as a means create new business ventures unto themselves.

By looking at the business processes surrounding the core of your company, you should be able to increase your competitive advantage by using the Internet, and its associated technologies, to expand your business, reduce or contain your costs, and develop tighter relationships with your "partners." All these lead to a more efficient, effective, and profitable business.

Requirements and Planning

Windows NT as Your Internet Server Platform

Y ou've decided Internet connectivity is the right direction; you have a good idea about the type of connectivity your company needs, and a preliminary estimate of what it will take and what you will run. The next stage is to evaluate the operating system software for your network needs. Obviously your choice, or at least major consideration, is Microsoft's Windows NT operating system.

This chapter explains the Windows NT choice for Internet connectivity, and details general Windows NT operating system information. The following topics are covered in this chapter to help you understand just what Windows NT has to offer, as well as the requirements for use.

The Windows NT Choice

For many years, variations of Unix dominated the network operating systems (NOS) market; PCs were predominantly the domain of MS-DOS and Microsoft Windows. As the importance of mission-critical, stable operating systems increased, Microsoft developed its own high-security, stable networking platform: Windows NT Server and NT Workstation. This completely redesigned version of Windows (with absolutely no dependency on DOS or 16-bit technology) has quickly become one of the leading network operating systems of the business world.

Although NT still lacks the widespread acceptance that Unix possesses as a network operating system, it is quickly becoming a platform of choice in business and research. An independent research firm recently reported that in 1995, licenses for Windows NT Workstation surpassed the combined workstation shipments of the two largest competitors, Sun Microsystems Inc. and Silicon Graphics Inc. NT's estimated growth in the next few years is expected to increase even more.

Microsoft is apparently very serious about steering the development of NT toward Internet-centric design goals. The latest evidence of this is the upcoming new release, NT 4. Before delving into the enhancements of 4, take a look at a few of the underlying concepts behind Windows NT, both design- and business-wise. These are few of several considerations for choosing NT for your Internet server. These considerations include the following:

❏ **Client-server design**—Windows NT networks are typically based on central servers that contain accounts, data, applications, and more. These servers are accessed across the network by client computers, not dummy terminals. Client-server computing enables distributed processing load and a much more efficient design. NT is also designed in this way at the software level.

❏ **Multiple protocols**—Windows NT enables multiple protocols on the same system, and are bound to the same network adapters. The protocol most important to the Internet server is TCP/IP. A site can isolate its server from the rest of the network, however, by running a different protocol on the other computers and running TCP/IP on only the Internet server. This is often used as a security measure to prevent external threats such as hacking.

❏ **Multi-threaded design**—Windows NT goes beyond the multiple process barrier and implements multiple threads of execution. Threads are the smallest portion of executable code, and are allotted CPU time just as processes are. Multiple threads can exist for one application, and can run on multiple processors. A multi-threaded graphics program, for example, can have several threads running on multiple processors. One thread can render the image, the other can continue accepting user input, while threads for other processes are still active in the background. The operating system assigns threads priority levels. The threads are synchronized to prevent simultaneous changes to one critical resource, such as a file. NT's multi-threaded architecture dramatically increases the overall speed and stability of the operating system, and is utilized in all high-quality NT software, including Internet servers.

❏ **File-level security**—Windows NT enables file-level security assignable to individual user accounts or groups of users. The NTFS file system is a secure and self-maintaining file system exclusive to Windows NT. This is a particular advantage to the Internet server administrator because permissions can be assigned and removed for any file, directory, or resource.

❏ **Additional security**—Windows NT has all the auditing and security features professional network administrators demand: security, application, and system event logging; customizable auditing of access to resources; ownership of files and other resources; and a kernel-mode protected login sequence at the physical computer to prevent password grabbing or packet sniffing programs.

NT has the capability to act as a C2 Secure, stand-alone system with minimal upgrades. C2 is the Department of Defense rating for a secure computer system. Although NT has not been evaluated for this as a network component, Microsoft is addressing this concern and is working with the National Computer Security Administration to evaluate NT as a C2 secure network operating system.

❏ **Scalability**—Windows NT addresses the concern of the scalable network architecture with not only multiple domain options, but also with enhanced features and excellent third-party support. Multi-threaded advantages were previously discussed. Threads executing on multiple processors provide yet another key advantage NT has for improved scalability. Microsoft is currently planning a 64-bit version of NT that would launch the OS into the heavy-weight realm of massive data warehousing and increased bandwidth networking.

❏ **Ease of configuration**—Before NT entered the Internet server market, most Internet sites were maintained with Unix servers. These servers required a fair amount of command-line and troubleshooting knowledge (often more trouble than it was worth). Installing and maintaining protocols and severs was the domain of a networking professional or a long-time user. With NT, you can easily configure all protocols and servers with a graphical user interface that abstracts all the complicated and often trivial command-line operations of Unix. Don't be fooled, however: NT enables very low-level administration of servers and protocols. The administrator can dig as deeply as required, or only skim the surface, to rapidly publish information on the Internet.

❏ **Compatibility**—Windows NT runs programs written for 32-bit Windows NT, many Windows 95 programs and 16-bit Windows apps, DOS applications up to DOS 5 (later versions of DOS make direct calls to hardware, which NT will not allow), POSIX-1 compliant programs, and some OS/2 text-based programs. Windows NT 3.51 has file system support for OS/2's HPFS file system; Microsoft has discontinued this, however, in NT 4 because the demand for OS/2 has dropped considerably.

❏ **Reliability**—Windows NT has several features for disk reliability including fault tolerance and self-maintaining file systems. NT Server enables RAID (Redundant Array of Inexpensive Disks) fault tolerance levels zero, one, and five by using software implemented fault tolerance. (NT, of course, can utilize RAID hardware.) Disk mirroring, disk duplexing, striping with parity, sector-sparing, transaction-based disk access, and a self-defragmenting file system are all tremendously important benefits to an Internet or file server. NT's advanced disk features are discussed later in this book.

❏ **Business solutions**—Windows NT networks benefit from the expansive set of network servers called Microsoft BackOffice. These include MS SQL Server for database query and administration, MS Exchange Server for mail and Internet mail, MS SNA Server (which bridges the gap between desktop and mainframe), Internet Information Server, and several other mission critical enterprise-wide servers. Because of the interoperability among these packages, the artful Internet server administrator can give a secure and dynamic view of any part of the corporation's Information System to the outside world.

Windows NT Essentials

NOTE

For more information about hardware requirements, see Chapter 6, "Hardware Requirements." For more information on software requirements, see Chapter 7, "Software Requirements."

This chapter provides an introduction to Windows NT, the latest release, NT 4, and an overview of NT architecture and networking. Before you delve into such specifics, be familiar with the overall operating system and its abilities. An Internet server administrator should be familiar with hardware requirements, networking protocols, file systems, and more. This section is not an attempt to educate the reader in administering a Windows NT server, but to list some of the advantages and capabilities of the NT operating system.

Hardware Requirements and Support

Windows NT is not an operating system designed for minimal hardware support; to achieve its potential as a high-end, client-server advanced operating system, it's going to need an adequate hardware platform. NT supports massive amounts of disk storage and other important network resources.

Minimal Requirements

Table 3.1 explains the minimal and suggested requirements.

Table 3.1 Hardware Support Differences	Capacity	NT Workstation	NT Server
	Memory MB	Minimum 12 MB	Minimum 16
	Recommended	16 MB	32 MB
	Hard Disk Requirements	110 MB	160 MB
	Supported Processors	2	32

Processor Support

Windows NT Server supports up to 32 separate processors, with Symmetrical Multiprocessing (SMP) support. Another benefit of the NT operating system is its portability across many popular processors. Both NT Server and NT Workstation support the following platforms:

- ❏ Intel 486 and Pentium +
- ❏ MIPS R4000
- ❏ DEC Alpha AXP
- ❏ PowerPC

Disk Storage

Windows NT supports huge amounts of hard disk storage. This is achieved with the NTFS file system—the preferred file system for use with Windows NT. NTFS can support both file and partition sizes of 16 exabytes (EB). An exabyte is approximately a billion gigabytes; a number that none of us should be able to fathom (and a hard drive none of us should be able to afford). The FAT file system, also supported under Windows NT, supports a much smaller file and partition size; both file systems are explained in more detail later.

The Hardware Compatibility List (HCL)

T I P

The latest online version of the Windows NT hardware compatibility list can be accessed via World Wide Web at Microsoft's Web site: `http://www.microsoft.com/BackOffice/ntserver/hcl/hclintro.htm`

With each shipment of Windows NT comes a hardware compatibility list, a growing booklet of virtually every hardware component guaranteed to work with the Windows NT operating system. Everything needed is listed here including processors, computer systems, and peripherals. An NT network administrator will find the HCL very handy when deciding on new hardware and systems. It is not recommended to use any hardware component not listed in the HCL or (in the case of hardware compatibility after publication of the recent HCL) not guaranteed to work with Windows NT.

Networking

Windows NT supports several widely used networking protocols and secure transmission protocols, including TCP/IP (the Internet communications standard). NT can coexist in heterogeneous networks along with Unix hosts, Novell NetWare networks, Apple Macintosh networks, IBM mainframes, the Internet, and potentially more networks. NT has built-in networking, and was designed from the ground up to be a network operating system that can easily incorporate new protocols and devices. NT networking is also enhanced with fault tolerance features built in to the operating system and NTFS file system.

Networking Protocols

Windows NT is designed to function in a heterogeneous networking environment; existing with other networks and network protocols. NT easily communicates with Unix, NetWare, Macintosh, and other networks. The following networking protocols are currently supported by both Windows NT Server 4 and NT Workstation 4:

❏ NetBEUI (Net BIOS Extended User Interface). The small scale plug and play networking protocol commonly used by small Microsoft-only based networks. It is easy to set up and largely self-tuning, but it is neither routeable nor scalable to a larger network model. It does not support Internet connectivity.

❏ NWLink IPX. This is Microsoft's extended protocol for use with Novell NetWare networks. This protocol is a much more scalable and reliable networking protocol for LANs.

❏ TCP/IP (Transmission Control Protocol/Internet Protocol). This is the standard Unix and Internet networking protocol. You will definitely need to install either during NT installation, or afterwards. TCP/IP is a routeable, very scalable protocol that enables interoperability with any Internet host.

❏ DLC (Data Link Control). This protocol is used primarily for communication with IBM mainframes via a 3270 emulator, or to print directly to Hewlett-Packard network printers. It is not used for direct communication between Windows NT computers.

Data Protection and Fault Tolerance

Windows NT Server provides several built-in data protection and fault tolerance benefits in both the operating system and file systems. Not only does the NTFS file system have its own data protection enhancements, but NT Server enables software configurable fault tolerance for hard drives by using software configurable RAID (Redundant Array of Inexpensive Disks). Windows NT Server supports the following levels of RAID fault tolerance, discussed in much more detail later in this book.

❏ **Level 0: Disk Striping.** While not an actual fault tolerance method, disk striping distributes data across two or more disks by writing equal blocks of information to each. This does not offer data redundancy.

❏ **Level 1: Disk mirroring.** Disk mirroring copies or "mirrors" all data written to one disk, onto another disk. While this takes up twice as much disk space, it provides total redundancy in case one drive crashes.

❏ **Level 5: Disk striping with parity.** Similar to regular disk striping, striping with parity creates a block of parity data, a copy of a segment of data, stored on a separate disk from the original segment. This method enables all data to be retrieved in the event of a single disk crash.

NT also offers data protection through sector sparing, a marking of bad sectors on a hard disk to avoid later use. If a bad sector is found while accessing the disk, NT not only marks the sector, but also stores the data in a new sector. Sector sparing is conventionally performed during formatting of the hard drive, but Windows NT uses this technique every time data is accessed (whether read or written) from the disk.

NTFS File System and File Security

The Windows NT file system, NTFS, is a high performance, secure file system. It is generally recommended over the FAT file system for use with Windows NT. NTFS provides file level security, permissions, and other performance benefits. The old MS-DOS FAT (File Allocation Table) file system is supported under Windows NT, but is a lower performance file system with no security benefits. Windows NT 3.51 supports HPFS, the High Performance File System used by OS/2. In NT 4, no support for HPFS is offered; Microsoft felt that HPFS support was no longer a crucial demand. Table 3.2 illustrates some of the major differences between the FAT and NTFS file systems.

Table 3.2 Major Differences Between FAT and NTFS File Systems	Functionality	FAT	NTFS
	Maximum File Size	4 GB	16 EB (exabytes)
	Maximum Partition	4 GB	16 GB
	Security, ownership, auditing	None	File level
	Accessibility	Windows NT, DOS, OS/2	Windows NT only

File Security with NTFS

Windows NT features both a system of ownership of files and directories, and file security permissions based on users and group membership. On an NTFS partition, a directory or file can be secured with varying levels of access permissions from no access to full access (able to take ownership of a file or directory). Windows NT security will not enable any user or service, without proper permissions, to access a file.

NTFS Defragmentation

Fragmentation, the placement of data on a disk in nonconsecutive sectors, affects hard drive performance and system responsiveness. The NTFS file system was designed to reduce the effects of fragmentation. By using smaller block sizes of data than FAT, NTFS enables much more efficient use of hard disk space. Fragmentation is also reduced because NTFS attempts to write each block of data to a consecutive sector; this isn't always possible, but it does increase efficiency and reduce fragmenting problems. Several third-party tools, such as Executive Software's Diskeeper, have been created to successfully handle NTFS file fragmentation—picking up where Microsoft left off.

Windows NT Server and Workstation

Microsoft's design goals in developing two versions of its high-end Windows NT operating system were to ensure two high-performance operating systems with identical architecture, both optimized for decidedly different environments and uses. It is a common misconception that NT Server and NT Workstation are essentially the same, with only minor network tweaking and security improvements. Although the architecture, kernel, and Win32 programming interfaces are identical in both Server and Workstation, numerous fundamental differences exist between the two platforms.

NOTE

Although the NTFS file system is a secure file system, accessible through a Windows NT computer only, shareware tools enable both the Linux and MS-DOS (including Windows) operating systems read-only access to NTFS partitions. This information is not meant to frighten a network administrator, but to illustrate that no operating system is impervious to hacking.

Optimization of network and application responsiveness have always been primary differences between the two versions of NT. With the release of NT 4, several new changes have been made in both design and attention to networking. NT Server 4, for example, now ships with many more Internet related servers and applications. This section describes the various areas in which NT Server and NT Workstation differ, with attention to the following:

❏ Hardware requirements

❏ Performance

❏ Functionality

❏ Included tools and servers

❏ Pricing and licensing

❏ The Internet

Essentials

Before delving into more advanced explanations of the differences between NT Workstation and Server, some essentials of hardware requirements, pricing, and licensing should be understood. NT Server, being a more high-end OS for advanced network server functionality, supports more connections, more processors, and offers more licensing possibilities than NT Workstation. Naturally, both versions of NT have installations for the RISC, MIPS, Intel, and PowerPC platforms and, the underlying operating system is identical in both versions. Refer to table 3.1 for an explanation of some fundamental hardware support differences of which every network administrator should be aware.

Licensing for Windows NT differs on each version, and is dependent on the number of connections that will be maintained. Because NT Workstation is only licensed for a maximum of ten inbound connections, no options exist for extended licenses. NT Server, which can facilitate almost limitless connections, ships under two standard licensing plans: a five license pack, and a ten license pack. Further connection licenses can be purchased from Microsoft. Obviously, NT Server is several times more expensive than NT Workstation. This is often a consideration for smaller businesses that need the stability of NT, but require a more cost-conscious alternative. (The uses and restrictions of NT Workstation are discussed later.) At the time of this writing, the retail prices (from Microsoft) of each product were as follows:

- ❑ Windows NT Workstation (10 licenses)—$319
- ❑ Windows NT Server 4 (5 licenses)— $809
- ❑ Windows NT Server 4 (10 licenses)—$1,129

Design and Application

The principle differences between Windows NT Server and NT Workstation lie in the design considerations of both a network server and a secure workstation environment. Windows NT Server was designed to be an I/O intensive network server, capable of handling thousands of connections as quickly and efficiently as possible. Windows NT Workstation provides a multitasking, secure workstation operating system devoted to such tasks as client-server application usage, multimedia intensive work, and software development. To ensure that each version of NT is optimized to do its primary function without sacrificing performance, different priority levels and capabilities exist on both platforms.

File and printer sharing, network traffic, and increasingly memory intensive mission-critical tasks are expected to perform optimally under NT Server. Highest priority and resource allocation is given to networking tasks in order to provide the fastest and most scalable version of the operating system. Windows NT Workstation, however, differs by placing the highest precedence on user oriented processes such as application responsiveness and more conservative memory allocation. A comparison of NT Server and NT Workstation performance tuning shows architectural contrasts that help explain why further customizations have been made.

There are other design and architectural differences between the two versions of NT that need to be addressed here. The overall differences largely are performance- and network-based, but also are end-user and administrative concerns. The following is discussed in detail:

❑ Memory Allocation
❑ CPU Time Slices
❑ Networking

Memory Allocation

Allocating memory for processes is accomplished differently in each version of NT. The two versions are tuned to use the most efficient memory allocation scheme for their primary uses. NT Server allocates more memory because of its memory intensive network uses, network applications, servers, and the demand to provide rapid file transactions. NT Server loads an application with all requested memory (assuming it is available). Applications and resources on a network server are accessed periodically and require quick return of results.

NT Workstation allocates the minimum required memory for each process, and thereby conserves resources because workstation applications are seldom accessed in one session with the same frequency as those on a server. NT Workstation, usually running with less RAM than an NT Server, allocates memory with attention to overall responsiveness of the environment. Networking components receive less memory allocation on Workstation than on Server because networking is a secondary concern to optimal use of applications.

CPU Time Slices

An operating system uses time slices to continuously give very small amounts of time to all processes, and thereby provides a multiprocessing, multitasking environment. Windows NT Server and Workstation task scheduling are optimized differently for the most appropriate use of time slicing. Windows NT Server uses longer slices of time per task because it must handle networking connections and infrequently loaded and unloaded servers. The longer time slices prevent the OS from being interrupted while handling critical network traffic. Optimized for networking, NT Server's longer time slices provide a more stable and dependable platform for scalable network servers using multiple processors. In Symmetrical Multiprocessing (SMP), an operating system uses multiple processors to evenly distribute the processing load. Both versions of Windows NT can use SMP, but NT Server's longer time slices make it more efficient as a scalable network server where multiprocessor synchronization is important. As mentioned earlier, NT Workstation supports up to two processors, while NT Server can currently support as many as 32.

Windows NT Workstation keeps its time slices small; this provides faster response time to each running task. Like the more efficient memory allocation for Windows NT Workstation applications, the shorter time slices enable a more manageable environment for the user. Task switching is quicker and more seamless; loading and unloading applications is faster, benefiting multitasking. NT Workstation, designed to also support the needs of a high-end graphics workstation, provides much faster rendering and overall graphics processing speed than NT Server. With the shorter time slices and better local application handling, NT Workstation is the preferred NT platform for any graphics, multimedia, or number-crunching work.

Networking

Because NT Server and NT Workstation have considerably different capabilities and intended uses, it is important to understand the networking roles of both. Obviously, NT Server is the better platform for running a network server. NT Workstation, however, because of its lower price and NT's multitasking and security features, often fits a niche among smaller networks or cost-conscious companies.

Administration

Windows NT Server and NT Workstation have decidedly different network administration capabilities. NT Server provides a centralized administration model that enables administrative control over all servers and workstations in a particular domain. NT Workstation's administrative support includes only limited remote capabilities for administrating servers or other workstations. A clear working example of the differences between NT Server and Workstation's administrative capabilities can be seen in the User Manager (for NT Workstation) and User Manager for Domains (in NT Server). Domain-wide account administration, even across trusted domains, is possible with NT Server.

File and Networking I/O

The speed and integrity of file and network I/O is a critical factor in a network server environment. Windows NT Server, as a file server, supports much heavier I/O loads than NT Workstation. A typical network server may share files or applications, run database servers such as SQL Server, or host an Internet Web site. All these functions can require massive I/O throughput that require a fully optimized network server.

Windows NT establishes queues to wait for and handle incoming network requests. NT Workstation only has one such queue, limiting its network I/O load, and insuring more processor time and resources are devoted to local applications. NT Server, however, benefits from several threads of execution, gathered in I/O queues waiting to handle incoming I/O requests. For smaller network server needs such as Web sites receiving only a few transactions an hour, small client-server file sharing, or other low-end needs, NT Workstation's scaled down network I/O feature may be suitable. Some of the more innovative uses of NT Workstation as a low-end network component are discussed later.

Networking Support Capabilities

Windows NT Server exists to provide a high-performance, stable and secure network operating system for small to enterprise-wide networks. Whether this role means a network file server, print server, Internet server, or SQL Server, it is designed to handle large throughput. Windows NT Workstation has several networking limitations besides network I/O mentioned previously. Workstation's networking role is primarily a client-to-server or a peer-to-peer relationship, and thus Microsoft only supports and licenses ten inbound connections for NT Workstation. This limitation has directed more attention to NT Server and Internet Information Server for NT Internet solutions, but has caused some aggravation among smaller businesses that need moderate server capabilities.

Another important factor in determining critical network support differences between the two platforms is fault tolerance capability. Fault tolerance data redundancy options are not present on NT Workstation as they are on Server. Although RAID can be implemented with hardware, disk mirroring, duplexing, and striping with parity can only be achieved natively with NT Server.

NT Server also supports more services for non-NT networks, such as NetWare, and services for Macintosh clients. Microsoft offers NetWare File and Print server additions for NT Server, as well as NetWare Directory Services Manager for NT Server. Neither product is compatible with NT Workstation, which generally could not support the connection overhead needed for such services. NT Server also comes with

NOTE

Microsoft is also extending the capabilities of NT Server with clustering, the capability to use multiple NT Servers as one logical server. This strategy enables much larger networks to be managed on the Windows NT platform. The project, code-named WolfPack by Microsoft, includes several major software and hardware development companies including Intel and DEC.

NOTE

RESOURCE Kit The Windows NT 3.51 Resource Kit includes the C2 Security Configuration Manager tool, which analyzes the security of an NT Workstation or Server and enables an administrator to implement many of the C2 security requirements with Windows NT. The C2 Security Configuration Manager is discussed in Chapter 14, "Security Practices."

Gateway Services for NetWare, which enables clients infrequent access to NetWare networks. NT Workstation ships with a NetWare client access service that enables direct access to file and print servers on NetWare networks. Both OS versions benefit from NetWare connectivity, but only NT Server can provide a solid server connection for multiple hosts on the network.

Another substantial concern is compatibility with Microsoft's BackOffice server suite. Only NT Server supports the various servers of BackOffice, ranging from SQL Server for database management to SNA Server for IBM mainframe integration. The need (or eventual need) for BackOffice products should be a consideration in choosing the right version of NT. Although third-party NT Workstation targeted alternatives to some of Microsoft's BackOffice suite exist, the need for such products often merits a dedicated NT Server anyway.

Security

Both versions of Windows NT have high security features and have undergone evaluation by the Department of Defense as C2 Secure operating systems. This rating only applies to NT as a stand-alone system; a network OS evaluation is currently taking place. For this reason, it is generally accepted that NT Workstation provides C2 level security; NT Server, seldom used on a stand-alone computer, maintains only certain features of C2 security. The NTFS file system is present in both versions, and logon validation takes place in essentially the same secure manner. One key benefit to NT's C2 secure features is that it is completely software configurable and does not require any external, third-party, or add-on products.

WINDOWS NT4

New to both versions of NT 4 are security features like the CryptoAPI, Secured Sockets Layer (SSL) protocol, and Point to Point Tunneling Protocol (PPTP). These innovations (not all Microsoft developments) are present in both Server and Workstation versions of NT 4. Windows NT Server running Internet Information Server can use SSL encryption to permit secured Internet/Intranet transactions.

CPU Utilization

The Windows NT operating system is a multi-threaded environment, meaning it can execute small parts of code in separate threads (somewhat similar to processes) of execution. This greatly improves scalability because multiprocessor systems can run threads symmetrically across all processors. Expectedly, CPU use is tailored differently for both versions of Windows NT for many of the same reasons the other resources are optimized. NT Server's CPU usage is based on requirements of file sharing and network I/O access. NT Workstation devotes much less CPU time to networking and file sharing demands, and concentrates on the local applications.

Microsoft has tuned NT Server to provide much more CPU time to networking throughput; an NT Server is, therefore, enabled to use close to 100 percent of its CPU for networking demands. On the other hand, NT Workstation has a significantly lower allowance of CPU time for networking tasks. NT Workstation network CPU usage, leveling off at around 20 percent of processor time at maximum supported connections, ensures that more processor time is afforded to local applications.

Table 3.3

Summary of Design Differences Between NT Server and NT Workstation

Performance Tuning	NT Workstation	NT Server
Memory Allocation	Minimum memory loaded for each application.	Maximum requested for each application.
Network I/O	Given lower priority. Only one network input queue to handle networking requests.	Given highest priority. Several I/O queues to handle requests.

continues

Table 3.3 Continued	Performance Tuning	NT Workstation	NT Server
	CPU Usage	More CPU time allocated for local applications.	More CPU time allocated for network connections.
	Time Slices	Smaller for increased user responsiveness.	Longer for handling network traffic with less interruption.

NT Workstation's Internetworking Capabilities

Although NT Workstation is less suited to perform as an Internet server than NT Server, in some areas Workstation is still a cost-effective and viable solution. Because NT Workstation only devotes a limited amount of CPU time to networking tasks, it is often suitable for a small file or Internet server on which local applications or processing must also be implemented—running a test bed Intranet server on an NT Workstation, for example, and developing software on the same system.

Initially, Microsoft instituted a ten connection, ten minute limitation on NT Workstation 4. This confined the operating system to only ten simultaneous inbound network connections in any ten minute time period, regardless of how long the connections were active. This was quickly changed before Workstation 4 was released, satisfying the growing market of third-party Internet server software developers. With part of this restriction raised, NT Workstation 4 can be used for several multiprocessing network roles. Following are examples of some of these uses:

❏ Server for telephony devices and servers.

❏ Small server for dumb terminals or diskless workstations.

❏ Single workstation with NetWare services client for occasional access to NetWare file and print servers, when a dedicated server would be too expensive or elaborate.

❏ Small intranet server, for businesses needing only occasional access.

❏ Limited one-connection dial-in server.

Windows NT Workstation versus Windows NT Server—Making the Decision

It is easy to determine that considerable differences exist between the two versions of Windows NT. With the release of NT 4, these differences have escalated and become even more apparent. This does benefit users of both versions of the operating system to a great extent. It may, however, mean pricing and connection support difficulties to smaller businesses. Windows NT Server is currently receiving massive attention from software developers (especially Microsoft) because of its new-found use as an Internet and intranet server. BackOffice is becoming an increasingly popular suite of server products, and has also branched out into the Internet-centric market with Internet Information Server and Microsoft Proxy Server. The purpose of providing network servers, however, is to enable client access; NT Workstation is not being neglected as a high-powered client or stand-alone operating system for advanced business, engineering, graphics, and scientific work. For applications requiring true multitasking and the most power from the computer and operating system, NT Workstation is the choice of the two. All the security, APIs, Windows 95 interface innovations, and general NT specific technologies are present in both versions of NT. With this tight compatibility, the other differences between the two versions can actually be seen as a benefit, keeping the cost of NT Workstation much lower, and its performance as a desktop operating system much more powerful.

Using Windows NT as an Internet Server

In the past year, the demand for Internet connectivity and the corporate Internet presence has increased so astronomically that companies are racing to get ahead or keep up. At roughly the same time, Windows NT rose from a well-supported network operating system to a platform capable of sustaining complex Internet server solutions. Although NT always offered the TCP/IP networking protocol that has become the de facto standard of the Internet, there was originally nothing too amazing about Microsoft's Internet server capabilities. In the last year, and especially with the arrival of Windows NT 4, Microsoft's new technology operating system has significantly increased its standing in the Internet technology marketplace.

Your Windows NT Internet server choice should not be exclusively based on NT's performance and stability records. There are numerous Internet specific-advantages to using Windows NT as your server platform. Among these benefits are the following:

❏ Multiple protocols that enable TCP/IP network isolation for improved security of your network.

❏ Several layers of security, including secured transfer protocols.

❏ The high-performance transaction based NTFS file system. Security, ownership, permissions, and auditing can be implemented at the file level.

❏ Windows NT Server is optimized to give highest priority to network I/O, making it a much more efficient file and application server than Windows NT Workstation.

❏ Tight integration with Microsoft's BackOffice suite of server products.

NT Server versus Workstation as an Internet Server

Microsoft's recent attention to Internet technologies has pushed Windows NT into a much more Internet-worthy network operating system. New advances in Web browser technology, security, and network optimization are quickly making NT a contender in the Internet server platform market. The two versions do, however, extremely differ when it comes to Internet functionality. These differences easily promote NT Server as the preferred Internet server platform between the two, based on network performance and Internet application support.

Internet Server

Just as with a LAN network file server, an Internet server must be capable of handling a large amount of simultaneous connections as efficiently as possible. I/O through-put, scalability, and CPU usage for networking transactions are also capital demands of an Internet server. As discussed later in this chapter, NT Server is much better suited to handle these needs compared to NT Workstation. Another key issue here is the number of connections that are possible on each platform. With Windows NT Server, any number of outside Internet connections are possible. Server not only supports almost limitless inbound connections, but does not require licenses for them. NT Workstation, however, only supports and licenses ten inbound network connections because of its primarily peer-to-peer networking role.

Internet Software and Support

One of the noticeable differences between the four versions of Windows NT Server and NT Workstation, is the bundle of Internet related servers and software applications shipping with the Server version. Microsoft's recent direction toward Internet and Intranet development has prompted the software company to ship its latest servers and Internet-centric development software with NT Server in order to create a complete solution for Internet/intranet networking. This also illustrates a more intangible difference between the two: Microsoft's Internet technology investments are placed on Windows NT Server 4, and thus Server will be the primary Internet platform from Microsoft. Development and enhancements will center around NT Server and software to run on NT Server. Workstation has considerably less support for Internet server software, and suffers in this area from the different design goals, discussed later, and licensing that does not support most Internet server requirements.

Microsoft's Internet technologies such as ActiveX and other Internet specific Win32 APIs will of course work seamlessly on both platforms, as will any client software such as Microsoft Internet Explorer. The principle difference between Server and Workstation is that NT Server is the only platform that supports Microsoft's Internet servers; NT Server is also equipped to handle demanding TCP/IP network needs. There is also the difference in Internet site support products. NT Server 4 ships with software to help create and manage Internet servers and Web sites. This, along with other Internet-specific differences between the two platforms, is demonstrated in the following table.

Table 3.4 Internet Specific Differences Between NT Workstation and Server	Usage	NT Workstation	NT Server
	Internet Server	Limited by licensing of 10 inbound connections. No server included.	Unlimited connections; ships with No Internet Information Server, FTP, WWW, Gopher.
	DNS Server	None included	Included and integrated into NT.
	DHCP Server	None included	Included and integrated into NT.
	WINS Server	None included	Included and integrated into NT.

continues

Table 3.4
Continued

Usage	NT Workstation	NT Server
Internet Support Server Products	None included or offered	
Microsoft Index Server		For full site content searches, available free for download.
Microsoft Proxy		Server for enhanced security and Intranet connectivity without TCP/IP, part of the BackOffice Server suite.
Site Management (FrontPage)	No software included	Microsoft software included with NT Server 4. Professional Web site authoring and management.
Browser Technology (Explorer)	Internet Explorer 3 and ActiveX compatible.	Internet Explorer 3 and Active X compatible. Free for download.

NOTE

Some third party companies have claimed that the differences between Windows NT Workstation 4 and NT Server 4 are software configurable by editing certain NT registry settings. These companies claim that NT Workstation 4 can be converted to a full featured NT Server 4 (minus the administration tools). Although Microsoft denies this, it would be against licensing agreements to make this change in the first place.

It becomes apparent after viewing the preceding table that Windows NT Server is the choice NT operating system for most Internet server needs. Although some still use NT Workstation because of its price and the continuing support of third-party Internet server vendors, Microsoft has made a strong argument for NT Server 4's capability as a Net server with new software, support, and licensing. With Workstation's limitation of only ten licensed inbound connections, the need for a heavy-traffic server invariably points to NT Server. Security and site management considerations are addressed with server software that runs only on NT Server. Workstation's lower cost and third-party Internet server support has often made it an effective server solution for smaller businesses that require only occasional access. For larger sites, however, NT Server is optimized for Internet/intranet server use, and comes bundled with all of the software needed to create and manage an Internet server.

Windows NT 4

The latest incarnation of the Windows NT operating system, version 4, makes up much of the sparse and unfriendly Internet services that initially existed for version 3.51. Windows NT Server 4 ships with Microsoft Internet Information Server 2 (IIS), a powerful and fast Web, ftp, and gopher server with add-on capability. Microsoft has already released several free tools and servers to enhance the Internet server capabilities of NT, and IIS specifically. Security considerations from the Internet community also prompted Microsoft to include several new technologies (not all developed by Microsoft) to version 4. Secure Sockets Layer (SSL), Point-to-Point Tunneling Protocols (PPTP), and the CryptoAPI programming interface are examples of these, and are discussed shortly. Other improvements in overall performance and ease-of-use are also present in NT 4. Following are examples of some of the new enhancements to the operating system, including those just mentioned.

The Windows 95 Interface

Finally, Windows NT steps into the 95 shell desktop arena with the same easy-to-use, sleek interface (see fig. 3.1). While an attractive interface is the first benefit one might realize, there are several new Microsoft technologies dependent upon the interface's application programming interface (API) and common controls. New Internet products such as Microsoft Internet Explorer 3 require the new interface. Ease-of-use and more customization complement Microsoft's continuing Internet specific designs, like more browser enabled access to your computer and your network.

Figure 3.1
The Windows 95 Interface on Windows NT Server 4.

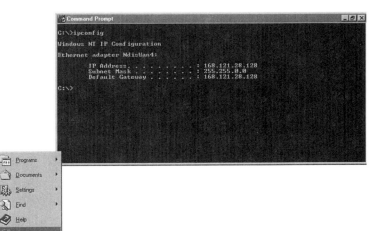

Network Performance Improvements

Both regular networking and Internet improvements have been made in NT Server 4, proving that the new version of the operating system received much more than cosmetic attention. File and print sharing see a large performance boost, especially on 100mbit LANs, where increases were recorded up to 66 percent over NT 3.51. Scalability has improved greatly as many third party tests have shown; NT 4 scales well with multiple processors, but the major improvements are seen when used with four or more processor systems. Better network diagnostic and monitoring tools, and former single system applications that now diagnose remote systems (such as the NT diagnostics program) provide much needed administration tools NT 3.51 lacked.

Improved Network Security

Network administrators often demand either very high levels of security or customizable options for secured resources. Windows NT 4 offers enhanced security at the API level, in new secure protocols and in its Internet server platform. Windows NT 4 has been designed not only with NT's long respected attention to C2 level security, but also with new Internet and intranet security considerations and standards, as in the following:

❏ Microsoft's new CryptoAPI provides a new set of cryptographic security features that enable software developers to write custom applications for use over networks or the Internet. CryptoAPI is an expandable set of API calls that can be augmented by new encryption keys.

❏ Secure Sockets Layer (SSL) is a networking protocol that enables secured network data transmission over a LAN or Internet by using a special encryption key. SSL is not a Microsoft invention, but is receiving much attention in Windows NT 4 and Microsoft Internet Information Server 2.

❏ Point-to-Point Tunneling Protocol (PPTP) enables private networks to be established dynamically over public networks like the Internet. NT 4 provides support for this emerging technology. Again, PPTP is not exclusive to Microsoft, but Microsoft is pushing to make this protocol an established standard for secure network data exchange.

New Performance Tools

Windows NT 4 comes with an impressive new utility for at-a-glance performance monitoring of your overall system. The Task Manager, available by right clicking on the task bar (the *Start* bar on the new interface), not only has an improved view of all applications running, with the capability to close and switch to, but also enhanced features for more control over the tasks of your system (see fig. 3.2). You can now view each process running on your computer, including 13 process specific attributes (such as CPU usage, page faults, thread count) of each. Processes can be killed, or given different priorities. A quick-glance performance monitor shows real-time graphs and meters of CPU usage and memory, as well as the number of threads and handles open.

Figure 3.2

Windows NT 4 Task Manager Performance screen.

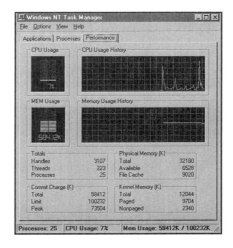

NT Server 4's Network Monitor is a new utility that captures and displays both network information on both incoming and outgoing packets (see fig. 3.3). Information such as network addresses, frames sent and received, percentages of network utilization, and impressively more data is reported on a single screen. Capture abilities enable a network administrator to save data from captured sessions and analyze it using a very advanced filtering system. Filtering expressions can be written using logical operators (AND, OR, and so on) for determining protocols, network addresses, and other properties. For tighter control and analysis of the network traffic on your system, the NT Network Monitor proves an important new tool, worth learning to utilize.

Figure 3.3
*Windows NT Server 4
Network Monitor.*

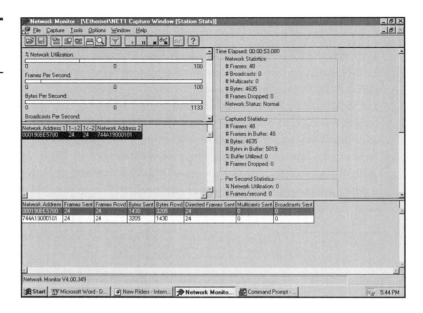

New Internet Server Integration

Windows NT Server 4 is quickly gaining ground in the Internet server market, which means new tools and innovations for developers and end users. One primary reason for NT 4's successful Internet integration is the wealth of server software Microsoft bundles with the operating system. From the new Internet Information Server, to enhanced DNS capabilities, Windows NT's Internet- and intranet-centric additions provide almost everything a company needs to create an Internet server presence. Still another attractive incentive is the free beta server software Microsoft offers for download on its World Wide Web site. Following is a partial listing of some of the Internet server additions to NT Server 4, and the current servers in development by Microsoft. For more detailed information on these products, see Chapter 13, "Other Services for Your Users."

Internet Information Server 2

Internet Information Server (IIS) 2 is the latest version of Microsoft's award winning Web, ftp, and gopher server. Since its first version, IIS has been rated the top Windows NT Internet server platform by several independent studies and tests. Its tight integration with the NT operating system provides a high-speed, secure, and stable Internet server platform. Another advantage is that IIS 2 ships with Windows NT Server 4, providing everything needed to create an Internet server in very little time. Although the documentation for IIS is not as thorough or easy to understand as it could be, but IIS is simple to set up and configure. Initial installation involves only choosing the appropriate directories; setup handles the rest, starts the server, and creates the necessary generic user account. Configuration and administration can be handled with an easy-to-use GUI administration application, or remotely over the Internet by using a Web browser and secure administration Web pages (included).

DNS Server

The old command-line DNS Server that shipped with the Windows NT 3.51 Resource Kit has been replaced with a feature-rich, graphically administrated commercial-quality DNS Server (see fig. 3.4). The DNS (Domain Name Services) Server enables seamless interaction with Unix and Internet servers by using standard domain names (like microsoft.com) mapped to IP addresses. This enables the administrator to provide Internet access to the network, as well as enabling intranets to work in the same manner. The DNS Server in NT 4 is can be administered remotely with the same administration utility. Microsoft's DNS server is based on accepted standards, meaning it can be integrated well with other DNS servers on the network; this makes migration easier. The DNS server is designed to work alongside Microsoft's WINS server and DHCP server, both of which are discussed in detail later in the book.

Figure 3.4
Windows NT DNS Server.

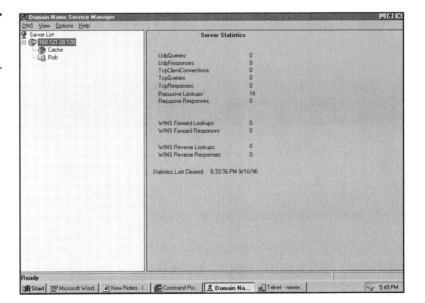

Microsoft FrontPage

Microsoft FrontPage, now shipping with Windows NT Server 4, is a Web site management utility that enables non-programmers and professional developers alike to create and manage entire Internet or intranet Web sites (see fig. 3.5). FrontPage is not just a Web page editing package; although it does offer wizards to help create dynamic and interactive Web pages (with database support), it also has advanced administration and management features. FrontPage can be used to administer an entire Web site, using password protected accounts for different administrators and managers. Secure updating in a team environment is one of the most enticing benefits FrontPage offers. By using server extensions, FrontPage enables Internet Information Server and other popular Web servers to host its managed Web sites. This easy integration is making it even more convenient and cost effective to use Microsoft's in-box Internet solutions.

Figure 3.5

Microsoft FrontPage's complete Web site editing capabilities include both design and administration.

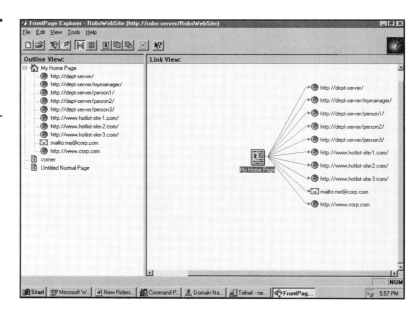

Microsoft Index Server

The Microsoft Index Server, an add-on for Internet Information Server 2, is a powerful site searching engine that can query and gather information on all documents, files, and Web pages it has permission to search (see fig. 3.6). By integrating with IIS 2, Index Server enables Web based searches of HTML documents, text files, and Microsoft Office documents such as Word, Excel, and PowerPoint files. The administrator can create customized search forms on the Web site, and enable viewers to search through material, creating indexes of information. Queries can be made on content, author of document, file creation times, and other specific attributes.

Administrators will benefit from network monitoring tools, automatic update, and crash recovery. Index Server also currently supports seven different languages.

Figure 3.6

Microsoft Index Server provides basic to complex Web site searches, available to any Web browser.

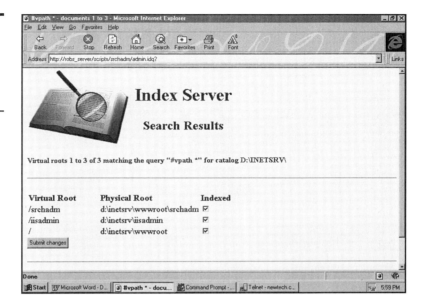

Microsoft Proxy Server

Microsoft Proxy Server, commonly referred to as *Catapult Server*, is an add-on to Internet Information Server 2 that enables you to bring full Internet access to all the PCs on your network, regardless of operating system or the lack of a TCP/IP protocol. Proxy Server works over Novell's IPX/SPX networking protocols, ensuring that TCP/IP services and costly administration are not needed in configuring an entire location with Internet access. Microsoft's proxy server, currently in beta testing, is one of the latest additions to the BackOffice suite of networking server products. For more information on the capabilities of Microsoft Proxy Server, refer to Chapter 13.

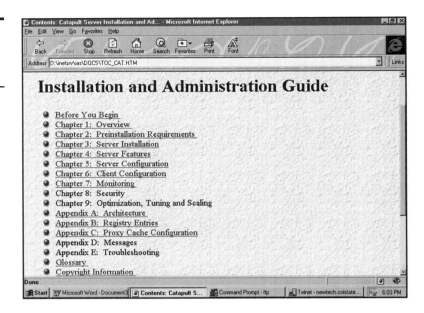

Summary

Windows NT rapidly is becoming a network operating system and Internet server platform of choice in the corporate world. Following are several advantages make NT an attractive solution for an Internet server:

- ❑ Ease of administration
- ❑ Excellent server and networking protocol security
- ❑ Scalability
- ❑ Third party and software design support

When choosing the best version of Windows NT for a company's needs, the roles and capabilities of NT Workstation and NT Server should be well understood. While NT Workstation can support small low-access Internet sites with a maximum of ten inbound connections, it is mainly a desktop workstation operating system for high-end business and technical software applications. Windows NT Server is not only equipped to handle unlimited connections, but version 4 also comes with Microsoft's Internet Information Server 2, providing the major components necessary for a Windows NT Internet of intranet server.

4

Basic Communication Fundamentals

A fundamental part of providing Internet services is the actual communication among computers. It will be your job, as the provider of Internet services, to connect the computer or computers that will provide these services. To accomplish this, you will need a basic understanding of data communications.

This chapter guides you in understanding the components of that make up your Internet connection. First, Local Area Networks, an important aspect of scalable Internet services are introduced. Following the section on local networks, various Internet connection options are explained. Next, you will learn what to look for when choosing an Internet service provider. Finally, everything you learn in this chapter is put together to demonstrate some example Internet access configurations. The topics covered are as follows:

Networking Basics

Two basic types of networks exist. One is referred to as local area network (LAN). The other is named wide area network (WAN). Most organizations that connect to the Internet connect their LANs to the Internet, thus forming a world wide WAN. This reveals what the Internet really is: A network of networks. Both LANs and WANs play an important part in the Internet. LANs are important because most individual hosts on the Internet reside on them. WANs are important because the Internet is essentially a huge WAN, and the Internet's infrastructure is based on WAN technologies. It is, therefore, important to have a good understanding of both types of networks. The following section provides a basic introduction to LANs. The section that deals with Internet connections covers the necessary information about WANs to connect to the Internet.

Local Area Networks: An Introduction

If you are serious about connecting to the Internet and do not currently have a LAN, consider installing one. A LAN gives you more flexibility and room for future growth in providing Internet services. A LAN enables you to split up services among computers when the services outgrow the capacity of a single computer.

A LAN refers to a group of interconnected computers in one physical location. The physical location may be a building, one floor of a building, or a particular room in a building. LANs can also stretch between buildings (usually the case in college campus networks). LANs are also known for speed, which is much higher than what can be achieved over normal WANs.

LAN Components

To create a LAN, you need the following three components:

❑ Computers that will make up the network
❑ Network hardware that ties the individual computers together physically
❑ Network software (including protocols and clients that enable the computers to talk to one another)

The following sections discuss these requirements in greater detail.

Computers and Workstations

Almost any type of computer can connect to a LAN. In addition to individual computers, often referred to as workstations, printers and other devices can connect directly to the LAN. You will often find LANs that have a very large computer called a server, perhaps with multiple processors. Servers are normally well equipped computers that house large amounts of data and applications for the rest of the computers on the network.

Network Hardware

Network hardware encompasses devices such as cables, network interface cards, hubs, bridges, and routers. All these devices together make up the physical network. Not all LANs have all these components on them. Some small LANs may only have two or three of these; larger LANs typically employ all these components and perhaps other custom hardware. Cabling is now available in two main forms: coaxial cables, and unshielded, twisted-pair (UTP) copper cable.

Coaxial cables come in two varieties: thick and thin. Thick coaxial cable, sometimes referred to as 10Base5 in Ethernet environments, resembles the coaxial cable used to transmit cable television. Thin coaxial cable is thinner and more flexible than thick coax; it is also more widely used.

Unshielded twisted pairs look similar to telephone cabling, except a bit thicker. UTP is also sometimes called 10BaseT. It uses an RJ45 connector that closely resembles a standard RJ11 telephone cable connection, only bigger. UTP is the most popular form of cabling in LANs because of its ease of use.

A network interface card is a hardware board or card that you put into an empty slot in the back of your client computer or server. This card physically connects to the cable that links your network. In addition to providing the physical connection to the network, they also perform the following:

- **Prepare data.** Network interface cards prepare the data so that it can transmit through the cable. The card translates data bits back and forth as they go from the computer to the cable and back again.

- **Address data.** Each network interface card has its own unique address that it imparts to the data stream. The card provides the data with an identifier when it goes out on to the Net, and enables data seeking a particular computer to know where to exit the cable.

- **Control data flow.** The card has RAM on it to help it pace the data so that it doesn't overwhelm the receiving computer or the cable.

- **Make (and agree on) the connection to another computer.** Before it actually sends data, the network interface card starts an electronic dialog with the other PC on the network that wants to communicate. They agree on things like the maximum size of data groups to be sent, the total amount of data, the time interval between data chunks, the amount of time that will elapse before confirmation that the data has arrived successfully, and how much data each card can hold before it overflows.

Hubs are boxes that enable multiple computers to connect at one single point. Bridges enable different types of networks to communicate. Bridges can be used to transfer data between Token Ring and Ethernet networks. Routers are intelligent pieces of hardware that control the flow of data between networks. Routers enable you to isolate traffic on separate networks, and enable only traffic destined from one network to another to pass through it. By separating networks in this manner, you can keep one network's traffic from being seen by a network that does not need to see that traffic.

Network Software

Windows NT Workstation includes network software. NT includes network card drivers, protocols, and client software that enables you to build a network easily. A network card driver needs to be installed for the type of network card installed in each client computer. The driver enables the client computer's operating system to communicate with the installed network interface card. Windows NT includes network card drivers for the most popular network cards available today. Network protocols are rules; when followed, these rules enable different types of computer systems to communicate over the network. The default protocol used in Windows NT 4 is TCP/IP, which is also the network protocol used by the Internet. Client software is the software that most users actually interact with on a first-hand basis. Client software implements services such as file sharing, printer sharing, and remote logins. Windows NT 4 includes a variety of network clients for networks based on Novell NetWare, Windows Networking, and TCP/IP.

LAN Topology

Topology refers to the cable layout of a physical network. Network topology is important because it can determine how easy it is to manage the network, what kinds of traffic patterns the network displays, and how resistant to failure the network is. The three most common types of topologies are called the star (see fig. 4.1), ring (see fig. 4.2), and bus (see fig. 4.3). Table 4.1 compares the three main network topologies:

Table 4.1
Comparison of Common LAN Topologies

Topology	Pros	Cons
Star	Most fault tolerant. Easy installation of clients. Centralized management and monitoring.	Higher initial cost.
Ring	Easy to install. Needs less cable than star. Even performance for all clients.	If one computer goes down, the network fails. Problems are hard to isolate.
Bus	Simple to install. Requires less cable than star or ring. Easy to extend.	Problems are hard to isolate. Network slows down during heavy use.

Figure 4.1
Star topology.

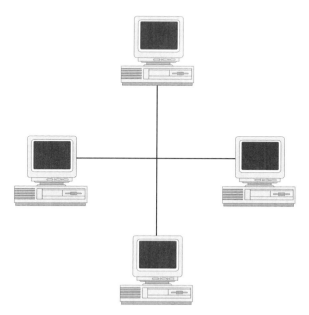

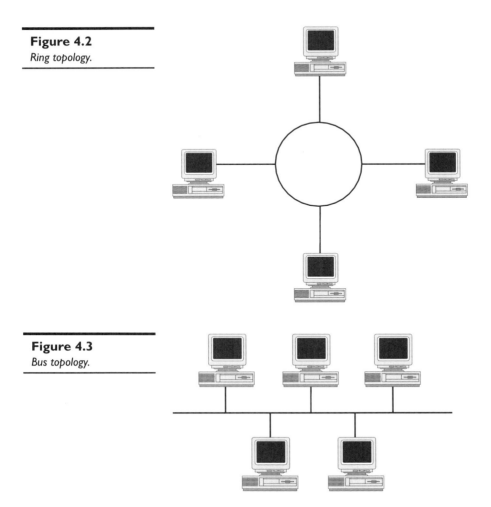

Figure 4.2
Ring topology.

Figure 4.3
Bus topology.

Network Architectures

When a number of people are working on networked PCs, inevitably several of them want to do the same thing on the network at the same time, such as print a file or use a fax modem. Specific LAN access methods (called architectures) are agreed-upon standards for how to send signals and regulate this network traffic in the most effective way. These methods work in conjunction with both the network and client operating systems, and are installed as part of the network adapter card. The two most commonly used architectures for PCs are Token Ring and Ethernet.

Token Ring

On a Token Ring network, a *token* (an electronic signal consisting of a set of bits) continuously circulates in one direction around the physical ring of PCs linked to the network. If the token is *free*, any PC can *grab* it. By doing so, the PC acquires the right to fill the token with data and then send it on to the data's network destination.

Ethernet

On an Ethernet network, the client PCs each *listen* for network traffic on the cable. If they don't hear anything, they transmit their information on to the network. Then, if two clients try to transmit information at the same time, they are alerted to the conflict. They stop transmitting, and wait for a predetermined period of time before trying again.

Ethernet is perhaps the most popular LAN access method. It uses either coaxial cable or UTP cable, transmits data at 10 megabits per second (although 100-megabit hardware is now available), and can be used in either the bus or the star topology. Ethernet has some real advantages. It's been around for a long time, so it's well understood and widely used. (Forty percent of LANs use it.) The percentage of use is even higher for small businesses. Ethernet also has a wide range of interface speeds and formats, and is relatively inexpensive.

Constructing a Simple LAN

A simple LAN can be constructed easily at low cost. To construct a LAN in this manner, use Ethernet as the network architecture and Windows NT as the network operating system. The necessary components are as follows:

❏ Computers with Windows NT installed.

❏ One 12 port 10BaseT hub.

❏ One Ethernet card for each computer in the network.

❏ Unshielded twisted-pair cabling, with connectors. You should purchase one cable for each computer you want to connect to the network. Make certain that the cable you purchase is the appropriate length.

To build a LAN, follow these steps:

1. Install the network cards on the computers.

2. Install the appropriate network card driver for your network card in Windows NT.

3. Connect one end of a cable to the computer and the other to one of the 10BaseT ports on the hub.

4. Connect all computers to the hub in the manner just described.

5. Install the protocol you want to use on every computer on the network.

6. Finally, make certain that all the computers are using the same protocol.

At this point, the network is ready for use. The network should look like that shown in figure 4.4. Some further configuration may need to be done on the computer you want to use as a server. Consult the Windows NT documentation for information on how to set up an NT LAN server.

Figure 4.4
A sample Ethernet network.

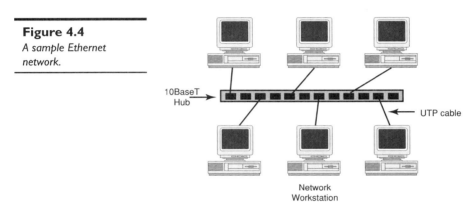

After following the preceding steps, you should have a small working LAN. If you are just starting out, you may just have a few of the 12 ports in your hub connected to a computer, but you now have more ports ready if your needs grow. The capability to expand your local network is important when delivering Internet services because you can offload certain services to computers that are specifically equipped to handle that type of service when your needs grow beyond the capacity of your primary Internet service. If your users demand a full UseNET news feed, for example, you can configure another computer specifically for news services, providing a large amount of disk space and memory, and migrate your news services to your new news server. Now that you have a LAN, you can connect it to the Internet or the world wide WAN, and still have room to grow.

Connecting to the Internet

After you have determined that you want to provide services on the Internet and have obtained all the necessary permissions, it is time to begin thinking about how you're going to connect to the Internet. Before deciding how you are to connect your organization to the world-wide Internet, it is necessary to understand what it means to be connected to the Internet. It is also very important to be as informed as possible about all the available Internet connection options.

In addition to knowing what is available, it is to your advantage to familiarize yourself with the strengths and weaknesses of the various Internet connection options. This information helps you determine which is the best way to link your organization to the Internet. This decision is based on such factors as availability of service in the area, initial and ongoing cost, performance, and integration into your existing network infrastructure.

After you have decided on the method by which your organization will access the Internet, the next decision you will have to make is who will be your network provider. Making an informed decision about the company who will provide you with Internet access can mean the success or failure of your Internet site.

The following sections cover all these important issues in greater detail, including some fairly technical discussions of the various Internet connection options available today and in the future.

What *Being Connected* to the Internet Means

You can connect to the Internet today in the following three basic ways:

- ❏ By remote access to a computer permanently connected to the Internet
- ❏ *On-demand* via modem over analog or ISDN phone lines
- ❏ Through a permanent, dedicated connection to the Internet via leased lines or some other wide-area networking communications medium

Remote access, or *terminal access*, to a computer permanently connected to the Internet is becoming less common; it is difficult, if not impossible, to provide Internet services by using this type of connection.

Dial-on-demand connections also have limited use for providing Internet services, but can still be viable connection options for certain types of applications. Dial-on-demand connections can be useful and cost effective in some circumstances. Examples of such include providing mail services to a small organization, providing batch UseNET news services, and providing e-mail lists or e-mail based information services. A dial up 128k ISDN connection is a good choice for implementing these services.

By the strictest definition, a computer *connected* to the Internet is one connected to the Internet 24 hours a day. A dedicated connection is the type of connection necessary to provide large-scale Internet services and is required for services such as World Wide Web, Gopher, and FTP. A full-time connection to the Internet can also provide users within your organization with Internet access from each desktop. Permanent Internet connections have also historically been the hardest and most complex to implement. Permanent connections to the Internet provide the user with the widest array of access methods from which to choose.

Components of a Permanent Internet Connection

Connecting an organization to the Internet requires the following three components:

❏ The physical connection

❏ Some type of Internet access, typically provided by an Internet Service Provider (ISP)

❏ The underlying networking hardware that acts as a gateway from the organization to the rest of the world

All three of these components depend very much on one another. The choice of an ISP may limit the media by which you may access the Internet to the ones supported by your ISP. Your choice of access medium also affects the type of networking hardware required. It is, therefore, important to have a firm understanding of each component and how each interacts with one another.

Physical Connection Type Overview

These days, many physical connection options are available to organizations wanting to connect to the Internet. The most commonly available today are leased lines (56k/ T1), frame relay, and ISDN. Other options becoming increasingly common include xDSL, cable modems, and local multipoint distribution services.

Leased Lines

Leased lines are by far the most common way to connect to the Internet at high speeds. A *leased line* is the casual, informal name for a connection to the Digital Data Network (the digital switching system used by the telephone companies). It provides a permanent, virtual circuit from one fixed location to another. It is not *dry copper* (plain copper wires running from your site to your ISP); it is an interface to the telephone company's internal bit-synchronous data system. The bandwidth available when using leased lines ranges from 56 kilobits/second to 45 megabits/second.

Leased Line Options

On the low end of leased line connections are so-called 56k lines. These lines are called 56k because they literally provide 56,000 bits per second or 56 kilobits per second (kbits/second) of bandwidth over the line. Also, 56k refers to a class of bit-synchronous digital data services provided by most telephone companies. This 56k class is also sometimes called *DS0* which stands for *Data Service Zero*.

The next, most common type of leased line connections are T1 connections, sometimes called *DS1* or *Data Service One*. T1 lines are very similar to 56k lines, except T1 lines are faster. A T1 line operates at the speed of 1.536 million bits per second (Mbits/ second). T1 lines are also more expensive and have lower latency than 56k lines. There is also Fractional T1 service, which sounds like what it is: Fractions of T1 speeds, generally in 128 K increments: 128 K, 256 K, 384 K, 512 K, 768 K, and so on. Fractional T1 uses full T1 equipment and, therefore, is not as inexpensive as you might think.

On the high end of leased line connection options is T3 service. T3 service operates at speeds of 45 Mbit/second. As you might expect, T3 service is very expensive and is mainly used by Internet backbone providers. Sometimes very large companies or extremely busy Internet sites, (such as Walnut Creek CD-ROM's FTP site `ftp://ftp.cdrom.com` which handles over 1,200 simultaneous ftp users at a time) opt for this high speed access method. Nobody really knows what happened to T2, .

Benefits of Leased Lines

You have probably noticed that a 56 K line is only twice the speed of a 28.8 K modem. This probably makes you wonder if hooking up a couple of 28.8 modems to some dedicated voice-grade telephone lines would achieve the same goal. But there are a few reasons why leased lines are better than an analog modem for serious Internet applications. Bytes-per-second throughput is only half the answer. For relatively simple *download* situations, flat-out speed transferring bulk data is the answer. On the Internet, however, interactivity is the norm, and client/server software puts great demands on command/response type activity. The limiting factor is not just bytes/second, but latency—or to put it another way, how much delay there is.

The best modems on the market now have latencies between 100 and 300 milliseconds, with most v.32bis models around 250–280, and v.FAST around 150. This is the lag you see on an otherwise idling system while typing in Telnet. Latency determines the overall response of the network, not bulk throughput. For short packets, which are common in interactive applications like remote logins, e-mail, WWW, Gopher, or UseNET news, your network's latency determines how responsive the network feels to you—how much delay you see whenever you ask for something.

Latency on a 56 K link is about 10 milliseconds ($1/100$ of a second), virtually unnoticeable, and does not vary much with load. Modem latencies vary greatly with load and the amount of instantaneous bi-directional data because modems are software-based. Latency on a T1 link is about 3 milliseconds.

Leased Line Setup

Both 56 K and T1 are four-wire interfaces: one pair for receive data, one for transmit, with 48V between them, and a steady clock frequency on the transmit pair. A device known as a CSU/DSU is required to convert computer-generated data (via RS-232, V.35, and so on) to the telco's four-wire scheme. Figure 4.5 shows a typical leased line setup.

The cost of a leased line to the Internet depends on two main factors. One factor is the distance between your organization's site and your Internet Service Provider. The second factor is the rate of speed at which you want to connect. As previously mentioned, T1 links are more expensive than fractional T1 or 56 K links. Another thing to consider is that equipment built for higher speed leased lines is also more expensive than for lower speed connections.

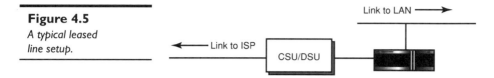

Figure 4.5
A typical leased line setup.

To order leased line service, you should first contact your local telephone company. In many cases, they may be the only provider of leased communication lines in a given geographic area. Telephone companies normally break the cost down per end, but it is important to note that you will need to get two ends. Telephone companies typically charge a one-time installation charge per end. If they charged $622 for installation per end, for example, your total one-time charges for the line would be $622 × 2 or $1,244. Typical monthly recurring costs on a leased line include a termination charge for each end and a per-mile toll on the distance the line spans. An example monthly recurring cost may be $152 for a ten mile line at $10 per mile and a $51 termination charge on each end.

Frame Relay

Frame relay is another fairly common way for organizations to access the Internet. It is similar to leased line options, and frame relay connections are often referred to with leased line nomenclature, such as Frame Relay T1 or 56 K services. Frame relay is different from a leased data communications line because it provides a connection to the telephone company's frame relay network, whereas a leased line is a direct point-to-point link. Frame relay can be described as being a wide area network technology that enables the creation of permanent virtual circuits (PVCs) that provide dedicated bandwidth over a vendor provided frame relay cloud. Frame relay facilitates the deployment of circuits optimized to meet the bandwidth requirements of your site. Frame relay connections are available at speeds ranging from 128 Kbps to 1.5 Mbps, or full T1 speed.

Frame relay connections are closer in nature to a normal switched telephone connection than a traditional leased line. To connect to a provider with frame relay, you run a leased line to the nearest frame relay access point. The connection is then made to your provider, even if it is a long distance away. The provider also runs a high speed connection to the nearest frame relay access point; this way a connection is established (see fig. 4.6). This makes it possible to have an Internet provider providing Internet access over frame relay, even if the provider's end of the connection is thousands of miles away.

Figure 4.6
Frame relay overview.

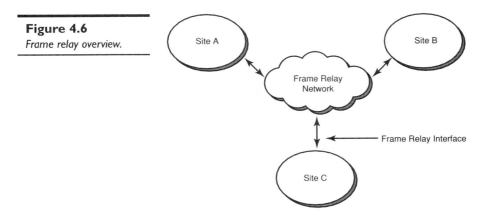

Frame Relay Specifics

Technically, frame relay is a multiplexed interface to a packet switched network. This means that on the customer equipment there is a single electrical interface into the switched network, but what appears to be many distinct interfaces to specific systems. These pseudo-interfaces are called PVCs, and are identified by numbers (names) called DLCIs or *Data Link Connection Identifiers*. The pseudo-connections are indirect; you are talking to a switch, which in turn is talking to the other end of the connection or another switch, and so on. Frame relay is optimized for carrying protocol-oriented data in discrete units of information (generic packets). Its capability to statistically multiplex provides the same bandwidth sharing efficiency as X.25.

The frame relay interface specification provides a signaling and data transfer mechanism between endpoints and the network. This interface enables communication bandwidth to be shared among multiple users, creating instantaneous bandwidth allocation on demand. Each frame (or packet) contains header information used to determine the routing of the data to the desired destination. This enables each endpoint to communicate with multiple destinations via a single-access link to the network. Rather than fixed amounts of bandwidth allocated to the resource, frame relay traffic receives full bandwidth for short transaction bursts.

A frame relay network consists of user devices and network devices that implement the standard interface. The user device is responsible for delivering frames to the network in the prescribed format. The network is responsible for switching or routing the frames to the proper destination user device.

A frame relay connection works in the following manner. An end-user device sends frames to the network. (Frames are information units that may vary in length.) The frames contain addressing information that the network uses to determine the destination of the frame. The network device reads this information and routes the frame to the proper destination. Note also that one physical frame relay connection can be connected to multiple PVCs at the same time. This enables providers to have only one large interface into the frame relay cloud, and to service many other smaller bandwidth circuits. Instead of having multiple 56 K connections to its customers, therefore, an Internet service provider can connect a single 1.5 Mbit connection to the frame relay switch; the packets are then switched over to the individual customer's 56 K hookups (see fig. 4.7).

Figure 4.7
Frame relay connection with multiple PVCs.

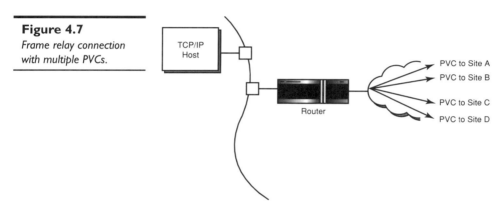

Because frame relay is really just an interface specification, the network may route the frames by any method that the network designers have chosen. Some providers, for example, keep the frames intact throughout the routing process. This is called *frame switching*. Other providers may choose to break up the frames into smaller fixed-length units called cells. This is called *cell switching*.

Committed Information Rate

Because frame relay data is carried over a switched network, the possibility exists that you will be sharing the switched connection with a potentially large number of users. This connection has a fixed capacity that must be divided between you and other potential users. Because of this possibility, your frame relay provider gives you a committed information rate (CIR), which specifies the minimum speed your line will connect at, no matter what the conditions may be. With frame relay, the provider has a system of switching ports that share the bandwidth of the frame network. Because a switched packet network is a non-dedicated data path, the equipment used to provide the service is normally the limiting factor in the amount of bandwidth everyone gets. If your provider is under-utilizing the capacity of the switch, all traffic in that switch may travel at the highest speed your line can handle. If the traffic in the switch gets heavy, the provider must add more bandwidth or limit the speed of the connections during peak periods—CIR. CIR is a provider-imposed limit on the speed of your connection. Most telephone companies sell a frame relay connection like this: You get a 56 K frame relay connection with at CIR of 30 K—you are guaranteed that the connection will go at least 30 K and will peak at 56 K. In reality, in most areas, the connection will do 56 K and might rarely drop to 30 K for brief periods. When buying a frame relay connection, you can also request that the CIR is the same as the maximum speed of the connection; this usually incurs a small surcharge.

Frame Relay Advantages

The main advantage of a frame relay connection to the Internet is cost. If it is important to your organization to have access to the Internet at high speeds and low cost, frame relay is the way to go. Frame relay can also cost less because if you need to connect a central site to many smaller sites, all you need is a single interface to the frame relay network to access multiple PVCs. If this were to be done with leased lines, a leased line would have to be run from each site to the central site and each would have its own price depending on the distance between it and the central site.

ISDN

ISDN, or Integrated Services Digital Network, is a suite of internationally-adopted standards for end-to-end digital communication over the public telephone network. As this network has been traditionally oriented for voice services, ISDN is an important step forward in the adaptation of the network to handle the increasing global demand for computer-to-computer data communications. ISDN brings the goal of a ubiquitous multiservice network closer, integrating voice, data, video, and image services in a digital format over a common, global network.

Although ISDN differs fundamentally from conventional telephone service (called Plain Old Telephone Service or POTS), ISDN has been designed to enable end-to-end compatibility for voice services. Voice calls can be made to or from an ISDN line from a POTS line anywhere in the world. Equally important, ISDN service can be carried over the existing telephone network infrastructure. This infrastructure represents a massive global investment over the past century in central office switches, which route calls and handle billing; in transmission systems, which carry the large volume of calls to remote destinations, largely over optical fiber cable today; and millions of miles of twisted-pair copper cabling to carry services to our homes and offices.

The Basic Rate Interface (BRI)

The term ISDN or ISDN line is often used synonymously with the Basic Rate Interface. The Basic Rate Interface defines a digital communications line consisting of three independent channels: two Bearer (or B) channels, each at 64 Kilobits per second, and one Data (or D) channel at 16 Kilobits per second. For this reason the ISDN Basic Rate Interface is often referred to as 2B+D.

The B channels are used for carrying the digital information, whether computer data, digitized voice, or motion video with appropriate equipment (such as the ISDN ISA boards available for PCs). These B channels can be bonded or linked together to provide an aggregate 128 Kilobits per second data channel. The D channel is used to carry signaling and supervisory information to the network, and can also be used to carry packet-mode data over an X.25 network.

Each of the two B channels is treated independently by the network, enabling simultaneous voice and data, or data only, connections to different locations. With specialized hardware and software, multiple B channel connections can be aggregated to achieve file transfer rates of several Megabytes of data per minute or more.

NOTE

Some other differences exist between ISDN and regular switched telephone service. ISDN lines do not provide their own power like normal analog telephone lines do, so it is necessary to power ISDN devices from external sources. It is also important to have battery backup devices; in the event of a power outage, your ISDN link will still function properly.

The Primary Rate Interface (PRI)

The Primary Rate Interface is designed for businesses with larger data needs, or with the need to set up their own local phone system. It is generally a much faster connection to the phone company, with several B channels. In the U.S., the most common Primary Rate Interface (PRI) is designed for 23 B channels and one D channel, which is the equivalent of a U.S. DS1 service. In Europe, the most common PRI is 30 B channels, and one D, which is the equivalent of Europe's E1 service.

With a PRI, you also have the option of combining several B channels into one bigger, fatter channel called an H channel. Several different speeds of an H channel exist. The most common, H0, is 384 Kbps, or 6 B channels. H11 is 24 B channels, or the equivalent of DS1 service. H12 is 30 B channels, or European E1 service. Above that, H21 provides 32 Mbps (512 B channels); H22 provides 44 Mbps (690 B channels); and H4 provides 135 Mpbs (2,112 B channels).

Connecting to the Internet via ISDN

To use an ISDN line to connect to the Internet, you should first contact the Internet Service Provider that you will be using to verify that the provider has an ISDN connect option. Next, you contact the local telephone company and order an ISDN line for your organization. The type of line, BRI, (Basic Rate Interface) or PRI, (Primary Rate Interface) you order depends on the connectivity needs of your organization.

For a single computer connection at BRI speed, a device known as a Terminal Adapter is necessary to interface with the ISDN line. To connect a PRI line, or if the BRI line will be used to connect your LAN to the Internet, you need to use an ISDN router.

A BRI ISDN connection is an adequate solution for a small organization or an organization whose Internet connectivity needs are modest. Using channel bonding, a BRI ISDN link can yield connection speeds of 128 Kbits/second. Rates like this are adequate for a limited UseNET news feed, or for providing e-mail and mailing list services to your users and others on the Internet. Even low-traffic Web sites can be established by using a 128 K link.

Using a PRI connection gives you more options and enables your organization to provide more services over the Internet. Because a PRI link can achieve speeds of up to 1.5 Mbit/second, its bandwidth can be equivalent to a leased-line T1 connection. Another advantage of using a PRI connection is that you can use different amounts of bandwidth for different purposes. A company can use some of the B channels in a PRI for voice communications, for example, and use the rest to make an H channel of a specified bandwidth.

Benefits of an ISDN Internet Connection

ISDN may be a good connectivity option for organizations located in an area where services such as frame relay are not available, or leased lines are very expensive. Using an ISDN connection also provides extra flexibility because of the capability to connect multiple devices to an ISDN line. An organization can use the same ISDN line for voice, faxes, and Internet data.

xDSL Technologies

DSL is an acronym for *Digital Subscriber Line*. Digital Subscriber Line describes a specification of high-speed data transfer over copper lines. Many types of DSL technologies exist, one of which is BRI ISDN (typically referred to as just *DSL*). Other forms of *DSL* include HDSL, SDSL, ADSL, and VDSL. Each of these *DSL* technologies has its own characteristics that make it suited for certain data communications tasks. Table 4.2 shows a summary of available DSL technologies, and their possible uses.

Table 4.2
Summary of copper-based transmission technologies

Name	Meaning	Data Rate	Mode	Applications
V.22, V.32, V.34	Voice, Modem, Band	1,200 bps to 28,800 bps	Duplex	Data Communications
DSL	Digital Subscriber Line	160 Kbps	Duplex	ISDN Service (Voice and data communications)
HDSL	High data rate, Digital Subscriber Line	1.544 Mbps to 2.048 Mbps	Duplex Duplex	T1/E1 service, WAN, LAN, server access
SDSL	Single line, Digital Subscriber Line	1.544 Mbps 2.048 Mbps	Duplex Duplex	Same as HDSL plus premises access for symmetric services
ADSL	Asymmetric Digital Subscriber Line	1.5 to 9 Mbps 16 to 640 Kbps	Down Up	Internet access, video on demand, LAN access
VDSL	Very high data rate Digital Subscriber Line	13 to 52 Mbps 1.5 to 2.3 Mbps	Down Up	Same as ADSL plus HDTV

An xDSL connection does not refer to a line; all DSL technologies use copper pairs as the transport medium (or to put it another way, plain old phone lines). In general, it is said that DSL signifies a modem, or a modem pair. It is the xDSL modem pair when applied to a line that creates the Digital Subscriber Line. When the telephone company deploys xDSL technologies, it buys modems, not lines, because it already owns those. Also note that *DSL* is one modem. To have an xDSL line, two modems are required (one at each end).

DSL

Simply put, DSL is the modem used for Basic Rate ISDN. A DSL transmits data in duplex—data in both directions simultaneously, at 160 Kbps up to 18,000 feet over 24 ga wire. The data stream is multiplexed into two 64 K, B channels and one 16 K, D channel by attached terminal adapter equipment. Figure 4.8 shows a simplified DSL connection.

Figure 4.8
DSL (ISDN) connection example.

HDSL: High Data Rate Digital Subscriber Line

HDSL is mainly a replacement for traditional T1/E1 service over twisted-pair copper lines. Traditional T1/E1 transmissions require repeaters to be situated 3,000 feet from the central office and every 6,000 feet thereafter. This method internally employs fairly crude protocols to transmit the data over copper. Conversely, HDSL uses less bandwidth and does not require repeaters. Using advanced modulation techniques, HDSL can transmit 1.544 Mbps or 2.048 Mbps, or bandwidth equal to T1/E1. HDSL provides these rates over lines that can be up to 12,000 feet in length. This distance is called the Carrier Servicing Area (CSA). HDSL uses two copper pairs for T1, and three for E1; each operates at half or third speed. HDSL is the most mature of the xDSL technologies, and is currently the most used. This is expected to change, however, in favor of ADSL and SDSL.

SDSL: Single Line Digital Subscriber Line

SDSL can be thought of as a single line version of HDSL, transmitting T1 or E1 speeds by using only a single copper pair. In most cases, SDSL can operate over POTS, and thus enable a single line to support POTS and T1/E1 simultaneously. In fact, this gives SDSL an important advantage over PRI and BRI ISDN service; when the power goes out, the line is not affected.

SDSL is also better suited for end-user access because it only requires one copper pair, which all organizations have—no need to install an additional copper pair (phone line). Applications needing symmetric access benefit the most from SDSL. Note that SDSL will not operate beyond 10,000 feet.

ADSL: Asymmetric Digital Subscriber Line

As the name implies, ADSL transmits data as an asymmetric stream, with much more transmitted downstream to the subscriber's end and less coming back to the provider. The reason for the imbalance in transmission rates stems not from ADSL technology, but from the copper cable network itself. A typical telephone network configuration places 50 or more copper pairs to a cable. These cable pairs can cause interference in one another if symmetric signals are sent down many pairs. Higher transmission frequencies and longer distances also increase interference. Avoiding this type of interference causes ADSL to be asymmetric.

ADSL downstream speeds range from a low of about 1.54 Mbps to a high of about 8.448 Mbps. Upstream speeds can range from 16 Kbps to 640 Kbps. The transmission speeds are determined by cable distance. Downstream speeds for ADSL depending on distance are as follows:

Distance	Speed
Up to 18,000 feet	1.544 Mbps (T1)
16,000 feet	2.048 Mbps (E1)
12,000 feet	6.312 Mbps (DS2)
9,000 feet	8.448 Mbps

One interesting thing about ADSL is that all transmissions take place in a frequency band higher than POTS operates at, leaving POTS service independent and undisturbed, even if the ADSL modem fails. Applications well suited for ADSL include video-on-demand and individual Internet access. Both of these uses require more downstream bandwidth than upstream bandwidth. Figure 4.9 demonstrates a typical ADSL connection.

Figure 4.9
ADSL connection example.

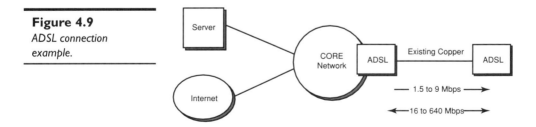

VDSL: Very High Data Rate Digital Subscriber Line

VDSL has not yet been fully defined by international standards committees, and therefore, is not available. Initially, VDSL will be asymmetric, and will operate at higher speeds than other xDSL technologies. Operating at higher speeds requires that VDSL have a shorter maximum line length than other xDSL technologies. After symmetric VDSL is developed, it will require even shorter line lengths. Although no standards for VDSL exist yet, standards-makers have almost decided on the following downstream speeds:

Speed	Distance
Mbps (1/4 STS-1)	4,500 feet of wire
Mbps (1/2 STS-1)	3,000 feet of wire
Mbps (STS-1)	1,000 feet of wire

VDSL is mainly targeted at ATM networks, and thus eliminates many of the complexities inherent in other xDSL technologies. VDSL will not have to do channelization and packet handling, such as is done by ADSL. VDSL will also employ passive termination, which enables more than one VDSL modem to be connected to the same line at a location, much like telephone lines enable more than one phone to be attached to the line.

Figure 4.10
VDSL connection example.

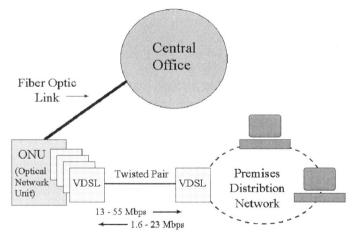

Using xDSL Technologies for Access to the Internet

If your organization wants to use any xDSL technology to connect to the Internet, first contact the local telephone company to determine which types of DSL services it offers. If they offer any xDSL service at all, it is more than likely an HDSL.

SDSL and ADSL are not widely deployed yet, but you can still use those methods to access the Internet if you are willing to do a little work. The first thing that must be done is to obtain a *dry pair* (running between your premises to your Internet provider) from the telephone company. A *dry pair* is a like normal telephone line installed by the telephone company except that it does not have any electrical signaling going over it.

Next, you must obtain two SDSL/ADSL modems. One is for your end, and the other to be located at your ISP's premises. Finally, you need to obtain a high-speed connect account from your ISP. You should contact your ISP first, before doing any of the above, to determine if it offers a high-speed connect option and whether the ISP will permit you to install the second modem on its premises. If your ISP has a high-speed connect option, it normally will not mind permitting you to install the modem on its end. The upstream bandwidth offered by ADSL may seem fairly small, but remember that 640 Kbps is still five times greater than a 128 Kbps BRI ISDN link. Small-to medium-sized organizations will find that this is adequate bandwidth for most of their needs.

Cable Modems

Cable modems are special broadband modems that connect to a normal coaxial cable television line to enable fast transfer of data. Cable modems are just now beginning to emerge. All the major cable companies are currently scrambling to test cable access to the Internet. In some areas, this type of Internet access is already available. Some industry experts believe that cable access to the Internet will become widespread by next year.

Cable access to the Internet is asymmetric such as ADSL. Most cable networks are not prepared to handle bi-directional traffic. It is estimated that only about 30 percent of all cable networks are ready now for cable Internet access, and that more will be ready as cable companies spend billions of dollars to upgrade existing cable infrastructure.

Using cable for Internet access and wide area networking is appealing to many. The use of coaxial cable results in this appeal. Coaxial cable used in cable television networks has much more bandwidth available than the copper telephone cable currently used to provide much of the Internet access throughout the world. Standard analog modems operate at a frequency of 3.3 Khz; the current speed of this technology, 33.6 Kbits/second, is almost at theoretical limits. Cable, on the other hand, operates at a frequency of 6 kHz per channel, and most cable systems can carry around 116 channels. This large amount of bandwidth enables cable modems to reach speeds of up to 30 Mbps downstream.

Cable modem access is asymmetric. The reason it is asymmetric is that cable networks were never really designed for two-way communications. Typical cable modem networks can deliver anywhere from between 540 Kbit/second to 4 Mbit/second upstream speeds. Some cable networks that are not equipped at all for bidirectional communications are expected to adopt a scheme that employs both cable and analog modems. This scheme works by having an analog modem to send upstream data and the cable modem to receive the downstream data requested.

One problem with cable modems is that the bandwidth of the coaxial cable is shared among all users on that feeder line. If you are using the cable modem, you are sharing the 30 Mbit/second bandwidth with anyone who may be on at the same time on that feeder line. On the other hand, it is entirely possible that the cable companies will dedicate another channel for data to alleviate the bottleneck when demand exceeds the available bandwidth. Also, cable companies who have Hybrid Fiber Coax (HFC) networks can activate unused fiber-optic pairs. Most cable companies run six fiber-optic cables to their fiber nodes, but currently only two are used. If the network demanded it, the two unused fiber pairs could be lit up and instantly triple the network bandwidth.

Cable Modem Internet Connections

To obtain a connection to the Internet by using a cable modem, a few steps must be taken. First, you should contact the local cable company to see if it offers Internet access through its cable network. If it does, the next step is to find out which type of cable modem the company recommends, and then buy one. Most cable modems currently available have an Ethernet port to interface to your own local area network. Having an Ethernet decreases complexity because no special network drivers are necessary for computers to access the cable modem.

The upstream speeds supported by most cable Internet-access schemes are adequate for deploying substantial Internet services. A 4 Mbps/second upstream speed is about three times faster than T1 leased line access. Even the low end of cable modem upstream speeds can be up to half as fast as a leased T1 link. With the widespread availability of cable-based Internet-access, cable modem technology will be an even more viable Internet access alternative.

Local Multipoint Distribution System

Local Multipoint Distribution System, or LMDS as it is commonly called, is a wireless two-way digital broadcast system that uses ground-based transceivers to transport data. Using a wireless solution like LMDS, it is possible to get around some of the limitations of wire-based wide area networking technologies. LMDS is currently not available because it needs a portion of the RF spectrum to be auctioned off soon by the U.S. government.

LMDS uses a 1 GHz wide portion of the RF spectrum that begins at the very high frequency of 28 GHz. The use of such a high frequency will enable the user's dish antenna to be smaller than the smallest antennas currently used to broadcast satellite television. User antennas will point to a neighborhood hub station mounted on a high roof or pole. Neighborhood hubs will communicate with a central station by using a transponder located in the hub. The central station is similar to the cable system's head end; it will handle all routing, switching, and bridging on to the Internet (see fig. 4.11).

Figure 4.11
LMDS network configuration.

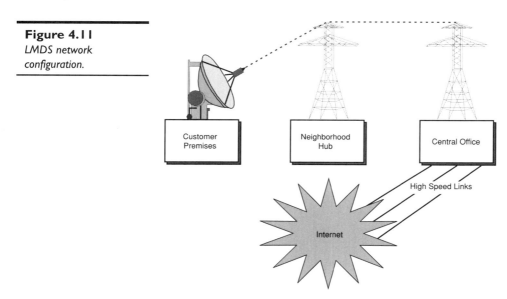

Like many other broadband networking solutions, LMDS will be asymmetric. Dividing the 1 GHz RF frequency into an 850 MHz downstream path and a 150 MHz upstream data path will yield 1.3 Gbps downstream speeds and 240 Mbps upstream speeds. This is shared by all users of the neighborhood hub. Typically, the LDMS network will assign each user a channel that is 20 to 40 MHz wide, which translates to around 64 Mbps of raw bandwidth, shrinking to 25 to 50 Mbps after error correction and other network overhead.

Using LMDS for Internet Connectivity

To use LMDS, a computer connects to a special LMDS modem via Ethernet. The modem connects to the dish antenna and on out to the neighborhood hub. Actual speed will depend on the number of users on the channel and the computer's I/O efficiency.

After the bureaucratic roadblocks are overcome, deploying LMDS will be easier than for cable companies to upgrade infrastructures to support data services. Companies deploying LMDS think they will be able to deliver data services at the same price point as the cable companies will deliver cable modem-based Internet access. Some telephone companies are also looking to LMDS as a way to provide interactive television, essentially making LMDS the way for telephone companies to deliver wireless cable programming.

Choosing an Internet Service Provider

Choosing an Internet provider can be compared to buying a computer. Much like buying a computer, your choice of Internet providers should be based on your intended use. If, for example, you are looking for a low-cost bare bones computer for your kids to play around on, you might look for the lowest priced computer you can find from a no-name vendor. On the other hand, if you are looking for a machine that will be a mission-critical component of your company, you will probably choose differently. For your business, you might think that getting the most expensive computer is a good idea, ascribing to the belief that you get what you pay for. After you have analyzed the situation further, however, you probably reach the conclusion that a mid-range system from a reputable company will meet your needs.

Some low-cost Internet service providers exist who claim that their service is as good as the others, but they may not be around next year to prove it. Likewise, high-priced providers out there will attempt to justify providing the same services as their competitors at an inflated price. As you can see, options can vary widely; it is, therefore, important to be an informed consumer. Following are some important criteria to consider when choosing an Internet Service provider:

- ❏ Network topology
- ❏ Network link speeds
- ❏ External network links
- ❏ High speed backbone
- ❏ Technology
- ❏ Lower level network infrastructure
- ❏ Technical staff
- ❏ Network operations center
- ❏ Full range of services
- ❏ Customer base
- ❏ Comparison shopping

Network Topology

Network topology is one of the most important criteria to consider when choosing a provider. By looking at the provider's network topology, you can understand how vulnerable the network is to outages. Network topology can determine how much capacity is available when the network is loaded more heavily than usual. More importantly, knowing the network topology can show you how well the provider understands network engineering. A provider should be glad to show you its network topology. By showing you its topology, a provider can show you how well it understands its business.

After you have obtained a map of its network, examine what the provider has given you closely. Some providers try to give you a virtual backbone map. Virtual networks are unimportant for the purpose of evaluating an ISP because your data does not travel on a virtual network; it travels over a physical network. Virtual networks serve only to show the theoretical paths that could be implemented by a provider's switching equipment. Providers who only provide virtual maps are normally trying to side-step the issue of physical capability. Your supplier needs to understand the physical network to understand what is important for serving its customers. If the provider tries to tell you that the physical network is unimportant, it either does not understand how to engineer a network or is trying to hide something. Nothing is wrong with the provider using technologies that implement virtual circuits as part of the backbone, such as frame relay or ATM. The provider still needs, however, to understand the physical network topology on which its virtual network is running.

Network Link Speeds

You should also find out the speed of your provider's backbone links. If you are not given this information, the provider is possibly trying to hide something. Remember that your network connection can only be as fast as the slowest link in the path. It does not matter that you are connected to the Internet via a T3 link if a 56 K link is between you and your destination—it is like hooking up a garden hose to a fire hydrant. The limit is the garden hose, not how much water the fire hydrant can pump out.

Find out whether the topology you are being shown is currently operational. Some providers like to include links that are not operational in their network maps. Some even go to the trouble of displaying planned links with solid lines and current ones with dashed lines, leading one to believe that the solid links are actually the ones in use. Also, do not confuse an announcement of a new high-speed network link with that link actually being operational. If your organization will be making heavy use of high-speed lines, look for a provider that has a connections to the Internet via DS3 (T3) circuits. For less bandwidth intensive applications, such as mailing lists and e-mail traffic, a provider with multiple T1 circuits should be adequate.

External Network Links

Take a look at the external links of your potential provider's backbone. Do they only have a single connection to the rest of the world? Is there a potential single point of failure? Look for multiple direct connections to other network providers—the more of these the better. Many connections to the outside world show that your provider is concerned about being dependent on one point for connectivity. If the provider has only one gateway to the rest of the world, find out how often it breaks down and how long it stays down when it does. If the provider cannot provide these statistics, you should think twice before opting for service from this provider. It is recommended that you use what are called *Tier One* Internet providers, if at all possible; that is, providers who actually own large chunks of the Internet's high-speed backbone. Tier One Internet providers normally connect to other Tier One providers at multiple points, and they provide the highest speed connections available. Some examples of Tier One providers include MCI, Sprint, CRL, and UUNET.

High-Speed Backbone

If the provider you are evaluating claims to have a high-speed backbone, check to see if it is available now or if it is just planned. Some providers claim that they have a T3 (45 Mbps) backbone, but if questioned further, you will find they mean T3 *ready*. The term T3 *ready* does not really mean much. A 2,400 baud modem can be considered T3 *ready* because it could be replaced by a T3 line at any time.

Another thing to consider regarding high-speed backbones is how useful they can be to you. Most Internet Service Providers require that the customer pick up the cost of the line from the customer premises to the ISP's Point Of Presence (POP). If the local line costs to the POP exceed the cost of the high-speed connect option, you might want to reevaluate how useful the high-speed backbone is to you.

Many providers boast that they have an astronomical number of POPs. Find out what makes up a POP by their standards. A major difference exists if a POP consists of a single customer at the tail end of a low-speed link, or if a POP houses high-end routers connected to each other via multiple high-speed lines.

Technology

Make certain that the equipment used to operate the network is of the highest quality. Plenty of advanced, high-quality networking equipment is currently available at reasonable costs. The provider is selling you a service, and it is incumbent on the provider to provide customers with the highest quality service by using the highest quality hardware. Sometimes providers try to use hardware and software developed in-house. Take this as a sign that you will have long-term problems if you decide to go with that provider.

Lower Level Network Infrastructure

Only the largest providers have the resources to establish the lower levels of their own network. This is the case when the provider is a telephone company that can lay its own fiber cable in the ground. Look for a provider who has strong relationships and partnerships with the companies that actually own the cable in the ground and on the poles. By establishing relationships with the phone companies, the service provider can provide a higher level of service than if it tried to do everything alone.

Technical Staff

One of the most important factors to consider when choosing a provider is the quality of the technical staff. The technical staff are the ones who get your connection running to begin with, and will continue to keep your network running in the future.

Find out how long the staff has been running TCP/IP networks. The provider should have several people who have been working with TCP/IP for close to ten years. Find out the average experience level. Knowing this is important because it is likely that you will not be dealing directly with the most senior engineers. Also, make certain that even the most junior technicians have prior experience with TCP/IP itself, and not just *networking-related* experience.

Make certain that the provider has adequate staffing to handle the usual situations. If the provider sends people to Interop for a week, how many people are back at the office running things and how skilled are they? If the provider has only a few technical people and they go to all the shows, what happens if your network connection breaks down while they are gone for a week? Find out the rate of technical staff turnover. If people are leaving, find out why and who is left to keep your connection going.

Network Operations Center

Check out the provider's network operation center (NOC). It should be staffed by at least one person at all times, including nights, weekends, holidays, and during important sporting events. A large number of providers who claim to have 24-by-7 operations really mean that someone is available to answer the phone, not that someone knowledgeable is available at all times. An answering service or a beeper is no substitute for a network engineer when one is needed. Insist that a network engineer be available at all times, and not just on call. You never know when your link will fail, and what crucial project that it can affect.

Ask how the NOC is staffed. You want to have senior engineers available during the normal business hours of 8 a.m.–8 p.m. Eastern time. If your network fails during the business day, you deserve to have the most senior people working on it to resolve the problem.

Full Range of Services

Ask yourself the following questions to determine the range of services a potential provider offers. Does the provider offer a full range of services, or is it only trying to target a niche? If you need to increase your access level, will you have to change providers? Does the provider offer true one-stop shopping? Does the provider supply equipment, manuals, training, consulting, and so on, as well as basic data services? If remote connectivity is important, can the provider provide connectivity throughout the country, or does it serve only a small region?

Customer Base

Find out how many subscribers the provider has. Do not be misled by the total number of customers the provider claims to have. Some providers count all the individuals they have connected; most others count only the organizations they have connected. The number of organizations willing to pay $1,000 per month is a better indicator of service quality than the number of individuals willing to pay $10 per month.

Comparison Shopping

Do a price/benefit analysis. Some providers may have lower prices than others. Do a fair comparison of providers. Do not compare one provider's no-frills service with another's full package. Do not be confused by product names. What one provider considers basic may be of no use to you. Ask for customer references and talk to them. See what issues current customers have. If you get a reference, make certain that person has no insider relationship with the provider. Find out where the provider's new customers are coming from. The most interesting thing to find out is how many of their customers have switched from other providers.

Internet Access Hardware

The hardware used to access the Internet varies with the medium you are using to access the Internet. Many Internet Service Providers sell or lease the necessary hardware used to access their services. In many cases, the Internet service provider offers installation of the networking equipment on the customer's premises. Also, many Internet providers offer the option of maintaining the networking equipment on the customer's end of the connection.

Although in many cases the Internet provider handles all or most of the hardware setup, it is still important to be familiar with the hardware. When choosing an Internet provider, you should make arrangements with the provider for maintenance of the communications equipment. Even if you have a service contract with the provider, it is impossible to tell when the connection will run into problems. If these problems occur when no qualified personnel are available to take care of the problem, it may be possible to troubleshoot them on your own. It may also be the case that your provider does not offer installation, or if they do, you choose not to purchase that option. In that case, you must do all the connecting yourself.

The main pieces that make up the hardware part of the Internet connection are the router, and the interface to whichever connection method was chosen to connect to the Internet. In the case of leased lines, a CSU/DSU is the interface to the line. For frame relay, a device known as a Frame Relay Access Device (FRAD) is necessary to convert computer data into frame relay frames. For ISDN, a terminal adapter is needed if one computer is going to connect as a stand-alone unit, and an ISDN router is used for a shared ISDN connection. For xDSL, the appropriate DSL modem pairs for the type of service requested must be used. In the case of a cable connection, a specially designed broadband cable modem is needed. And finally, for satellite and wireless connections, a transmitter/receiver appropriate for the type of service is necessary.

Routers

A router is a dedicated computer whose job is to determine if packets on your internal network are destined for the Internet, and to send them out. This may sound like a simple task, but the routing must be done at very high speeds, and error-free. You should purchase a high quality router. A router is needed at both ends of the connection. Most Internet Service Providers charge a one-time startup fee. The provider uses this fee to pay for the equipment on its end, including a router or a connection to a large multiport router.

Major manufacturers of routers include Cisco systems, Wellfleet, and Synoptics. Many people recommend Cisco routers because Cisco is the market leader and tends to be the de facto standard. Your provider may sell or lease you the router you need as part of a connection package. If the ISP provides the router, it will configure it for you; this is the recommended method.

 It is also possible to use an NT 4 server as a simple router. If you are on a tight budget, this might be a good option. To use the Multi-Protocol Router service for Windows NT, you need to install the MPR service. Installing and configuring a router is not for the faint of heart. If you do not feel comfortable configuring the router yourself, you should allow your ISP to configure your router for you, even if it stretches the budget a bit; it's worth it.

If you decide to go with a software-based router such as the MPR for NT, consider this: Many networking experts believe that a router should only do just that, route packets, not run application software, Web servers, and so on. A danger exists that if some hacker breaks into the machine hosting your router and causes some damage, your connectivity will be compromised. Also, if other services are hosted on the machine acting as your router, you will have periodic downtime for periodic maintenance of the other components. These periods of downtime, although unrelated to routing, cause your connectivity to be broken.

CSU/DSU

DSU stands for *Digital Service Unit*, CSU for *Customer Service Unit*. Originally they were two boxes—one owned by the phone company, the other by the customer. After the government forced the phone company to enable you to connect your own equipment directly to the phone company's lines, the boxes were merged into one for convenience. Sometimes a CSU/DSU is called just a *DSU*.

A CSU/DSU is basically a modem for leased lines. It converts reasonably standard computer electrical protocols such as RS-232 or V.35 to the four-wire scheme that the telephone companies use. It also provides, and generates, status about the line itself and the state of the DSU and other equipment on the *far* end of the leased line. Most are able to perform tests of the line and remote DSU when commanded to do so.

Like modems, you need one at each end of a leased line. The ISP normally provides one for its end of your connection; you need to have one for your end.

Frame Relay Access Devices (FRADs)

A frame relay access device, or *FRAD*, is very similar to a CSU/DSU. Whereas a CSU/DSU is a modem for leased lines, a FRAD is the functional equivalent for frame relay connections. Frame relay access devices convert a data stream in a standard format as delivered from a router or a computer to frames that the frame relay network can route to the appropriate destination.

Frame relay access devices are also available as cards that can be installed inside a computer so that the computer can be connected directly to the frame network. Using a card inside a computer can be somewhat limiting because only one computer is connected to the frame relay link. Conversely, if a stand-alone unit is used, you can connect it to a router and enable your entire LAN access to the frame relay network.

ISDN Terminal Adapters and Routers

To use ISDN, some hardware is necessary to interface with the ISDN network. For a stand-alone computer connected to the ISDN link, you need what is known as a terminal adapter (TA). A terminal adapter is just like a modem for ISDN. Two types of TAs exist, internal and external. External terminal adapters normally connect to the computer's serial port. You want to get a terminal adapter that supports bonding of the ISDN B channels. Beware that if you use an external terminal adapter, and want to use it to bond two channels, you might have to upgrade your computer's serial ports so that they can support the full 128 Kbit/second bandwidth offered by the bonded channels.

Another ISDN hardware option is to use an ISDN router. This solution is typically used when it is necessary to connect more than one computer to the Internet over the ISDN link. An ISDN router is essentially a router with a built-in terminal adapter. Ascend is a well-known maker of this type of ISDN device.

xDSL Modems

Although many telephone companies do not yet offer ADSL/SDSL services for Internet access, it is still possible to create an access solution by using this technology. By using a *dry* copper pair between two locations and ADSL/SDSL modems on each end of the connection, you can have low-cost, high-speed WAN/Internet links.

Companies such as Pair Gain Technologies have offered ADSL/HDSL modems for quite some time. These products have been targeted as *campus access* solutions (an alternative to leased lines) for organizations that have multiple locations in one city or geographic location. Remember that when using xDSL modems, use the same company's modem on both ends of the link. ADSL/SDSL are relatively new technologies and vendors vary in their implementations. ADSL/HDSL/SDSL modems normally have an Ethernet port for connectivity to your network. A router is still necessary on both ends of the connection to route packets between you and the Internet.

Cable Modems

Cable modems are currently available from manufacturers such as Motorola and Zenith Electronics. Find out which modems the local cable company recommends, and use those if you can. Cable modems, such as xDSL modems, normally have Ethernet ports for interfacing to the LAN. If your aim is to connect your entire LAN to the Internet, a router is necessary at both ends; otherwise, a protocol like PPP is used.

LMDS Modems and Antennas

No one is deploying LMDS yet, but expectations are that it is coming soon. The equipment that will be used for an LMDS connection will consist of two pieces. One will be the dish antenna that communicates via RF with the neighborhood hub. The other will be an LMDS modem that connects to the LAN on one end via an Ethernet port and to the dish antenna on the other end. LMDS equipment will probably cost around $1,000 initially, and will soon drop as manufacturing increases.

Putting It All Together

At this point, you should be familiar with some of the connection options available, the hardware required to make them work, and what to look for in an Internet Service Provider. The only thing left is to see how all the pieces fit together. The following sections identify typical connection scenarios and explain how it all works.

A Leased Line Internet Connection

Figure 4.12 shows the typical configuration of a leased line-based connection linking a LAN to the Internet. Your Internet server connects to the LAN by way of a port on a 10BaseT Ethernet hub. The router interfaces to the local network via the hub. Next, the router is connected to the CSU/DSU via the router's V.35 interface. Finally, the CSU/DSU connects to the four-wire leased line interface provided by the telephone company. Internet-bound traffic from your server travels in this manner:

1. A packet is sent along the LAN via the hub.
2. The router determines whether the packet is destined for the local or remote network.
3. If the packet is bound for the remote network, the router retransmits it over its interface to the CSU/DSU.
4. The CSU/DSU transmits the packet over the leased line to a CSU/DSU on your ISP's end of the connection.
5. The ISP's CSU/DSU passes the packet over to the ISP's router, which then sends the packet to the Internet to be routed by other routers along the way to its destination.

Figure 4.12

A typical leased line connection.

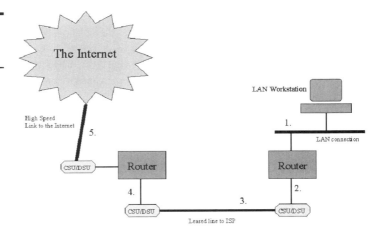

A Frame Relay Internet Connection

Figure 4.13 shows how a frame relay network connection transports your traffic to the Internet. The connection is exactly the same as the leased line connection, except that the data is not sent over a dedicated wire; it is sent over the provider's frame relay network. Rather than the router being connected to the CSU/DSU, the router may be connected to a frame relay access device, providing access to the frame relay network. Traffic travels in the same way as it does over the preceding leased line example, except that the data travels over the frame relay cloud to the provider's end of the frame connection.

Figure 4.13

A frame relay connection.

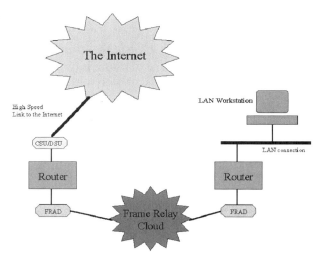

Two Types of ISDN Connections

Figures 4.14 and 4.15 show two types of ISDN connections. Figure 4.14 demonstrates a single computer using an ISDN terminal adapter attached to the ISDN network. The computer in the stand-alone example may also be connected to a LAN by using an Ethernet card. In this case, it is possible for the computer to act as a router by using the MPR service for Windows NT Server. Figure 4.15 shows a typical dedicated ISDN connection using an ISDN router over a BRI or PRI ISDN link. This setup is very similar to the leased line setup, except that an extra piece of hardware is not needed between the router and the actual line because the ISDN interface is built into the ISDN router.

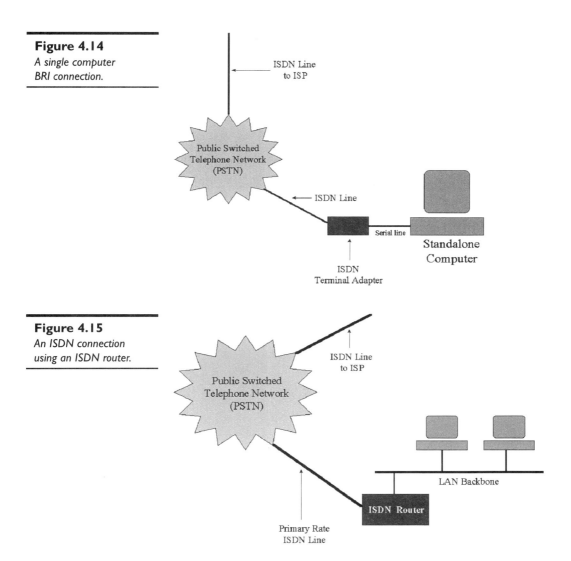

Figure 4.14

A single computer BRI connection.

ISDN Line to ISP

Public Switched Telephone Network (PSTN)

ISDN Line

Serial line

Standalone Computer

ISDN Terminal Adapter

Figure 4.15

An ISDN connection using an ISDN router.

ISDN Line to ISP

Public Switched Telephone Network (PSTN)

LAN Backbone

ISDN Router

Primary Rate ISDN Line

xDSL and Cable Modem Connections

xDSL and cable modem connections are exactly the same as leased line connections, except there is no CSU/DSU in either case. The xDSL modem or cable modem takes the place of the CSU/DSU in this scenario. Both of these technologies can also be used in non-networked environments, much like the BRI ISDN connection shown in figure 4.14. No need exists for a router when the link is direct because a point-to-point protocol such as PPP is used to make the connection.

LMDS Connections

LMDS connections will be like many of the Internet connections previously mentioned. A single machine configuration would consist of a LMDS modem connected to the computer via an Ethernet. The LMDS modem connects to the dish antenna on the outside of the building. Communications in such a setup are point-to-point, using PPP.

Connecting more computers to the Internet via LMDS will be essentially the same as the single machine option, but will include the use of a router. The router determines which traffic is local and which is Internet bound. Location of the router will be between the LAN and the LMDS modem (see fig. 4.16).

Figure 4.16
An LAN connection using LMDS.

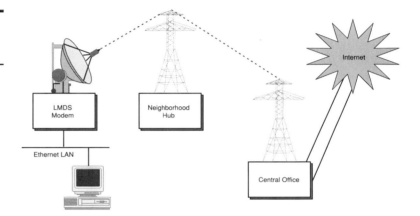

Summary

An important thing to keep in mind when making a connection to the Internet using any of the previously described methods is to follow the hardware manufacturer's instructions carefully, because their equipment may require a special configuration that was not described in this chapter. Also, work closely with your Internet Service Provider: Ask them what hardware/software combinations they recommend, or have had good success with. Your ISP also may do much of the work of connecting you to the Internet as part of their setup fee, and you will only have to set up your LAN computers for access. The important thing to remember is to ask questions of your hardware vendor, ISP, Telco, and so on, whenever you are in doubt. Procedures and options vary from vendor to vendor, so it is best to get as much information as you can. After doing all these things, you are ready to connect your organization to the Internet.

Understanding the Transport Layer: TCP/IP

The TCP/IP, or Transmission Control Protocol/ Internet Protocol, is the data communications protocol of the Internet, and is used to coordinate the exchange of information between two network devices. TCP/IP is so important to the Internet that Microsoft has included TCP/IP support in the base Windows NT system. Before setting up the Internet server, it is a good idea to understand the basic fundamentals of the protocol and how it is used.

The following topics will be covered in the review of TCP/IP:

❑ The One Minute History Lesson
❑ The Layered Approach
❑ Addressing in TCP/IP
❑ Routing IP Data

- ❏ Applications Based on TCP/IP
- ❏ Introduction to Dynamic Host Configuration Protocol
- ❏ Introduction to Windows Internet Name Service
- ❏ Installing TCP/IP on the Windows NT Server

The One Minute History Lesson

With its roots in the Advanced Research Projects Agency Network of the United States Department of Defense, the Internet grew from its 1971 base requirements—a means for ARPAnet to transfer files and support remote logins. The first requirement led to the File Transfer Protocol (FTP), and the second to the development of Telnet.

In 1983, the University of California at Berkeley released a version of Unix that incorporated TCP/IP as a transport protocol. Because of the extensive use of Unix at ARPAnet, the adoption of TCP/IP was widely accepted within ARPAnet—the Internet boom was on.

As the de facto standard of Internet communication, TCP/IP has become supported by almost all computer systems manufactured today.

As previously stated, TCP/IP stands for the Transmission Control Protocol/Internet Protocol. It is actually a suite or *stack* of protocols, and aides in the movement of data between computers. The next section introduces the major protocols and provides a brief description of their functions.

The TCP/IP Protocols

TCP/IP is not a single protocol; it is a family of protocols that work together to move data between two computers or nodes. The following are the major protocols that make up the TCP/IP family:

- ❏ Transmission Control Protocol (TCP)
- ❏ Internet Protocol (IP)
- ❏ User Datagram Protocol (UDP)
- ❏ Address Resolution Protocol (ARP)
- ❏ Internet Control Message Protocol (ICMP)
- ❏ Routing Information Protocol (RIP)
- ❏ Domain Name Service (DNS)

The preceding list is not exhaustive. Other protocols exist, such as Simple Mail Transfer Protocol (SMTP), Telnet, and File Transfer Protocol (FTP), which are part of the TCP/IP protocol stack. Later chapters in this book cover Telnet and FTP. For more information on TCP/IP protocols and a more in-depth review, see *Inside TCP/IP* by the New Riders Development Group, November 1994.

Microsoft TCP/IP is a full-featured implementation of the protocol stack and related services, including: TCP, IP, UDP, ARP, and ICMP. Support is also provided for PPP and SLIP, which are protocols used for dial-up access to TCP/IP networks, including the Internet.

Transmission Control Protocol (TCP)

The Transmission Control Protocol (TCP) takes the data to be sent between two nodes of the internetwork and breaks the transmission into smaller components for transmission. TCP assigns *ordering information* to the packets of data that make up the whole transmission and, upon receipt, uses this ordering information to reassemble the original data set. If any packets are missing, TCP causes the missing packets to be resent. If the data cannot be delivered to the application, TCP reports back to the application that it has not been able to complete the transmission.

Internet Protocol (IP)

The Internet Protocol is a routing protocol independent of the hardware used. A discussion of it in greater detail follows later in this chapter. The main benefit of IP is that it turns physically distinct and separate networks into a network that appears homogeneous. This internetworking results in an *internet*—different from the Internet, which is the official name of one global Internet.

User Datagram Protocol (UDP)

The User Datagram Protocol (UDP) puts a maximum size on the amount of data to be sent in a single transmission. Unlike TCP, UDP is not a *reliable* protocol. UDP is a best-effort protocol, which means that the protocol itself does not handle reliable data transfer. If the UDP packet is lost or corrupted during its transmission, it must be noticed by the application sending the data. This is sort of like losing your luggage on the airline—after it is lost by the airline, your luggage is gone.

Address Resolution Protocol

Devices on a network are connected to each other by some form of cable (wireless is also possible) and protocol. The Address Resolution Protocol is used to map the Internet Protocol (IP) addresses—there is a section in this chapter that discusses IP addresses in detail—to the Ethernet addresses, for example, of the physical devices on the network. When ARP wants to find the Ethernet address corresponding to a given IP address, it uses the *broadcasting* feature of Ethernet by sending out a datagram to all stations on the network. This ARP datagram contains a query for the IP address and is reviewed by each host on the network and compared to its own IP address. If there is a match, the matching host sends an ARP reply back to the inquiring host, which in turn extracts the sender's Ethernet address.

Internet Control Message Protocol (ICMP)

A routing protocol, the Internet Control Message Protocol (ICMP) was introduced to provide a dynamic means to ensure an up-to-date routing table (the section on routing IP data later in the chapter discusses this in more detail). ICMP is automatically enabled in any TCP/IP implementation and requires no configuration. Route redirection is one of the functions that ICMP performs—if the user's computer sends a packet to a router and that router is aware of a shorter path to the destination, the router sends the user's computer a *redirection* message informing it of the shorter route.

Routing Information Protocol (RIP)

The Routing Information Protocol (RIP) was introduced in 1988 to assist *intelligent* routers, connecting networks together, in learning about the other networks to which it can connect. A router knows which networks to which it is physically connected. RIP is a distance-vector routing protocol and, as such, keeps a routing table of its perspective of the network (see the section "Routing IP Data" later in this chapter for more details). RIP is probably the most common routing protocol at this point in time due to the ease of implementation.

Domain Name Service (DNS)

The Domain Name Service helps to match the numeric IP address with the name associated with that particular device. DNS maintains a table that maps the Internet (or intranet) addresses to names.

The Layered Approach

The TCP/IP protocol's design is based on a layered model. With each layer independent of the others, changes in the services affecting one layer should not affect the others. The layered model also enables the development of a number of small services for a specific task. Initially more difficult to design, a layered model is easier to maintain and enhance. As such, it is more efficient.

According to the original model, as information moves from one computer to another through the protocol, control over the data passes from one layer to the next, starting at the application layer in one of the systems. The data proceeds down through the stack on the first computer, travels across the wires to the second computer, and then travels up the stack in the second system. Figure 5.1 outlines this process and lays out the hierarchy of the TCP/IP stack.

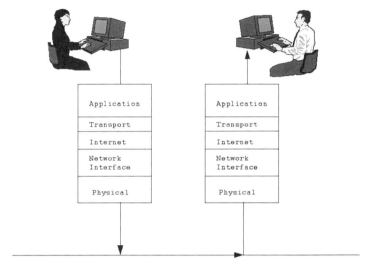

Figure 5.1

Transport of data across the TCP/IP stack.

Physical Media - Network Cable

The TCP/IP protocol has five layers. Each adds its own header and trailer data, encapsulating the message from the layer above. At the receiving end, the data is stripped one layer at a time and the information is passed up the stack to the application layer. The layers are as follows:

❏ *Application Layer* (Layer 5)—applications such as ftp, Telnet, and SMTP relate to this layer.

❏ *Transport Layer* (Layer 4)—TCP and User Datagram Protocol (UDP) add transport data to the information packet and pass it to the Internet layer.

❏ *Internet Layer* (Layer 3)—this layer takes the packet from the transport layer and adds IP information before sending it off to the network interface layer.

❏ *Network Interface Layer* (Layer 2)—this is the network device as the local computer (or host) sees it and through which the data is passed to layer 1, the physical layer.

❑ *Physical Layer* (Layer 1)—this is the layer where the Ethernet, Point-to-Point Protocol (PPP), or Serial Line Interface Protocol (SLIP) protocols exist and permit the use of TCP/IP over the wires connecting the computer to the Internet—the LAN cables or the phones lines.

Addressing in TCP/IP

The Internet Protocol is the base on which the other major protocols of the TCP/IP stack are built. TCP and UDP are *encapsulated* within IP like an invitation in an envelope. To get to the recipient, the envelope needs to be addressed to arrive at the correct destination. IP provides the address required to get the data packet to the correct intranet computer.

The Basics of IP Addressing

An analogy to the addressing scheme of TCP/IP is the corporate phone system that includes an automated, voice-response system. With many employees, companies often publish one main number in the phone book. Each employee has an individual extension, thus when someone calls the main number, he is instructed to dial the extension of the person he is trying to reach.

An examination of the phone number dialed reveals that it is made up of an area code, the local phone number, and the extension of the individual in question. TCP/IP is similar in nature in that the addresses are divided into components that help to specify the location of an individual resource on the network.

An *IP address* is a 32-bit number, but is broken down into four segments of eight bits each. These eight-bit segments are called an *octet*, and are converted into decimal numbers separated by dots (.). The result is a *dotted octet*, such as 205.211.4.4.

The IP address is made up of two parts: the network portion and the host portion. To make efficient use of the addresses available, the designers divided the IP addresses into classes based on the demand for the number of hosts on a network. The most important classes of addresses are A, B, and C.

In building an Internet server that will provide access to external sites, such as customer or competitor sites, your organization should, if it has not done so already, contact the InterNIC registration services (http://www.internic.net) at Network Solutions Inc. The InterNIC will assign an official, unique network number to the company. You can now assign the host IDs for that network as you see fit.

Registration with InterNIC requires that you first try to have IP addresses assigned to you by your local provider. This is in attempt to stem the number of addresses being used and to prevent a situation where there is a shortage of IP addresses. New addressing schemes are being developed; until they are in use, however, InterNIC will only grant IP addresses in special cases. See InterNIC's site for more information.

Currently, InterNIC also requires that you provide two IP addresses for each domain name. This system provides redundancy in case one name server goes down; clients will still be able to negotiate their way to your site.

As pointed out in the Note, if you do not already have an IP address, it may be simpler to obtain an IP address by connecting through an Internet Service Provider. Having the service provider set you up with the network number that is part of its network address space is called *subnetting*.

If you already have Internet connectivity, an internal network administrator may be responsible for assigning IP addresses to individuals. Check with your system administrators to determine the appropriate solution.

After you have been assigned an IP network number, you can start to assign specific addresses (from that network) to individual devices on your network. An electronic *log book* provides the most efficient way to keep a record of assigned IP addresses and their corresponding devices. If it is on the internal network of your company, appropriately protected, your systems administrator can check the list from any machine in the organization.

Networks grow in size. New users are added with new computers, new printers, and new servers to support their work efforts are added. As you build the Internet server for use inside a network, keep two things in mind when configuring new devices into the network that support the Internet server, as follows:

❏ All devices on the network must have the IP address configured with the same network number.

❏ Each device must have a unique host portion of the IP address; otherwise, the two or more devices with the same IP address will not work properly.

After the IP addresses are properly installed and configured for all the devices on the network, a node uses the IP address to determine which packets to receive and which to ignore. Only the nodes with the same network ID portion accept each other's broadcasts. In determining which part of the IP address represents the network ID and which represents the host ID, netmasks are used.

Netmasks are used primarily to split the network into subnets when there are a number of local area networks (LANs) within your network. Rather than applying for class C network addresses for each LAN—and dealing with the cost and maintenance of each of these distinct networks—you could apply for a class B network address, for example, which enables multiple LANs to have class C-like functionality. Netmask numbers resemble an IP address, using the dotted octet form, but use only two numbers, 255 and 0.

An octet of 255 indicates that this is reserved for the network ID. A zero indicates that the octet is reserved for the host ID. The default netmask for a class C network is 255.255.255.0, for example—the first three positions signify the network ID and the last is the host ID. This netmask enables you to effectively break a class B address into class C subnets by using the third position to assign a network ID to the individual LANs to use across their nodes. Nodes are assigned unique host IDs using only the last position and the netmask of 255.255.255.0. They discard any packets that do not match its network ID.

In the final analysis, communications by computers take place by moving data from node to node on a network using some form of link. Some of the more common links are Ethernet, Token Ring, FDDI, and Point-to-Point Protocol (PPP). The addressing schemes of these links are different from that of IP addresses—most of the addresses used here are built right into the hardware of the device (usually a Network Interface Card) by the manufacturer.

On an Ethernet network, for example, every device on the network has a built-in Ethernet address assigned to the device: The first three bytes identify the vendor of the device, and the last three are unique to each device manufactured by that vendor.

Because not all computers, or other network devices, have Ethernet support, IP addresses enable devices connected to other types of links to communicate. IP addresses are based on network topology and not on the vendor—this makes for a much more effective routing scheme to move data from point to point. Ethernet connects network hardware—users and services on a network communicate with other users and services, not network devices.

For an IP node on an Ethernet network to communicate with another IP node with the same network number, IP makes the assumption that the two nodes are on the same segment of wire. Ethernet sends out a broadcast message that all Ethernet devices hear—this is a specific Ethernet address that all devices accept as if it were addressed to them. Each device receiving the packet and supporting IP checks its own IP address to see if it matches the *recipient* IP address in the message. If this is the case, that device sends a response back to the Ethernet address of the originator with the correct Ethernet address of the intended recipient. The originator then encapsulates the IP packet in an Ethernet packet, and sends it on its way to the correct Ethernet address.

TCP/IP Addresses and Names

In terms of finding and using services on the Internet, the people behind the keyboards are not good at remembering numbers. What is your Social Security number? What is your partner's? It is much easier to remember names. TCP/IP services are usually found by names—at least, that is how the users ask for these services. It is easier to remember *www.magmacom.com*, for example, than to remember *204.191.36.1*.

Because IP packets cannot be addressed to a name, a service name can be mapped to an IP address and maintained in a *hosts file*. This works for small networks, but an up-to-date file on each single IP device in a large network would not be practical to maintain. The Domain Name Service (DNS) is one way to maintain a network-accessible database of name-to-IP mappings.

To maintain such a database, you should designate a machine to be the DNS site and have all other machines send requests to these servers to have names converted to an IP address or vice versa. In configuring each device on the network during the installation of the TCP/IP stack, enter the address of the machine to which the device should go to use the DNS service.

As many organizations and home computer users have acquired Windows 95, this chapter discusses shortly how to configure a Windows 95 desktop to access a DNS service.

Routing IP Data

Sending packets along the wire of a network is not really a difficult concept to grasp. But what about sending information between two networks (LANs, or even corporate networks)? If the destination is on another network, how do you send the packet from *our wire* to *their wire* when you are not directly connected?

Routers are used to connect networks. To interconnect networks, the router is a network device whose duty it is to get the IP packet from one *end node* to another in a series of *hops* between routers.

In the Ethernet example, the originating node encapsulates the IP packet in an Ethernet packet addressed specifically to the router.

NOTE

TCP/IP end nodes need to be configured with the address of at least one router—the *default gateway*. This is usually a manual task when installing the stack on the node.

Upon receipt, the router examines the internally stored *routing table* to determine where it should forward the packet. If the network is not directly connected to the router, the routing table indicates which router is the next one to send to. The router sends a request to the next *hop* router and encapsulates the packet in the link layer packet, addressed to the next router. The receiving router checks its routing table to determine if it needs to route the packet to yet another router or can deliver the packet to a node on a network directly connected to this router.

Routing tables can be set in two ways: manually or through dynamic acquisition. Manual configuration and maintenance is difficult in a changing network environment, and downright impossible in a large network. Dynamic acquisition of routing tables is usually done through the Routing Information Protocol. This protocol enables the router to communicate with other routers about its routing table and to receive reciprocal information from them. In addition, many routers are clumped together in a default route, the IP network 0.0.0.0, and advertise their connectivity to this default route. If a router does not see a specific network address anywhere, it can send the packet to this default route, and the packet should be delivered from there.

Applications Based on TCP/IP

TCP/IP offers a standard, routable networking protocol supported by all modern operating systems. Most large networks rely on TCP/IP for much of their network traffic. Microsoft TCP/IP for Windows NT Server and Windows NT Workstation provide a technology for connecting disparate systems. Many standard utilities are included with Windows NT to access and transfer data between systems—for example, File Transfer Protocol and Terminal Emulation Protocol (Telnet).

Microsoft TCP/IP includes the following in its implementation of TCP/IP:

❏ Support for network programming interfaces such as Windows Sockets, network dynamic data exchange (Network DDE), remote procedure call (RPC), and NetBIOS.

❏ Basic connectivity utilities including *finger*, *ftp*, *lpr*, *rcp*, *rexec*, *rsh*, *telnet*, and *tftp*—enable users running Windows NT to interact with and use resources on non-Microsoft hosts such as Unix machines.

❑ TCP/IP diagnostic tools such as *arp*, *hostname*, *ipconfig*, *lpq*, *nbtstat*, *netstat*, *ping*, *route*, and *tracert*—used to detect and resolve TCP/IP networking problems.

❑ Services and related administrative tools including Dynamic Host Configuration Protocol (DHCP) service for automatically configuring TCP/IP on computers running Windows NT, Windows Internet Name Service (WINS) for dynamically registering and querying NetBIOS computer names on an internetwork, and Domain Name System (DNS) Server service for registering and querying DNS domain names on an internetwork.

❑ A Simple Network Management Protocol (SNMP) agent that enables a computer running Windows NT to be remotely monitored and managed—includes SNMP support for DHCP and WINS servers.

❑ Server software for simple network protocols that include Character Generator, Daytime, Discard, Echo, and Quote of the Day—enables a computer running Windows NT to respond to requests from other systems that support these protocols.

❑ Support for the Internet Group Management Protocol (IGMP) used by workgroup software products.

Microsoft TCP/IP for Windows NT does not include a full set of TCP/IP connectivity utilities or server services (daemons) because many of these applications are available in the public domain or from third-party vendors and are compatible with Microsoft TCP/IP.

Standards Supported by Microsoft TCP/IP

Table 5.1 outlines the TCP/IP standards defined in the Requests for Comments (RFCs) published by the Internet Engineering Task Force (IETF) and other working groups. RFCs are an evolving series of reports, proposals for protocols, and protocol standards used by the Internet community.

Table 5.1 Requests for Comments (RFCs) supported by Microsoft TCP/IP	RFC	Title
	768	User Datagram Protocol (UDP)
	783	Trivial File Transfer Protocol (TFTP)
	791	Internet Protocol (IP)
	792	Internet Control Message Protocol (ICMP)
	793	Transmission Control Protocol (TCP)

continues

Table 5.1
Continued

RFC	Title
816	Fault Isolation and Recovery
826	Address Resolution Protocol (ARP)
854	Telnet Protocol (TELNET)
862	Echo Protocol (ECHO)
863	Discard Protocol (DISCARD)
864	Character Generation Protocol (CHARGEN)
865	Quote of the Day Protocol (QUOTE)
867	Daytime Protocol (DAYTIME)
894	IP over Ethernet
919, 922	IP Broadcast Datagrams (broadcasting with subnets)
950	Internet Standard Subnetting Procedure
959	File Transfer Protocol (FTP)
1001, 1002	NetBIOS Service Protocols
1034, 1035	Domain Name System (DNS)
1042	IP over Token Ring
1055	Transmission of IP over Serial Lines (IP-SLIP)
1112	Internet Group Management Protocol (IGMP)
1122, 1123	Host Requirement (communications and applications)
1134	Point to Point Protocol (PPP)
1144	Compressing TCP/IP Headers for Low-Speed Serial Links
1157	Simple Network Management Protocol (SNMP)
1179	Line Printer Daemon Protocol (LPD)
1188	IP over FDDI
1191	Path MTU Discovery
1201	IP over ARCNET
1231	IEEE 802.5 Token Ring MIB (MIB-II)
1332	PPP Internet Protocol Control Protocol (IPCP)
1334	PPP Authentication Protocols

RFC	Title
1518	An Architecture for IP Address Allocation with CIDR
1519	Classless Inter-Domain Routing (CIDR): An Address Assignment and Aggregation Strategy
1533	DHCP Options and BOOTP Vendor Extensions
1534	Interoperation Between DHCP and BOOTP
1541	Dynamic Host Configuration Protocol (DHCP)
1542	Clarifications and Extensions of Bootstrap Protocol
1547	Requirements for Point to Point Protocol (PPP)
1548	Point-to-Point Protocol (PPP)
1549	PPP in High-level Data Link Control (HDLC) Framing
1552	PPP Internetwork Packet Exchange Control Protocol (IPXCP)
1553	IPX Header Compression
1570	Link Control Protocol (LCP) Extensions

Source: Microsoft Windows NT Server Networking Guide

TCP/IP, Third-Party Software and Windows NT

TCP/IP is the common denominator for internetworking and Windows Sockets is a standard used by applications developers—together they facilitate cross-platform client/server development.

Windows Sockets defines a networking API that developers use to create applications for all versions of the Windows operating systems. Windows Sockets is a public specification based on the Berkeley Unix sockets and enables Unix applications to be ported quickly and easily to Windows NT. Windows Sockets provides a single standard programming interface supported by all the major vendors implementing TCP/IP for Windows systems.

The Windows Sockets standard ensures compatibility with Windows-based TCP/IP utilities developed by many vendors including applications for X Windows, NFS, and e-mail. Windows NT is compatible with 16-bit Windows Sockets which enables applications created for Windows 3.x Windows Sockets to run over Windows NT without modification or recompilation. Typical Windows Sockets applications include terminal emulation software, Simple Mail Transfer Protocol (SMTP) and electronic mail, SQL client applications, and corporate client/server applications.

Sample Applications That Use TCP/IP

When you have to *get it done yesterday*, instant access to information is essential. A variety of tools and utilities that use TCP/IP have been developed over the years. The following list outlines just a few of the tools, not discussed elsewhere in the book, that have been developed and will be introduced briefly in the following sections:

❑ Gopher
❑ Ping
❑ Finger
❑ Whois

Gopher

Gopher was the first *easy-to-navigate* information service. Gopher clients display a menu of text-labeled choices, and the user selects one, which may result in the display of another menu or a text document. The architecture is easy to administer if well organized. The file and subdirectory names become menu items to the gopher client. The user has only to click on the appropriate item and it will be delivered to the user's screen.

The service is essentially text-oriented; it currently only displays ASCII text data. You can transfer binary data from a Gopher menu and display it with other software at the user's workstation. When searching a Gopher site for information, only the menu headings can be searched. This means that the critical information about the content of the file has to be captured succinctly within the title, or the searcher will not find the document.

Ping

Ping enables you to check any host on your network or any other network to see if it is up and running. It enables you to see if you are both receiving and sending packets on your computer. The simple syntax is to issue the ping command followed by the name of the host you want to check. When you have difficulty connecting to a resource on the internetwork, you can *ping* the resource to see if it is working. Many times the systems administrator of the other host will appreciate knowing if you have found the host *down*.

Finger

Finger is used to query any system on the network to determine who is logged on to that system. With finger, you can determine who is logged on to a particular system that is running a finger daemon. As well, you can query any user on a particular system for more detailed information about the user. Typical implementations of finger enable you to write the information obtained to file.

Whois

In some cases, you want to know more about the individuals who contact your system. Using whois, or applications that extend the capabilities of whois, you can find information on registered computer network users, domains, and organizations. In some implementations, you can search whois databases and obtain addresses, telephone numbers, e-mail addresses, and full names. If you are trying to find the e-mail address of someone that you met at a conference, whois may be able to help you locate the address you need.

Introduction to Dynamic Host Configuration Protocol

Administering a network is often considered a *fixed cost*. To keep expenses down, companies must manage internal reorganization quickly and efficiently, minimizing the amount of time required by both the technician and the user waiting for his system to be part of the corporate network.

With the typical naming structure, for example, the DNS implementation of network addresses requires that each time a computer is renamed or physically moved to a new location, it must be reconfigured with both the new TCP/IP network address (to reflect its new subnet) and the DNS tables must be updated (to reflect the new client configurations).

Even a simple configuration change, such as a computer name, requires that the DNS tables be updated in order to locate the new computer on the network.

To ease this burden, the Dynamic Host Configuration Protocol enables dynamic configuration of IP addresses and related information. DHCP provides centralized management of IP address allocation. The network administrator assigns a *lease duration* to an assigned IP address that specifies how long a computer can use the assigned address before having to renew the lease with the DHCP server.

If a computer is moved from one subnet to another within the organization, for example, the leased IP address is released for the DHCP client computer, and a new address for the new subnet is assigned when that computer reconnects on the other subnet. Neither the user nor the network administrator need to supply new configuration information. This is significant feature for both mobile users with portable computers and for frequently moved computers (those used to give demonstrations throughout headquarters, for example).

DHCP operates on a client/server model and on leases for IP addresses. The following are the steps in the acquisition of an IP address from a DHCP server:

NOTE

After sending the *IP Lease Request*, the client waits for *IP Lease Offers* to come back. The client sends the *IP Lease Request* four times every five minutes, going to sleep between retries, until it does.

1. A DHCP client computer sends an *IP Lease Request* broadcast message on the network during startup.
2. Each DHCP server that receives the client's request responds with an *IP Lease Offer* containing an IP address and the valid configuration information required by the client that sent the request.
3. The DHCP client selects one of the *IP Lease Offers* and responds with an *IP Lease Selection*—usually, the first Offer is selected—responding to the DHCP server with an *IP Lease Selection* indicating the acceptance of the offered IP address.
4. The DHCP server whose Offer was accepted sends an *IP Lease Acknowledgment* that contains the IP address first sent in the *IP Lease Offer*, as well as a valid lease for the address and the TCP/IP configuration parameters for the client.

As the expiration date of the lease approaches, the client attempts to renew the lease by doing the following:

❑ After 50 percent of the lease timeframe has expired, the client tries to renew the lease with the DHCP server that originally assigned the IP address.

❑ If unable to communicate with the original DHCP server and 87 ½ percent of the lease timeframe has expired, the client tries to renew the lease by broadcasting to any available DHCP server.

❑ If the lease expires, the client must immediately discontinue using the IP address and begin the process again by broadcasting a new *IP Lease Request*

In the Windows NT Server, the DHCP Manager is used to define the local policies for address allocation, leases, and so on.

DHCP Administration

The DHCP administration tool is designed to group the configuration of the network resources into logical groupings of computers on the same cable. The administration tool enables the network administrator to define global and scope-specific configuration settings in order to identify routers connecting the various segments of the network together.

Each scope within the overall network is defined by specific properties established by the DHCP administrator. The administrator defines the subnet ID, the subnet mask, and the primary DHCP server. The network administrator also defines the pool of available IP addresses in that specific scope and any exclusion ranges to avoid. This enables legacy systems to retain their established IP addresses. Figure 5.2 displays some of the scope properties.

Figure 5.2
DHCP Administrator Scope Properties dialog box.

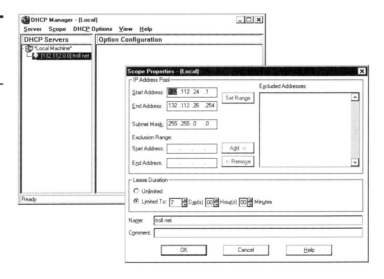

Each scope definition receives a name so that it can be easily identified by any network administrator, along with additional comments or questions.

Another option with the DHCP Administrator tool is the capability to review the client lease information. This enables the administrator to review the outstanding leases and associate them with the client names and their MAC-layer addresses. Figure 5.3 shows the active lease information for a sample DHCP server.

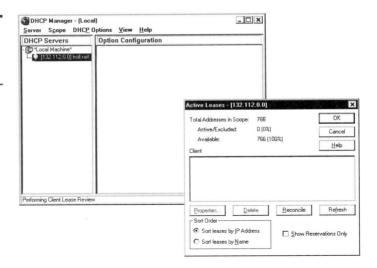

Figure 5.3

DHCP Administrator Client Lease Review dialog box.

Options can be configured for each scope-member for the scope to provide additional configuration information to the scope members. Note that this same information can be set globally as well, via a similar Global Option Settings dialog box.

Introduction to Windows Internet Name Service

Name resolution services under Windows NT are handled as a session-layer network service that performs name-to-IP address mapping for name resolution. Under Windows NT, it is implemented through the Windows Internet Name Service (WINS).

N O T E

Two general categories exist for name resolution services for Windows NT: NetBIOS over TCP/IP (NetBT) and Domain Name System (DNS). WINS is the Windows NT implementation of NetBT.

WINS was developed to address the problem of locating network resources in a TCP/IP-based Microsoft network. It does this by automatically configuring and maintaining the computer name and IP-address mapping tables, while serving basic functions such as preventing duplicate network names. WINS is a complementary service to DHCP and has its own complete, centralized tool for administration and configuration of the WINS servers.

After the DHCP client is configured and bound, the client proceeds to register its name with the designated WINS server.

1. The client issues a NAMEREGISTRATIONREQUEST message to the WINS-based server with the DHCP client's computer name and leased IP address.

2. The WINS-based server checks to see if the requesting computer name is unique on the network, and responds with a positive or negative WINS name registration response message—if positive, the registration response includes the Time To Live (TTL) for the name registration; if negative, the name registration to the new DHCP client is declined, and the user is advised of the name conflict.

WINS Renewal

The NetBIOS over TCP/IP support (NetBT) automatically registers the computer name with the WINS-based server when a NetBT client process is started. In many cases, therefore, the renewal process is automatic, with the WINS-based server automatically reissuing a new TTL with each NetBT registration. With each new TTL, a timer is reset in the system. Its function is to issue a NetBT name registration with the WINS-based server should the computer be in a state of inactivity, causing the timer to expire.

Locating a Resource

What happens when a computer in one domain wants to locate a resource in another domain? To locate the computer's IP address, the requester sends a NAMEQUERYREQUEST to its primary WINS server, which it knows to be at a given IP address. It requests that the server look in the database to find the entry for the other computer and responds with the IP address of the desired computer. The WINS-based server responds with a NAMEQUERYRESPONSE to the requester with the computer's IP address, at which time the entry is cached at the requesting client computer.

Now that the requester has the necessary IP address, it establishes a TCP connection, followed by a session message (request) to the other computer and the establishment of the resource connection.

WINS Administration

The WINS administration tool is designed to assist the network administrator in configuring the WINS-based servers and monitoring activity. The information presented is very detailed in nature. Following are the key pieces of information:

❑ Number of name queries received by the WINS-based server

❑ Number of successful and less-than successful responses (see fig. 5.4)

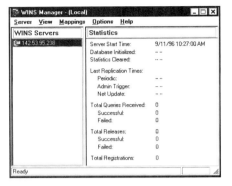

Figure 5.4

The WINS Administrator tool.

The WINS Administrator tool enables the network administrator to configure various parameters for the WINS-based server, including which WINS-based server to focus on, the static mappings for the server, the replication information, and the database in use. Figure 5.5 outlines a sample of this information.

Figure 5.5

WINS Administration options.

The Static Mapping options enable the network administrator to manually configure WINS mapping information for non-WINS clients, similar to the old host table information. Figure 5.6 displays the Static Mapping dialogue box. For example, connecting someone on an Unix machine to the WINS information system would require a Static Mapping of the IP address.

Figure 5.6

Static mappings (local).

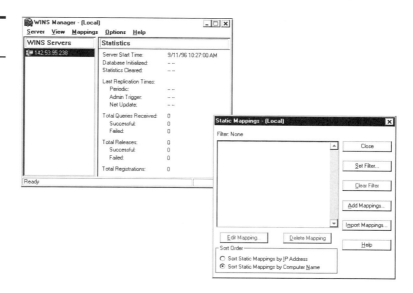

This static mapping information can be entered individually for each computer, or it can be loaded from a file containing the necessary mappings. Loading from a file minimizes the amount of work required to create an interoperative environment by importing the DNS host tables from a Unix DNS server.

WINS-based servers specify the name registration TTL by specifying an Extinction Interval, which is defined by the network administrator. Should a NetBT client's renewal not be received prior to the extinction time, the name will no longer be registered with the WINS server.

Installing TCP/IP on the Windows NT Server

To connect to the services that utilize the TCP/IP protocol, you must have the TCP/IP stack installed on every machine that you want to connect to the Internet—this includes the server.

Microsoft recognized the importance of TCP/IP as the most accepted transport mechanism in the world, and provided native support for TCP/IP in Windows NT. The discussion here assumes that you have already installed the NT software and are adding the TCP/IP functionality.

1. Log on as the administrator.
2. Open the Control Panel and select the Networks icon.
3. Select Services.
4. Click Add Software.
5. Select TCP/IP Internetworking, Connectivity Utilities, and Simple TCP/IP Services.
6. Click Continue.

Windows NT copies over the file necessary for the installation of the TCP/IP protocol stack. After the software has been copied to the NT computer, you must provide some basic configuration information in order for the computer to function within the Intranet. The information requested follows:

NOTE

Up to three IP addresses can be entered, but ensure that they are listed in the order you want the server to search. Use the arrow buttons on the side to change the order.

NOTE

The domain suffixes are added to the host names during resolution to create a Fully Qualified Domain Name (FQDN) of host_name.domain_name. Thus, if the host name is *subscription* and the domain name is *busint.com*, the FQDN is *subscription.busint.com*.

1. Windows NT asks for a valid IP address. Enter the IP address of this machine.
2. Enter the subnet mask (see the discussion earlier in this chapter).
3. Enter default gateway, or router, address (see discussion earlier in this chapter).

At this point, you should set up the access to the Domain Name Service that will resolve the system names with IP addresses. Follow these steps to set up the system:

1. Click DNS.
2. If you have a HOSTS file on the computer, enter the name of the file.
3. Enter the DNS server's IP address, and then click Add.
4. If you desire, enter up to six domain suffixes to be used in resolving host names—if several domains exist within the Intranet that you want to have searched, for example. This helps to identify to the DNS which domains it should search first.
5. Click OK to close DNS Configuration.
6. Click OK to close the TCP/IP Configuration dialog box.

Following these steps should enable the TCP/IP stack on the computer so that the computer will operate as an Internet server.

Summary

This chapter has introduced you to the concepts encapsulated with the TCP/IP protocol, and has discussed briefly the Microsoft TCP/IP implementation. As well, the reader should be familiar with how IP addresses are used within the Internet and how IP packets are routed between two or more computers. Integral to this functionality is the understanding of how names and IP addresses are resolved. WINS is one method of resolving addressing issues in the Internet.

Finally, you should be able to configure TCP/IP on the Windows NT Server and be able to continue on with the development of an Internet server.

6

Hardware
Requirements

B uilding an Internet server with Windows NT requires a
lot of planning, including planning what kind of hardware your server will use. The hardware that you decide
to use is mainly dictated by what you plan on using the
server for. After you have determined what your intended use will be, you can begin exploring the types of
hardware that you will need to achieve that goal.

This chapter provides an overview of the various hardware options you need to consider when setting up your
Windows NT Internet server. It helps you make the right
decisions in choosing the architecture to use and selecting
a CPU, chipset, and motherboard. This chapter also
discusses memory and storage considerations, as well as
video and network cards.

Determining Your Hardware Needs: Preliminary Considerations

In general, you can go by the usual criteria that you apply when choosing the hardware for a normal server on your internal network. The machine you choose for an Internet server will be just that, a server. Applying normal server criteria to it will give you a baseline configuration you can add to. It is not wise to skimp on hardware for your planned Internet server, especially if you are expecting a lot of traffic. Remember that the server should have the capability to handle as large a load as possible; there is, after all, no telling how many clients will attempt to use your Internet service simultaneously. This is unlike a normal server in your network, where you know how many clients can access the server, and you design the server accordingly. Because the load on the server is unknown, it is always best to get as powerful a machine as possible. Nothing is more annoying to a potential user trying to connect to your service than to see an error message that states that the server is unavailable because of too many connections.

Certain services also require more horsepower than others. A typical Web server does not need as much hard disk space or CPU power as a dedicated UseNet news server. UseNET news requires great processing capabilities and large amounts of disk space to keep news flowing smoothly. You need to know, therefore, which services you plan to implement so that you can select appropriate hardware. See the section "Determining Storage Requirements," for specific information on how much disk space you need for various services.

Deciding Which Computer Architecture To Use

Windows NT 4 has the great advantage of having the capability to run on multiple computer architectures. Users of Windows NT can leverage NT's multiplatform support by choosing hardware tailored exactly to their computing needs.

Before you can begin to consider the individual pieces that will make up your Internet server, you must decide which architecture your server will use. The choice of architecture determines the requirements of the other components that make up the system. An example of how other hardware choices are affected by the architecture chosen is the minimum and recommended memory requirements of Windows NT. An Intel architecture computer's minimum memory requirement to run Windows NT is 12 MB, and the recommended amount is 24 MB. On the other hand, a RISC architecture computer's minimum memory requirement under Windows NT is 16 MB with 32 MB recommended.

Windows NT 4 is available for the following processor architectures:

❏ Intel 486/Pentium/Pentium Pro
❏ Mips
❏ PowerPC
❏ Digital Alpha AXP

An Overview of the Intel x86 Architecture

If you are using Intel, you can choose from Intel 386, 486, Pentium, and Pentium Pro architechture. Although you can use a 386-based computer with Windows NT, it is not recommended, especially for a server application. For this reason, the 386 processor is not be discussed in this section. Following is an overview of each type of machine and how each functions. This section familiarizes you with the advantages and drawbacks of each choice.

The 80486

To non-technical people, the 80486 is a fast 80386DX with an on-board math coprocessor and 8 K of cache memory. It is not really a newer technology as such (only second generation), but better use is made of its facilities. It takes fewer instruction cycles to do the same job, for example, and is optimized to keep as many operations inside the chip as possible. A more in-depth analysis of the processor reveals some important changes in the processor's design. The 386 pre-fetch unit was replaced by 8 K of SRAM cache, and pipelining was replaced by Burst Mode, which works on the theory that most of the time spent getting data concerns its address. Burst enables a device to send large amounts of data in a short time without interruption.

Pipelining on the 386 requires two clocks per transfer; only one is needed with 486 Burst Mode. Memory parity checks also take their own path at the same time as the data they relate to. The 486 has an on-board clock, so the motherboard runs at the same speed as the CPU. In addition, the bus system uses a single pulse cycle.

Generally speaking, at the same clock speed, a 486 delivers between 2–3 times the performance of a 386. A 486 can perform well in a system that has light traffic load, as in a departmental e-mail server.

Clock Doubled Chips

The DX/" chip runs at double speed of the original, but it is not the same as having a proper high-speed motherboard because the bus will still be running at the normal speed. Unfortunately, high-speed motherboards are more expensive because of having to design out RF emissions and the like.

Actual performance depends on how many accesses are satisfied from the chip's cache, which is how the CPU is kept busy, instead of waiting for the rest of the machine. If the CPU has to go outside the cache, effective speed is the same as the motherboard or, more properly, the relevant bus (memory or data); best performance is obtained, therefore, when all the CPU's needs are satisfied from inside itself. Performance is still good if it has to use cache, however, because the hit rate is around 90 percent. As an example, the DX4 has a larger cache (16 K) to cope with the higher speed.

The Pentium

The Pentium essentially has two 486s in parallel (or rather an SX and a DX), so more instructions are processed at the same time (typically two at one time). This, however, depends on whether software can take advantage of it and can get the timing of the binary code just right. It has separate 8 K caches, for instructions and data, split into banks that can be accessed alternately. It has a 64-bit bus to cope with two 32-bit chips.

The Pentium Pro

The Pentium Pro is very much like a RISC chip with a 486 hardware emulator on it. This chip uses several techniques to produce more performance than its predecessors; speed is achieved by dividing processing into more stages, and more work is done within each clock cycle; three instructions can be decoded in each one, as opposed to two for the Pentium.

In addition, instruction decoding and execution are decoupled, which means that instructions can still be executed if one pipeline stops. (When one instruction is waiting for data from memory, for example, the Pentium stops all processing.) Instructions are sometimes executed out of order—that is, not necessarily as written down in the program. Instead, the instructions are executed when information is available, although they will not be much out of sequence (just enough to make things run more smoothly).

The Pentium Pro has an 8 K cache for programs and data, but it will be a two chip set, with the processor and a 256 K L2 cache in the same package. It is optimized for 32-bit code, so will run 16-bit code no faster than a Pentium.

The Mips Technologies R4x00 Architecture

The Mips R4x00 family of processors are the cornerstone of the Mips R4x00 architecture. These processors are high-performance RISC processors suited to a variety of compute-intensive tasks. Systems capable of running Windows NT are available from vendors such as NEC and Siemens Nixdorf.

The Mips R4400 supports a wide variety of processor-based applications from 32-bit desktop systems through high-performance 64-bit online transaction processing (OLTP) systems manipulating large databases. The R4400 provides complete upward application software compatibility with the R3000 family of microprocessors, as well as with the R4200 family. Microsoft Windows NT support ensures the availability of thousands of application programs geared to provide a complete solution to a large number of processing needs. The R4400 provides a good balance of integer and floating-point performance by using a super-pipelined architecture. It also is a true 64-bit processor with a 64-bit address space, as well as 64-bit computing; at the same time, it enables 32-bit applications to run as well.

R4400 Family

The R4400 processor is available in three different configurations: the R4400MC and the R4400SC, which include a 128-bit secondary cache bus, and the R4400PC, with no secondary cache.

R4400PC

The R4400PC is available in a 179-pin Pin Grid Array (PGA). This configuration does not support a secondary cache interface directly, nor does it implement cache coherency in hardware. This is ideal for applications such as high-performance embedded applications or low-cost desktop systems.

R4400SC

The R4400SC is available in a 447-pin Pin Grid Array (PGA). This processor supports a secondary cache interface and is suited for high-performance applications. The component supports a 128 KB to 4 MB secondary cache that can be designed using standard static RAM.

R4400MC

The R4400MC is also available in the 447-pin Pin Grid Array (PGA). Like the R4400SC, the R4400MC supports a secondary cache interface that can be used to design a system with secondary cache ranging from 128 KB to 4 MB by using standard static RAMs. In addition, it supports configurable cache coherency protocols for multiprocessing systems.

R4400 Operating Modes

The R4400 has three operating modes:

❏ User mode
❏ Supervisor mode
❏ Kernel mode

These modes are available to system software to provide a secure environment for user processes. In the user mode, the R4400 provides a single, uniform virtual address space of 2 GB. When operating in the supervisor mode, the R4400 provides a virtual address space of 2.5 GB, divided into two regions based on the high-order bits of the virtual address. In the kernel mode, the R4400 provides a virtual address space of 4 GB. Any attempt to access an address space not permitted results in an address error.

Summary of Features Found on Mips R4x00 Processors

The Mips R4x00 family of processors implement a 64 bit high-performance architecture. These processors are true 64-bit processors throughout, including a 64-bit external bus. The following is a summary of the features found in the Mips R4x00 family of processors:

❏ True 64-bit microprocessor
   ❏ 64-bit integer operations
   ❏ 64-bit floating-point operations
   ❏ 64-bit registers
   ❏ 64-bit virtual address space

❏ High performance microprocessor
   ❏ Super-pipelined architecture
   ❏ No issue restrictions for dual instruction issue
   ❏ Over 90 SPECint and over 100 SPECfp at 75 MHz

- ❏ 50/67/75 MHz input and output clock frequency
    - ❏ On-chip clock doubler for internal 100/134/150 MHz pipeline
- ❏ High level of integration
    - ❏ 64-bit integer CPU
    - ❏ 64-bit floating point unit
    - ❏ Direct mapped, separate instruction and data caches (16 KB each)
    - ❏ Flexible MMU with 48-entry TLB mapped into even/odd page pairs (96 pages)
- ❏ 64 GB physical address space
- ❏ Available in 179-pin PGA (R4400PC) & 447-pin PGA (R4400SC/MC)
- ❏ Write-back cache
- ❏ Burst reads and writes of 32 or 64 bytes
- ❏ Fully binary compatible with the R3000A family of microprocessors
- ❏ Standard operating system support includes:
    - ❏ Microsoft Windows NT
    - ❏ UNIX System V.4
- ❏ Processor family for a wide variety of applications, including the following:
    - ❏ Personal computers running NT
    - ❏ Desktop workstations
    - ❏ Deskside or departmental servers
    - ❏ High-performance embedded applications

The PowerPC Architecture

The PowerPC architecture is a computer architecture based around the PowerPC microprocessor. The PowerPC is a RISC microprocessor designed to meet a standard jointly developed by Motorola, IBM, and Apple Computer. The PowerPC standard specifies a common instruction set architecture (ISA), enabling anyone to design and fabricate PowerPC processors, which will run the same code. The PowerPC architecture is based on the IBM POWER architecture, used in IBM's RS/6000 workstations. Currently IBM and Motorola produce PowerPC chips.

The PowerPC architecture specifies both 32-bit and 64-bit data paths. Earlier implementations are 32-bit; future higher-performance implementations will be 64-bit. A PowerPC has 32 general purpose (integer) registers (32- or 64-bit) and 32 floating-point (IEEE standard 64-bit) registers.

Summary of Available PowerPC Processors

Following are descriptions of the available PowerPC processors. Information is provided to help you in your decision-making process.

❏ PowerPC 601. The very first PowerPC. It was designed as a bridge between the POWER architecture and the PowerPC architecture. For this reason, it incorporates the user-level POWER instructions, which were eliminated from the PowerPC specification.

❏ PowerPC 601+. This is a 601, implemented in a 0.5u CMOS 2.5V process. This effectively means that it runs faster and draws less power.

❏ PowerPC 602. A processor aimed at consumer electronics (set-top boxes, game consoles, and so on), PDAs, and embedded controller applications.

❏ PowerPC 603. A low-power processor, intended for portable applications (notebook computers, for example). Performance is roughly comparable to the 601.

❏ PowerPC 603e. A higher-performance 603 with a faster clock and bigger caches (originally called the 603+).

❏ PowerPC 604. A higher-performance processor, intended for high-end desktop systems.

❏ PowerPC 604e. A 604 with larger caches.

❏ PowerPC 620. An even higher-performance processor, aimed at high-end systems and multiprocessors. The 620 is the first 64-bit PowerPC implementation.

❏ G3 Series. The next generation of PowerPC processors, expected to ship in 1997.

❏ G4 Series. Expected in 1999.

Clock Speeds of the Different PowerPC Microprocessors

Table 6.1 lists the clock speeds of the PowerPC microprocessors.

Table 6.1 Clock Speeds of PowerPC Micro-processors	PowerPC Processor	Clock Speeds
	MPC601	50, 66, 80

PowerPC Processor	Clock Speeds
MPC601+	100, 110
MPC602	66
MPC603	66, 80
MPC603e	100, 120, 150, 160, 166, 180, 200
MPC604	100, 120, 133, 150, 166, 180
MPC604e	166, 180, 200, 225
MPC620	133

The Digital Alpha AXP Architecture

The Alpha AXP is a 64-bit computer architecture designed for high performance and longevity. Focusing on multiple instruction issue, the Alpha architecture is said to be superscalar. The architecture contains a good shared-memory model, atomic-update primitive instructions, and relaxed read/write ordering for the support of multiprocessing. It is well known that the microprocessors that make up the Alpha architecture are the fastest single-chip microprocessors in the world. These blindingly fast microprocessors are also optimized to run multiple operating systems, using a mechanism called PALcode.

The Alpha AXP architecture is a traditional RISC load/store architecture. All data is moved between registers and memory without computation, and all computation is done between values in registers. Most implementations pipeline instructions, meaning they would start execution of a second, third, and so on instruction before the execution of a first instruction completes. This degree of pipelining in the Alpha keeps latency in the processor to a minimum.

The Alpha AXP architecture uses a linear 64-bit virtual address space. Registers, addresses, integers, floating-point numbers, and character strings are all operated on as full 64-bit quantities. No segmented addresses are in this architecture.

Alphas have a reputation for sheer performance. Their large horsepower is leveraged by many companies through the use of Windows NT Server in high-performance applications. The Alpha architecture used with Windows NT makes for an excellent high-performance platform, combining the speed and raw power of the Alpha microprocessor with the stability and ease of use of Windows NT.

Making the Choice

After evaluating the available architecture options, you must make a decision. In many cases, the decision of platform will not be made by the person who is implementing the Internet server, but by organizational policy and hardware requirements. If your organization already has servers based on one of the advanced RISC platforms previously discussed, it would be a good idea to stick with that and to implement the Internet server on the organization's choice of RISC platform. Most NT users, however, use the various Intel architectures described in a previous section. These platforms have a great advantage in terms of price and performance. Also, a large existing base of applications is already available under the Intel platforms. The high end of the Intel architecture is rapidly approaching the performance of the RISC platforms, and at a fraction of the cost.

Other factors can cause you to choose one architecture over another. If, for example, you have neither a policy nor an existing hardware preference, the choice of platform is entirely up to you. You are free to choose the least expensive architecture or the highest performance platform based on the needs at hand. In essence, it is important to find out what your existing setup requires and to go with what that dictates. An example of this would be if your organization already has a roomful of Alpha-based RISC servers, and your technicians are already knowledgeable about that hardware, then you should make your server an Alpha-based system. If there is no existing setup, make the choice based on predetermined performance, expandability, and scalability needs.

Choosing The Right CPU for the Job

Choosing a Central Processing Unit (CPU) for your Internet server is one of the most important decisions you must make. By choosing a certain CPU, you can dictate what architecture your server will be and how much your server will be capable of doing. If a low-end, low-speed CPU is chosen, your server will not be capable of handling some of the more resource-intensive Internet services such as UseNET news. On the other hand, if you run the latest and greatest CPU in a server that is lightly loaded, you may be wasting a valuable resource. The hardware investment you make should be applied to the most performance-intensive parts of your Internet service.

Although Pentium class CPUs are very common, many World Wide Web servers are still run on 486s (and some even on 386s). Simple Web sites with few scripts and images are well suited to these type of processors because the HTTP protocol used by the WWW is very lightweight. Pentium class and Pentium Pro CPUs should be used to power highly interactive sites that have high amounts of traffic. Interactive scripts can take up large chunks of processing power if many users are connecting to the system and using those scripts simultaneously. Database-driven Web sites should definitely invest in the latest CPUs because the Web server often hosts the database housing the site's data.

For sheer speed, nothing can beat the Digital Equipment Corporation Alpha CPU. These CPUs currently run at speeds over 400 MHz. Only the largest Internet sites employ such fast machines. altavista.Digital.COM is one such site, hosting databases containing billions of records.

The vast majority of Windows NT servers in use today run on Intel-based hardware. Because of this, Windows NT supports more hardware on the Intel-based platforms than on any other. The following sections focus on hardware options for the Intel-based systems because the Intel architecture is the most widely used NT supported architecture.

Intel and Compatible CPUs

Two main CPUs are currently being shipped by Intel: the Pentium and the Pentium Pro. Both of these processors are adequate performers in the Internet server arena.

Intel Pentium and Pentium Pro

The Pentium can scale well in an Internet environment, and many of the world's Web servers run on the Pentium processor. Pentium processors can be considered the staple of Intel-based machines and Internet servers. On the other hand, the Pentium Pro is at the bleeding edge of Intel's processor offerings. Offering RISC-like performance at a low price, the Pentium Pro can be a low-cost solution for a large Internet site. The Pentium Pro is very useful in situations where there are many interactive users, such as FTP servers. On high-capacity FTP servers, there may be hundreds of file transfers occurring simultaneously and hundreds of users interactively navigating the site. A high-performance processor such as the Pentium Pro can rise to this type of challenge, managing the myriad tasks to be performed in serving multiple gigabytes of data per day. An important thing to note about the Pentium Pro is that the processor is optimized for 32-bit operation, and because Windows NT is a full 32-bit operating system, the two go hand in hand.

Compatible Processors

Other CPU offerings are available in the processor world that offer Intel x86 compatibility. Many of these processors provide cost effective solutions because they often have lower prices than the performance-equivalent Intel processor. Price-conscious organizations can benefit from these CPU choices. The main suppliers of Intel clone chips are AMD and Cyrix.

Cyrix

The Cyrix 6x86, or M1, as it was called before, is a strong contender to the Intel Pentium and is capable of outclassing the Pentium in a few respects. This CPU might also be capable of pushing technology forward more than the current Pentium CPUs; since the 6x86 P200+ was released, a new bus speed of 75 MHz turned up at the horizon to replace the old maximum of 66 MHz of Intel CPUs. This will require new memory technology, as well as new chipsets and, therefore, new motherboards.

The new bus speed, however, is also the downside of the new 6x86 P200+ because you cannot run this chip in a Triton FX or HX board because they do not support a bus speed of 75 MHz. The 6x86 P200+ runs at a clock speed of 150 MHz, which is a multiple of the 75 MHz bus speed by a factor of 2. Were you to run this CPU with a bus speed of only 50 MHz and a multiplier of 3, you would lose all the speed advantages due to the slower bus speed. The next generation of processors will also include MMX Technology.

The new generation of the 6x86, code named M2, will be released at the beginning of 1997. It will contain a new 64 KB L1 cache and the new MMX technology to again be better than the new Pentiums with MMX.

AMD

AMD's Pentium competitor is a fifth-generation processor named the K5. The K5 at its core is a RISC processor providing x86 compatibility. This processor is designed to compete with the Pentium by delivering greater performance on a clock-by-clock basis at a lower cost. Important in the success of the K5 processor is the fact that the CPU is pin compatible and voltage compatible with the Pentium. There is no need to redesign motherboards or to use different motherboards when using the K5 as your CPU. All in all, the K5 is an exciting option available to those needing x86 compatibility at a lower price.

Making a Decision

Whichever CPU you choose depends on your performance needs and your budget. If you must absolutely have the highest performance available on the market to deploy your Internet service, one of the faster CPUs, such as the 200 MHz Pentium Pro, is what you need. If, on the other hand, Pentium performance at a low price is more important, some of the slower Pentium models, or the new Pentium clones, like the AMD K5 and the Cyrix 6x86, provide the solution you require.

Selecting a Chipset

This section helps you make the best choice in selecting a chipset for your server. The chipset can dictate the expansion capabilities of your system. The amount of memory, number of expansion slots, and expansion slot types are all governed by the chipset of the system board used on the server. Therefore, it is important to be familiar with the basics of chipsets.

What is a Chipset?

A PC consists of different functional parts installed on its motherboard: ISA (Industry Standard Architecture), EISA (Enhanced Industry Standard Architecture), VESA (Video Enhanced Standards Association), and PCI (Peripheral Component Interface) slots, memory, cache memory, keyboard plug, and so on. Not all of these are present on every motherboard. The chipset enables a set of instructions so that the CPU can work (communicate) with other parts of the motherboard. Most of the discrete chips—that is, PIC (Programmable Interrupt Controller), DMA (Direct Memory Access), MMU (Memory Management Unit), cache, and so on—are packed together on one, two, or three chips: the chipset.

Because chipsets of a different brand are not the same, for every chipset there is a BIOS version. Now there are fewer and fewer chipsets that do the job. Some chipsets have more features, some less. OPTi is one commonly used chipset. In some well-integrated motherboards, the only components present are the CPU, the two BIOS chips (BIOS and Keyboard BIOS), one chipset IC, cache memory (DRAMs, Dynamic Random Access Memory), memory (SIMMs, Single Inline Memory Module, most of the time), and a clock chip.

Factors Affecting Hardware Performance

Although computers may have basic similarities (they all look the same on a shelf), performance differs markedly between them (just the same as it does with cars). The PC contains several processes running at the same time, often at different speeds; a fair amount of coordination is required to ensure that they do not work against each other.

Most performance problems arise from bottlenecks between components that are not necessarily the best for a particular job, but a result of compromise between price and performance. Usually, price wins out, and you have to work around the problems this creates.

The trick to getting the most out of any machine is to make certain that each component is performing at its best and then to eliminate potential bottlenecks between components. You can get a bottleneck just by having an old piece of equipment not designed to work at modern speed—a computer is only as fast as its slowest component. Bottlenecks can also result from badly written software.

System Timing

The clock is responsible for the speed at which numbers are crunched and instructions executed. It results in an electrical signal that switches constantly between high and low voltage several million times a second. This is how CPU speeds are measured, in cycles per second, *Hertz*.

The Motherboard

This is a large circuit board to which are fixed the central processor (the CPU), the data bus, memory and various support chips, such as those that control speed, timing, the keyboard, and so on. The CPU does all the "thinking" and is told what to do by instructions contained in memory; there is a direct two-way connection between them. The data bus is actually a part of the CPU, although it is treated separately.

Extra circuitry in the form of expansion cards is placed into expansion slots on the data bus, so the basic setup of the computer can be changed easily. (You can, for example, connect more disk drives or a modem there).

A math coprocessor is frequently fitted alongside the main processor, which is specially built to cope with floating-point arithmetic (decimal points, for example). The main processor has to convert decimals and fractions to whole numbers before calculating them, and then has to convert them back again.

The Central Processor

The central processing unit, or CPU, can also play a role in performance bottlenecks. It does not matter if you have large amounts of RAM or the fastest disk controller, if the CPU cannot keep up with the processing load placed upon it, it becomes a data bottleneck. Upgrading the CPU is sometimes not the answer because other subsystems are not capable of getting data to the CPU fast enough. In those cases, a processor upgrade only gets you higher performance on massive calculations.

Summing Up Performance Factors

In principle, the faster the CPU, the better, but only if your applications do a lot of logical operations and calculation (where the work is centered around the chip) rather than writing to disk. In a typical word processing task, for example, replacing a 16 MHz 386 with a 33 MHz one (doubling the speed) only gets you something like a 5–10 percent increase in practical performance, regardless of what the benchmarks might say. It is often a better idea to spend money on a faster hard disk.

Also, if you put only 8 MB RAM in your computer, you will not see much of a performance increase from a DX2/66 until you get a Pentium 90 (none at all between a DX4/100 and a Pentium 75). With Windows, this is because the hard disk is used a lot for virtual memory (swap files), which means more activity over the data bus. Because motherboards below the 90 run at 33 MHz (only the chips run faster), the bottleneck is the disk I/O, running at much the same speed on them all. This is especially true if you use Programmed I/O (PIO), where the CPU must scrutinize every bit to and from the hard drive (although Multi-sector I/O or EIDE will improve things). As the Pentium 90's motherboard runs faster (66 MHz), the I/O can proceed at a much faster pace, and performance will more than double (a more sophisticated chipset helps).

With 16 MB, on the other hand, performance will almost double, regardless of the processor because the need to go to the hard disk is reduced, and the processor can make a contribution to performance. The biggest jump is from a DX2/66 to a DX/4, with the curve flattening out progressively up to the Pentium 90.

Buying a Motherboard

The first decision you must make before buying a Pentium motherboard is which chipset you would like to use. Next, you must choose the manufacturer. You really should go for a brand-name motherboard, preferably a brand present on the Web, because that is by far the best way to get the latest Flash BIOS update, drivers, and information about the board you might require. In the first place, you obviously should look for the best performance, but the features of the motherboard are very important too. At the moment, the most popular manufacturers are Asus, Supermicro, Tyan, Intel, Gigabyte, and ECS. Better or more feature-rich boards may, however, be on the market. The best thing to do is to find out as much as you can about the board and its manufacturer. That way you can make an informed decision and not be pressured into buying something that you do not want just because it has a brand name.

The following is a list of questions to consider when purchasing a motherboard:

❏ *Does the motherboard support Pentium-compatible CPUs, like the 6x86 (BIOS, big voltage regulator and 55 MHz bus speed for P133+) or the 5K86?*

This gives you the option of choosing a different CPU manufacturer in the future.

❏ *Does the motherboard have a decent voltage regulator, which is cooled in an easy-to-reach place and capable of supplying a good current?*

A good voltage regulator will help avoid power supply problems.

❏ *Can you change the CPU supply voltage (Standard/VRE)?*

If the motherboard allows you to change the voltage, it will enable you to use CPUs that require special voltages without having to get a new motherboard.

❏ *How many PCI/ISA slots does the motherboard have?*

The number of expansion slots can determine how many peripherals (network cards, SCSI controllers) your system can have connected.

❏ *How many SIMM banks does the motherboard have?*

You will want as many banks as you can get, allowing for large amounts of memory.

❏ *Which RAM types are supported?*

It is necessary to know which types of RAM the motherboard supports, so you can purchase the appropriate type (EDO, FPM, and so on).

❏ *Do you want an ATX board?*

ATX boards have a smaller form than normal boards and have an improved layout for easy access to memory slots and expansion slots.

❏ *Is the CPU in the way of long slot cards (such as SCSI cards or SB AWE 32)?*

If the CPU obstructs the expansion slots, you might limit the number of slots you can actually use on the board.

❏ *Do you need an IR (infrared) Communications Port?*

IR ports are commonly used for communicating with a laptop that is similarly equipped.

❏ *Do you want a motherboard with USB (Universal Serial Bus)?*

USB is a new expansion bus type that delivers higher performance and expandability than existing serial com ports.

❏ *Are any disk controllers built in to the motherboard?*

Some motherboards come with integrated SCSI or IDE controllers. This is useful if the board has few expansion slots, freeing one up for use with some other peripheral.

❏ *How much cache and what types of cache memory can the motherboard use?*

Cache memory can greatly improve system performance. It is good if the motherboard supports cache upgrades.

Memory

The memory contains the instructions that tell the central processor what to do, as well as the data created by its activities. Because the computer works with the binary system, memory chips work by keeping electronic switches in one state or the other for however long they are required. Actually, memory chips consist of a capacitor and a transistor; the *capacitor* stores a charge (data), which represents a 1, and the *transistor* acts as a switch that turns the charge on or off. Where these states can be changed at will, it is called Random Access Memory, or RAM. The term derives from when magnetic tapes were used for data storage, and the information could only be accessed sequentially. A ROM, on the other hand, is a memory chip with its electronic switches permanently on or off, so they cannot be changed (hence the name, Read-Only Memory).

Memory Types

Your server uses two main types of memory. One is dynamic memory, which is usually used as main system memory. The other is static memory, normally used as cache memory.

Dynamic RAM

Dynamic RAM (DRAM) uses internal capacitors to store data (a single transistor turns it on or off) that lose their charge over time. They need constant refreshing to retain information; otherwise, 1s will turn to 0s. The end result is that between every memory access, an electrical charge is sent that refreshes the chip's capacitors to keep data in a fit state, which cannot be reached while recharging is going on. Reading a DRAM discharges its contents. They must, therefore, be written back immediately to keep the same information.

Enhanced DRAM

Enhanced DRAM (EDRAM) replaces standard DRAM and the SRAM in the level 2 cache on the motherboard, typically combining 256 bytes of 15 ns SRAM inside 35 ns DRAM. Because the SRAM can take a whole 256-byte page of memory at one time, it gives an effective 15 ns access speed when you get a hit (35 ns otherwise). The level 2 cache is replaced with a SIC chip to sort out chipset versus memory requirements. System performance is increased by around 40 percent. EDRAM has a separate write path that accepts and completes requests without the rest of the chip.

Synchronous DRAM

Synchronous DRAM (SDRAM) takes memory access away from the CPU's control; internal registers in the chips accept the request and enable the CPU to do something else while the data requested is assembled for the next time the CPU talks to the memory. As they work on their own clock, the rest of the system can be clocked faster. A version is optimized for video cards.

Extended Data Output

EDO (Extended Data Output) is an advanced version of fast page mode (often called Hyper Page Mode), which can be up to 30 percent better and only costs 5 percent more. As it replaces level 2 cache and does not need a separate controller, space on the motherboard is saved, which is good for notebooks. It also saves battery power.

EDO is very similar to normal FPM RAM, but what makes it different is that it keeps requested data available for the CPU for a longer period of time. This is important for fast CPU's such as the Pentium and is also what gives the RAM its name (Extends the time the Data is available for Output). In short, EDO gives an increased bandwidth due to shortening of the page mode cycle, but it does not appear to be that much faster in practice. It is the most commonly used type of memory on new Pentium-based systems. EDO RAM comes in three flavors: 70 ns, 60 ns, and 50 ns. If you should get EDO, do not get 70 ns, or you will never be able to upgrade to a 100, 133, 166, or 200 MHz processor. Get 60 ns or, if your motherboard supports it, get 50 ns EDO RAM.

The Fast Page Mode RAM (FPM RAM)

FPM RAM is the oldest and least sophisticated among all these RAM types. It now comes in two different flavors: 70 ns and 60 ns access time. You will need the 60 ns type if you have a Pentium with a bus speed of 66 MHz (in 100, 133, 166, and 200 MHz Pentiums). You are probably familiar with this kind of RAM; it is also used by default on video cards, referred to as DRAM and sometimes with an access time of only 48 ns there.

Burst Extended Data Output RAM (BEDO RAM)

The BEDO RAM reads data in a burst; this means that after the address has been provided, the next three data are read in only one clock cycle each. At present, this RAM type is only supported by the VIA chipsets 580VP, 590VP, and 680VP. The main downside of the really fast BEDO RAM seems also to be its incapability to cope with bus speeds faster than 66 MHz.

Synchronous Dynamic RAM (SDRAM)

This is another type of RAM. It might get very popular soon because it is supported by the new Intel Triton VX chipset, all new VIA chipsets, the 580VP, 590VP (for Pentiums, 6x86) and the 680VP (for Pentium Pro). This RAM is able to handle all input and output signals synchronized to the system clock. That feat is quite amazing; until recently, only the Static Cache RAM was able to achieve this. The best thing about SDRAM, however, is that it easily handles bus speeds up to 100 MHz. This memory speed is what is needed in the near future because expansion bus speeds will soon reach these dimensions. SDRAM is the only memory capable of keeping up with very high bus speeds.

Static RAM

Static RAM (SRAM) is the fastest available, with a typical access time of 25 nanoseconds. Static RAM is expensive and can only store a quarter of the data that DRAM is able to because it uses two transistors to store a bit against DRAM's one (although it does retain it for as long as the chip is powered). The transistors are connected so that only one is either in or out at any time; whichever one is in stands for a 1 bit. Synchronous SRAM enables a faster data stream to pass through it—which is needed when used for caching on 90 and 100 MHz Pentium.

Asynchronous Static RAM (Async SRAM)

This is the good old cache RAM used for years—ever since the 386 with the first level 2 cache came out. The simple trick of this type of cache RAM is that it is just faster to access than DRAM; depending on your CPU clock, you can still get it in a 20, 15, or 12 ns flavor. The shorter the access/data time, the faster it is and the shorter burst accesses to it that can be chosen. Nevertheless, as the name states, it is not fast enough to have the capability to be accessed synchronously, which means that the CPU has to wait on this cache RAM as well, only shorter than it has to wait for DRAM.

Synchronous Burst Static RAM (Sync SRAM)

With current bus speeds up to 66 MHz, the Sync Burst SRAM is the fastest available RAM. The reason is that as long as the CPU does not run too fast, the Sync Burst SRAM can indeed offer the data synchronously. This means that there is no delay to the CPU. As soon as CPUs do cross the 66 MHz bus speed barrier (as the Cyrix 6x86 P200+ already does), however, the Sync Burst SRAM becomes strained and delivers in slower bursts, which makes it significantly slower than Pipelined Burst SRAM.

Pipelined Burst Static RAM (PB SRAM)

By employing input or output registers, a SRAM may be pipelined. Loading the registers takes an extra lead-off cycle, but after loading, enables early access to the next address location while supplying data from the current location. It is, therefore, the fastest cache RAM for new systems with 75 MHz bus speeds or faster. Actually, PB SRAM can work with bus speeds up to 133 MHz. Furthermore, it is not that much slower than Sync Burst SRAM in slower systems. You can see how fast it is by its address/data times: 4.5 to 8 ns.

Cache Memory

For a long time, a 256 KB L2 cache was state of the art. The Pentium P54C then came out, and you could install 512 KB cache on your motherboards. The latest VIA Pentium chipsets now support up to 2048 KB level 2 cache.

Up to the time when DOS and Windows 3.1/WfW 3.11 were the most popular operation systems, there was no point in installing more than 256 KB L2 cache as long as you did not have more than 64 MB RAM. Since 32-bit operating systems (such as NT) have come on the scene, it is possible to see an increase in system performance with a 512 KB cache with even a RAM size of only 16 MB. Currently, many organizations are moving to Windows NT 4 and other operating systems; this demonstrates a trend to 32-bit multitasking operating systems.

In 32 bit OSes with multitasking, an increased level 2 cache size up to 2 MB makes sense and will result in increased performance. This increased performance results from the larger size of the actual programs and the larger number of programs that are running at the same time. Obviously, it is not overkill to think of getting more than 512 KB L2 cache, as long as you are using a modern operating system.

Following are several major design implementations with synchronous burst SRAMs that make them far superior to asynchronous SRAMs in high-speed cache design:

❑ Synchronized to the system clock: In its simplest form, this means that all signals are triggered on a clock edge. The availability of signals on a clock edge simplifies high-speed system design.

❑ Burst capability: Synchronous burst SRAMs provide high speed operation by incorporating a small amount of logic that enables the memory to self-cycle through sequential locations. The four-address burst sequence is interleaved for Intel compatibility or linear for PowerPC and others.

❑ Pipelining: By employing input or output, registers such an SRAM may be pipelined. Loading the registers takes an extra lead-off cycle, but after enables early access to the next address location while supplying data from the current location.

The features mentioned in the preceding list enable the microprocessor access to sequential memory locations faster than the underlying SRAM technology would otherwise support. Although some vendors are able to provide 3.3V asynchronous SRAMs with clock-to-data times of 15 ns, pipelined synchronous burst SRAMs utilizing a similar technology can achieve clock-to-data times of less than 6 ns.

The purpose of L2 cache is to enable the microprocessor to run closer to its theoretical limit. Any time the microprocessor is waiting for instructions or data, it is that much further from its performance limit. When discussing SRAM as cache, the most consistent way to compare one solution to another is to compare the number of SRAM accesses per cycle during a burst. (All present and future general purpose microprocessors support either interleaved or linear burst schemes.) When using the burst mode for cache accesses, the first access takes the microprocessor two cycles. The second, third, and fourth access require only one cycle. A zero-wait-state cache, for example, would add no delays to this 2-1-1-1 sequence. As bus frequencies increase, maintaining a zero-wait-state cache becomes increasingly difficult and prohibitively expensive for most system designs.

How Much Memory Do You Need?

After determining which type of RAM you will use in your Internet server, you need to decide how much of each kind. For an average Web server, 32 MB of RAM is enough. If the WWW server will be doing a lot of database access or cgi scripting, you should consider getting more. UseNET news has a minimum real-world requirement of 64 MB of RAM; although if you do not have a large newsfeed or have few users, you may be able to get away with less.

Storage

Consider two things when choosing the storage solution for your Internet server. The first thing to consider is how much space you are going to require. As stated earlier, different types of Internet services have different hardware requirements. Having an idea of the type of services you wish to offer will, therefore, dictate your storage requirements. The second thing to consider is the storage interface you wish to use. Currently, two main storage interfaces are supported by Windows NT: SCSI and IDE. In many cases, the interface you choose is dictated by your service's storage needs. Larger size drives, for example, are only supported under SCSI.

Determining Storage Requirements

There are a few rules of thumb to follow when determining the storage requirements for your service. The following sections provide a guide in determining how many gigabytes you will need, depending on the services for which you will be using your server.

WWW

If you only want to have a WWW server, two gigabytes is a good disk size. Two gigabytes gives you enough room for the operating system, the HTTP server, and a great amount of space left over for Web pages containing moderate amounts of images and multimedia files. The equation changes slightly if you plan on using multimedia extensively. AVI movies and WAV files can take big chunks of disk space very quickly. If your Internet server is the main server for a large organization, you will need more space. Various departments and units of your organization will want to place their pages and information on the main server. More disk space may be required if the WWW server will contain large databases that will be made available over the World Wide Web. Other Internet services, such as Gopher, generally have the same (or lower) storage requirements as WWW servers.

Mail Services

The disk space requirement for providing mail services for an organization varies depending on the number of users to be serviced. When providing mail services, the mail server will store users' mail for long periods of time. Four gigabytes will handle about a thousand users fairly well. Four GB may seem like a large number, but mail is a service that normally grows continually. Users may not make great use of the mail system at first, but as time goes on, they will become more comfortable with the system and will make greater use of it, and thereby increase the mail volume the server must handle. Users' subscription mailing lists normally generate a large amount of mail and increase the need for mail storage space. The increasing use of mail will be more of an issue if you implement a mail system that keeps a user's mailbox on the server (and the mail is never downloaded to the user's local machine using POP, IMAP, or some other remote mail access protocol).

UseNET

UseNET news is the Internet service that has the greatest storage demands of them all. A decent news feed should have at least four gigabytes of disk space and more is recommended. Tens of thousands of UseNET news groups are available, and if you would like to provide access to all of them, six to eight gigabytes of disk space is a more realistic estimate. The amount of storage that UseNET requires also is dependent on how long you wish to keep articles available for your users. Holding news from a full newsfeed for one week requires less space than if you hold the same newsfeed for two or three weeks.

It is also better to have large numbers of smaller disks than it is to have one large disk on which to store news. Four 2 GB disks will yield better performance than one 9 GB disk. Having more disks enables more articles to be retrieved in parallel from all the disks simultaneously because many disk heads can read different parts of the news system at the same time.

Table 6.2 Recommended Gigabytes of Disk Space for Various Services	If Using Your Server for...	Recommended Gigabyte
	World Wide Web	2
	Mail Services	4
	UseNET	4–8

Hard Disk Interfaces

Two types of hard disk interfaces are available for Intel-based systems, IDE and SCSI. These interfaces determine the characteristics of the system's external storage facilities. Storage interfaces can determine what type of storage devices can be used, such as hard disks, CD-ROM drives, tape drives, and so on. These interfaces also dictate how many storage devices can be connected to the system, and how fast the data is transferred from the storage devices to the rest of the system.

IDE

IDE stands for Integrated Drive Electronics, sometimes called ATA (AT Attachment). IDE is a disk drive implementation designed to integrate the controller on to the drive itself, and thereby to reduce interface costs and make firmware implementations easier. This reduction of costs and the high level of integration has made IDE the most popular drive interface for PCs. DE is the interface of choice if you have a very limited budget. Now a more advanced implementation of IDE exists called EIDE (Enhanced IDE) or ATA-2. EIDE enables faster data transfers using PIO mode 3 or better. It also enables up to four devices to be put into a computer through the use of a secondary controller and BIOS support. EIDE/IDE hard drives are normally very inexpensive when compared to other drive types. Capacities range from 5 MB to 2 GB.

SCSI

SCSI, pronounced *scuzzy*, stands for Small Computer Systems Interface. It is a standard for connecting peripherals to your computer via a standard hardware interface that uses standard SCSI commands. The SCSI standard can be divided into SCSI (SCSI1) and SCSI2 (SCSI wide and SCSI wide and fast). SCSI2 is the most recent version of the SCSI command specification and enables scanners, hard disk drives, CD-ROM players, tapes, and many other devices to connect.

A SCSI subsystem is composed of three components: the host adapter, the devices, and terminators. A host adapter is a circuit board, normally plugged into a computer's expansion bus to connect the computer to the SCSI bus. Devices consist of any SCSI piece of hardware: scanners, tape drives, hard disks, CD-ROM drives, and so on. Terminators are resistors placed on the ends of the SCSI to dampen signals on the bus, preventing the signals from bouncing off the end of the cable.

SCSI is the recommended interface for server storage peripherals. SCSI has some significant advantages over EIDE/IDE in a server environment, such as the following:

- ❏ Flexible device attachment (up to 7 or 15 devices per SCSI bus).
- ❏ Support for almost any peripheral type (disk, tape, CDROM, scanner, and so on).
- ❏ All commands can overlap with commands on other devices.
- ❏ Usually uses DMA to transfer data (which frees CPU for other tasks).
- ❏ Interface and protocol is carefully specified by ANSI.
- ❏ Largest, highest performance devices are available in SCSI before IDE.
- ❏ Most adapters can do scatter/gather DMA, which is a necessity in virtual memory systems (such as NT, OS/2, and Unix).

The natural multitasking capability of SCSI can be a huge performance advantage with a modern operating system such as Windows NT. Most modern SCSI adapters are bus mastering, which means that no CPU intervention is necessary for transferring data from the device into memory. This frees up the single most expensive chip on the computer to do some worthwhile tasks instead of spending time waiting on data. In such a system, due to virtual memory, a 64 KB *contiguous* read requested by a process may be spread to 16 separate physical pages. A good SCSI controller, given a single request, can perform this *scatter/gather* operation autonomously. EIDE/IDE requires significant interrupt service overhead from the host CPU to handle this.

Another thing worth considering is that EIDE/IDE does not enable more than one I/O request to be outstanding on a single cable, even to different drives. SCSI enables multiple I/O requests to be outstanding, and they may be completed out of order. Process A, for example, needs to read a block. The request is sent to the drive, the disk head starts to move, and process A blocks waiting for it. Process B is then enabled to run; it also reads a block from the disk. Process B's block may be sitting in a RAM cache on the SCSI controller or on the drive itself. Or the block may be closer to the head than process A's block, or on a different drive on the same cable. SCSI enables process B's request to be completed ahead of process A's, which means that process B can be running sooner; the system CPU, therefore, tends to spend less time waiting for data transfers to complete. Under ATA, the process B request cannot even be sent to the drive until the process A request is complete. These SCSI capabilities are very valuable in a true multitasking environment and especially are important in a busy file server, such as an Internet server.

SCSI drives are available in larger capacities than EIDE/IDE drives, enabling you to add large amounts of storage to your server when it is required. SCSI Drives also have longer MTBFs than comparable EIDE/IDE drives have; your investment in hard disks will last longer. The large number of devices supported on a SCSI bus also enables you to reuse your older drives when you upgrade the system serving as your Internet server.

RAID

RAID is one other storage-related technology that you might consider using when creating an Internet server. RAID stands for Redundant Array of Inexpensive Disks and is a storage technology designed for applications where data availability is important. Various levels of RAID exist, ranging from 0 to 5 with RAID 5 being the highest. Windows NT supports certain RAID levels through software, enabling disk mirroring, disk striping, and disk striping with parity. For an Internet server, the only levels of RAID worth considering are RAID levels 1 and 5.

RAID 1

RAID level 1 is disk striping. This enables disks or portions of disks to be seen as one large disk by the operating system. Disk striping yields greater performance than having stand-alone disks. The greater performance results from the data being spread throughout several physical drives and, therefore, more disk heads could be active trying to get the requested data at one time. RAID 1 is good for things like the news spool in a UseNET news server because you want maximum performance. It does not matter, however, if the data is lost or damaged; the only thing you need to worry about is the server's system files.

RAID 5

RAID level 5 is disk striping with parity. This level of RAID does not have the performance gain attributed to RAID level 1, but what you lose in speed you gain in data integrity. Data is written across all drives and also on to a special drive called the parity drive, which is used to recover data in the event of a drive failure. It would be a good idea to implement RAID 5 on any server containing information not easily replaced, or better yet deploy it anywhere you can.

Hardware Versus Software RAID Solutions

Although you can use the built-in RAID capabilities of Windows NT, hardware RAID solutions also exist. These hardware RAID solutions often come as an adapter that fits into the SCSI bus and appear to the main system as a single disk. Frequently, these types of hardware RAID solutions have higher performance than the built-in RAID software has. Note that hardware RAID solutions often come in chassis that enable hot swapping drives. Hot swapping means that if one drive fails, it can be pulled out of the chassis and replaced without having to power down the system.

A good RAID 5 implementation requires seven drives. Four of the drives are used as data drives. One drive is used by the RAID subsystem as the parity drive. You should really use one more drive inside the chassis as a hot spare. A *hot spare* is a drive that is ready to go in case of failure. This will keep performance up; in the event of a failure, the RAID subsystem can begin regenerating the data from the failed drive just as soon as the failure occurs. In addition to a hot spare, you should ideally have a shelf spare (just in case).

Backup Hardware Options

After having an Internet server up and running for some time, you will want to consider installing a tape backup device on the computer. As your Internet service grows, you will continue to expand your service offerings and the amount of work put into the site will become substantial. This means that you will want to protect the time and money you have invested in your Internet server. One of the best ways to protect your data is by using tape backup devices.

Digital Linear Tapes (DLT)

For large applications such as servers, the only real backup solutions available have SCSI interfaces. DLT, or Digital Linear Tapes, are high speed, high capacity tape drives frequently used to backup network servers. These types of tape drives are very robust and very expensive.

Digital Audio Tape (DAT)

DAT drives are another solution. These drives come in two sizes: 8 mm and 4 mm. DAT drives have a capacity from 1.3 to 8 GB. They are also decent performers and do not cost as much as DLT drives.

Understanding Expansion Buses

The expansion bus (where expansion cards go) is an extension of the central processor. When adding cards to it, therefore, you are extending the capabilities of the CPU itself. The relevance of this with regard to the BIOS is that older cards are less capable of coping with modern buses running at higher speeds than running at the original design of 8 or so MHz. When the bus is accessed, the whole computer also slows down to the bus speed. To speed things up, it is often worth altering the speed of the bus or the wait states between it and the CPU. The PC actually has four buses. The processor bus connects the CPU to its support chips, the memory bus connects it to its memory, the address bus is part of both of them, and the I/O (or expansion) bus is what is addressed here. The following are expansion bus types:

- ❏ ISA
- ❏ EISA
- ❏ MCA
- ❏ Local Bus

ISA

ISA stands for Industry Standard Architecture. The 8-bit version came on the original PC and the AT, but the latter uses an extension to make it 16-bit. It has a maximum data transfer rate of about 8 megabits per second on an AT, which is actually well above the capability of disk drives or most network and video cards. The average data throughput is around a quarter of that. Its design makes it difficult to mix 8- and 16-bit RAM or ROM within the same 128 K block of upper memory; an 8-bit VGA card could force all other cards in the same (C000-DFFF) range to use 8 bits as well, which was a common source of inexplicable crashes where 16-bit network cards were involved.

EISA

EISA stands for Extended Industry Standard Architecture. An evolution of ISA and (theoretically) backward compatible with it, including the speed (8 MHz); the increased data throughput is mainly due to the bus doubling in size, but you must use EISA expansion cards. It has its own DMA arrangements that can use the complete address space. One advantage of EISA (and Micro Channel) is the ease of setting up expansion cards; plug them in and run the configuration software that automatically detect their settings.

MCA

The Micro Channel Architecture it is a proprietary standard established by IBM to take over from ISA. It is, therefore, incompatible with anything else. It comes in two versions: 16- and 32-bit. In practical terms, it is capable of transferring around 20 mbps.

Local Bus

The local bus is one more directly suited to the CPU; it is next door (hence local), has the same bandwidth, and runs at the same speed. The bottleneck is, therefore, less (ISA was local in the early days). Data is moved along the bus at processor speeds. The following two varieties of local bus exist:

❏ VL-BUS is a 32-bit bus that enables bus mastering and uses two cycles to transfer a 32-bit word, peaking at 66 Mb/second. It also supports Burst Mode, where a single address cycle precedes four data cycles, meaning that 4 32-bit words can move in only 5 cycles, as opposed to 8, giving 105 Mb/second at 33 MHz. The speed is mainly obtained by enabling VL-Bus adapter cards first choice at intercepting CPU cycles. It is not designed to cope with more than a certain number of cards at particular speeds; examples include 3 at 33, 2 at 40, and only 1 at 50 MHz; even that often needs a wait state inserted. VL-Bus 2 is 64-bit, yielding 320 MB/sec at 50 MHz. Two slot types exist: master and slave. Master boards (SCSI controllers, for example) have their own CPUs that can do their own things; slaves (video cards, for example) do not. A slave board will work on a master slot, but not vice versa.

❑ PCI is a mezzanine bus divorced from the CPU, giving it some independence and the capability to cope with more devices. It is, therefore, more suited to cross-platform work. It is time multiplexed, meaning that address and data lines share connections. It has its own Burst Mode that enables 1 address cycle to be followed by as many data cycles as system overheads allow. At nearly 1 word per cycle, the potential is 264 MB/second. It can operate up to 33 MHz or 66 MHz with PCI 2.1, and can transfer data at 32 bits per clock cycle so that you can get up to 132 MB/second (264 with 2.1). Each PCI card can perform up to eight functions, and you can have more than one bus mastering card on the bus. Note, however, that many functions are not available with PCI (sound, for example)—not yet, anyway. It is part of the plug-and-play standard, assuming your operating system and BIOS agree. It is, therefore, auto configuring (although some cards use jumpers instead of storing information in a chip); it will also share interrupts under the same circumstances. The PCI chipset handles transactions between cards and the rest of the system, and enables other buses to be bridged to it (typically an ISA bus to enable older cards to be used). Not all of them are equal, though; certain features, such as byte merging, may be absent. The connector may vary according to the voltage the card uses (3.3 or 5v; some cards can cope with both).

Selecting Video And Network Cards

Not many demands are placed on an Internet server in terms of a video display. A standard 15-inch monitor is just fine for a server. As for video cards, a standard video card with 1 MB of memory suffices for running at 1024-by-768 resolution with 256 colors. The display subsystem in an Internet server and on any other type of server is mainly used for administration of the server and, therefore, video requirements are quite modest.

The Ethernet card you choose for your server is somewhat important. You should get a network card that has a large amount of memory on board. This memory queues up the data transmission if the speed of the transmission is overwhelming the CPU. In essence, the larger the card's buffer, the better performing that Ethernet card will be.

SMC, 3COM, and NE2000 compatible cards are directly supported by Windows NT and generally do a good job. More than likely, it will not be your Ethernet card that will be a potential bottleneck in Internet traffic; your network card transmits at 10 Mbps, and most Internet connections are currently only 1 Mbps.

Summary

Windows NT gives users the ability to choose from a wide variety of specialized and off-the-shelf hardware with which to build a robust server platform. The first step of the process requires deciding which processor architecture to deploy your Internet service on. The choice of architecture then dictates your other hardware choices. SCSI is the only real storage option, for example, available under RISC-based systems.

If you choose to use the more widely supported Intel architecture, the range of choices is generally broader.

In terms of the system CPU, many choices exist from vendors such as Intel, Cyrix, and AMD. Motherboards supporting all these types of microprocessors are widely available and vary in their features (also called the chipset).

When it comes to storage, two main options exist under the Intel architecture: IDE and SCSI. EIDE supports only up to four hard disks and is generally not a good performer under multitasking systems. SCSI, on the other hand, shines under multitasking. The SCSI system itself can handle data transfers in parallel, and thereby greatly improves multitasking performance. Most SCSI controllers are bus mastering, meaning that the CPU is not needed for data transfers between devices and system memory. The Intel architecture supports a wide variety of memory types, including EDO RAM and pipeline burst cache RAM, two of the most widely used memory types in the Intel world. Under the Intel architecture, there are five types of expansion buses to choose from: ISA, EISA, MCA, VL, and PCI. PCI is the bus of choice for modern Intel machines.

Finally, video in an Internet server should be minimal; it is not, after all, a graphics workstation. On the other hand, network cards are a bit more important because they can determine how fast your server can send data over an Internet connection. In short, Windows NT provides the widest variety of hardware options as an Internet server platform.

7

Software Requirements

Windows NT 4 comes with many useful software components. Although it is not required that you use all of the software components, you will find it useful to get to know the different parts. This chapter discusses related background on licensing issues, as well as an overview of all the software tools included with Windows NT 4, including the following:

- ❏ Administrative Wizards
- ❏ Task Manager
- ❏ Network Monitor
- ❏ Windows NT Diagnostics
- ❏ Microsoft Windows NT Directory Service (NTDS)
- ❏ Internet Information Server (IIS)

Background: In the Beginning…

Those who have been around a bit will recall the early days of networks. Networks usually consisted of wires running under the floor or hanging from the ceiling. The configuration issues with the wiring, at least, were pretty simple. In the case of Novell, for example—again in the *good old days*—the network was called S-NET. S-NET had a one-to-one relationship between the server and the users. The server had connections or physical ports on it. New employees got a port and that was that. If a new employee was on the third floor, you ran a line to her desk, within the limits of NetWare—nothing to it. If she reported a *network problem*, it was easy as pie to check it out. Although troubleshooting was not as easy as sticking your tongue on a 9-volt battery (you did do that, right?), it was not a tough situation to manage.

We got smarter over the years. Instead of running a single continuous wire from the server to the employee, we created patch panels, smart closets, and tons of other gizmos to make the network look a whole lot more complicated than it really was. But in the end, it basically was one physical connection for each machine *on the network*.

This history is meant to provide some perspective on the evolution of networks. In some cases, software has replaced hardware. In some situations, your troubleshooting will be a lot more complex than just checking a blinking red light or a jumper switch. This chapter reviews what comes with Windows NT 4 and provides an idea of how it fits into the big picture, and what you might want to think about when you get into problems.

Normally, when you think of software, you may not give the hardware much thought. In the case of Windows NT 4, it is important to get a sense of what the hardware can do and where software has replaced hardware. As mentioned previously, for example, older networks tended to have a one-to-one relationship with data servers. Obviously, the Internet would not be what it is if you had to run dedicated wires from each computer to each data server to which you wanted access. Hence the importance of routers. In some cases, using routers lowers costs and makes things easier, but in others, that dedicated hardware is a more reliable method of deploying services.

The point to all this is to understand your options. As you read about the networking software components built into Windows NT 4, make sure you understand what hardware or other methods have been replaced. Remember, at its core, the Internet server you are going to deploy will rely heavily on the network infrastructure you have in place.

Understanding Windows NT Licensing

Before delving into the network components that come with Windows NT, you are going to get a short course in Windows NT licensing. This will bore you to tears, but there are some really good reasons why you should pay attention.

If you are familiar with the way insurance companies work, you are familiar with a term called *risk assessment*. Insurance companies make money by placing big bets on events such as your life span. The company's actuaries spend the day creating math tables and other such items with the sole purpose of getting the odds in favor of the insurance company. Think of the following as risk management.

Despite all the Information Superhighway hype, this is new territory. No one has really figured out such things as fair use, copyright, access rights, and so on. This means risk. Knowing the licensing arrangement of the operating system gives you some knowledge that might come in handy if you get a letter from a lawyer some day. In addition, many software developers do not have a clue how all this licensing stuff works, so they could, inadvertently, sell you a product that by its design or implementation violates the operating system licensing you have. As you review the software components mentioned in this chapter, think in terms of performance and licensing. These two concepts will aid you in your deployment planning.

Finally, as the following section demonstrates, a good understanding of the licensing scheme can save you money.

Microsoft's Answer to Baskin Robbins: Two Flavors

Two versions of Windows NT exist: Workstation and Server. The versions serve two very different markets. They have features and optimizations designed to meet two customers' unique requirements. It is important to know these differences because you can have one flavor of NT act in the capacity of the other under certain circumstances. The most common example is a print server. In some cases, using a copy of Windows NT Workstation is a perfectly acceptable solution.

Given this two-version approach, you should be aware of the licensing issues Microsoft has with the different versions of NT. Some of those pesky connection limitations are licensing and marketing issues and not technical ones. This will be made clear in a minute, so keep reading.

Software Cops: License and Registration, Please

Microsoft has created a rather complex method to ensure that you are *legal* from the perspective of having the appropriate licensing for Windows NT. The phrase you will hear a lot from Microsoft is *Client Access License*, or CAL.

Next, there is a notion of physical connection versus application connection. The CALs apply to the physical simultaneous connection to the server. In practical terms, this refers to the number of users logged on to the server at the same time. If you have 20 people in your organization and you want them all to be logged onto the server at the same time, you need to have 20 CALs. If you only have two workstations and one dial-up connection, you could get away with three CALs because only three people could ever be connected to the server at any time.

Now assume that you add an application to this NT machine (mail, for the application example). If you have a mail application that enables 20 mailboxes, but you only have the three access points already mentioned (two machines and the dial-up), you still need only three CALs. The reason is the same mentioned previously—only three people will be on the server at any given time.

Here's the point. Assume that you take this server and put it on the Internet. You have only one user ID (guest) on the machine. That guest ID is used by *the world* to get at your Internet Web server. How many CALs do you need to purchase? If you answered a zillion or higher, the employees and stockholders of Microsoft thank you and will name a company cafeteria after you. The correct answer is *one* because Microsoft views accessing that Web server as one ID (or CAL) being used by the Web server application to service multiple requests. The Web server software is licensed as an unlimited user application. So, yes, a zillion people can log onto the Web server via one guest ID (or CAL).

Of course, Microsoft got testy about people using NT Workstation as an Internet server and saving money, so they have a licensing restriction in place. If you are using the Workstation version, the licensing only enables 10 simultaneous *IP* connections at any one time. The Server version has no such restriction. As far as Microsoft is concerned, running an Internet Server such as Netscape's or Microsoft's IIS does not have a simultaneous limit. If you run your Internet server on NT Server, a zillion people can hit it at once—no problem. Several Web server products that run just fine on NT Workstation are on the market. For obvious reasons, companies such as Netscape are not particularly pleased about this because Windows NT Workstation is cheaper than NT Server, and Netscape's server software runs just fine on it. Because Microsoft wants you to buy the NT Server versions, they have created this limit in the Workstation version.

Microsoft says that you need the Server version of the product to run Web server software and, surprise, the Windows NT Server version has a Web server built into it.

To give you one more twist on this issue, consider this example. The same previously discussed server is now on the Internet. How does that change the CAL issue for the 20-user base? It changes if you enable the 20 users to access the server via the Internet. Assume, for example, that Sally has an AT&T Internet account. Assuming that your server is set up correctly, Sally could log on to the server from anywhere on the Internet. She would not have to be on one of those two stations mentioned earlier, nor would she have to use the dial-up connection mentioned previously. That means you must rethink the CAL issue. If you have all 20 employees using an Internet connection of some type, and they all can get at the server, you have the potential for a license violation if more than three people log on to the server at one time. You can do several things to solve this from a technical and software perspective, but the point here is to get you thinking about the licensing issues that come up when your server goes on to the Internet.

An Evolving Headache

To wrap up this thorny and admittedly boring issue is to remind you of the two most important issues: CALs and application access issues. Remember that for users to log on to your Windows NT Server simultaneously for the purpose of using NT services such as file and print, you need an appropriate number of licenses that match the simultaneous usage you will have. From the perspective of Web applications, such as a Web server, remember that Windows NT Server has no limit on Net connections using a single log on ID to access that application. Windows NT Workstation has a 10-user limit. In some cases, the 10-user limit is fine, and you should consider deploying Windows NT Workstation as the solution. Finally, remember that when the server goes on to the Internet, you must pay close attention to how you have the system set up from an access perspective.

Looking at Software Components of Windows NT 4

Now that you have a basic understanding of licensing issues, this chapter moves on to a discussion of the major software components included with Windows NT 4 that you should be familiar with.

This section covers the admininstrative wizards, naming services, registry entries, and some of the monitoring tools available within the operating system.

Windows NT Administrative Wizards

Windows NT Server has always provided a complete set of utilities for server administration. Windows NT Server 4 adds a set of administrative wizards that gives a single pane view of eight commonly used administrative functions (see fig. 7.1). This enables centralized administration of common server and directory service tasks. Administrative wizards coaches system operators through the most commonly performed operations. Although you might not think of this as a feature that matters, give it a review; you might find something to help on those days when things get a little crazy around the shop.

Figure 7.1

Windows NT Administrative Wizards.

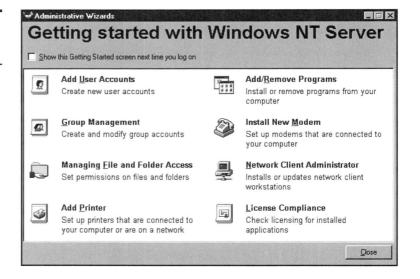

The following sections describe the the administrative wizards included with Windows NT 4.

Licenses

The License wizard enables you to keep track of the software licenses used for servers and clients applications. This has limited value for straight Web work; it may come in handy if you have applications that are for the company, but are accessed via the Internet.

T I P

The reason to think about using the wizard is what I call *checklist mentality*. If you fly in the Air Force, you don't do anything without a checklist. Pre-flight, landing, getting lunch, and so on was all done by the book. The wizards act like mini-checklists. This increases efficiency and decreases problems.

User Accounts

The User Accounts wizard enables you to add new users to a Windows NT Server. You can, of course, use the other administrative utilities to create users. In fact, you can write your own utility to create users. When you use the wizard, however, you can be certain that you have covered all the bases every time. The wizards ask the questions. What is the full name? Starting password? Do you want to have them change the password on log on? Most of the time, you would remember this stuff. Using the normal administrative tools in those instances is fine. It is that one percent that you forget that this author worries about, such as the accidental assignment of some goof ball to the Administrators group. There goes the neighborhood.

Group Management

Assume that you create and manage groups of users. The Group Management wizard is particularly handy when setting up groups of people having various Web assignments (see fig. 7.2). You could create groups for Webmasters, database people, Web designers, and so on. Spend the time to think this through carefully. This can be a great help or a security nightmare.

Figure 7.2

The Group Management
Wizard dialog box.

When you create groups, think about what they are authorized to do. Suppose that you give group A the right to delete certain accounting log files. You also have group A authorized to create directories or read some material on a particular server directory. On Thursday, Fred joins the company and is part of group B, which doesn't have the read rights that group A has. So someone wanting to get this done fast makes Fred a member of group A so that he can get at the files to read. Oops! Fred makes a mistake, forgets he is on a network drive, and types "delete *.*" the log place. The person who put Fred in group A should have just added the read rights to group B.

Again, the point is to really think through how you set up groups so you avoid giving people more power than they need.

File and Folder Access

The File and Folder Access wizard provides the capability to share drives and folders. After you have the groups set up, you then can assign by groups access rights to various folders. The Webmaster might have all access, but the database people only get *write* access to certain files. You want to carefully review who has access to what. After all, who wants that late night phone call about those weird pictures suddenly appearing on the network.

Printers

The Printers wizard helps you to set up printers connected to the network and to share them. It also helps install printer drivers on the server. Some administrators claim that four out of seven support calls relate to printers. This wizard helps by giving you a checklist approach to the installation of the printer. After printers are correctly installed, printer troubleshooting can at least look at other causes other than a messed up server installation.

Add/Remove Programs

Installing or removing a program incorrectly can be the kiss of death for a workstation. For a server, it is worse. Workstation death kills a user. Server death wipes out access for a lot of people. Windows NT is not that old .INI or autoexec stuff. The operating system likes to install and remove programs in a set and orderly manner. Use the Add/Remove Programs wizard each time you install something so that you can, later on, remove it via the system. More than one server has died because someone deleted some tiny little file that just happened to be running the Web server. Don't let this happen to you.

Modems

The Modem wizard detects and sets up modems connected to your computer. If you have a newer modem that has its own drivers and files, this is a handy way to have the computer walk you through the process. Like other tasks, this too can be done via other methods. The wizard's benefit in this case is to give you an orderly installation that helps when the troubleshooting starts.

Network Client Administrator

The Network Client Administrator wizard helps to install or update client workstations. It is handy for LAN management, but is not really an Internet issue.

Task Manager: What's Really Going On

In general, Windows NT Server is easy to manage. Task Manager in Windows NT Server 4 offers extensive applications information, graphical readouts of CPU, and memory use that gives administrators easier control over system status checking. Task Manager gives you a very granular view of what is going on in the system.

Granular view refers to a very detailed view of the tasks and how they use resources on the machine. This becomes vital when you are trying to determine why the server is slow or some other vanilla complaint. Task Manager enables you to see exactly what is happening with the CPU, tasks, processes, and other system-level information.

System managers with Unix or mainframe familiarity especially will welcome the added control. In addition to the detailed Processes display, Task Manager offers graphical readouts of CPU and memory utilization for easy, at-a-glance status checking. With the added level of information provided by the improved Task Manager, spotting potential trouble sources, such as CPU-intensive or memory-sapping applications, can be done in seconds.

Network Monitor: Paying Attention to Packets

Windows NT Server 4 now includes the Network Monitor, which has the capability to monitor network traffic, making it easy for administrators to troubleshoot the network's performance.

You might be familiar with a product from Network General called the Sniffer. The Sniffer, when first introduced, was a lifesaver for network managers. It was deployed by connecting the box to the network and turning it on. Within seconds, the Sniffer showed the data on the network in the form of the packets that were moving from network card to network card. It is an amazing tool. You could watch, for example, somebody type the Dir command on a network drive. This request was then handled by the server, and the requested information was returned to the requesting user. At this level of troubleshooting, you were able to see network cards sending out bad data. You could spot a machine that had the wrong network address and which machines were causing errors on the network. This hardware tool saved hundreds of troubleshooting hours. For those with a nostalgic bent, the Sniffer looks like a Kaypro or one of the early portables from Compaq.

The Network Monitor Tool is a tool that acts like a Sniffer, only it works with software. Many limits exist, and it does not replace the Sniffer in the heavy-duty troubleshooting adventures. It does, however, perform some reasonable functions and can be helpful in informing you of the data coming over your wires.

With the Network Monitor tool, you can spot problems such as performance robbing cross-router traffic. This is a fancy way of saying that you can be alerted to packets of data that your particular system should not be seeing or dealing with. Remember that with Windows NT, you are likely to have an Internet server running many different applications and services. To make certain that users are getting the best response rates they can, you want to make certain that the server is dealing with the data appropriately. In the case of router traffic, you can set up a filter to isolate traffic bound for that router's MAC address.

How Network Monitor Works

Network Monitor monitors the network data stream, which consists of all information transferred over a network at any given time. When you click on a Web hyperlink, for example, you are asking your computer to jump to a certain location. The computer figures out what information the Web site you are currently pointed to needs and creates a request that will be transmitted to this server. Prior to transmission, this information is divided by the client network software into smaller pieces, called *frames*, or *packets*. Each frame contains the following information:

❏ The source address of the computer that sent the message
❏ The destination address of the computer that received the frame
❏ Headers from each protocol used to send the frame
❏ The data or a portion of the information being sent

To ensure that security is maintained on your Windows NT network, Windows NT Network Monitor displays only those frames sent to or from your computer, broadcast frames, and multicast frames. In a practical sense, this means that you can watch requests come into your Web server and the results sent by your Web server. You can watch this data flow at the packet level, which is the lowest level of data you are going to care about.

As things get more complex, you are going to need to be able to see the Information Superhighway as nothing more than a lot of packets moving along a bunch of wires. When you are able to think this way, you will have a mental edge in your troubleshooting activities.

You will see things in a completely different way by using Network Monitor. When response times appear slow, you will be able to do more than just display a browser and take a look. You will be able to see exactly what your Web server is doing at the lowest level. When you combine this data with the information you can get from the Task Manager, you will be in a much stronger position to make decisions. When you decide to run a database of restaurants against which customers can run queries, for example, you will be able to work with designers, programmers, and others at a very detailed level. Determining how much traffic you generate is another important skill that you can enhance with this information.

Filtering the Data

Network Monitor is *memory bound*—it can capture only as much information as fits in available system memory. In most cases, this is not a big deal because you are normally looking for something specific. To get this isolated data, you need to design a *capture filter*, which functions like a database query. You can create filters against things like source and destination addresses, protocols, protocol properties, or by specifying a pattern offset.

Triggers

To have a running capture respond to events on your network as soon as detected, you can design a capture trigger. Triggers are important because they enable you or the system to act upon various activities. The most obvious example would be to have a trigger execute when the system starts getting packets from particular source.

A capture trigger performs a specified action (such as starting an executable file) when Network Monitor detects a particular set of conditions on the network. This means that you could have the Web server trigger launch an executable program that fires off a message to your pager. You can combine this with other monitoring functions such as watching hard drive space, and so on. Network Monitor supports dozens of popular protocols, including NetBIOS (NetBEUI), IPX, SPX, and many TCP/IP-related protocols.

After you have captured data, you can view it. Network Monitor does much of the data analysis for you by translating the raw captured data into its logical frame structure. Of course, you can also save it to be used later by other applications. You might want, for example, to do a trend graph with Excel.

Network Monitor Security

The Network Monitor does not replace sniffer type hardware for a number reasons; the most important reason is the security limitations built into the product. Windows NT Network Monitor captures only those frames, including broadcast and multicast frames, sent to or from the local computer. This means it cannot, and does not, deal with network traffic going from a workstation to some distant Web site. This tool is only concerned with the traffic that involves the server it is running on. Network

Monitor displays overall network segment statistics for broadcast frames, multicast frames, network utilization, total bytes received per second, and total frames received per second.

This information can be helpful when you are attempting to get a big picture of the overall health and traffic management of your server. If you are hosting a site that is being talked about on live TV, for example, you might see a massive increase in the traffic that hits your site all at once. Tools such as this enable you to watch things "as the server sees it" or at the basics level. You can watch, for example, the number of bad data or delayed data that comes in. This might be an indication that somebody is making a mistake when they transfer information to your server. The point here is that Network Monitor is not a network spy tool, and it does come with some limitations.

To help protect your network from unauthorized use of Network Monitor installations, Network Monitor provides two features:

❏ **Password protection.** It appears obvious, but you would be amazed at how many people ignore this feature. Unless your server is under lock and key and you have the only key, password protect access to this application.

❏ **Other NM Installations.** The product has the capability to detect other installations of itself on your network. You would probably want to know if somebody else was trying to watch packets on your network.

Windows NT Diagnostics

Again, Windows NT Diagnostics are not a feature or component in the traditional sense. The diagnostic parts of the operating system are "built-in," but often get overlooked by folks building Internet Servers. You should think of them as software tools that are at your disposal. The reason you should look at and understand the improved NT diagnostics program is that it now provides extensive information on device drivers and network use, and thereby makes troubleshooting desktop systems much easier than before (see fig. 7.3). If you are considering NT for an intranet, you face all the normal issues that LAN support people face. You should be aware of the tools that come with your operating system. You may never need this, but it's that one time the boss can't *see* the server, and that demo for the customer is ten minutes away, and so on. The diagnostic software can tell you that the server doesn't have a TCP address correctly entered and that's why the boss's machine cannot log on or "see" the server.

This new version of the tool contains information on device drivers, network usage, and system resources such as memory and Input/Output address. This information is in an easy-to-view graphical tool that can also be run on a remote Windows NT-based system.

Uses for Windows NT Diagnostics

You can use Windows NT Diagnostics to view configuration information for a local or remote computer. You will find Windows NT Diagnostics in the Administrative Tools folder. Following are the items you can view:

❑ Operating system information, such as the version number and system boot options, plus process, system, and user environment variables.

❑ Hardware details such as BIOS information, video resolution, CPU type, and CPU steppings.

❑ Physical memory, paging file information, and DMA usage.

❑ The current state of each driver and service on the computer. Pay particular attention to this one. It can tell you things such as whether the FTP service is running on the machine. This would be one of the first places to look if someone complains about not being able to log on.

❑ Drives and devices installed on the computer, plus related interrupt (IRQ) and port information.

❑ Network information, including transports, configuration settings, and statistics. This is helpful when looking at traffic levels and which settings you have for TCP/IP, retries, packet sizes, and so on.

❑ Printer settings, fonts settings, and system processes that are running.

Figure 7.3

The Windows Diagnostic Memory tab.

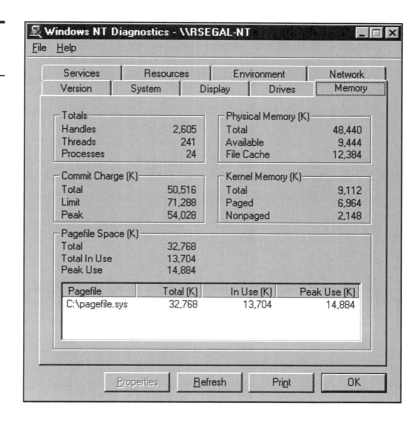

Policy Editors: Who Can Do What

You can skip this part if you are only going to have the guest ID, simple Web pages, and no worries about anybody getting on the machine.

Well, it's no surprise that most of you chose to stick around! If you remember nothing else, remember that Windows NT thinks of those Internet users just like a LAN user in the office—there's no difference. This means that you can get very specific about what you want people to do on your machine, and who can even get on the machine.

The System Policy Editor and User Profiles software provides Windows NT Server 4 the capability to generate Policy Files for network clients, which gives administrators the ability to have a consistent environment for users. Big deal, right? Yes, this is a big deal. Although it is simple to set up a Web server or ftp service on a Windows NT Server, you miss opportunities if you don't think of this Net as users wanting data, just like the corporate LAN.

Suppose, for example, that you were asked to set up a place where users could upload and download materials for a training class. Clearly one simple way to do this is to use an ftp program, set up users, and do all the management tasks required from within the ftp program. But there is much more you can do. If you set up user accounts on the NT server, those users could log on to the server with a client, just like they would log on to a corporate LAN server. This means that to the users, it is just another disk drive letter. So the person finishing up the training assignment could save it from the word processor to the server on the Net.

The point, again, is to change the way you think about that Web server or Internet box. Think of it and manage it like a box on your business LAN. Although at one level you can have standard Web services, such as HTML pages, ftp, and so on, by understanding all the management pieces within Windows NT, you are empowered to get much more out of your server investment.

Policy Editor Tools

Included with Policy Editor are the following tools that enable you to manage various work environments. Environments refer to situations in which a user can log on or to which services from a particular machine users have access.

❑ **User Profiles.** The User Profile contains all user definable settings for the work environment of a computer running Windows NT, including display settings and network connections. All user-specific settings are automatically saved into the Profiles folder within the system root folder (typically, C:\winnt\profiles). This is where a WEB_SURFER profile would reside. You might not want this user to have access to a certain date or the capability to save things to the server, and so on.

❏ **System Policy Editor.** The System Policy Editor enables you to control the user-definable settings in Windows NT and Windows 95 user profiles, as well as system configuration settings. You can use the System Policy Editor to change desktop settings and restrict what users can do from their desktops. Remember that these system policies apply to users that log on to your server, regardless of how they do it. If your server is on the Net, and you allow logons, you can create policies to protect the system.

Microsoft Windows Directory Service (NTDS)

Microsoft Windows NT Directory Service (NTDS) has been available since the first release of Windows NT Server in 1993. Most persons who are doing straight Web server work probably did not pay much attention to this feature. NTDS is used by Windows NT Server customers to simplify management of corporate networks. The odds are that you also can find some benefits in understanding NTDS.

Understanding NTDS

Directory services are operating system features that simplify the use and administration of computer networks. Take a quick look at the key things you should know:

❏ **Directory database.** NTDS is based on a secure directory database containing user IDs, passwords, access rights, and organizational information.

❏ **Distributed architecture.** The NTDS directory database can be automatically replicated to multiple locations for backup reliability, load-balancing performance, and reduced network impact. This matters to you when you create databases on the Internet that require multiple locations for data storage and access.

❏ **Location-independent single logon.** With one logon, users can access a globe-spanning network, even when dialing in remotely or accessing the network over the Internet. The key here is maximizing your server's usefulness. By using NTDS, you can give the users the same sign-in-one-time routine they are used to on the business LAN. To the remote worker dialing in or accessing your information via an Internet service provider, having a good directory service set up and running is very important.

- **Easy, location-independent administration.** Network administrators use NTDS to set up new users, authorize access to network resources, and respond to changes in company personnel, organizations, and information technology.
- **Comprehensive management of resources, services, and applications.** NTDS provides secure access to all the services, information, devices, and applications managed by Windows NT Server. One observation to note when buying server-based software is the Microsoft BackOffice Logo program. If the developer has gone to the trouble of getting this logo, the software the developer sells you should be easily integrated in the management services of Windows NT, including the NTDS.

Internet Information Server (IIS)

Traditionally, file and print services have been the most common services on most servers. With the obvious explosion and increased popularity of the Internet and standardization on TCP/IP for networking, Web servers are rapidly becoming just as important as the file and print functions. Microsoft Internet Information Server 2 (IIS) has taken the two functions of a Web server that are fundamental to the network operating system—transfer of data via the standard HTTP protocol, and the Internet Server API (ISAPI)—and has integrated them into Microsoft Windows NT Server 4.

Integration into Windows NT Server offers the Internet Information Server several unique advantages, including the following:

- Set up of all Internet Information Server services (Web, FTP, and Gopher) as part of the Windows NT Server installation. The Web server is up and running with the system.
- Integration with the Windows NT Server security model makes IIS a secure Web server on any platform that runs Windows NT.
- IIS has good performance; it has been optimized through a lightweight single-process design with a multithreaded architecture. What this means is that the developers of IIS did a good job of understanding NT's threading methodology, and integrated IIS into the system to maximize performance.
- IIS will run on thousands of Windows NT Server-supported hardware platforms, including single- and multiprocessor servers using Intel 486, Pentium and Pentium Pro, Digital Alpha, MIPS, and Power PC. Servers can be easily migrated to more powerful hardware.

Internet Information Server used with Windows NT Server is a good intranet/ Internet platform to deploy server applications beyond just the obvious Web server. There are a couple of good reasons for this, the most important being that security and administration are integrated into the Windows NT management model. Large numbers of Web servers and Web applications can be quickly deployed across an existing network, and that existing network can function as an intra/Internet at the same time. In addition, the extensibility through ISAPI gives developers a good development target to create applications that are both network aware and good Windows NT "citizens."

The extensibility of IIS enables you to create services or features that are not built into IIS. For example, you might want to create a database of interesting dog pictures. You then might want to make those pictures available to Internet users via a form they fill out on the screen. With the Information Services API (ISAPI), you have the capability to create the form and then to have IIS make requests to the database you build in Access, SQL Server, or any other database. Although IIS does not have a search or database engine, you can easily extend the functions of your Internet server.

IIS also does a good job of making it easy to publish and share existing documents and databases on the Web. Several tools are included with IIS and Windows NT Server to help build compelling Web sites. They include the following:

- ❏ Content creation and management with Microsoft FrontPage
- ❏ Document indexing and searching with Microsoft Index Server
- ❏ Choice of administration tools, configuration setting, and monitoring options
- ❏ Built-in connectivity to ODBC databases for accessing existing information
- ❏ Secure APIs for building new Internet applications
- ❏ Integration with the Microsoft third-party, server-based solutions

Internet Information Server as an Integrated Service

Microsoft Internet Information Server is an integrated service of Microsoft Windows NT Server. This is an important distinction between it and other solutions. As you may know, an application on NT Server can be designed to run as either a service or as a traditional executed application. As a service, the program essentially runs as part of the operating system.

To the nontechnical person, the most important aspect of running as a service is unattended operations upon boot up or restarts. When the machine fires up, the service just starts to run. If you have ever been called out in the middle of the night to restart some application because a batch file failed or because the reboot didn't start up the applications, you will love this feature. If the machine takes a power hit and comes back up, for example, IIS starts back up. You don't have to log on to the machine or be there. As an application, you have to have some form of log on and application execution. Most smart and well-written Windows NT Server applications run as a service on the server.

Microsoft Internet Information Server (IIS) enables you to make a Web server on existing hardware instantly because it is installed with Windows NT Server. If NT runs on your hardware choices, the odds are excellent that IIS will run just fine. Before the Internet became a widespread phenomenon, the issues surrounding the difficulty of deploying a traditional Unix-based Web server were no big deal. Tools were not really tied into operating systems. That was not a major problem, however, because expert Unix people were available to deal with the issues that came up.

In implementing a site, you must take into account two issues if the site is to survive. First, implementation must be simple and integrated into the existing infrastructure. If you have made the commitment to Windows NT Server, your relationship with the Web must be a natural extension of what you do, or you just create a separate infrastructure that ends up costing you additional (and probably wasted) dollars. A natural extension of what you do is best explained by way of example.

If you are Ford Motor company, your business is selling cars. If you were doing the Ford Web site, it should extend the buyer's need for information on buying a car, right? So, you would expect "easy payment" calculators or long lists of specifications or other things that relate to the car buying experience. It would be a waste of time and Web resources to create some silly Net game if it didn't bring customers to the dealer.

The second and probably most important issue is the people costs. Rolling out a Web site needs to be low maintenance from a support perspective. That means dollars and people are deployed to the content issues of the Web site, and not simply to keep the server alive. Again, to make that happen, the technology and software you deploy must be an integral part of the operating system and its underlying infrastructure. It must work seamlessly with all other network services across all your servers.

IIS Security

One important concern that managers face is site security. More and more Internet users consider it an extension of their own local and wide area networks. That is why understanding the NT security model is so important to you. Because the Windows NT security model is the same across all system functions, you can deal with security in the same way regardless of how that user gets to your data.

The same protection required for file servers and database servers is available to the Web server, with no extra work for system administrators. Under Windows NT, new users can be given access to network resources, such as HTML pages, shared files and printers, corporate databases, and legacy systems on all servers under one model.

IIS Performance

Performance is the next critical issue for Webmasters. The Internet Information Server is a fast product that compares favorably with other NT-based Web server offerings. Surprisingly, it is not one of those famous little *applets* that Microsoft usually tosses in the box. IIS is snappy and has the capability to run on thousands of hardware platforms.

Additional IIS Features

Everybody has a view that the Web is becoming the land where all information, of any kind, is shared on servers everywhere. Although all Web browsers can read standard HTML documents, there is very little produced solely in HTML. Getting information shared and accessible requires supporting documents in many different formats and languages. IIS makes it easy to build a useful and secure Web site with information in existing file servers and databases, created in popular formats such as Microsoft Word and Excel.

IIS offers a choice of administration tools, monitoring and auditing, and configuration options that make it easy to manage both single servers and multiple servers across your entire network. This goes a long way toward being able to have content available in native formats, on disparate servers around the company, being updated by colleagues around the world. Some of these choices and options include the following:

❏ FrontPage wizards and templates to help create Web sites without having to deal with HTML tags and coding issues. FrontPage, which is reviewed later, has excellent graphical site management tools to keep information organized. In addition, FrontPage has a variety of automatic verification of links, and updates when a file is moved. This is tied into the NT user/security model so that users creating Web pages with FrontPage or any other tool cannot upload pages to server areas for which they have no permissions.

❏ The Index Server add on to IIS provides advanced searching of HTML, plain text, Microsoft Word, Excel, and PowerPoint documents and properties in seven languages. This is handy for publishing information in a native format and getting users access to material as it is produced. Hopefully, the HTML zealots of the world won't picket my house, but truth be told—content developers like to use what they know. That nice lady down the hall who has finally figured out how to work in PowerPoint is not going to be happy to to have learned about HTML tags. She is pretty familiar with saving files on to the network server. What you, the Webmaster, want to be able to deal with is that native PowerPoint presentation on the Web site. Integrating the viewers that people need is one aspect, but enabling the slides to be indexed as content on the server that users can be made aware of is equally important. By setting up your PowerPoint slides and other data on your server to be indexed on a regular basis, you give users access to the most current information through automatic incremental updates of indexes as documents change in the file system. Finally, our old friend security comes into play as the integration with Windows NT Security enables users to see only those documents for which they have permissions, not every file on the site that matches their search.

❏ You have two choices for administration: Any Web browser or the Internet Service Manager for Windows NT and Windows 95. Internet Service Manager enables you to monitor the status of all your servers on all machines so that you can manage these Web servers as resources on the Net just like you manage servers today.

❏ IIS supports both the Internet-standard common log file format, as well as custom logs with only certain fields. You can feed this data into any SQL/ODBC source, such as Microsoft SQL Server and then perform analysis of your site with standard tools such as Access and Excel.

❏ Windows NT has real-time monitoring through the Windows NT Performance Monitor. After IIS is installed, the monitoring functions enable you to monitor performance of the Web server, growth of your disk space, and other perform-ance issues. The security auditing through the event log tracks security issues in the same way as they are handled for the core OS.

Internet Services API (ISAPI)

Through ISAPI, the Internet Services API, server applications can be created that take advantage of the Web server as well as being tightly linked to the OS itself. If you are a programmer, read on. If you are not a programmer, read anyway so that you can bug your programmers to create some of these new applications.

Accessing information in databases, for example, is rapidly becoming the most popular feature of any Web site that has content to offer. It has not been easy to offer this feature. It was a programming nightmare to put a really good database access program in place. IIS includes an interface called the Internet Database Connector (IDC). This is an example of an ISAPI applications. The IDC enables projection of databases to the Web without programming. By using various graphical tools, such as FrontPage, you can now create a Web page that has database access on it without having to code it.

Summary of IIS Capabilities

Table 7.1 shows the primary capabilities of the Microsoft Internet Information Server. Note that all the different protocols are supported. You can set up an FTP site within IIS, which is important if you want to have a place for people to download and upload files. Also note that IIS uses the NT security model. As mentioned previously, this enables you (as the Webmaster) to treat this as just another network resource. Gopher is also supported.

IIS also supports the Open Database Connectivity (ODBC) standard, which is handy if you have other databases you want people to access through your Web server. Note also the remote management, which often is overlooked. This is handy when you are on vacation and get that midnight phone call.

Table 7.1
Primary Capabilities of Microsoft Internet Information Server

Component	Purpose	Description
World Wide Web Service	Hypertext document publishing, integration with BackOffice and Web application solutions	High-performance multimedia document publishing and application development platform for Windows NT Server
FTP Service	File Transfer Protocol server for binary or ASCII file transfers	High-performance FTP service for Windows NT Server

Table 7.1 Continued	Component	Purpose	Description
	Gopher Service	Distributed Gopher space server	High-performance Gopher server for Windows NT Server
	Internet Database Connector	ODBC Database gateway for the World Wide Web service	Flexible Web/database integration through ODBC for developing organizational information applications
	Secure Sockets Layer	Client/server private communication	Encrypted communication between server and client
	Internet Service Manager	Server administration	Remote, secure administration of all Internet Information Server services
	Browsers	Hypertext clients for Windows 3.x, Windows for Workgroups 3.x, Windows NT, and Windows 95 HTML browsers	Internet clients for all Windows platforms support HTML 3.0, plus additional markups on Windows

Upgrading an IIS 1.0 Installation to Version 2

As was mentioned previously, IIS is integrated into the Windows NT 4 setup. IIS 2 also requires Windows NT 4. When you upgrade to Windows NT 4, the setup guides you through the process of upgrading Internet Information Server. Table 7.2 is for those who already have a 1.0 version of IIS. These are the primary upgrade points with which you will want to be familiar.

Table 7.2 Upgrading IIS 1.0 to IIS 2 for Windows NT Server 4	Fully Integrated with Windows NT Server 4	
	Installation integrated into Windows NT Server 4 installation	Installation integrated into Windows NT 4 setup—enables you to easily install IIS while installing Windows NT Server
	Integrated with Windows NT Server 4 directory and security services	Fully integrated with security and directory services
	High-performance Web server	Over 40 percent faster than IIS 1

Comprehensive Web Server Solution

Microsoft Index Server	Provides content indexing and search capabilities of HTML and Microsoft Office documents (free downloadable component)
Microsoft FrontPage	Microsoft FrontPage is now included free of charge
FrontPage Extensions	Microsoft FrontPage extensions facilitate remote content authoring on your Web server without the need for file shares.
HTML-based Administration	Server administration of IIS from any Web browser in addition to the Internet Service Manager.
Internet Service Manager Enhancements	Internet Service Manager now also runs on Windows 95. The TCP/IP port that IIS listens on is now configurable.
Key Manager Tool	Easier to set up SSL security.
Configurable TCP/IP port	The Internet Service Manager enables specification of the port on which the server operates.
Supports standard administration tools	IIS now includes support for SNMP administration tools, as well as Systems Management Server.

Easy platform for building Internet applications

Improved programmability using the Internet Server API (ISAPI)	Several additional server variables are now exposed and nested IF statements are supported, providing greater programming capabilities. ISAPI filters can now receive notification when a request has been denied.
Improved database programmability with the Internet Database Connector (IDC)	IDC now supports multiple queries from a single HTML page and associated result sets. In addition, all server variables are now exposed to IDC scripts.

continues

Table 7.2 Continued	Easy platform for building Internet applications	
	HTTP Read Byte Range	Enables clients to resume reading a file from where they left off in the event that the network connection is lost.
	Image Map file enhancements	Support for both NCSA and CERN style image map files facilitates porting from Unix systems. IIS 2 will always send redirects on image map lookup.

Index Server

Dumping a bunch of material on the Internet and letting people have at it was a popular thing to do when the Internet craze first started. It was a cheap thrill to wade through zillions of documents and hyperlinks for hours on end—not any more! People now want to take advantage of indexing and searching technology to help their users find the right documents quickly.

NOTE

The key concept in this section is the importance of providing users an easy way to find things on your Web site. Index Server is one such solution.

Index Server is Microsoft's content indexing and searching solution for Windows NT Server 4. This section provides an overview of the index server.

Index Server is designed to index the full text contents and properties of documents served by Microsoft Internet Information Server. It gives your users a way to formulate queries by using any World Wide Web browser after filling in the fields on a form. IIS then forwards the request to the Index Server, which services the request and returns the results to the client in the form of a Web page.

Because Index Server can index more than just standard Web pages, you can have native format documents on your server. People can still search for data, however, as if everything were an HTML document. Should a user find something he would like to view, you can launch the appropriate viewer or helper application to work with the user's browser. If a user searches for Cats, for example, and you have a spreadsheet with cat food listings, the user will see this in the search results. If the user wants to look at the spreadsheet, it is retrieved and viewed with the native application or a

viewer as appropriate. This method of indexing and viewing native documents eliminates the need to convert the past into HTML as well as not restricting a content developer to just HTML.

Index Server Architecture and Features

Microsoft designed Index Server to take advantage of the Windows NT Server operating system environment. The unique features of a multipurpose file server and applications server operating system were considered when the Index Server features were selected and the architecture designed. System file change notifications, Windows NT security, recoverability, and logging, for example, are some of the Windows NT Server-specific features that Index Server exploits—as you would expect.

Index Server works well in a busy, yet smaller network environment. An environment such as this typically uses a number of different document formats, and documents will be changing frequently as users create new documents and modify existing ones. In smaller businesses, which represent the vast majority of companies in the world, the server hardware may be limited compared to typical indexing super-server environments. Index Server was built to have a minimum impact on day-to-day servers, even on smaller server configurations and it does not assume it is the only process running on a server.

Index Server was designed to use a number of different utility modules so that indexing features can be extended by third parties. This is important because document formats usually change with new revisions, and new applications with their own new formats are always being introduced. To support this, Index Server uses format- specific content filters to extract textual information from a document. Microsoft has published the programmatic interface specification so developers can create their own Index Server content filters and expose their document formats to the indexing engine. Be aware, however, of what file formats are going up on your server. Make certain that the formats are supported by the index server you use, either Microsoft's or somebody else's.

Table 7.3 summarizes the features of Microsoft Index Server:

Table 7.3 Using Microsoft Index Server in Windows NT Server	Feature	Microsoft Index Server in Windows NT Server Architecture
	Integration with Windows NT Server architecture	Yes
	Integrated with Windows NT Server security	Yes
	Indexed updates	Automatic. Real-time updates using change notification, in addition to directory re-scans
	Robustness and recoverability	Automatic detection and repair
	Comprehensive Functionality	
	Supported document PowerPoint formats	HTML, Text, Word, Excel,
	Support for other document formats	Via published filter interface
	Select files to index	Automatic. Based on IIS virtual roots, and document type
	Index document properties	Yes
	Foreign language support	French, German, Dutch, Spanish, Italian, Swedish, English, Japanese
	Limit queries by directory	Yes. Can limit search by specifying physical or virtual path to search
	Restrict query results based on security settings	Yes
	Search against any document, HMTL, or text at the same time	Yes
	Free-text search (no syntax required)	Yes
	Text operators	AND, OR, NOT, NEAR (proximity searching)
	Property operators	text operators for textual properties, $<$, $<=$, $!=$, $=>$, $>$ for numeric properties

Comprehensive Functionality	
Linguistic analysis (stemming, inflection)	Stemming and inflection in all supported languages
Return document properties in query results	Any document property, including auto-generated document summaries

FrontPage

To assist in creating and managing your intranet and Internet Web sites, Windows NT Server 4 includes a complete Web site authoring and administration tool—Microsoft FrontPage 1.1. Designed for nonprogrammers, yet robust enough for experienced Web site developers, Microsoft FrontPage is a fast, easy way to create and manage professional-quality Web sites. FrontPage includes easy-to-use functionality, such as WYSIWYG editing, wizards to walk you through the creation of your Web site, and integration with Microsoft Office.

FrontPage provides a Web-publishing application created for nonprogrammers, with wizards to guide you through the process. Microsoft FrontPage reduces the need to know Web-based programming languages by providing WebBot components that you can use to create advanced interactive functionality automatically, without programming.

Microsoft FrontPage also makes it easy for large teams to work together to create and manage sites. Its combination of flexible client/server architecture, passwords, user authentication, and other security features enables contributors in different locations to securely update different pages simultaneously on the same site. After developing your Web site, use the one-button publishing capability of Microsoft FrontPage to host it on a server within your own organization or company, or to the Internet on a server that's accessible to the whole world. Wherever you publish it, you can take advantage of flexible Web server tools for easy site administration.

The following list highlights some of the advantages of FrontPage:

❏ Microsoft FrontPage Editor enables you to create and edit Web pages without knowing HTML. It's all as easy as writing a letter because the FrontPage Editor automatically generates the correct HTML code behind the scenes for you.

❏ FrontPage Explorer supports the latest Web standards. It automatically imports and converts existing text files into HTML, generates HTML 2 and the latest

HTML 3 styles (such as bulleted and numbered lists and centered text), and displays hidden formatting and authoring commands so that you can control every aspect of a page's design.

❑ Working with graphics is easy with automatic conversion of images into GIF or JPEG. Create hot spots in seconds—just trace an area and turn it into a clickable image map with the hot spot editor.

❑ Hyperlinks have never been this simple. Use drag-and-drop or click on a button to create hyperlinks within a page, to other pages, or to other Web sites.

❑ With the flexible forms editor, you can easily create entire forms with text fields, check boxes, radio buttons, drop-down lists, and push buttons.

❑ Wizards and templates help you generate entire Web sites or individual pages automatically. You can now create WYSIWYG tables and build custom pages and backgrounds—saving them as page templates, or using the new Frames wizard to generate custom frame grids.

❑ WebBot components provide rich functionality that would otherwise require complex CGI programming. Just drop them on your page to add interactive features such as navigation bars, threaded discussion groups, full-text searches, and forms handling.

FrontPage does a good job of giving you some site-management tools that make it easier to control dynamic sites. The important points about these tools and features are

❑ Microsoft FrontPage Explorer gives you intuitive views of your complete Web site. Use the Outline View to see a hierarchical representation of your site, the Link View to see a graphic display of your site, or the Summary View to see a list of pages and other files in your site.

❑ Auto-recalculate automatically links updates Web hyperlink references when you rename a file or move it to a new directory.

❑ Auto-verify links lists all broken links, both to local and external Web sites. What's more, if you correct a broken link, you can choose to correct all or just some of the pages that contain it.

❑ FrontPage Explorer's site-management tools enable you to assign multiple team members to your Web site and to enable those users to work on the site simultaneously, either locally or remotely.

❑ The To Do List makes it easy to name, track, and complete all unfinished Web tasks. Different groups can maintain their respective parts of a Web site. And you can add To Do List items manually or automatically, using a Web wizard.

❏ FrontPage Explorer automatically launches the corresponding Microsoft Office application whenever you open any imported Web file created by that application. After you edit the file, FrontPage automatically adds it to the Web import list.

Remote Access Service (RAS)

Here is yet another one of those NT features that you might think to skip over given that you are providing Internet services and not some business server. The Remote Access Service (RAS) feature within Windows NT Server does have some interesting possibilities for the Internet-focused administrator, though, so stick around. This might give you some cool ideas for your Internet site. This section introduces RAS and discusses some potential uses for it.

Understanding Remote Access Service

As networks became more prevalent, the ability for people to dial in and access then became increasingly important. With RAS, businesses have been able to extend their networks to phone lines. RAS enables mobile and work-at-home users to access networks seamlessly. It provides small businesses with a cost-effective, easy-to-use dial-up server. With RAS, large organizations get a standards-based, dial-up server that enables client/server computing for remote users. RAS works with different protocols and most computers already include software that enables end users to use it.

Windows NT Server's RAS enables remote users to connect their computer to a phone line and to access a corporate network in another location. Such remote users can securely access files and printers on the remote network, as well as run applications such as Microsoft Back Office across a network in another location as though the user were actually at the location of the network. With RAS, a business can extend its network across long distances by making use of existing phone lines.

RAS Is Built-In

RAS is built-in with Windows NT Server so that customers do not have to buy extra software to get dial-up services. Most operating systems include client software for RAS; users can, therefore, use operating systems out of the box to connect to networks.

RAS Supports ISDN

RAS enables users to dial in across phone lines as well as ISDN. As ISDN becomes increasingly available at lower costs, this helps users get higher-speed access to networks and increases productivity.

RAS Supports Numerous Clients

RAS supports all the mainstream networking clients, including the following:

Windows for Workgroups-based clients	Windows NT Server-based clients
LAN Manager-based clients	Unix-based clients
Windows 95-based clients	Macintosh-based clients
Windows NT Workstation-based clients	NetWare clients, OS/2-based clients

RAS Is Secure

With RAS, small business employees can connect their PCs to a phone jack at home and seamlessly access the business' network. Users can enable all data to be encrypted and sent across phone lines to a network in another location. RAS also authenticates users securely by using industry standard protocols.

New Communications Features

Windows NT Server 4 has some new communications features. Table 7.4 provides an overview of the changes.

Table 7.4	New Feature	Description
RAS and Dial-Up Networking Features	PPP Multilink	Now, you can combine the bandwidth of two or more physical communication links to increase your remote access bandwidth and throughput by using RAS Multilink. Based on the IETF standard RFC 1717, RAS Multilink enables you to easily combine analog modem paths, ISDN paths, and even mixed analog and digital communications links on both your client and server PC. This speeds up your access to the Internet or to your intranet and cuts down on the amount of time you have to be remotely connected. It can, therefore, reduce your costs for remote access.

New Feature	Description
Point-to-Point Tunneling Protocol (PPTP) Support	Now, you can use the Internet for low-cost, secure remote access to your corporate network with virtual private networking support on Windows NT Server 4 and Windows NT Workstation 4. The new Point-to-Point Tunneling Protocol (PPTP) enables you to use a local call to an Internet service provider to gain secure remote access to your corporate network via the Internet. PPTP supports easy, flexible networking: the most prevalent network protocols (IP, IPX, and NetBEUI); and is an open, industry standard. Many companies will also use PPTP to outsource their remote dial-up needs to an Internet service provider or other carrier to reduce cost and complexity.
Restartable file copy	This feature automatically begins retransferring a file upon reconnection whenever your RAS connection has been lost. Nearly all who have used a modem can probably remember times when they have nearly completed a file transfer across a modem only to have their remote connection disabled before the transmission was completed. Reestablishing the connection and starting the file transfer process all over again can be frustrating, time-consuming, and expensive. Restartable file copy addresses these problems by remembering the status of your file transmission and continuing the transfer from that point after you reconnect.
Idle disconnect	This new feature automatically terminates your RAS connection after a certain period of time if there has been no activity over the remote dial-up communications link. The user or administrator can specify the amount of time before this feature is activated. Idle disconnect reduces the cost of remote access carrier service and can even enable a company to reduce the capacity of its dial-in communications links, all based on the reduction of wasted remote connect time.

continues

Table 7.4 Continued	New Feature	Description
	Autodial and Log-on Dial	Windows can now map and maintain an associate between a Dial-up Networking entry and a network address to seamlessly integrate Dial-Up Networking with files and applications. This means that if you double-click on an icon to open a file (and that file is only accessible over a dial-up connection), Dial-up Networking automatically initiates to provide you with quick and easy access to information you need.
	Client and server API enhancements	A number of new APIs are now available to extend Remote Access Service capabilities on Windows NT Server 4 and Dial-Up Networking with Windows NT Workstation 4. These APIs enable third-party developers to add value to RAS and Dial-up Networking, making an already great platform for remote access and communications even better. For a complete list and detailed descriptions of how to use the new RAS APIs in Windows NT 4, please refer to the Microsoft Developer Network.
	Windows 95 look and feel	Windows NT Server 4 and Windows NT Workstation 4 now share the on-screen look and feel of Windows 95. These user interface improvements are also available with the Dial-Up Networking and RAS, so it has never been faster and easier to use these important features.

Multilink PPP

To provide maximum flexibility for remote users, Microsoft has expanded the Remote Access Service component of Windows NT Server 4 to support Multilink PPP connections.

Multilink PPP provides bandwidth aggregation from multiple links, including analog and ISDN, which gives customers higher communications throughput. When used with two or more modems, Multilink PPP supports the simultaneous transfer of data across parallel connections, which effectively delivers scalable bandwidth for maximum efficiency.

With RAS Multilink PPP, you can combine the bandwidth of two or more physical communication links to increase your remote access bandwidth and throughput by using RAS Multilink. Based on the IETF standard RFC 1717, RAS Multilink enables you to easily combine analog modem paths, ISDN paths, and even mixed analog and digital communications links on both your client and server PC.

By way of example, notice how cool this is when you have phone line or network limitations. Pretend that you are in a room to do a demonstration, and instead of providing a high-speed line for your demonstration, the telephone technician got you two Plain Old Telephone lines (POTS). Because you need to show some intense graphics off a networked machine, the 28.8 modem is looking mighty lame; enter Multilink. Two phone lines, two 28.8 modems, and you have a 56 KB line into your Windows NT Server. This speeds up your access to the Internet or to your intranet, and cuts down on the amount of time you have to be remotely connected; it can, therefore, reduce your costs for remote access.

As another example, a Windows NT Workstation with three 28.8 bits per second (bps) modems can connect to a Windows NT Server with multiple modems and can achieve a transfer rate of more than 86 K bps. This example can be extended across any number of modems or ISDN lines to achieve even greater bandwidth. The speeds of the modems and ISDN lines can vary, but Multilink coordinates transfers across the various links to achieve performance equal to the combined speed of the devices.

Point-to-Point Tunneling Protocol (PPTP)

The Remote Access Service in Windows NT Server 4 enables remote users to access their networks via the Internet by using the new Point-to-Point Tunneling Protocol. PPTP is a networking technology integrated with RAS that supports multiprotocol virtual private networks (VPNs). PPTP uses the Internet as the transfer mechanism instead of long distance telephone lines or toll-free (800) services, which greatly reduces transmission costs.

A RAS server is usually connected to a PSTN, ISDN, or X.25 network, enabling remote users to access a server through these networks. RAS now enables remote users access through the Internet by using the PPTP.

PPTP enables remote users to access networks securely across the Internet by dialing into an Internet Service Provider (ISP) or by connecting directly to the Internet.

PPTP offers the following advantages:

❏ **Lower transmission costs.** PPTP uses the Internet as a connection rather than a long-distance telephone number or 800 service. This can greatly reduce transmission costs.

❏ **Lower hardware costs.** PPTP enables modems and ISDN cards to be separated from the RAS server. Instead, they can be located at a modem pool or at a communications server (resulting in less hardware for an administrator to purchase and manage).

❏ **Lower administrative overhead.** With PPTP, network administrators centrally manage and secure their remote access networks at the RAS server. They need to manage only user accounts instead of supporting complex hardware configurations.

❏ **Enhanced security.** Above all, the PPTP connection over the Internet is encrypted and secure, and it works with any protocol (including, IP, IPX, and NetBEUI).

Applications for PPTP

This feature enables you to extend your private network over the Internet. This means providing applications beyond simple Web services. You can, for example, have a secure way for people to get directly to your server, secured, by using whichever Internet service provider they are using. So, for example, if you want to allow someone to connect to your server just as they would any server on a LAN, this would be the way to do that in a secure manner. Think of this as a method to extend your LAN, secured, through the Internet, to a desktop or another segment of the network.

PPTP provides a way to route PPP packets over an IP network. Because PPTP enables multiprotocol encapsulation, you can send any type of packet over the network. You can, for example, send IPX packets over the Internet.

PPTP treats your existing corporate network as a PSTN, ISDN, or X.25 network. This virtual WAN is supported through public carriers, such as the Internet.

Compare PPTP to the other WAN protocols: When you use PSTN, ISDN, or X.25, a remote access client establishes a PPP connection with a RAS server over a switched network. After the connection is established, PPP packets are sent over the switched connection to the RAS servers to be routed to the destination LAN.

In contrast, when you use PPTP instead of using a switched connection to send packets over the WAN, a transport protocol such as TCP/IP is used to send the PPP packets to the RAS server over the virtual WAN.

The end benefit for both the user and the corporation is a savings in transmission costs by using the Internet rather than long distance dial-up connections.

The following three sections describe how PPTP can be used: for outsourcing a dial-up network, for client connections directly through the Internet, and for client connections through an ISP.

PPTP in Outsourced Dial-Up Networks

Communications hardware available for supporting dial-up needs can be complicated and not well integrated. For a large enterprise, putting together a Windows NT RAS server requires modems, serial controllers, and many cables. Furthermore, many solutions do not provide a single integrated way to efficiently support V.34 and ISDN dial-up lines.

Many corporations would like to outsource dial-up access to their corporate backbone networks in a manner that is cost effective, hassle free, protocol independent, secure, and that requires no changes to the existing network addressing. Virtual WAN support using PPTP is one way a service provider can meet the needs of corporations. This also gives those users wanting access or *inbound* service an additional method of obtaining access.

By separating modem pools from a RAS server, PPTP enables you to outsource dial-up services or geographically separate the RAS server from the hardware. A telephone company can manage modems and telephone lines, for example, so that user account management can be centralized at the RAS server. An end user would then make a local call to the telephone company, which connects to a Windows NT RAS server using a WAN link. The client then has access to the entire network.

This type of solution leverages existing, proven PPP authentication, encryption, and compression technologies.

The RAS client does not need to have the PPTP protocol; the client just makes a PPP connection to the modem pool or communications server. Note that the communication server or modem pool must implement PPTP for communication with the RAS server.

An Outsourced Dial-Up Network Using PPTP

A RAS client that has PPTP as its WAN driver can access resources on a remote LAN by connecting to a Windows NT RAS server through the Internet. Two ways enable users to do this: by connecting directly to the Internet or by dialing an ISP, as shown in the following sections.

NOTE

Connecting directly to the Internet means direct IP access without going through an ISP. Some hotels, for example, allow you to use an Ethernet cable to gain a direct connection to the Internet.

Secure Access to Corporate Networks over the Internet (Virtual Private Networks)

In this first example, a client directly connected on the Internet dials the number for the RAS server. PPTP on the client makes a tunnel through the Internet and connects to the PPTP enabled RAS server. After authentication, the client can access the corporate network.

Connecting Through an Internet Service Provider

In this second example, the same functionality is achieved by calling an ISP rather than being directly connected to the Internet. The client first makes a call to the ISP. After that connection is established, the client makes another call to the RAS sever that establishes the PPTP tunnel.

Security Considerations

Data sent across the PPTP tunnel is encapsulated in PPP packets. Because RAS supports encryption, the data will be encrypted. RAS supports bulk data encryption using RSA RC4 and a 40-bit session key that is negotiated at PPP connect time between the RAS client and the Windows NT RAS server.

PPTP uses the Password Authentication Protocol and the Challenge Handshake Authentication Protocol encryption algorithms.

In addition to supporting encrypted PPP links across the Internet, a PPTP-based solution also enables the Internet to become a network backbone for carrying IPX and NetBEUI remote-access traffic. PPTP can transfer IPX traffic because it encapsulates and encrypts PPP packets so that they can ride TCP/IP. Thus, a solution does not depend only on TCP/IP LANs.

Windows NT Server MultiProtocol Routing

Windows NT Server 4 includes Windows NT Server MultiProtocol Routing support, which enables routing over IP and IPX networks by connecting LANs to WANs without needing to purchase a dedicated router.

NOTE

AppleTalk routing support is provided in the Services for Macintosh component, which is included with Windows NT Server 4.

After you install Windows NT Server MultiProtocol Routing and enable the Routing Information Protocol (RIP) routing options, your Windows NT Server computer should be capable of routing network packets between two or more network adapters using RIP on Internet Protocol (IP), Internetwork Packet Exchange (IPX), or both. Your computer can also be a DHCP Relay Agent (depending on your configuration), which enables a computer to relay DHCP messages across an IP network.

DNS Server

Windows NT Server 4 adds a complete Domain Name System (DNS) server. DNS is integrated with WINS, and it offers new graphical administration tools to make dynamic DNS updates and DNS administration easier. TCP/IP has emerged as the preferred protocol for most types of networks. Managing addresses and host names on a TCP/IP network, however, presents a challenge. Previous versions of Windows NT Server provided the following features to ease the administrative burden of address and host name management:

❏ The Dynamic Host Configuration Protocol (DHCP) service, which automatically and dynamically assigns IP addresses to hosts.

❏ The Windows Internet Name Service (WINS), which provides a distributed, dynamically updated database of host names mapped to IP addresses. This enables users to use friendly host names rather than IP addresses to locate network resources.

Microsoft DNS server, running under Windows NT Server 4, is an RFC-compliant DNS name server that you use to manage and administer DNS services on your TCP/IP network. Microsoft DNS server supports RFCs 1033, 1034, 1035, 1101, 1123, 1183, and 1536, and is also compatible with the Berkeley Internet Name Domain (BIND) implementation of DNS.

Because Microsoft DNS server is an RFC-compliant DNS server, it creates and uses standard DNS database files and record types referred to as resource record types. It is interoperable with other DNS servers and can by managed by using the standard DNS diagnostic utility—*nslookup*. Nslookup is included with the TCP/IP utilities provided with Windows NT Server 4.

Microsoft DNS server also has features above and beyond those specified in the RFCs, such as tight integration with Microsoft Windows Internet Name Service and ease-of-administration by using the graphical DNS Manager.

Integration of DNS and WINS services is an important feature that enables interoperability between non-Microsoft and Windows-based TCP/IP network clients. DNS and WINS integration provides a method to reliably resolve name queries for Windows-based computers that use dynamic (DHCP-based) IP addressing and NetBIOS computer names.

The other important new feature of the Microsoft DNS server implementation is *DNS Manager,* a graphical user-interface used to manage local and remote Microsoft DNS servers and database files. Microsoft DNS server enables you to use a computer running under Windows NT Server 4 to administer an entire domain or subdivisions of the domain referred to as zones, subzones, and domains. These subdivisions are dependent on your enterprise requirements for name and administrative groupings of computers, integration of Windows NT-based domains into the DNS domain model, or your role as an Internet service provider to other enterprises.

The structure of a DNS zone changes whenever a new host is added or when an existing host is moved to a different subnet. Because DNS is not dynamic, someone must manually change the DNS database files if the zone is to reflect the new configuration. This results in increased administrative overhead, especially on zones that change frequently.

Coupling WINS and DNS

WINS was created to ease this type of administrative burden. Coupling DNS with WINS capitalizes on the strengths of each to provide a form of Dynamic DNS. This coupling is supported by the DNS service that runs under Windows NT Server 4. With it, you can direct DNS to query WINS for name resolution of the lower levels of the DNS tree in your zones. All this is transparent to the DNS resolvers, which perceive the DNS name server as handling the entire process.

Summary

This chapter discussed many of the software components that come with Windows NT 4.

NT was designed with Internet users and their need to access information stored on the NT machine in mind. This is a simple yet important concept when designing and laying out your Internet server. Use the built-in NT security where appropriate, and use the Administrative Wizards to help you set up your users and profiles.

Windows NT 4 comes with a full-featured Internet Server and the capability function as a full-fledged Internet machine by way of its Domain Naming Services, WIN Services, FTP, Gopher, and, of course, HTTP services.

Finally, remember that the improvements in Remote Access Communications give you the maximum flexibility in putting your server on the Internet. From simple modem aggregation to sophisticated secured connections, Windows NT 4 server can provide excellent Web access and service delivery.

part

Site Construction

8

Getting Windows NT Up and Running

T he exciting time has arrived for you; you are now ready to install Windows NT Server, either from a CD or over a network. This chapter a guides you step-by-step through the entire installation.

You set a variety of variables throughout the installation. The Setup program provides default values and enables you to check those settings graphically.

Setup is further automated by automatic detection of hardware and peripheral devices, although you need to make certain NT correctly identifies your hardware. If your hardware device in not on the list of hardware that Microsoft supports, specify a generic hardware device such as *modem* rather than *Twincom 14.4 DF*.

If you are changing from Windows 95 to Windows NT, be aware that many software titles that run on Windows 95 do not run on Windows NT. This chapter mentions some of the incompatible software titles. Some software titles even prevent Windows NT from installing correctly.

The following sections guide you through the installation process:

- ❏ Getting ready
- ❏ Running setup
- ❏ Connecting to the network
- ❏ Configuring Windows NT
- ❏ Troubleshooting installation problems

Before beginning the installation, you must make certain that your computer meets the system requirements for Windows NT.

Getting Ready

Before running Setup, which installs Windows NT, do a little homework. *Please* do not skip this section. You probably are anxious to install Windows NT and get your server up and running. The problem with installing a new operating system, however, is that you are about to fundamentally change the way in which your computer is operating. If you have a new computer or are installing Windows NT on a clean hard disk, you have far fewer worries than those who are replacing an older operating system with Windows NT. The danger is that you can lose all the information on your hard disk. If the information on your disk becomes corrupted, you will kick yourself for not backing up all the information on the disk. So please, follow the steps in this section. Even if Setup proceeds without error, you will have a backup of all your data on the disk. This may prove invaluable at a later time.

This section examines the requirements your system must meet, as well as the backup steps you should take before initiating the installation.

System Requirements

Because your computer is going to serve many other computers, it should be the fastest computer you can afford. A slow server is almost worse than no server. Consequently, your computer should have the latest and fastest CPU available for your platform.

The following sections list the minimum requirements that enable Windows NT to run. Please be forewarned that you should strive to exceed the minimum requirements as much as your budget allows. A biplane can take you across the country, but flying in a 747 provides a far more pleasant trip. The same goes with your computer.

The entire feeling about your server will be based on its performance. Do not underestimate the necessity for speed and reliability.

Following are the minimum requirements for Windows NT to work:

❑ 16 MB of memory is the absolute minimum for a x86-based system, but 32 MB or even 64 MB are preferable. The more RAM you have, the more programs your computer can keep in memory at the same time—the less swapping your computer has to do. Swapping programs to disk is a far slower process than accessing programs in memory. If you spend extra money anywhere in your system, spend it on RAM.

❑ 16 MB of memory for a RISC-based system (again, the more the better). 32 MB or more of RAM really improves the performance of your server.

❑ Although a mouse is optional, it is a practical necessity.

❑ CPU requirements include one of the following:

  ❑ 32-bit, x86-compatible microprocessor, such as the Intel 80486/33 or higher or Intel Pentium.

  ❑ Supported RISC-based microprocessor, such as the MIPS R4x00, Digital Alpha, or PowerPC.

Other hardware requirements include the following:

❑ Your monitor must have VGA or better resolution.

❑ Your server computer must have:

  ❑ One or more hard disks.

  ❑ A minimum of 125 MB of free disk space in the partition where Windows NT Server will go on a x86-based computer.

  ❑ A minimum of 158 MB of free disk space in the partition where Windows NT Server will go on a RISC-based computer.

❑ Because your Windows NT server is only half of the equation, you need to make certain that your Windows NT workstations also meet the minimum requirements of Windows NT Workstation:

  ❑ A minimum of 117 MB of free disk space in the partition where Windows NT Workstation will go on a x86-based computer.

  ❑ A minimum of 124 MB of free disk space in the partition where Windows NT Workstation will go on a RISC-based computer.

❑ For anyone *not* installing Windows NT Workstation or Windows NT Server over a network, the computers must have a CD-ROM drive.

❏ A 3.5-inch, high-density floppy drive for x86-based computers. If your computer has only a 5.25-inch drive, you can only install Windows NT Server over a network, regardless of whether you have a CD-ROM drive.

❏ One or more network adapter card. The whole point of installing Windows NT Server is to enable other computers to access this server. The network adapter cards connect your server to a network to facilitate that communication. The computers that will act as a client (running Windows NT Workstation) for your server also must have a network adapter card.

Hard Disk Partitions

NOTE

The preceding list identifies the minimum requirements for installing Windows NT Server and Workstation. The other hardware requirement assumed is that you have the networking hardware already in place. Networking hardware, besides the network adapter cards in the server and client computers, includes the network wiring and, potentially, a router. Setting up a network, however, is beyond the scope of this book.

Dividing your hard disk into partitions is not a requirement for installing Windows NT. This section is included for people who need further explanation of partitions. If your hard disk is not partitioned, or you already understand partitions, skip to the next section.

A *partition* is a subsection of a hard disk. When you format your hard drive, the hard disk can either be one big disk with one name, such as C:, or you can divide your hard disk into two or more partitions, each with its own name. You could, for example, divide one hard drive into three partitions; the names of the partitions could be C:, D:, and E:.

One reason to divide your hard drive into partitions is that the disk drive might be so large that your system cannot access all of it. In this situation, you need to partition your disk or use a disk manager that breaks the disk-memory barrier of 640 MB. In general, it is better to upgrade your system to include a disk manager. A disk manager usually comes with your hard drive or with a SCSI board that controls large hard drives.

Final Checklist and Backing Up Your Data

If your computer passes the hardware requirement test, you are about ready to install Windows NT Server. The danger in installing Windows NT Server, however, is that all the data on your hard disk could become corrupted. If no data is on your disk, you are lucky; you do not have to back up anything. If you are installing Windows NT Server on a system that was running another operating system, it is paramount that you back up your system data.

This section consists of a checklist for tasks you should complete before installing Windows NT Server. Go ahead and use a pencil to check off the items as you complete them.

❏ Read the release notes that come with Windows NT Server. They contain last-minute information unavailable at the writing time of this book and at the writing time of the manual that comes with Windows NT. Most important, they might include updated information about hardware compatibility or errors found in the manual.

❏ Back up the data on your hard disk to a network server, a tape drive, or to floppy disks. By far, the most tedious choice of the three is to back up to floppies. You will be happy to have the data backed up, however, if the data on the hard drive becomes corrupted. Do not get caught by someone saying, "I told you so!"

❏ Windows NT Server comes with a book, *Windows NT Hardware Compatibility List*, that contains all the hardware with which Windows NT Server is compatible. Make certain that all the hardware components in your system are listed in that book.

You can get the latest version of the hardware compatibility list if you have an Internet connection by checking the following URL:

```
http://www.microsoft.com/ntserver/hcl/hclintro.htm
```

If you do not have a World Wide Web browser, you can download the latest hardware compatibility list by using FTP at the following site:

```
ftp://ftp.microsoft.com/bussys/winnt/winnt_docs/hcl
```

Remember that Microsoft does not guarantee the success of the installation if your hardware is not listed in the *Windows NT Hardware Compatibility List* book. If your hardware is not listed, try the installation. You can specify generic hardware for the installation. If the installation is not successful, however, it is time to find out if your hardware will be supported by Windows NT Workstation in the future. You can find this out from your hardware manufacturer. It also is time to consider replacing the hardware with supported hardware.

❏ Gather together the device driver disks for all the hardware in your system. Although Windows NT Server tries to set up all the hardware in your system automatically, it is not always successful. In this case, you might need to reinstall the device drivers for your peripheral equipment. You also might need to secure an updated version of the hardware driver that supports Windows NT from your hardware manufacturer.

❏ Write down the configuration settings for your device drivers. Configuring devices is sometimes a hard-won battle. If your device drivers require configuration, record the settings you currently have in case you have to reinstall the drivers.

NOTE

If you are already using Windows 3.1 and plan to replace it with Windows NT server, make copies of your autoexec.bat and config.sys files. Configuration information often appears in these files for devices and software.

❏ Create an emergency boot disk. An operating system forms the groundwork on which all the other software in your system runs. If the Windows NT installation is not successful, nothing on your computer will start, except for preliminary hardware items such as the system BIOS. Although it is uncommon, if Windows NT does not install correctly, your system will be useless unless you have an emergency boot disk. (It's not unheard of to kick a computer's plug out of its socket during installation!)

Table 8.1 summarizes the information required for each kind of adapter.

	Adapter	Information Required
Table 8.1 Information Required for Various Adapters	Network	IRQ, I/O address, DMA (if used) connector type (twisted pair, BNC, and so forth)
	SCSI Controller	Adapter model or chipset, bus type, and IRQ settings
	Video	Chipset type or adapter name

To create an emergency disk, consult your current operating system. For Microsoft Windows-based operating systems, you need to format a high-density floppy disk after checking the System option. Copy on to the floppy disk your autoexec.bat, config.sys, and command.com files. Using the emergency disk will enable you to boot your computer and to retry the installation of Windows NT Server. If you have repeated installation failures, it will enable you to reinstall your old operating system. Remember that if you do not have an emergency disk, your system may be totally useless if the installation fails. At that point, you will have to create an emergency boot disk using another computer with its configuration information (that might be incompatible).

❏ If the disk on which you are going to install Windows NT is compressed, remove the data and uncompress the disk. Windows NT does not install or work with compressed disks unless it is compressed with NTFS compression.

- ❏ Ensure that you have the Windows NT Server installation CD-ROM, or that your network connection is working if you are installing Windows NT Server over a network.

- ❏ If the installation of NT fails, you or your system administrator might need the following information about your computer:

  - ❏ The previous operating system

  - ❏ The name of your computer

  - ❏ The name of your computer's workgroup or domain if it is already connected to a network

  - ❏ Your computer's IP address (The IP address is a number that identifies your computer on the network.)

- ❏ Remove any third-party network service or client software. Other network operating systems can conflict with Windows NT server. Ensure that third-party network client software also is removed from all Windows NT Workstation computers that will use this server.

In general, it is not a good idea to install Windows NT Server on a computer already running Windows 95. Although their interfaces look the same, they cannot occupy the same directory. You cannot replace Windows 95 with Windows NT by installing Windows NT in the same directory as Windows 95. Windows NT must occupy its own directory. This fact creates some problems, including the following:

- ❏ Having Windows 95 and Windows NT creates a dual-boot system. Although this, in itself, is not a major concern, it means that every time you boot the computer, you must choose which operating system you want to use.

- ❏ When you install software for Windows 95, you also must install it for Windows NT. One installation of the software does not suffice for both operating systems.

NOTE

You can choose the default operating system to boot by editing the boot.ini file.

- ❏ When you install new hardware devices in your computer, you must install the hardware drivers for both operating systems separately; one installation does not suffice for both operating systems.

- ❏ Windows 95 might configure software differently from Windows NT. Depending on whether you are using them with Windows 95 or Windows NT server, you might need to reconfigure software titles.

❑ If you are installing Windows NT on a mirrored partition on your disk, disable mirroring before starting Setup. You then can restart mirroring after you complete the Windows NT installation.

NOTE

None of these problems are insurmountable. If you have the choice *not* to install Windows 95 on the same computer as Windows NT Server, how-ever, exercise that choice. It will make your life that much simpler.

❑ If your computer has a DOS and OS/2 dual boot, boot the computer with the operating system you want to continue to use in addition to Windows NT. When Setup creates a dual boot, it uses Windows NT and whichever of the other two operating systems was last run.

❑ If you are installing Windows NT on a portable computer with a Personal Computer Memory Card International Association (PCMCIA) port, and you want Windows NT to configure a device attached to that port, you must attach the device and restart your computer before starting Setup.

If you have faithfully completed all the tasks in this section, congratulations! You are ready to run Setup and install Windows NT Server.

Running Setup

Setup is the program that installs Windows NT Server. It is a graphical program that enables you to make choices about a variety of system settings, to watch the progress of the installation, and to check on the accuracy of such installation procedures as the automatic detection of your hardware devices.

The procedure for starting Setup varies depending on the following:

❑ Your computer platform (x86, RISC, or PowerPC)
❑ Your access to the Setup program (on a CD-ROM or over a network)

Consequently, this section is divided into two parts: installing Windows NT from the CD-ROM disk, and installing Windows NT over a network.

The following instructions pertain to x86-based systems. Variations for RISC-based systems are included in notes. If you are using an x86-based system, you can skip all the notes pertaining to RISC-based systems.

Creating Setup Installation Disks

Regardless of whether you are installing Windows NT Server over a network, you need Setup Installation floppy disks. If you do not have those disks for some reason, use one of the following procedures.

If you are installing Windows NT Server from a CD-ROM, insert the CD-ROM and follow these steps:

NOTE

You do not need Setup Installation floppy disks if your computer's BIOS supports the El Torito Bootable CD-ROM format. In this case, Setup can boot directly from the CD-ROM. If you are using a RISC-based system, you also boot directly from the CD-ROM.

1. Change to your CD-ROM drive.
2. If your computer is already running Windows NT at the system prompt, type the following:

   `> winnt32/o`

   If your system is running Windows 3.1, Windows for Workgroups, or Windows 95, type the following:

   `> winnt/o`

3. Press Enter and follow the on-screen instructions.

If you are installing Windows NT Server over a network, you can create the Setup boot disks by performing the following steps:

NOTE

The Setup boot disk is unrelated to the Emergency Boot disk. You need to make both.

1. If your computer is already running Windows NT, type the following:

   `> winnt32`

   If your system is running Windows 3.1, Windows for Workgroups, or Windows 95, type the following:

   `> winnt`

2. Press Enter and follow the on-screen instructions.

The Setup Installation disks also enable you to start Windows NT after a system error. Together, the Setup Installation disk and the Emergency Boot disk can restart your system.

Using the CD-ROM to Install Windows NT Server

If you are going to use the CD-ROM supplied with Windows NT Server to install the product, use the following procedures. If you do not have the Setup Installation floppy disks, create them by following the directions in the preceding section, "Creating Setup Installation Disks."

1. With your computer turned off, insert the Setup Installation floppy disk into the 3.5-inch drive.
2. Turn on your computer.

Setup starts automatically on an x86-based system. If you are installing Windows NT Server on a RISC-based system, perform the following steps:

1. Choose the Install Windows NT from CD-ROM option on the ARC screen.
2. Setup starts.

If the preceding option is not available on the ARC screen, complete the following steps:

1. Choose the Run A Program option.
2. At the system prompt, type the following and then press Enter:

   `cd:\systemdir\setupldr`

   Where *systemdir* is the name of your CPU type: **MIPS**, **PPC** (for PowerPC), or **ALPHA**.

   Setup starts.

Completing Setup Tasks

After Setup starts, it provides a step-by-step guide through the process of installing Windows NT Server. You can ask for additional help at any time by pressing the F1 key. The help screen contains context-sensitive information that provides further explanations of options on-screen.

T I P

To cancel the installation procedure, press the F3 key.

Setup begins with a screen that welcomes you to the installation of Windows NT Server. It enables you to confirm that you want to proceed with the installation. If this is the first time that Windows NT is being installed on your computer, click on the Next button to begin the installation.

Detecting and Configuring Mass Storage Devices

After you decide to proceed with the installation, Setup attempts to detect the mass storage devices, such as CD-ROM drives and SCSI adapters, that are connected to your system. Hard drives are not scanned for in this step. Setup also scans, but does not display, all Integrated Device Electronics (IDE) and enhanced Small Device Interface (ESDI) drives.

Setup displays all the mass storage devices it finds and gives you the opportunity to confirm that it has detected the correct hardware. If Setup has missed some of the devices attached to your system, you can either add them later (after the installation procedure is finished) or you can choose to add them now. Whenever you choose to add the devices, you need to install the device drivers that accompany the device. If your device is old, you probably want to contact the manufacturer to get the latest Windows NT compatible version of the driver. In this case, install the device drivers later.

To install or change the SCSI drivers later, after Windows NT is running, click on the following icons:

Start→Settings→Control Panel→SCSI Adapters

To install device drivers at this time, press S.

Hardware Detection

After detecting mass storage devices, Setup automatically checks for other hardware connected to your system, such as network adapter cards and modems. Setup displays a list of the hardware components it finds in your system.

If any members of the list need to be changed, click on the up and down arrows on your keyboard until you highlight the correct component, and then press the Enter key to see the list of options for that component. Make the appropriate selections from the list of options.

Partitioning Your Disk

WARNING

Be forewarned that formatting a disk erases all the information on it. You can, however, use the NT convert utility to convert FAT partitions to NRFS partitions without erasing the data on the disk.

A disk may be partitioned into slices from 1 MB in size to the size of the entire disk. When installing Windows NT, the partition you install the system on must be at least as large as the minimum system requirements specified in the section, "System Requirements." (An x86-based system needs at least 148 MB of free disk space in a partition.)

You partition a disk when you format it. This process is part of Setup.

Each partition can have a different format type. The possible format types include NTFS and FAT. NTFS is for use with Windows NT only. You cannot, for example, run Windows 95 with an NTSF-formatted disk. If you intend to run a dual boot of Windows 95 and Windows NT, therefore, you must choose to have at least some of your disk partitions formatted in FAT.

If you are only going to run Windows NT on the server, you might want to format the disk with NTFS. It contains some performance and security enhancements unavailable with the older FAT system.

WARNING

Be forewarned again, however, that changing the format of the disk erases all the information on the disk. Change the format of a disk only when you have made a complete backup of it.

The next section describes in further detail which disk format to choose.

Choosing a Disk Format

The following considerations should help you in deciding how to partition your hard disk:

❏ **If you are running only Windows NT Server or Workstation on the computer**

If you do not have data on the disk that you need to save, make your disk a single partition and use the NTFS format. (Remember that on RISC-based computers, you need a 2 MB FAT-formatted partition. Leave the remainder of the disk as one NTFS-formatted partition.)

If your disk contains data that you want to keep, maintain all the current partitions. If you do not have a partition of adequate size, you need to back up all the information on the disk (which you should have already done!), and then repartition the disk making at least one partition of adequate size. After installing Windows NT, return the data from the backup system to the disk.

If you plan to use another operating system in addition to Windows NT on this computer, follow these steps:

1. To run DOS or a DOS-based operating system, install DOS before installing Windows NT. If you install Windows NT first, DOS overwrites files in the boot sector that make it impossible to run Windows NT without an Emergency Repair disk.

2. Ensure that the system partition of the disk is formatted in FAT. The system partition contains hardware information that your computer needs at startup. DOS and Windows 95 work only with FAT-formatted disks.

3. To use the NTFS file system, you must partition your disk into at least two partitions: one that uses the FAT file system for your DOS or Windows 95 operating system and files, another that uses the NTFS file system for use with Windows NT and its files.

Remember that when saving programs, you have a disk partitioned with different file systems. Save DOS and Windows 95 programs to the FAT partitions and Windows NT programs to the NTFS partitions. If you try to save the programs to the wrong partition, the information will not be saved. Note that NT can access both FAT and NTFS partitions, whereas DOS and Windows 95 cannot access NTFS partitions.

Setting Up the File System

In the partition of your disk on which you are installing Windows NT, you can choose whether you want to use the FAT or the NTFS file system. The following points should help you in making a decision:

❑ If you have a partition currently unformatted (and therefore empty), you can choose the NTFS or the FAT file system. Choose the FAT file system if you want to use the same files in Windows NT, Window 95, OS/2, or MS-DOS. To take advantage of the security and performance enhancements afforded by NTFS, choose that file system.

❑ If a disk is already partitioned, keep the current partitions; otherwise, you lose all the information on them.

You can convert a FAT file system partition to an NTFS partition as long as you do not need to access the partition by anything other than Windows NT. This option preserves the information in the partition. If, however, you choose to convert an existing partition to *reformat* an existing partition to FAT or NTFS, all the data in those partitions will be lost. Luckily, Setup gives you plenty of advance warning when you are about to lose data.

If you choose to reformat a partition, you must save all its data, reformat the partitions, and then restore the data. For more information about this procedure, see the *Windows NT Workstation Resource Kit Version 4.0.*

A variety of differences exist between FAT and NTFS, as the following sections explain.

N O T E

If you already have a system with a DOS and OS/2 dual boot, Setup sets up a new dual boot with Windows NT and whichever of the other operating systems was last run before installing Windows NT.

If you choose to use OS/2 as part of your dual boot, you need to re-enable it after the installation of Windows NT. To do this, click on the following choices:

Start button→Programs→
Administrative Tools→

Disk Administrator→OS/2 Boot
Manager partition→

Mark Active in the Partition
menu

Operating System Compatibility

FAT can work with all operating systems, whereas NTFS can only work with Windows NT. Even when running OS/2 or DOS from within Windows NT, these other operating system cannot access the data on the NTFS partitions. To access the data in the partition from any operating system other than Windows NT, you must use the FAT file system.

Security

Windows NT provides a variety of security features, such as permission sets, that are only enabled if the data is saved in an NTFS file system. FAT file systems do not afford any of the security features offered by Windows NT. If security is an important consideration in the implementation of your server, you should use the NTFS file system.

Size of Files

NTFS can support larger file sizes, up to 64 GB, depending on the size of the clusters. FAT file systems have a maximum file size of 4 GB. If you are running database or other applications that require saving files larger than 4 GB, choose the NTFS file system.

File Compression

When you run Windows NT, you can compress any file on a per-file basis if you are using the NTFS file system. Windows NT cannot compress files on a FAT system. Remember that you cannot install Windows NT on a compressed disk.

Data Sharing

NTFS is Windows NT-specific, in that files on a NTFS partition can only be read by Windows NT. To share files with other operating systems, such as Windows 95, in the same partition, you must use the FAT file system.

Selecting a Directory for Windows NT

Now that you have partitioned your hard drive and chosen a file system, Setup displays the name and location of the directory in which Windows NT can be installed. In general, the location and name of the directory is fine as is. You can, however, elect to change the name and location of the directory.

If your computer currently runs Windows NT 3.*x*, Windows 3.*x*, or Windows 95, Setup displays a special window that asks whether you want to overwrite your current operating system with Windows NT. Except for Windows 95, Setup defaults to overwriting your previous operating system. Whether you accept the default depends on the following considerations:

❏ Do you want to keep your old operating system so that you can use it with Windows NT as a dual boot system? If you are going to use this computer for something other than a dedicated server, you might consider keeping the old operating system. Windows NT is incompatible with many applications that run under Windows 3.*x* and Windows 95. Norton Utilities for Windows 95 and Seventh Guest, for example, do not run under Windows NT.

❏ Do you want to maintain the same registry settings from your previous version of Windows NT or Windows 3.*x*? If you replace your older version of Windows NT with version 4, Registry settings automatically migrate into the new installation.

As mentioned previously, it is not possible for Windows NT to replace Windows 95; they are incompatible and must run as a dual boot system.

The following lists summarize your options, which depend on which systems you are running:

❏ **If you are running Windows 3.***x*

Installing Windows NT in the same directory migrates the Registry settings to Windows NT, and also enables you to use a dual boot system.

Installing Windows NT in a new directory does not migrate the Registry settings to Windows NT, but it does enable you to use a dual boot system.

❏ **If you are running a 3.***x* **version of Windows NT**

Installing Windows NT in the same directory migrates the Registry settings to Windows NT, but overwrites the old version so that it is effectively lost.

Installing Windows NT in a new directory does not migrate the Registry settings to Windows NT, but it does enable you to use a dual boot system.

If you are running Windows 95, you have no choice but to install Windows NT into a new directory. You also must run the two as a dual boot system.

Setting Up Your Computer Accounts

At this point in the installation, you have made all the choices required to define where, what, and how Windows NT will be installed. Setup copies this information to the hard drive and restarts.

After the restart, you enter phase two of Setup called Setup Wizard, which prompts you to define a lot of variables, such as the name of the computer. Setup displays a screen for each of these definitions.

During the Setup Wizard phase, you can go back and forth between screens by using the Back and Next buttons on the screen so that you can easily change information you previously entered.

The following sections take you through each step of the Setup Wizard.

Choosing Your Installation

The first screen in the Setup Wizard enables you to define the type of installation with which you want to proceed. You have four choices:

❏ **Typical Setup.** This installation is the most common one; it installs all the optional elements in Windows NT, such as Microsoft Exchange and HyperTerminal, and it also configures your system for you. Because the Typical Setup does it all, this installation asks the minimum number of questions.

❑ **Portable Setup.** This option is useful only if you are installing Windows NT on a portable computer. If you are using this system as a server, this would be an uncommon choice.

❑ **Compact Setup.** This option installs Windows NT automatically without all the optional elements that automatically get installed with the Typical Setup. You would choose this option only if your disk space is severely restricted, or if you are certain that you are not interested in using any of the Windows NT Server optional features.

❑ **Custom Setup.** This option enables you to choose which optional features you want to install. If you are familiar with Windows NT and its optional features, and you know that you want to use some but not all of them, this is the appropriate choice. Custom Setup avoids flooding your disk with optional features you do not want (included in the Typical Setup), yet it gives you the optional features you want to use (not included in the Compact Setup). This option does assume, however, that you will have some familiarity with the choices you must make.

Supplying Personal Information and Preferences

Setup next displays six dialog boxes that enable you to set various variables. You must fill in these entry fields for Setup to continue. Those windows include the following:

❑ **Name and Organization.** This window enables you to identify yourself and your organization. These settings are important for other tasks you perform later.

❑ **Licensing Mode.** Choose Per-Seat if you have multiple servers and the number of Client Access Licenses is equal to or greater than the number of computers on your network. Otherwise, choose Per-Server. If you are uncertain which option to choose, choose Per-Server. It is legal and free for you to switch from Per-Seat to Per-Server one time.

❑ **Computer Name.** When choosing a name for your computer, the name must be 15 characters or less and must be different from the name of all other computers on the network. The name cannot be the same as any domain or workgroup name in the network. This name identifies your computer, which is important for such things as sending e-mail to the right location. (It is much easier to identify your computer by its name than by its IP address, which also uniquely identifies it.) In general, you need to ask your system administrator whether the name you have chosen has already been used for another computer.

❏ If you choose to use the Custom Setup, Setup displays a dialog box in which you select the optional features, such as games and accessories, you want Setup to install.

Selecting the Server Type

After entering your personal information and preferences, Setup displays a dialog box in which you specify the type of server you want to install. Following are the three choices offered in that dialog box:

❏ **Primary Domain Controller (PDC).** A PDC tracks the changes made to all the accounts in all the computers in a domain. It is the account administrator for the domain. Each domain has only one PDC; it is the only one to receive this kind of information.

❏ **Backup Domain Controller (BDC).** A BDC is a backup system for the PDC. The BDC is periodically synchronized with the PDC. If the PDC server fails for some reason, the BDC is promoted to the role of the PDC. The BDC also authenticates user logon operations. Many BDC servers can exist in the same domain.

❏ **Stand-Alone Server.** If your server does not function as the account administrator (PDC) or its backup (BDC), it functions as a stand-alone server. This choice is the most common.

Setting Up the Administrator Account

One of the security systems in Windows NT involves having different user types. Each user type is capable of performing a certain set of functions. An administrator can perform all the possible functions in the system, and can assign users to a restricted permission set.

Setup creates an Administrator account; there must be at least one administrator per server. The administrator's job includes assigning users different permission levels, assigning users to specific groups, and managing the system's overall configuration.

Because the administrator's functions are far reaching, Windows NT enables you to assign a password for the Administrator account so that only people who know the password can perform the tasks of an administrator. You can choose, however, not to make the tasks of the administrator password protected; in this case, leave the input box for the administrator's password blank.

Make certain to write down the password so that you do not forget it. If you forget the password, there is no way to perform the tasks of an administrator except by reinstalling Windows NT Server—and once is enough!

Correcting Floating Point Errors

If you are installing Windows NT on an x86-based computer, Setup checks your CPU to determine whether it might commit a floating-point error when dividing specific values. If Setup detects that such an error might occur, Setup gives you the option of turning off your computer's floating-point hardware module. Instead, Windows NT performs the floating-point operations.

Unfortunately, Windows NT performing these operations is an order of magnitude slower than the hardware performing the division. If, however, you expect to do a large amount of floating-point math, allow Windows NT to perform the operations; if you won't do much floating-point math, allow the hardware to handle the operation.

Creating an Emergency Disk

At this point, the Setup Wizard prompts you to create an Emergency disk. The Emergency disk records all the configuration settings that you have already defined. Included are the Registry settings, the config.sys file, and the autoexec.bat file. You can use the Emergency disk if these files get corrupted.

NOTE

In addition to the Emergency disk, you need the three floppy disks that you used during installation. (You may have created the disks before you began the installation.) The only case in which you do not need these additional disks is when your computer can boot from the Windows NT CD-ROM directly. For this to be the case, your computer's BIOS must support the El Torito No-Emulation CD-ROM Boot Specification.

Although this step is optional, it really should not be. No one plans for computers to fail or files to get corrupted, but these things happen, and often at the worst times. It is next to essential that you create an Emergency disk to protect your system. You should also update the Emergency disk when you make major changes to your system, such as when you add additional hardware, change your partitions, change device drivers, or install new applications.

Regardless of whether you create a floppy Emergency disk, the same information is available on your hard disk. System errors, however, often make this information inaccessible.

If you have a 2.88 MB floppy drive, the Emergency disk may not work. Reformat the drive to 1.44 MB and recreate the Emergency disk. If you choose to create an Emergency Repair disk, you must supply a floppy disk. Setup overwrites any information on the disk, so be careful when choosing the floppy.

Setting Up Optional Features

If you selected the Compact Setup, Setup skips the next step, which is to install optional features such as Microsoft Exchange, games, multimedia, and other accessories. The Windows NT Components window enables you to install the optional features or skip the process. If you choose to install optional features, Setup displays the Select Components window.

The Select Components window displays a list of optional features that you can install along with the amount of disk space they will consume. A Description box to the right of the list of optional features provides a short description of any optional feature that you highlight.

To install one of the optional features, click on the box next to the name of the feature so that a check appears. If you change your mind, you can choose not to install the optional feature by clicking again on the box so that the check disappears.

After you select all the optional features you want to install, click the Next button. At that point, Setup displays the Windows NT Setup window, which notifies you that Setup is ready to install all the selected optional features.

To change your selection list in any way, click on the Next button to return to the previous window.

When ready to install the optional features, click the Next button.

Congratulations! You have now completed the installation of Windows NT Server on your computer. You still, however, must connect your server to the network and configure it correctly so that it can act as a server for all the clients on the network.

Configuring Network Connections

Setup continues with the process of configuring your system so that it can communicate with client computers across a network.

The first Windows NT Server Setup window asks you to specify how your computer is connected to the network.

If your computer is connected to a remote network through a modem, click on the Remote access to the network option. If your computer is connected to a network, click on the Wired to the network option. You can click on both these options, if both apply. Although you also can click on the Do not connect this computer to a network at this time option, this option prevents your computer from acting as a server to others because it does not set up the network connections.

Setting Up an Internet Server

The next window asks if you would like to set up the computer so that it acts as a server on the Internet.

If you choose to set up your server in this fashion, Setup installs the Microsoft Internet Information Server (IIS) files.

NOTE

If you chose not to install the network connection features, these windows will not appear. If you want to set up your computer to act as a server for a network, you must go back in the installation process and select to install the network connection features.

Making your server an Internet server presumes that you already have a connection to the Internet or an intranet. To provide a welcome, you also must supply an HTML document in the \Wwwroot directory.

You can install the IIS files at any time after Setup by running Inetstp.exe from the \Inetsrv directory in the directory matching the name of your computer platform, such as I386 on the Windows NT CD-ROM disc.

Setup installs the IIS files with default configuration values. In almost all situations, these value are appropriate. If you find that you need to reset some of these values, consult the online IIS documentation.

Detecting Network Adapter Cards

Assuming that your computer is wired directly into a network, it must have a network adapter card. Setup tries to identify that card at this time.

NOTE

Chapter 7, "Software Requirements," tells you more about the Microsoft Internet Information Server.

Setup automatically detects the network card currently in your computer. If you plan to change network cards, you must specify the card you intend to use. Before you do, check the Windows NT hardware compatibility list to make certain that the card is compatible with Windows NT. You also need the device driver for the network card supplied by its manufacturer.

To start the automatic detection of the network adapter card, click on the Start Search button. Setup searches your computer for a network adapter card and displays the first one that it finds. If your computer has more than one network adapter card, click on the Next button to find each succeeding network adapter card.

NOTE

If your computer is connected to a network only through a modem, Setup does not try to detect a network adapter card.

Unfortunately, Setup cannot detect all makes of network adapter cards. In this case, you must click on the Select from list button, and then click on the name of the card you want to install. You also click on this button if you intend to install a network adapter card not currently in the computer. If you do not know the name of your network adapter card and Setup has not identified it, you need to ask your system administrator for the name of the card, or to run the hardware query tool.

You can install additional network adapter cards after completing Setup by double-clicking on the Network icon in the Control Panel.

Setting Up Network Adapter Cards

Now that you (or Setup) have identified the network adapter cards you will use, you need to configure them. Many network adapter cards are automatically configured to the correct IRQ and I/O base port address settings. In this case, accept the default settings.

Other network adapter cards present a dialog box in which you can choose an IRQ and I/O base port address setting. For information on setting these values, consult the documentation that came with your network adapter card.

Setting Network Protocols

The next step is to specify the network protocol you want to use. A *network protocol* is the language that computers can use to communicate with one another. Protocols specify things such as how information is packaged, and how to arrange the information packages. Windows NT enables you to install one of the following protocols:

❑ **TCP/IP.** This protocol provides communication across a wide variety of hardware platforms on a network. If you expect to communicate with systems running Unix, for example, choose this protocol. If you are setting your server up as an Internet server, you can choose this option.

❏ **NWLink IPX/SPX.** Choose this option if this server will support routing and NetWare client-server applications, where Sockets-based applications work with IPX/SPX Sockets-based applications. You also can choose this protocol if you want to set up this server as an Internet server.

❏ **NetBEUI.** Only use this protocol for networks that use the NetBEUI transport protocol. This protocol is designed for use with small (up to 200 clients) network installations. This protocol can only use the Token Ring routing system.

If you are uncertain which protocol to select, accept the default or ask your system administrator for guidance. You can change the protocol settings after completing Setup by double-clicking on the Network icon in the Control Panel.

If you want this server to act as a server on the Internet, choose the TCP/IP option.

Choosing Network Services

After you configure the first network adapter card, Setup next displays the Network Services dialog box. This window enables you to install additional network components for each network adapter card. Some of the components might require that you insert the disks from the network card manufacturer.

Installing the Network Component Options

Now that you have selected all the network options, Setup is ready to actually install them. If you need to change any of the settings you have chosen, use the Back button to return to the appropriate screen, make the changes, and then use the Next button to return to the screen.

The following steps guide you through the process of installing network options:

NOTE

Alternatively, your Internet service provider can assign you an IP address automatically if the provider uses DHCP. Contact your Internet service provider for details.

1. To begin the installation, click the Next button.

2. Some of the network options you chose might cause Setup to display a dialog box. In general, accept the default settings as prescribed by Setup.

3. If you are installing an Internet Information Server, register the IP address given to you by your Internet service provider.

Changing Network Bindings

Network bindings are the connections between network services, adapters, and protocols on your computer. Setup presents a screen so that you can adjust the bindings to increase the performance of network services among multiple networks. Setup also displays the default communication paths. You should not change the communication paths if you are a novice at setting up networks.

To enable or disable communications between a service and an adapter or protocol, double-click on the service name and then click on the adapter or protocol. Click the Enable or Disable button to set up the communications path.

Setting Up Workgroups and Domains

Workgroups and domains represent groups of users with the same permission set. The administrator uses these tools so that each user's permission set does not have to be configured individually; instead, a user is made a member of a particular workgroup or domain whose permissions are already set.

Workgroups

Workgroup and domain permission settings often are oriented around the tasks these groups need to complete in the work place (hence the name, workgroup). If one group needs access to the entire information tree, it receives the permissions to do so. If another group only needs access to part of the information tree to adequately complete its tasks, that group receives permission to only that part of the information tree.

Workgroups also share the same network resources, such as tape drives, printers, and servers. Computers belonging to the same workgroup appear under the same workgroup name when your browse through network resources.

Windows NT supplies some generic workgroups; often, however, the administrator creates his or her own workgroups tailored to the work tasks completed in the organization. You can create a workgroup just by typing its name in the text entry field.

Domains

A domain also is a grouping of computers. Unlike workgroups, however, domains have to be set up by an administrator. Users cannot create their own domain; they must petition the administrator to join an existing domain.

If you do not know whether your computer is part of a workgroup or domain, you can either bypass the dialog box or you can fill in a workgroup name and later revise it. To change these settings after completing Setup, double-click the Network icon in the Control Panel.

If the network starts up successfully, you can confirm or re-specify your computer's domain, workgroup, or both.

If the network does not start up, you can reconfigure the network and try to start it again. If it still does not start successfully, click the Next button; Setup adds your computer's name to a temporary workgroup.

Final Adjustments

You now have made all your configuration choices and Setup has copied your choices to disk and installed the systems and options that you chose. The final steps of Setup involve setting up your computer regardless of Windows NT Server.

Setting Time and Video Displays

Setup displays the Date and Time window. You should adjust all these settings so that they are correct. Setup next enables you to configure your video display. Before you click the OK button, make certain to test your configuration; if you make a mistake, you will need to reinstall Windows NT because your monitor will not work properly.

After Setup completes, you can reset the time, date, or the monitor by clicking the Time/Date or the Display icon in the Control Panel.

Starting Windows NT Server

At this point, everything is ready. Setup prompts you to reboot your computer. The following steps guide you through the process for starting Windows NT Server.

1. When you choose to reboot your computer, make certain that no disks are in your A: drive. When you choose the Reboot option, your computer screen goes black for a second.

2. The boot loader menu then appears if you have more than one operating system on your computer. At this point, you choose which operating system you want to run. In this case, choose Windows NT and then press the Enter key.

3. The Welcome logon window appears. Press Ctrl+Alt+Del to log on.

4. The Welcome dialog box appears. Enter your name and password, and then click the OK button. If your computer is already part of a domain, choose a domain in the Frame box in order to log on.

5. Congratulations! You have successfully installed, configured, and run Windows NT Server.

Troubleshooting

Hopefully, this is a section you will not need to read. On the other hand, if you find that your installation was unsuccessful, this section will prove very useful. It contains some of the most common installation problems and suggestions for solutions.

Hardware Incompatibility

❑ Windows NT Server works with many pieces of hardware, but not all. If Windows NT cannot detect one of your devices or the device cannot be accessed even after you have reinstalled the device's drivers, Windows NT may just be incompatible with it.

❑ Check the hardware compatibility list for the list of support hardware. For the latest updates, check the URL or FTP site given earlier in this chapter.

❑ If a piece of hardware is listed but still not responding, check to make certain that an IRQ conflict does not exist.

Incompatible Software

❑ Although many pieces of software that run on Windows 95 also run on Windows NT, not all do. Some manufacturers can provide updated versions of the programs so that they function properly under Windows NT.

❑ For a complete list of incompatible software, or for further explanations of exactly what is incompatible, look at the release notes for Windows NT Server.

Printer Problems

❑ Printer drivers that worked under previous versions of Windows NT no longer work under version 4. Check with your manufacturer for an updated driver.

❑ In Windows NT 4, only the administrator and users can access the Registry; guests cannot. Because you need access to the Registry to access a printer, guest accounts may have problems with using printers.

❑ Although Windows NT can handle very long printer names, some applications cannot. To resolve printer problems in this case, make the name of the printer 31 characters or less.

❑ If you try to print in a printer's non-primary colors (black, red, blue, cyan, green, magenta, white, or yellow), the printer may print in white, in which case you may not see the print.

Summary

You have now installed and configured Windows NT Server to run in a network. This chapter has provided you with a step-by-step installation guide and a short trouble-shooting guide. If you find that you continue to have problems, check the Microsoft Internet site to discover if there are known problems with Windows NT Server or if there are known incompatibility problems between Windows NT Server and other software applications.

At this point, you should have a system up and running and servicing your network. Congratulations.

9

Getting Web Services Up and Running

N ot long ago, the world was perceived as being flat— two-dimensional. The written word and knowledge traveled very slowly. Today we live in a technological age of advancements that enable us to view the world in a new way. Since the advent and acceptance of the Internet as a global publishing medium, knowledge is now distributed to millions of people in a matter of seconds. The WWW server on your NT Server will be your tool to publish information to the global Internet community. This chapter guides you through the steps necessary to install and configure Microsoft's Internet Information Server that ships with the Windows NT Server, covering the following topics:

❏ Web Server 101
❏ Web Server Choices
❏ Internet Information Server Installation
❏ Understanding the Internet Service Manager

❑ Installing the WWW Publishing Service

❑ Configuring WWW Publishing Services

❑ O'Reilly's WebSite Server Installation

Web Server 101:
An Introduction to Web Servers

This chapter is geared toward getting you started on building your own Internet server. Of immediate concern is how Hypertext Markup Language (HTML) documents are normally moved between a server and a client (browser).

In the course of *normal* interaction, a Web browser requests a document from a Web server, processes the HTML codes, applies the appropriate formatting, and displays the document to the user. If the returned document contains a hyperlink to another document, and is activated by the user, the Web browser retrieves and displays the linked document. All this is undertaken via the Hypertext Transport Protocol (HTTP)—the protocol that moves data between computers. Web servers are also commonly referred to as HTTP servers.

The browser running on Desktop 1 obtains a document from Server A that contains a link to a document on Server B.

By activating the link, the client requests the file from the Web server running on Server B and presents it to the user at the desktop.

The communications between the browser and the Web server are defined by the Hypertext Transfer Protocol (HTTP). If you need to review how the communications work or would like to brush up on your HTTP knowledge, please read George Eckel's *Intranet Working* (New Riders Publishing, 1996).

After you have become acquainted with HTTP and the operation of an HTTP server, the remainder of the chapter guides you through the process of setting up the Internet Information Server on the Windows NT Server.

The HTTP protocol can be looked at simplistically as the browser sending out a message that roughly says:

```
"This is who I am: my name and
➥address
This is the version of software
➥that I am operating under:
➥product X version y.z
These are the file formats that I
➥can display dynamically within
➥my display: formats a, b,
➥c, d, ...
This is the file that I would like
➥to receive from you, the server,
➥if it is one of the file formats
➥that I can use: name of file"
```

The server's response is along the lines of:

```
"Ok, this is what you told me:
➥name, address, file requested
Here is the file that you wanted,
➥in the following file format
➥that you, the browser, can use"
```

There is a great deal more involved within the HTTP protocol, but the whole of it revolves around the negotiation process of request/response format, until the information requested by the browser is delivered to the browser or a determination is made by the browser and the server that the information requested is just not accessible by the user.

A Quick Review of Hypertext Transfer Protocol (HTTP)

The Hypertext Transfer Protocol (HTTP) has been in use in the World Wide Web since 1990. The first version, HTTP/0.9, enabled the transfer of raw data across the Internet. Since then, HTTP/1.0 has evolved to provide messages in Multi-purpose Internet Mail Extensions (MIME)-like formats that contain metadata about the data being transferred. MIME is discussed in more detail later in the chapter.

Given the demand for new functionality and features, a revised specification, HTTP/1.1, is under development. This new specification seeks to address functions and services beyond the scope of this book. (Suffice to say here, the version change is necessary to enable two communicating applications to determine each other's real capabilities—such as determining whether a browser supports extended HTML tags or Java.) The new version (HTTP/1.1) will be backward-compatible with HTTP/1.0, but has tightened up the requirements to ensure more reliable implementation of HTTP's features.

The Purpose of HTTP

When obtaining information from the Web browser, and to indicate the purpose of the browser's request—today's information systems require more than just retrieval; they need to have the capability to search, update, and annotate—HTTP permits an open-ended set of methods to be used. Open-ended refers to the capability to add new functionality to the methods of passing information, such as GET and POST, between computers.

The messages transmitted are passed along in a MIME-like format.

The Uniform Resource Locator (URL) of the document on Server B might appear something like the following:

```
http://ServerB.domain_name.orginization_type/i_want_this_file.html
```

In other words, something has to enable you to retrieve different types of documents on a variety of different machines running a variety of different operating systems and server programs. To this end, HTTP enables the browser to select a resource by selecting a hypertext link, and the server responds with not only the file, but with information about what the browser should do with the file or how it should be displayed. Because there are many file formats that people want to provide, and this number is increasing rapidly as new ways to prepare and deliver information are explored, the current version of HTTP is being rewritten to accommodate new file formats and to provide greater functionality within the Internet and the intranet.

HTTP also permits other Internet protocols (SMTP, FTP, Gopher, and so on) to communicate with browsers. This provides hypermedia access to a wide range of resources in a variety of application types.

Web Server Choices

As you go through the implementation of the Internet server, first you must ensure that you have the Internet Web server up and running. Because this is an HTTP server, you need to make certain that you understand the basics of how the HTTP protocol works and have the equipment necessary to put the server into place.

There are several *flavors* of HTTP servers that can be implemented as the heart of the Internet for your organization; table 9.1 provides a list of currently available servers. Several of them have, traditionally, been free of charge in terms of acquiring and implementing them, as well as being *unsupported* by the authoring groups. More and more, however, commercial versions of HTTP servers are appearing on the market and are fully supported. The demands of companies putting in place mission-critical applications on these servers have caused businesses to move toward the selection and implementation of a *commercial* server. Like any product list dealing with the Internet technologies, errors and omissions will occur in this list. Best efforts have been expended, however, to make the list as accurate as possible.

When determining the correct server software for your Internet service, you should make a list of the types of information services that you will be providing (FTP, database access, and chat servers, for example) to determine the requirements of your server software. By comparing the list of your requirements to the capabilities of the server software provided in table 9.1, and others that come along, you can develop a short list of products that meet your needs. From that list, you can pilot one or more of the programs to test its capability to function within your Internet environment.

Table 9.1 A Listing of HTTP Servers	Server	HTTP Address
	Alibaba	`http://www.csm.co.at/csm/`
	Amiga Web Server	`http://www.phone.net/aws/`
	Apache	`http://www.apache.org/`
	Apache-SSL-US	`http://apachessl.c2.org/`
	Common Lisp Hypermedia Server	`http://www.ai.mit.edu/projects/` `➥iiip/doc/cl-http/homepage.html`
	Commerce Builder	`http://www.ifact.com/ifact/` `➥inet.htm`
	COSMOS Web Server	`http://www.ris.fr/`
	OSU DECthreads server	`http://kcgl1.eng.ohio-state.edu/` `➥wwwdoc/serverinfo.html`

	EMWAC Freeware HTTPS	`http://emwac.ed.ac.uk/html/`
		`➥internet_toolchest/https/`
		`➥contents.htm`

	EnterpriseWeb	`http://www.beyond-software.com`
	Esplanade	`http://www.ftp.com/esplanade`
	ExpressO HTTP Server	`http://www.capitalcity.com:4321/`
	Fnord Server	`http://www.wpi.edu/~bmorin/fnord/`
	FolkWeb	`http://www.ilar.com/`
	GN	`http://hopf.math.nwu.edu:70/`
	GNNserver	`http://www.tools.gnn.com/`
	GoServe for OS/2	`http://www2.hursley.ibm.com/` `➥goserve/`
	IBM Internet Connection Server	`http://www.ics.raleigh.ibm.com/`

Table 9.1 Continued	Server	HTTP Address
	IBM Internet Connection	`http://www.ics.raleighSecure` `➥Server.ibm.com/JSB`
	INTRAnet Jazz Server	`http://www.intranet.co.uk/`
	MacHTTP from Quarterdeck	`http://www.starnine.com/`
	Microsoft Internet Information Server	`http://www.microsoft.com/` `➥infoserv`
	NCSA HTTPd	`http://hoohoo.ncsa.uiuc.edu/`
	NetPresenz	`http://www.share.com/stairways/`
	Netscape Enterprise Server	`http://home.netscape.com/`
	Netscape FastTrack Server	`http://home.netscape.com/`
	NetWare Web Server from Novell	`http://www.novell.com/`
	OmniHTTPd	`http://www.fas.harvard.edu/~glau` `➥httpd/`
	Open Market Secure WebServer	`http://www.openmarket.com/`
	Open Market WebServer	`http://www.openmarket.com/`
	Oracle WebServer	`http://www.oracle.com`
	Purveyor WebServer	`http://www.process.com/`
	Quarterdeck WebServer	`http://www.quarterdeck.com/`
	Sioux	`http://www.thawte.com/products` `➥sioux/`
	Spinnaker Web Server	`http://www.searchlight.com`
	Spinner	`http://spinner.infovav.se/`
	SPRY SafetyWeb Server	`http://server.spry.com/`
	SPRY Web Server	`http://server.spry.com/`
	Stairways Web Server	`http://www.share.com/stairways/`
	SU/httpd	`http://www-swiss.ai.mit.edu/scsh` `➥contrib/net/sunet.html`
	SuperWeb Server	`http://www.frontiertech.com/` `➥products/superweb.htm`
	TECWeb Server	`http://www.tecs.com/`

Server	HTTP address
thttpd	`http://www.acme.com/software/` `➥thttpd/`
VBServer	`http://wwwdev.com/products/` `➥vbserver/vbserve.htm`
Web Commander from Interactive	`http://www.luckman.com/Luckman` `➥WebCommander/webcom.html`
Web Server/400	`http://www.inetmi.com/products/` `➥webserv/webinfo.htm`
Webshare	`http://www.beyond-software.com/` `➥Software/Webshare.html`
WebSite from O'Reilly & Associates	`http://website.ora.com/`
WebSTAR 95/NT from Quarterdeck	`http://www.quarterdeck.com/`
WebSTAR Mac from Quarterdeck	`http://www.starnine.com/`
Webware Commercial Edition	`http://www.edime.com.au/webware/`
WN	`http://hopf.math.nwu.edu/`
Zeus Serve	`http://www.zeus.co.uk/`

Internet Information Server Installation

When preparing to install the Internet Information Server as your Internet Web server, you should have an overall understanding of the possible methods of installation, as well as the common terms used when discussing the operation and configuration of the Internet Information Server. You must also understand the prerequisites necessary to install the Internet Information Server.

Within this section of the chapter, you will cover the following topics:

❑ Installation methods
❑ Understanding related terms

Installation Methods

A variety of methods are available to install the Internet Information Server. All methods provide the same results. The installation method you choose will largely depend on your particular needs.

Configuration of the individual Internet Information Server component services is performed after the initial installation procedure is completed by using the Internet Service Manager. The Internet Service Manager is located in the Microsoft Internet Server folder. The use of the Internet Service Manager is discussed later in this chapter (see the section entitled, "Understanding the Internet Service Manager").

 The possible installation methods are as follows:

❏ The first method of installation is to select the installation of the Internet Information Server during the process of NT 4 setup. During NT 4 setup, a dialog box appears, asking whether you want to install the Internet Information Server.

❏ The second method is to run the Install Internet Information Server icon located on the desktop. This may not be present on your NT Server installation, depending on whether your NT 4 installation was an upgrade or a fresh installation.

❏ The third method requires you to add the Internet Information Server by selecting the Services Tab from the Network icon, located in the Control Panel. You then choose the Add button, and select Microsoft Internet Information Server 2.

❏ The fourth method is to run the Internet Information Server installation setup program from the NT CD-ROM.

❏ The fifth method is to run the Internet Information Server installation program from a network drive. This method may be selected if you do not have a compact disk drive available on your NT Server. Often, the option to install the Internet Information Server is bypassed during the initial NT 4 Server setup procedure. When the decision is made later to install the Internet services contained within the Internet Information Server, the most commonly used method is the installation procedure from the CD. This installation procedure is discussed later in this chapter (see the section entitled, "Installation Procedures").

Understanding Related Terms

The WWW Publishing Service is the key component of Internet Information Server. Many other components of the NT Server installation process relate to IIS installation. You should have a general understanding of each of the terms and components involved in planning the WWW Publishing Service installation.

The following terms and components are discussed here:

❏ Internet
❏ Intranets
❏ HTML and HTTP
❏ Hyperlinks
❏ Internet Information Server
❏ URLs
❏ Browser requests
❏ ISAPI filters
❏ ISAPI applications
❏ Dynamic HTML pages
❏ Static HTML pages
❏ CGI scripts

Internet

The term *Internet* refers to the global network of computers that communicate using the TCP/IP protocol. The Internet is the largest network of computers in the world.

One aspect of the Internet is the World Wide Web. The World Wide Web is the most common perception of the Internet. The Web enables information to be viewed in graphical manner. When information is published on the Web, it can be interrelated and linked to other sources of information. This global structure of interrelated and linked information comprises the World Wide Web.

Intranets

The term *intranet* refers to a TCP/IP network not directly connected to the Internet. An intranet network is usually considered to be a private network, or private network segment.

Many intranet networks have a secure connection to the Internet through a firewall. Often, computers on an intranet can be allowed access to the Internet through a firewall implementation. A firewall implementation can restrict and prevent access to computers on an intranet from computers on the internet.

IIS operates on an intranet in the same manner as when connected to the Internet. All features and functionality are available to users on the private network.

HTML and HTTP

HTML and HTTP are abbreviations that have recently made their way into everyday vocabulary. These abbreviations are becoming commonplace in advertising.

The WWW Publishing Service transmits information written in the HyperText Markup Language (HTML), using the HyperText Transport Protocol (HTTP). Information published on the World Wide Web is usually in the form of HTML Pages.

Hyperlinks

When viewing HTML pages of text and graphics with a Web browser, you will often see highlighted text in a different color, or graphics with a similarly colored border. These are links to other sources of information on the World Wide Web. These links are referred to as hyperlinks.

Hyperlinks are text and graphics, defined within HTML pages, that have Web addresses embedded in them. When you click on a hyperlink, you send a Web server a request for an HTML page located elsewhere on the Internet.

Internet Information Server

The Internet Information Server is an NT Server running one or more integrated Internet services. The WWW Publishing Service, the FTP Publishing Service, and the Gopher Publishing Service are the Internet services that comprise the Internet Information Server. An NT Server running any or all of these services is also commonly called an Internet Server.

By using the Internet Information Server, you are able to publish information in a variety of ways. Home pages, newsletters, informational documents, catalogs, database information retrieval, and interactive programs are but a few examples of the potential and power of publishing on the Internet.

The Internet Information Server's operation can be equated to this simple process: it listens for requests for information from other computers, and responds.

The following sections discuss terms related to the Internet Information Server.

URLs

The Uniform Resource Locator, known as the URL, is the full address used by a Web browser to request information on the Web. The format of an URL begins with the specific protocol, the domain name, the path to the requested information, and then the name of the file.

```
ftp://ftp.yourcompany.com/software/updates/versions.txt
     ¦             ¦                    ¦     ¦
  Protocol         ¦                    ¦     ¦
             Domain name               ¦     ¦
                                     Path    ¦
                                          File name
```

Here are a few sample URLs:

```
gopher://gopher.yourcompany.com/marketing/reports/index.html
http://www.yourcompany.com/sales/catalog.html
https://www.yourcompany.com/sales/orders.html
```

Note

The protocol descriptor https:// requests a secure session. If you choose to implement server software that provides for secure transactions, such as the entry and transmission of credit card numbers, the use of the https: within the URL indicates to the browser that it is entering a secure space.

Browser Requests

Browser requests are URLs sent from a Web browser to the Internet Information Server. When the Internet Information Server receives the URL, it responds accordingly, sending the requested information back to the Web browser.

ISAPI Filters

An Internet Server Application Programming Interface (ISAPI) filter is a software DLL loaded with the Internet Information Server. It enhances the functionality or operation of the WWW Publishing Service. ISAPI filters are loaded by modifying a Key Value in the Registry.

ISAPI Applications

An ISAPI application is a DLL that performs a specific search as a result of a request. You may choose, for example, to enable searches for information within your WWW server documents. In this case, you implement an ISAPI filter that would perform the task of searching through your WWW server documents. The WWW Publishing Service can be enhanced by utilizing customized ISAPI applications.

Following is an example of an ISAPI URL:

```
http://www.yourcompany.com/isapi/search.dll?TEXT=findthis
```

Dynamic HTML Pages

A dynamic HTML page does not exist as an HTML page on a drive. It is created as a response to a request, dynamically on-the-fly, by an application or process running in association with the Internet Information Server. A dynamic HTML page name is not explicitly called out from within an URL.

Dynamic HTML page generation is of great benefit to the Webmaster, or administrator in charge of maintaining the Web site. If a Web site has a catalog of thousands of products, for example, each product usually needs its own HTML page stored on the WWW server. Each HTML page needs to be created and maintained by the Webmaster or administrator. If the HTML pages were generated as dynamic HTML pages, the task of Web server administration is greatly reduced.

Static HTML Pages

A static HTML page is a term used to refer to an existing HTML page stored on a drive. You can edit static HTML pages. To request a static page, the URL might look like this:

```
http://www.yourcompany.com/sales/catalog.html
```

CGI Scripts

A CGI script performs a specific task as a result of a request. The functionality of the WWW Publishing Service can be enhanced by utilizing customized CGI scripts. Here is an example of a CGI script URL:

```
http://www.yourcompany.com/cgi-bin/counter.pl?homepage
```

See Bill Weinman's *The CGI Book* (New Riders Publishing, 1996) for more information.

Understanding the Internet Service Manager

In the past, the most common complaints related to managing and maintaining a Web server have been the difficulty involved with configuration programs, or the lack of a friendly configuration program. The primary program used to configure the WWW Publishing Service is the Internet Service Manager. This program is well designed, and is easy to use. After you have completed and tested your installation, you can use the Internet Service Manager and other programs to configure advanced features of the WWW Publishing Service.

Within the Internet Service Manager, you can configure advanced features of the WWW Publishing Service, the FTP Publishing Service, and the Gopher Service.

Configuration of the WWW Publishing Service is discussed in this chapter. Advanced configuration issues related to the WWW Publishing Service are discussed in the book *Unlocking IIS* (New Riders, 1996).

Configuration of the FTP Publishing Service is covered in the next chapter, "Getting FTP Services Up and Running."

The following is a list of what you can configure within the Internet Service Manager:

- ❏ Default settings
- ❏ Home directories and virtual directories
- ❏ Access permissions
- ❏ Bandwidth usage
- ❏ Logon security
- ❏ Multiple domain virtual servers
- ❏ Encryption requirements
- ❏ Other Internet Information Servers
- ❏ Comments and messages
- ❏ Logging

Internet Service Manager Views

When working in the Internet Service Manager, three views are available. You can select a view to display the available servers and services, as needed. The views available from the Internet Service Manager are as follows:

- ❏ Servers view
- ❏ Services view
- ❏ Report view

Servers View

The Servers view displays Internet Information Server Services running on NT Servers, by server name. You can click on the plus symbol next to a server name to see which services a server has available. You can double-click on a service name to see and configure its property sheets. The Servers view is usually selected when you have multiple computers that you need to configure, or when you need to know whether a service is running or stopped, and the services installed on a specific computer. Figure 9.1 shows the Servers view.

Services View

The Services view, shown in figure 9.2, enables you to list the Internet Information Services on selected NT Servers, grouped by service name. You can click on the plus symbol next to a service name to see which servers are running that service. You can double-click on the server name under a service to display and configure its property sheets. The Services view is usually selected when you need to configure, or when you need to know which computers are running a specific service.

Figure 9.1

The Servers view.

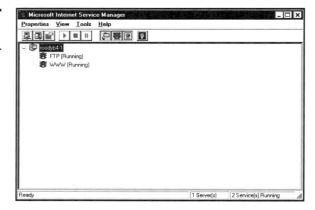

Figure 9.2

The Services view.

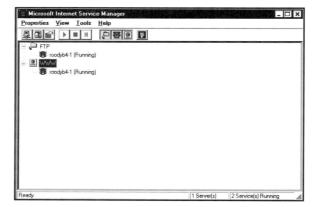

Report View

The Report view is the default view, and is the most commonly referred view. The Report view lists Internet Information Servers alphabetically, with each available service shown on a separate line. The list can be sorted alphabetically by clicking on the column headings. The Report view, shown in figure 9.3, is usually selected when you only have one or two servers running Internet Information Server.

Figure 9.3

The Report view.

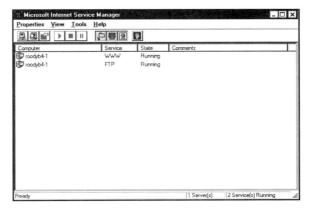

Connecting to an Internet Information Server

To connect to an Internet Information Server from the Internet Service Manager, you have two options. You can have the Internet Service Manager find available servers, or you can select a specific server to connect to.

Finding Available Servers

To find and connect to available Internet Information Servers, follow these steps:

1. From the Properties menu in the Internet Services Manager, choose Find All Servers.
2. From the list of servers displayed, double-click on the server that you want to connect to.

Selecting a Server

To select a specific server to connect to, you need to know the server name, IP address, or the NetBIOS name of the server. To select a specific server to connect to, follow these steps:

1. From the Properties menu in the Internet Service Manager, choose Connect to Server.
2. In the Server Name box, type the server name, IP address, or NetBIOS name.

Starting, Stopping, and Pausing Services

The Internet Service Manager enables you to start, stop, or pause individual services on a specific server, as necessary. When installing a new ISAPI filter, for example, you need to stop the WWW service and restart the service after the ISAPI filter has been installed. This enables the WWW service to load the ISAPI filter. If you pause a specific service, all users connected to the service will be disconnected. Figure 9.4 shows the dialog box that appears.

To start, stop, or pause a service, follow these steps:

1. Connect to an Internet Information Server.
2. Select the service you want to start, stop, or pause.
3. From the Properties menu, choose Start Service, Stop Service, or Pause Service (see fig. 9.4).

Figure 9.4

Starting, stopping, and pausing services.

Installing the WWW Publishing Service

The WWW Publishing Service is one of three component services that may be selected during the Internet Information Server installation. The other services are the FTP Publishing Service and the Gopher Publishing Service. The Internet Information Server installation Setup program enables you to selectively install the individual component services. To install the WWW Publishing Service, therefore, the general procedure to install the Internet Information Server is followed.

Installation Prerequisites

To install the WWW Publishing Service, you must first be logged on as a member of the Administrators group. You can verify if you are a member of the Administrators group by looking in the User Manager for Domains, located within the Administrative Tools folder.

In addition, you should confirm the following:

❏ NT Server is installed on an NTFS partition, and your server is functioning normally. For security reasons, your WWW Publishing Service must be installed on an NTFS partition.

❏ TCP/IP Protocol is loaded and has been properly configured.

❏ Name Resolution has been set up through the use of either DNS, WINS Server, HOSTS file, or an LMHOSTS file.

❏ Security procedures have been reviewed, and are in order. Do not allow unauthorized access to your NT Server from the Internet. Ensure that all users defined in the User Manager have unique passwords. See Chapter 14, "Security Practices," for detailed security information.

Installation Procedures

The following procedure guides you through the WWW Publishing Service installation. During the installation process, you can change some of the installation options. Keep in mind that the default installation configuration is fully operational, and may be reconfigured later using the Internet Service Manager.

To perform the WWW Publishing Service installation, follow these steps:

1. **Insert the NT Server compact disc.**

   Insert the NT Server compact disc into an available compact disk drive. If you do not have a compact disc drive on your NT Server, the installation can be performed from a network drive.

2. **Access a directory.**

   Run either the Explorer, File Manager, or open a Command Prompt window.

3. **Change to the INETSRV directory.**

   Locate and change to the INETSRV directory within the appropriate directory for your hardware platform. Change to I386\INETSRV for Intel platform, for example. If your NT Server was loaded from a network drive, you may copy the entire contents of the appropriate INETSRV directory tree to an available network drive. Figure 9.5 shows the INETSRV directory listing in Explorer.

Figure 9.5
Explorer.

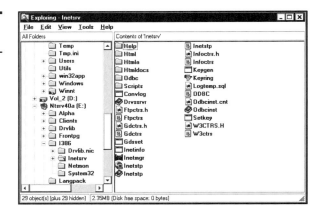

4. **Run INETSTP.EXE.**

   In the Explorer or File Manager, locate and run the file named INETSTP.EXE by double-clicking on the file name. If you are working in a Command Prompt window, enter **INETSTP** to start the installation program. When the Microsoft Internet Information Server Setup Welcome dialog box appears, choose OK.

5. **Choose install/remove option.**

   A list of available options appears in the Add/Remove, Reinstall, Remove all options dialog box (see fig. 9.6). Choose Add/Remove.

Figure 9.6
The Add/Remove, Reinstall, Remove All options dialog box.

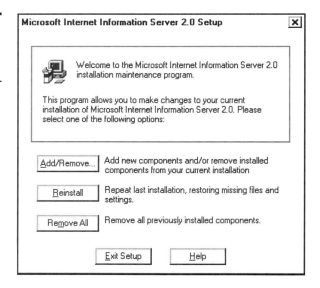

6. **Choose the location of the install files.**

   In the Location dialog box, choose the location of the installation files (see fig. 9.7). Choose OK.

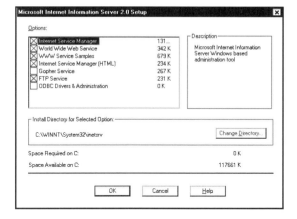

Figure 9.7

The location of installation files dialog box.

7. **Verify installation options.**

   A list of installation options is now visible in the Installation Options and Directory Location dialog box. For a complete installation of the WWW Publishing Service, you must verify that the following boxes, located on the Installation Options and Directory Location dialog box, are checked:

   ❏ Internet Service Manager: The Internet Information Server Configuration Manager.

   ❏ World Wide Web Service: The WWW Publishing Service.

   ❏ Help and Sample Files: Online Help and sample Hypertext Markup Language files.

   Other installation options appear on the list (see fig. 9.8). If you do not want to install a particular option, clear the check box next to it.

   If you plan to provide access to databases through the Internet Information Server, you need to check the box next to ODBC Drivers and Administration. This installs the Open Database Connectivity drivers, commonly referred to as ODBC, and the ODBC Control Panel applet. This option is required for logging to ODBC database files and for enabling ODBC access for the WWW Publishing Services Internet Database Connector. If you currently have an application running that uses ODBC, you may encounter an error message telling you that one or more ODBC components are in use. Before proceeding, close all applications and services currently using ODBC components.

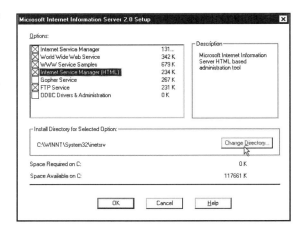

Figure 9.8

The installation options and directory location dialog box.

If you have chosen to include ODBC Drivers and Administration, the Install Drivers dialog box appears (see fig. 9.9). After you have made your ODBC selections, choose OK.

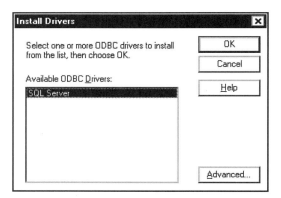

Figure 9.9

The Install Drivers dialog box.

8. **Choose your installation directory path.**

   You now can choose the installation directory path. You can accept the default path or specify a new directory path. If this is your first time installing the Internet Information Server, you can change the installation directory path. If you have previously installed Internet Information Server, and want to reinstall into a different directory path, you must first remove the *INetStp* key from the Registry. The following is the Registry path to the key:

   `\HKEY_LOCAL_MACHINE\SOFTWARE\Microsoft\INetStp`

If this key is present in the Registry from a previous installation, the Change Directory button will be dimmed, and you cannot change the directory path. If you get to this point and decide that the key must be removed, you need to re-start the installation setup program after you delete the key.

To accept the default installation directory path, choose OK.

To specify a new directory path, click on the Change Directory button, and then type the new directory path. Choose OK.

The installation program begins a partial file copy process.

9. **Specifying your WWW Server home directory.**

The directory you specify in this dialog box becomes your World Wide Web Server home directory. This is where the default home page is located for your domain. You may choose to accept the default directory path for the WWW Publishing Service, or you may change the directory path to another location. Figure 9.10 displays the dialog box that appears.

Figure 9.10

The publishing directories dialog box.

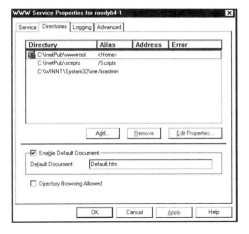

If you already have HTTP files ready to publish that exist elsewhere on the same drive as Internet Information Server, you can enter the full path to their location. If you accept the default directory path, you can move your HTTP files to the default location.

If your HTTP files are located on an accessible NTFS network drive, you should accept the default directory for the moment. After setup has completed, you can use the Internet Service Manager to change your default home directory to the path for the network directory containing your HTTP files. The following is an example network path:

```
\\ServerName\ShareName\WebFileDir
```

You also need to verify that the security permissions on the network drive are correct. See Chapter 14, "Security Practices," for more information.

The Installation Setup program prompts you to create the WWW Publishing Service directory. Click on Yes.

10. **Creating an Internet account.**

This is the user account name assigned for all anonymous access to the Internet Information Server. You have the option to enter a password and confirm the password for this user account name. See Chapter 14, "Security Practices," for more information.

Choose OK.

The Installation Setup program copies all the remaining Internet Information Server files to your drive. The Installation Setup completion dialog box appears. Click OK.

You may use the Installation program later to add or remove individual components. You also can use the Installation program to reload or remove all Internet Information Server-related components.

Testing the Installation

To test the WWW Publishing Service, you need access to a Web browser. Ideally, you should test from another computer on your intranet, or from the Internet. You can test the basic functionality of the WWW Publishing Service from your NT Server; this, however, may not confirm the proper operation of other related components. To test the WWW Publishing Service, follow these steps:

1. Start your favorite Web browser.
2. Enter the URL for your Web server into the Location field of your Web browser. The URL you enter begins with http://, and is followed by the name of your Web server, and ends in a slash (/). It should appear similar to the following example: *http://hostname.domain.com/*.

If you performed a default installation, and everything is functioning properly, a sample home page displays in your Web browser. The HTML file being displayed was loaded with the Help and Sample Files option, and is called default.htm.

3. Close your Web browser.

Configuring WWW Publishing Services

Configuration of the WWW Publishing Service is primarily performed using the Internet Service Manager. You can also use many other programs, related to advanced configuration and management.

The following sections describe configuration, and provide an understanding of related configuration programs.

Viewing and Configuring Property Sheets

In the Internet Service Manager, property sheets are used to view and configure the individual Internet Information Server Services. Each Internet Information Server Service has its own set of property sheets.

The WWW Publishing Service has four main property sheets for viewing and configuration. Many configuration options exist within each property sheet. The property sheets are listed as follows:

❏ Service
❏ Directories
❏ Logging
❏ Advanced

To view or configure the property sheets of a selected server, follow these steps:

1. Select a server.
2. Double-click on a service to view or configure.
3. Choose the property sheet to view or configure by clicking the tab at the top of the property sheet display page.

4. View or configure options as necessary.

5. Click OK to return to the main Internet Service Manager window.

You can find detailed information about advanced property sheet configuration options in chapters relating to security, multi-homing, and logging in the book *Unlocking IIS,* (New Riders Publishing, 1996).

Service Property Sheet

The Service property sheet is used to control access rights to the WWW Publishing Service. The account name used for anonymous client requests must be specified. The default user name, in the format *IUSR_computername,* is used for anonymous logons. The default user name is set up during the Internet Information Server installation. All anonymous logons to the service use this user name. If you decide to allow anonymous logons, you should still verify that the security permissions for this user name are correct.

You have the option to specify another user name. You can specify an existing user name, or create a new user account. In either case, you must configure its security permissions relevant to your requirements. It is recommended that the default account name be used. Use the default account name relevant to your security requirements unless you have a specific need to implement another one.

The password you select is used internally by the NT Server. The password is not presented by another computer during the logon process. See Chapter 14 for more information about security.

In the Comment option field, you can enter a comment or note, which will be visible in the Internet Service Manager, Report View window. This comment is sometimes used as a reference for the service. For reference purposes, for example, you could enter the IP address or the physical location of the server (see fig. 9.11).

Directories Property Sheet

Within the Directories property sheet, you can configure directory paths available to users, set access permissions, configure virtual servers, and define virtual directories (see fig. 9.12).

You also can define the Default Document, and decide whether to enable Directory browsing. Default Document and Directory Browsing options are discussed later in this chapter.

Figure 9.11

*The Service property
sheet.*

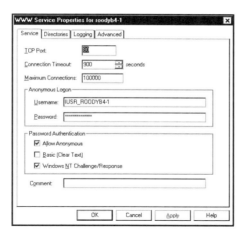

Figure 9.12

*The Directories property
sheet.*

The following sections discuss the Directories property sheet options related to a single domain WWW Publishing Service.

The WWW Publishing Service can also be configured for multiple domains on a single Internet Information Server.

Directory Paths

During the Internet Information Server installation procedure, a default home directory for the WWW Publishing Service was created. The default directory name is \wwwroot. This is also known as the default home directory for your Web server, and the root of your Web server directory tree. You can change this directory path as needed.

You can also place your home page or Default document into the home directory. You can create other directories within this directory. By default, files you place within the home directory tree of the WWW Publishing Service are available to Web browsers.

You can also add other directories, outside of the home directory tree structure, as needed. These directories appear to a Web browser as subdirectories of the home directory and are called virtual directories. They can be elsewhere on your NT Server, or on an available network drive.

In addition to being able to configure virtual directories, you can assign alias names to physical directories. You may want to assign an alias to a physical directory for reasons of security, or to simplify the physical directory name. If the physical directory name was long, for example, you could assign a shorter, simplified alias to the directory name.

The following is an example of a long directory name. The second line is its alias:

```
F:\SouthwesternSalesGroupMarketingReports
/SWReports
```

If you assign virtual directories to network drives, be certain that you specify a user name and password to connect to them from your NT Server. Ensure that your security procedures are correct. See Chapter 14 for more information.

Default Document

The WWW Publishing Service has the capability to respond to browser requests that do not specify a specific file name. If you enable the default document option, specify a default document name, and place a default document in each directory, the WWW Publishing Service returns the default document to the Web browser when it receives an URL request that does not specify a file name. If your default document is named *index.html*, for example, and you place an HTML page of this name into your home directory, this HTML page becomes your home page.

The following is an example of an URL used to access the default document, which in this case is the home page of the Web site:

```
http://www.yourcompany.com/
```

In another related example, if you place an HTML page named *index.html* into another directory within your WWW service tree structure, and an URL that does not specify a specific file name is used to access the directory, the WWW Publishing Service returns the default document named *index.html* to the Web browser.

The following is an example of an URL used to retrieve the default document from another directory and to place it within the WWW Service directory tree structure:

```
http://www.yourcompany.com/catalog/
```

If an HTML page with the same name as the document name configured within the default document option for the WWW Publishing Service exists in the home directory, it is known as the home page. The home page is typically an HTML page used to greet Web browsers, and usually contains hypertext links to other pages within your Web server.

The default document option is a global setting used by the WWW Publishing Service for the entire directory structure.

Directory Browsing

Directory browsing and the Default Document option are interrelated. If the WWW Publishing Service receives a browser request without a specific file name, and the Default Document is not present in the directory, a hypertext directory listing of the directory is sent to the Web browser.

Most often, directory browsing is not enabled. If it is enabled, Web browsers can see all the files and navigate through directories within your WWW Publishing Service tree structure. If you have files or directories within your Web server tree structure for administrative purposes only, for example, you usually would not want to make them available to Web browsers. This option is a global WWW Publishing Service setting, and affects all the directories within the Web server.

Logging Property Sheet

The Internet Information Server can log the activity of the WWW Publishing Service. Enabling logging is recommended. Logs can provide important information, and can be used for security and statistical review. The logs can tell you how your server is being used.

The IIS log file contains the IP address of the Web browser, date and time of access, service name, host name of service, service IP address, service status codes and bytes sent, and the name of the file accessed. For detailed information on how to read IIS log files, see Chapter 11, "Monitoring Server Activity and Performance," in *Unlocking IIS*, (New Riders Publishing, 1996).

The following is an example of an IIS log file:

```
206.27.214.226, -, 7/13/96, 10:52:51, W3SVC, KAHUNA, 206.173.231.39, 1011, 291, 4809, 200, 0,
➥GET, /jobs.html, -,
206.27.214.226, -, 7/13/96, 10:52:53, W3SVC, KAHUNA, 206.173.231.39, 80, 231, 5623, 200, 0,
➥GET, /images/jobsites_header.gif, -,
206.27.214.226, -, 7/13/96, 10:52:53, W3SVC, KAHUNA, 206.173.231.39, 0, 219, 1397, 200, 0, GET,
➥/images/ltb.gif, -,
206.103.73.9, -, 7/13/96, 10:56:29, W3SVC, KAHUNA, 206.173.231.39, 11, 224, 111, 404, 2, GET, /
➥cmed.html, -,
206.171.21.21, -, 7/13/96, 11:15:31, W3SVC, KAHUNA, 206.173.231.34, 0, 169, 476, 403, 5, GET, /
➥webdesign.html, -,
206.173.231.39, -, 7/13/96, 11:21:05, W3SVC, KAHUNA, 206.173.231.39, 120, 185, 29, 304, 0, GET,
➥/index.html, -,
206.173.231.39, -, 7/13/96, 11:21:07, W3SVC, KAHUNA, 206.173.231.39, 70, 293, 29, 304, 0, GET,
➥/images/coolsites_bb.gif, -,
```

You can choose to have the log data written to files or to an SQL/ODBC database. If you have multiple Internet Information Servers or Services on your network, you can log all their activity to a single file or database on a specific network computer.

If you would like to have individual log files for specific services, you can choose Log to a file. Individual log files can simplify the task of viewing the statistics for a specific service. If you choose Log to File, you must also specify how often to create new logs and where to log files. Check the box for the frequency of how often you want the Internet Information Server to create new log files, and specify the Log file directory location.

If you want to log the World Wide Web Service activity to a SQL/ODBC data source, you must specify the ODBC Data Source Name (DSN), table, user name, and password to the database. Logging to an SQL/ODBC database enables you to review the statistics for all your IIS services from a single file.

Advanced Property Sheet

The Advanced property sheet can be used to configure access restrictions to the WWW Publishing Service, and to limit the total outbound bandwidth of the Internet Information Server Services (see fig. 9.13). You may want to restrict access to your Web server for security reasons, or to limit outbound bandwidth from your IIS server to satisfy network bandwidth limitations.

Figure 9.13

The Advanced property sheet.

Restricting IP Access

The WWW Publishing Service can be configured to have the Internet Information Server grant or deny access from specified IP addresses. You can use this option to restrict access to your server from a specific computer or a group of computers. If the content of the Web server is intended for your research and development engineers only, for example, you can restrict access to the Internet Information Server from only the designated IP addresses associated to the engineers' computers.

By default, access to your WWW Publishing Service is granted to all IP addresses. You can choose to specify the IP addresses of computers to which you want to deny access.

You can choose to change the option to deny access to all IP addresses. If you choose this option, you can specify the IP addresses of computers from which you want to grant exclusive access.

Limiting Network Bandwidth

You can limit the outbound network bandwidth used by all the Internet Information Server Services on your NT Server. This option controls the maximum outbound network bandwidth for your Internet Information Server. If you have limited bandwidth, or are running other Internet services on the NT Server, you may want to enable and set this option to meet your needs.

If you choose to limit the outbound bandwidth used by the Internet Information Server Services, you must have an understanding of the possible implications:

❑ When the actual bandwidth usage remains below the level you set, the read, write, and transfer functions remain enabled.

- ❏ If the actual bandwidth usage approximates the limit you have set, reads are temporarily blocked.
- ❏ If the actual bandwidth exceeds the limit you set, reads are rejected, and file transfers are temporarily blocked.

The Internet Information Server returns to normal operation when the bandwidth usage equals or falls below the maximum limit.

Other Configuration Programs and Utilities

The Internet Service Manager is the primary configuration program used to configure the WWW Publishing Service. You can use other programs and utilities included with NT Server 4 to enhance functionality, perform advanced configuration, and monitor the Internet Information Server Services. This section references other configuration programs and utilities, and explains how they relate to the WWW Publishing Service.

This section discusses the following:

- ❏ HTML Administrator
- ❏ Control Panel Configuration Options
- ❏ Explorer
- ❏ User Manager for Domains
- ❏ Registry Editor
- ❏ Performance Monitor
- ❏ Event Viewer

HTML Administrator

The WWW Publishing Service can be remotely administered across the Internet with your Web browser by accessing the HTML. The HTML Administrator program is loaded during the Internet Information Server installation. The HTML Administrator program has the same configuration options as Internet Service Manager.

To securely log on to the remote Internet Information Server, you should use a Web browser capable of Windows NT Challenge/Response authentication. The Microsoft Internet Explorer has this capability.

If your Web browser is not capable of a secure logon, you can log on using basic, clear text. Be aware, however, that to use the HTML Administrator, you need to log on to the remote Internet Information Server as a user with Administrator's Rights. For this reason, a logon using basic, clear text across the Internet is not recommended; such a logon could compromise the security of your password. To use HTML Administrator, follow these steps:

1. Run your Web browser.
2. In the Location field, enter the URL in the following format:
   `http://www.yourcompany.com/htmla/htmla.htm`
3. Log on as a user who is a member of the Administrator Group.
4. View or configure options as needed.

Control Panel Configuration Options

The Control Panel contains the applets related to basic and advanced configuration options of the Internet Information Server. You can configure options related to the Internet Information Server, and its Services, in the following applets:

- ❑ Network applet
- ❑ Services applet
- ❑ ODBC applet

The following sections discuss each of these applets.

Network Applet

The Network applet can be used to configure your TCP/IP protocol settings and other network services and protocols. The TCP/IP protocol advanced configuration property sheet can be used to add additional IP addresses, up to a total of five, for use with multiple domain names within your Web server. When more than five IP addresses need to be added to the TCP/IP protocol configuration, you must use the Registry Editor to manually add additional IP addresses.

Services Applet

The Services applet can be used to start, stop, and pause the individual Internet Information Server Services, as well as control startup options.

After you highlight a service name, you can use the Startup button to enable or disable the individual Internet Information Server Services from loading during the NT Server boot process.

You can also configure the Log On As option for the WWW Publishing Service. The Log On As option contains the user name used internally by the Internet Information Server to log on to the service. The default setting for the Log On As option is set during the Internet Information Server installation. You usually need to change this setting for security reasons only. If you change the account user name in the Internet Service Manager Service property sheet for an Internet service, for example, you must also change the Log On As name for the service to the same name.

ODBC Applet

The ODBC applet is used to configure ODBC connectivity options. The ODBC applet will be present if you chose to install ODBC during the IIS installation procedure, or if it was installed as a necessary feature of other software.

Within the ODBC applet, you can add, remove, and configure User Data Source Drivers and System Data Source Drivers. Configuration and selection of ODBC Data Source Drivers depends on your specific needs and installed software related to the IIS.

Setting Permissions with the Explorer

By default, security permissions placed on files and directories within the individual IIS services directory tree structure are adequate for most installations. You may need to modify the security permission for files or directories within your IIS tree structure for security reasons.

If you find it necessary to change security permissions on files or directories within the WWW server directory tree structure, you can use the Explorer. If you have a file or directory that contains sensitive or secure data, and you want to restrict access to a specific user or group of users, for example, you can use the Explorer to set or change the security permissions.

To use the Explorer to set or change directory and file permissions on Windows NTFS drives, follow these steps:

1. Right-click on a file or directory name.
2. Click on Properties.
3. Click on the Security tab.
4. Click on the Permissions button.
5. Set the Permissions as needed.

User Manager for Domains

The User Manager for Domains is used to manage security policies, user accounts, and groups for your NT Server. The User Manager for Domains is located in the Administrative Tools folder.

You can use the User Manager for Domains to modify and implement security procedures relevant to the operation of your Internet Information Server.

Registry Editor

The Registry Editor can be used to edit Registry Keys and Values related to the Internet Information Server.

One of the most common uses for the Registry Editor, related to the Internet Information Server, is for adding IP addresses for use with multiple domains. If you are running a multiple domain Web server, and need more than five IP addresses or five domain names linked to your NT Server, you must use the Registry Editor to manually add the additional IP addresses to the registry.

You may also find it necessary to use the Registry Editor for other uses, such as loading ISAPI filters. The procedure for loading ISAPI filters, in most instances, requires that you manually edit or add a registry key or value in the registry.

Performance Monitor

The Performance Monitor is a powerful and useful tool, which provides a graphical interface that can be used to view real-time statistics and evaluate the overall operation of the Internet Information Server Services. It can also be used to evaluate and diagnose problems related to the individual Internet Information Server component services, such as the WWW Publishing Service.

With the Performance Monitor, you can view statistics in real time. You can use the Performance Monitor, for example, to show how many connections are active on all IIS services or an individual Internet service.

HTTP Performance Counters

The Internet Information Server installation loads Windows NT Performance Monitor counters for the WWW Publishing Service, the FTP Publishing Service, and the Gopher Publishing Service.

The Object name used in the Performance Monitor for the WWW Publishing Service is HTTP service. The following is a list of counters used to monitor the HTTP service object:

Bytes Received/second: The rate that data bytes are received by the HTTP Server.

Bytes Sent/second: The rate that data bytes are sent by the HTTP Server.

Bytes Total/second: The sum of Bytes Sent/sec and Bytes Received/second. This is the total rate of bytes transferred by the HTTP Server.

CGI Requests: Custom gateway executables (.exe) that the administrator can install to add forms processing or other dynamic data sources.

Connection Attempts: The number of connection attempts that have been made to the HTTP Server.

Connections/second: The number of HTTP requests being handled per second.

Current Anonymous Users: The number of anonymous users currently connected to the HTTP Server.

Current CGI Requests: The current number of CGI requests that are simultaneously being processed by the HTTP Server. This includes WAIS index queries

Current Connections: The current number of connections to the HTTP Server.

Current ISAPI Extension Requests: The current number of Extension requests that are simultaneously being processed by the HTTP Server.

Current Nonanonymous Users: The number of nonanonymous users currently connected to the HTTP Server.

Files Received: The total number of files received by the HTTP Server.

Files Sent: The total number of files sent by the HTTP Server.

Files Total: The sum of Files Sent and Files Received. This is the total number of files transferred by the HTTP Server.

Get Requests: The number of HTTP requests using the GET method. Get requests are generally used for basic file retrievals or image maps, although they can be used with forms.

Head Requests: The number of HTTP requests using the HEAD method. Head requests generally indicate a client is querying the state of a document the client already has to see if it needs to be refreshed.

ISAPI Extension Requests: Custom gateway Dynamic Link Libraries (.dll) that the administrator can install to add forms processing or other dynamic data sources.

Logon Attempts: Logon Attempts is the number of logon attempts that have been made by the HTTP Server.

Maximum Anonymous Users: The maximum number of anonymous users simultaneously connected to the HTTP Server.

Maximum CGI Requests: The maximum number of CGI requests that have been simultaneously processed by the HTTP Server. This includes WAIS index queries.

Maximum Connections: The maximum number of simultaneous connections to the HTTP Server.

Maximum ISAPI Extension Requests: The maximum number of Extension requests that have been simultaneously processed by the HTTP Server.

Maximum Nonanonymous Users: The maximum number of nonanonymous users simultaneously connected to the HTTP Server.

Not Found Errors: The number of requests that could not be satisfied by the server because the requested document could not be found. These are generally reported as an HTTP 404 error code to the client.

Other Request Methods: The number of HTTP requests that are not GET, POST, or HEAD methods. These may include PUT, DELETE, LINK, or other methods supported by gateway applications.

Post Requests: The number of HTTP requests using the POST method. Post requests are generally used for forms or gateway requests.

Total Anonymous Users: The total number of anonymous users that have ever connected to the HTTP Server.

Total Nonanonymous Users: The total number of nonanonymous users that have ever connected to the HTTP Server.

IIS Global Performance Counters

The Object name for the Internet Information Server is Internet Information Services Global.

The following is a list of counters used to monitor the Internet Information Services Global object:

Cache Flushes: The number of times a portion of the memory cache has been expired due to file or directory changes in an Internet Information Services directory tree.

Cache Hits: The total number of times a file open, directory listing, or service-specific object request was found in the cache.

Cache Hits %: The ratio of cache hits to all cache requests.

Cache Misses: The total number of times a file open, directory listing, or service-specific object request was not found in the cache.

Cache Size: The configured maximum size of the shared HTTP, FTP, and Gopher memory cache.

Cache Used: The total number of bytes currently containing cached data in the shared memory cache. This includes directory listings, file handle tracking, and service specific objects.

Cached File Handles: The number of open file handles cached by all the Internet Information Services.

Current Blocked Async I/O Requests: The number of current async I/O requests blocked by bandwidth throttler.

Directory Listings: The number of cached directory listings cached by all the Internet Information Services.

Measured Async I/O Bandwidth Usage: The measured bandwidth of async I/O averaged over a minute.

Objects: The number of objects cached by all the Internet Information Services. The objects include file handle tracking objects, directory listing objects, and service-specific objects.

Total Allowed Async I/O Requests: The total number of async I/O requests enabled by bandwidth throttler.

Total Blocked Async I/O Requests: The total number of async I/O requests blocked by bandwidth throttler.

Total Rejected Async I/O Requests: The total number of async I/O requests rejected by bandwidth throttler.

Event Viewer

The Event Viewer, located in the Administrative Tools folder, is a tool that you can use to monitor system, security, and application events. You can use the Event Viewer to view and manage system, security, and application event logs. The Event Viewer can notify administrators of critical events, such as a stopped or failed service and unauthorized access attempts, by displaying pop-up messages or by adding event information to log files. The information enables you to better understand the sequence and types of events that lead to a particular state or situation.

O'Reilly's WebSite Server Installation

O'Reilly and Associates produces a Web server called WebSite that you can implement on your Windows NT Internet server as an alternative to the IIS from Microsoft. The following sections take you through the steps to install and test your installation of the WebSite product:

Basic System Requirements

WebSite runs on Windows NT and Windows 95 platforms. Before installing the software, the following lists the requirements for implementing the product:

- ❏ 80486 or higher microprocessor; Pentium recommended
- ❏ 16 MB RAM for Windows NT; 32 MB recommended
- ❏ 12 MB RAM for Windows 95; 24 MB recommended
- ❏ 10 MB free hard disk space (for program files only)
- ❏ VGA video display adapter; SVGA recommended
- ❏ Windows NT 3.51 or higher, with Service Pack 4 installed recommended; WebSite runs successfully under Windows NT 4
- ❏ Web browser
- ❏ TCP/IP stack installed and running
- ❏ IP Address:_____._____._____._____
- ❏ Fully Qualified Domain Name (FQDN) for your server (for example, hostname.domain) name: _____
- ❏ Internet e-mail address for WebSite server administrator: _____
- ❏ Domain Name System (DNS) server (optional, but highly recommended) DNS Server 1:_____._____._____._____ DNS Server 2:_____._____._____._____
- ❏ WebSite server registered with DNS (optional, but highly recommended)

If you expect high-volume traffic or intend to implement database access services, you should expand your hardware. Perhaps the single most significant hardware component that affects performance is RAM. WebSite performance increases substantially with increased amounts of RAM.

For WebSite, you need to know the fully qualified domain name for your server. A fully qualified domain name (FQDN) includes the full hierarchical name of the computer—that is, the host name and the name of the domain. An FQDN is written from the most specific address (a host name) to the least specific address (a top-level domain). If your server's host name is *troll*, for example, and the domain is *dancing.com*, then the server's FQDN is *troll.dancing.com*.

Installing WebSite

Installing WebSite takes only a few minutes. The installation wizard guides you through the process. Following installation, you must test the server to make sure that the server is running. Running these tests is important to ensure that the server is installed correctly and operating properly.

To set the basic parameters for the server, during installation WebSite uses the information you provide (from the preceding bulleted list) as well as information from your Windows NT system Registry and configuration files. This general information is recorded in the General property sheet page of Server Admin.

The following steps take you through the installation of WebSite, guided by the Installation Wizard:

1. If you are running other Windows applications, close them before starting installation.
2. Start the WebSite Setup program by opening the WebSite folder on the distribution media with File Manager or Windows Explorer and double-clicking on setup.exe.
3. Enter your name and company or organization information to personalize your copy of WebSite.
4. Choose the destination directory for the WebSite software—the default is \WebSite, but you can install the software in another directory. Click Next to accept the default, or click Browse to choose another directory.
5. If you have an existing Web document structure, provide the full path name for the existing document root. If you don't have an existing Web on your computer, accept the defaults for the document root and home page in the Existing Web dialog box.
6. Choose the server run mode. Following are the possible options:
   - ❏ Application (manual start): Installs the WebSite server as an application that you must start each time you log in to Windows NT and is the default setting.

❑ Application (login start): Installs the WebSite server as an application in the Startup Group, causing it to start automatically when you login to Windows NT.

❑ Service (invisible): Installs the WebSite server as a service. The WebSite server icon does not appear on the desktop. The advantage of running WebSite as a service is that it runs even when no one is logged on to the computer. This is a good idea if you don't want to leave an open account on an unattended computer while running your Web site all day. In addition, running WebSite as a service enables it to restart automatically when the operating system reboots.

❑ Service (icon visible): Installs the WebSite server as a service. The WebSite server icon appears on the desktop and you can interact with it. If you are installing under NT 4, the icon is placed in the tray. You can later change it to a Task Bar icon, if desired.

7. Enter the fully qualified domain name for the server (see the description provided in the previous section).

8. Enter the administrator's e-mail address. This address can be at this site or at another site, depending on the location of your site administrator.

   At this point, the WebSite program files are copied to the destination directory that you specified in step 6.

9. Test the server's operation from the local computer. Using your browser, open the file (using the appropriate drive and directory names from your installation), as in the following:

   `file:///C:/WebSite/wsdocs/index.html`

   Select the hypertext link Click Here in the Important paragraph of the document that is shown within the browser. The link is for the following URL:

   `http://localhost/wsdocs/index.html`

   The browser sends out the request for this URL, which is interpreted by the browser and server as the Welcome page document on the local computer.

10. Run the server self-test. Click the link Server Self-Test and Demonstration that appears in the file that is currently being viewed from the preceding point.

After you complete these steps successfully, the WebSite server software has been installed and is running successfully.

To review the WebSite server properties, should you need to adjust any of the information regarding the installation and operation of the WebSite server, point to the

WebSite server icon, right-click your mouse and select the WebSite server properties menu option. Refer to your documentation for instructions on how to modify any of the information that you need to change.

Summary

In this chapter, you learned about the installation issues for the WWW Publishing Service. Prior to showing you the installation procedure, many of the installation concepts needed to understand the Internet Information Server configuration, such as installation methods and understanding related terms, were discussed. The Internet Service Manager was discussed in detail, and other configuration tools were noted. As well, an alternative product, O'Reilly and Associates' WebSite, was introduced through the installation procedures, to enable you to compare the IIS with another product.

The installation and configuration procedures discussed in this chapter should suffice for the majority of installation situations. The next chapter discusses getting your FTP services up and running.

10

Getting FTP Services Up and Running

Within the Windows NT Server software, support is provided for File Transfer Protocol (FTP). This means that the computer can be set up as an "FTP server," enabling you to deliver files to users. The FTP service provides a means to collect files together—put them into an *archive*, and make them available for retrieval.

FTP stores data in any format. It takes a bit of effort to set up the server itself and to maintain the lists of available files. This chapter discusses how to set up the server, but it also covers some basics on managing the service. Following is a breakdown of the chapter:

- ❏ FTP 101
- ❏ FTP Configuration with IIS
- ❏ Understanding the FTP Publishing Service
- ❏ Installing the FTP Publishing Service
- ❏ Configuring the FTP Publishing Service

- ❏ Creating Annotation Files
- ❏ Monitoring FTP Session Connections
- ❏ Directory Management: Maintaining the FTP Archive
- ❏ Troubleshooting
- ❏ Some FTP Choices

FTP 101: An Introduction to FTP Servers

File Transfer Protocol Servers have become a common service available in Internet sites, taking on some of the burden of making files accessible to users. Webmasters have several options when making their files available for downloading, including from FTP services and directly from the pages of the Web site.

The port numbers of HTTP (Web site) and FTP services differ—at least they should. Typically, the HTTP server runs on port 80 and the FTP service runs on port 20. If you operate a Windows NT server that is on the Internet and has high traffic volume to the HTTP site, enabling users to download files from the HTTP site might slow the response time for other users trying to access the site through the HTTP port. Forcing or permitting users to download files from another port, the FTP port, relieves pressure from a busy Web site.

Two types of access types to FTP sites are available—anonymous and nonanonymous. The most familiar method of FTP on the Internet is *anonymous FTP*, and it is on this that this chapter focuses. This method enables people to log on whether or not they have an account on the server. By specifying *anonymous* for the user name, users can log into the FTP server. The convention is to ask people for their e-mail address as a password so that the server administrator will have a record of who has been using the system.

The anonymous FTP users are restricted to seeing only part of the file structure on the actual server. The FTP server only enables the users to view directory listings, upload files to designated areas, and to download files to their workstations from designated areas. Because you can restrict the FTP access to certain areas of the server, it is relatively safe to set up and use.

FTP Configuration with IIS

The FTP Publishing Service—one of three component services within the Internet Information Server that comes with the Windows NT 4 server—is based on the File Transfer Protocol, known as FTP. FTP is one of the earliest protocols to be implemented on TCP/IP networks, and is still widely accepted today. FTP enables file transfers between computers. FTP is especially useful in transferring files between computers of different operating systems, which may have no other means of compatibility. Implementing the capabilities of FTP on the Internet Information Server requires some fundamental knowledge of Windows NT and creative tweaking abilities. This chapter prepares you to create a successful FTP site by discussing the following:

❑ Understanding the FTP Publishing Service
❑ Installation
❑ Configuration
❑ Related Tools

Understanding the FTP Publishing Service

The first FTP client programs used were character-based. Users were required to enter commands manually at a command prompt to be able to log on, list, and copy files. Character-based FTP programs are still widely used today. Windows NT includes a character based FTP program that can be run from the command prompt (see fig. 10.1).

Figure 10.1
FTP command prompt.

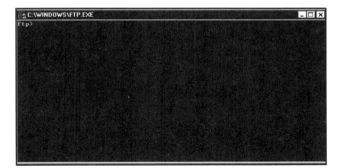

The FTP service displays directory listings to Web browsers as dynamically generated hypertext links. These hypertext links are displayed in the Web browser as directory listings (see fig. 10.2). The directory listings of hypertext links enable the user to navigate through directories with the simple point and click of a mouse. In the same manner, a click on a file name within the directory listing requests the file from the FTP service, and starts the file transfer process.

Figure 10.2
Internet Explorer FTP directory listing.

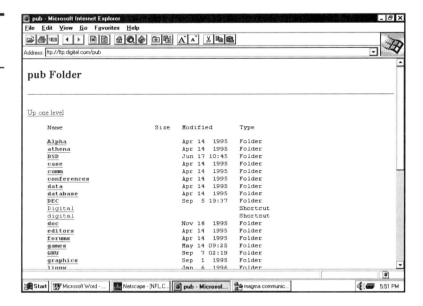

In addition to enabling anonymous logons, the FTP service can be configured to enable secure user logons. After a user performs a secure logon, access can be granted to enable the user to transfer files either to or from the FTP service. Secure, non-anonymous FTP logons are usually accomplished by using an FTP client. Most Web browsers enable only anonymous FTP logons.

The WWW service has replaced much of the functionality of and need for FTP. The WWW service enables users to request and transfer files from the Internet Information Server. (For more information on configuring a WWW service, see Chapter 9, "Getting Web Services Up and Running.") Of the three IIS component services, however, only the FTP Publishing Service can be used to transfer files from a remote computer to the Internet Information Server. If the FTP Service is used to distribute shareware files, for example, authors can send the latest versions of their shareware to the FTP service to create a dynamic repository for new software.

The content and format of the files made available through the FTP service are without restriction. Text, multimedia, executable, and compressed files can be made available for transfer.

Installing the FTP Publishing Service

The FTP Publishing Service is one of three component services that may be selected during the Internet Information Server installation. The IIS installation setup program enables you to selectively install the FTP Publishing Service. To install the FTP Publishing Service, refer to the general procedure for installing the Internet Information Server, previously outlined in Chapter 9, and substitute the FTP options for the WWW options.

Configuring the FTP Publishing Service

The FTP Publishing Service is configured through property sheets accessed from within the Internet Service Manager. The FTP service has five main property sheets for viewing and configuration. Many configuration options exist within each property sheet.

Configuration issues, related to the following, are discussed here:

- ❏ Service property sheet
- ❏ Messages property sheet
- ❏ Directories property sheet
- ❏ Logging property sheet
- ❏ Advanced property sheet
- ❏ Creating Annotation files
- ❏ Directory structuring

Configuring the Service Property Sheet

The Service property sheet, located in the Internet Service Manager, enables the administrator to control access to the service, set the connection timeout, set maximum connections, and enter connection messages (see fig. 10.3).

Figure 10.3

Service property sheet.

The following sections discuss the Service property sheet configuration options for the FTP Publishing service.

Connection Timeout

The Connection Timeout option sets the length of time (in seconds) for a connection before the server disconnects an inactive user. This is often referred to as the inactivity timeout. As a guideline, you should not set this number lower than 100 seconds. The default connection timeout value is 900 seconds (15 minutes). The maximum connection timeout value you can set is 32,767 seconds. This value ensures that all connections are closed if the FTP protocol fails to close a connection.

Maximum Connections

The Maximum Connections option limits the number of simultaneous user connections to the FTP server. If bandwidth is limited, and you have many users transferring files from the FTP server, you can lower the setting value to help conserve bandwidth usage.

Allow Anonymous Connections

By default, anonymous connections are allowed on the FTP Publishing Service. If you disable anonymous connections, only authorized, secure logons are allowed.

If you choose to allow anonymous connections, the account name and password used for anonymous client requests must be specified. The default account user name, in the format *IUSR_computername*, is used internally by the Internet Information Server for anonymous logon security. Anonymous logon users are linked to this account user name. The default account user name is set up during the Internet Information Server installation. All anonymous logons to the service use this account user name. To clarify this issue, when an anonymous user logs on to the FTP server, the IIS server uses the account user name for security restriction information.

The password you select for the account user name in the Service Property Sheet is used internally by the NT Server. This password is not known or set during the anonymous user logon process by the remote computer.

Anonymous FTP users usually log on using their e-mail addresses as passwords. Web browsers, such as the Internet Explorer, are, by default, configured to present the e-mail address of the user as the password during an anonymous FTP logon.

If you decide to allow anonymous FTP logons, you should still verify that the security permissions for this account user name are correct. You have the option to keep the default user name, specify another existing user name, or create a new user account. In any case, you must configure its security permissions relevant to your requirements. Use the User Manager for Domains to configure or verify security permissions. Refer to Chapter 14, "Security Practices," for more information.

Allow Only Anonymous Connections

In addition to anonymous FTP logons, FTP clients are also permitted to log on with a valid Windows NT account user name and password.

Select the Allow Only Anonymous Connections check box, located in the Service property sheet, to prevent valid Windows NT users from accessing the FTP service through user name account logons. With this check box enabled, only anonymous connections are allowed. For security reasons—to prevent unauthorized access and protect user passwords—this option is usually enabled.

Comment Option

The Comment option, located in the Service property sheet, is most often used to enter the text description of the service. The Comment option is commonly used for reference purposes. This comment will appear in the Internet Service Manager, Report View window. On networks with many IIS services, some systems administrators enter the IP address of the service for reference.

Configuring the Messages Property Sheet

The Messages property sheet, located in the Service property sheet, is used to customize the Welcome, Exit, and Maximum Connections messages (see fig. 10.4). By default, these entries are empty. Typically, these message options are used, and should be configured to meet your needs. These messages are usually used to personalize the FTP server.

The Welcome Message is displayed to the user during the logon process. This is commonly used to tell users something about the FTP server's content.

The Exit Message is displayed to a user when disconnecting from the FTP server.

The Maximum Connections Message is displayed to a user when the maximum number of connected users has been exceeded.

Figure 10.4

Messages property sheet.

Configuring the Directories Property Sheet

Within the Directories property sheet of the FTP Publishing service, you can configure directory paths available to users, set access permissions, define a home directory, define virtual directories, and select a directory listing style. Figure 10.5 shows the FTP Directories property sheet.

The following sections discuss the Directories property sheet configuration options of the FTP Publishing service.

Figure 10.5

FTP Directories property sheet.

Home Directory

During the IIS installation, a default home directory for the FTP Publishing Service is created. The default directory name is \ *Ftproot*. By default, this directory is actually a subdirectory within the existing IIS directory tree, and is not created in the root of the drive. The actual directory path will appear similar to the following example:

```
C:\WINNT\System32\InetSrv\Ftproot
```

You can change the location of the FTP home directory as long as the directory you assign is located on an NTFS drive within your domain.

WARNING

The FTP server will not operate properly without an assigned home directory. Assigning a home directory is a requirement for the proper operation of the FTP server. If you do not assign a home directory, all users will be denied access during FTP logon.

When configuring or changing the FTP home directory, you must choose another important option. You must select the type of access permission for the directory. By default, the home directory is assigned Read access permission only. If you want to allow users to upload files to the home directory, you must also select the Write option. It is generally not recommended to enable the Write option for the home directory. Only enable the Write option for the home directory if you have a specific need.

To allow users to be able to upload files to the FTP server, you should create other directories to accept transfers, and then configure them with the Write permission.

The home directory is perceived as being the root directory of the FTP server tree structure. You can create other directories within the home directory. By default, other directories and their contents will be available to anonymous logon users.

The following is an example of an FTP server home directory tree structure:

```
C:\WINNT\System32\InetSrv\Ftproot
                            \public
                            \info
                            \software
```

In the preceding example, the FTP server does not allow FTP clients to gain access to the \InetSrv directory. By default, the FTP server allows FTP clients to gain access to the \public, \info, and \software directories within the \Ftproot home directory.

You can place your FTP files into the home directory and other subdirectories that you create within the home directory. Directories created within the home directory can be created to organize your FTP contents. By default, the files you place within the home directory tree of the FTP server are available to anonymous users.

During an anonymous logon, when accessing the IIS server with a domain-name only URL such as ftp:\\www.yourcompany.com\, the FTP service operates in a slightly different manner than the WWW service operates. The WWW service looks for the default document or lists the directory contents of the home directory. The FTP service will first look for the presence of an \anonymous directory within the FTP home directory. If it exists, the anonymous user is given the \anonymous directory contents in the form of a hypertext listing. If the \anonymous directory does not exist, the user is given the contents of the actual FTP home directory in the form of a hypertext listing.

The following is an example of an FTP home directory tree structure with an \anonymous directory:

```
C:\WINNT\System32\InetSrv\Ftproot
                            \public
                            \info
                            \software
                            \anonymous
```

During the FTP logon process, the FTP service always looks for a directory that matches the user name. If a matching directory name does not exist, the user is directed to the FTP home directory.

The creation and use of an \anonymous directory within the FTP home directory is optional. You may want to use an \anonymous directory to direct anonymous users to specific content, for example, when the FTP service is configured to also allow nonanonymous logons to the FTP server.

The following is a sample domain URL, used to access the WWW service:

```
http://www.yourcompany.com/
```

The following is a sample domain URL, used to access the FTP service, on the same Internet Information Server:

```
ftp://www.yourcompany.com/
```

Create or Change the FTP Home Directory

You can change the home directory path, if needed. The home directory can be located on a local NTFS drive or on an available NTFS network drive within your domain.

To create or change the FTP home directory, follow these steps (see fig. 10.6):

1. In the Internet Service Manager, choose a server.
2. Choose the FTP Service for which you want to change the home directory.
3. Click the Directories tab.
4. In the Directory list, select the Home directory.
5. Click Edit Properties.
6. In the Directory properties box, type the full directory path, or choose a directory by using the Browse button.
7. In the Access box, choose the type of access needed.
8. Click OK.
9. Click Apply.
10. Click OK to return to the main window.

You can create other directories within the home directory. By default, these directories are both available and visible to FTP clients. You can create other directories within the home directory by using the Explorer.

Figure 10.6

The Directory Properties dialog box.

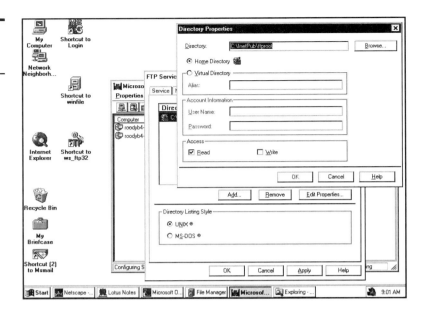

The following are examples of other directories created within the default home directory.

```
C:\WINNT\System32\InetSrv\Ftproot\public
```

```
C:\WINNT\System32\InetSrv\Ftproot\info
```

```
C:\WINNT\System32\InetSrv\Ftproot\software
```

Virtual Directories

You can also add other directories outside of the home directory tree structure. These directories appear to a user as subdirectories of the home directory. These directories are called virtual directories, and can be located anywhere on your NT Server or on an available NTFS network drive. For security reasons, you should use NTFS drives to store your FTP files.

Virtual directories are effectively implemented when you want to access directory contents existing on another NT server within your domain or network.

When you configure virtual FTP directories, you must assign the virtual directory an alias name. An alias name is a name linked to the actual physical directory. Users can

access the physical directory only if they know the alias name. You may want to assign an alias name to a physical directory for security reasons or to simplify the physical directory name.

If you assign virtual directories to network drives, you must specify a user name and password. The user name must have sufficient security permission to access the network directory. Ensure that your security procedures are correct. Refer to Chapter 14, "Security Practices," for more information.

When you use virtual FTP directories, the virtual directories are not visible to the user browsing the FTP home directory. This is a technical limitation of the FTP protocol as implemented within the FTP publishing service. Users can browse a virtual directory if they know the alias of the virtual directory.

Read and Write Permission

By default, the Read permission is enabled for all directories within the FTP server. You can use the Read and Write options in various combinations.

Read: The Read option enables an FTP client to see a directory listing and to transfer files from that directory.

Write: The Write option enables an FTP client to transfer files to a directory. Enabling the Write permission on a specific directory enables users to transfer files to your FTP server.

If you disable the Read option and enable the Write option on a specific directory, users can transfer files to that directory, but cannot see a directory listing or transfer files from the directory. If the Read and Write options are both enabled for a specific directory, users can transfer files to and from the directory, and see a directory listing. If you need a directory to accept file transfers from users, and do not want the files transferred to be visible to other users, enable only the Write option.

Directory Listing Styles

The Directory Listing Style option enables you to choose how the directory listing appears to an FTP client. You can choose from two styles—Unix and MS-DOS. It is usually recommended that this option be set to the Unix-format directory listing style.

This ensures maximum compatibility for Web browsers that require a UNIX-format directory listing.

Logging Property Sheet

The Internet Information Server can log the activity of the FTP Publishing service. Enabling logging is recommended. Logs can provide important information and can be used for security and statistical review. Fundamentally, logs can tell you how your server is being used.

You can choose to have the log data written to a file or to an ODBC database. If you have multiple Internet Information Servers or Services on your network, you can log all their activity to a single file or database on a specific network computer.

To log the FTP service activity to files, specify how often to create new logs and where to log files.

To log the FTP service activity to an ODBC data source, specify the ODBC Data Source Name, table, user name, and password to the database. The advantage of logging to an ODBC data source is that the activity from all three IIS services can be logged to one file and set up as parsed HTML information to be viewed on a Web page. Figure 10.7 shows the Logging property sheet.

Figure 10.7

Logging property sheet.

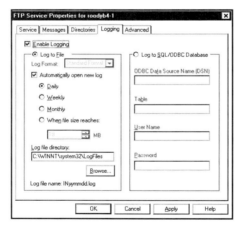

Advanced Property Sheet

The Advanced Property Sheet enables the administrator to configure access restrictions to the FTP Publishing service and to limit the total outbound bandwidth of the Internet Information Server services (see fig. 10.8).

Figure 10.8

The Advanced property sheet.

Restricting IP Access

The FTP Publishing Service can be configured to have the Internet Information Server grant or deny access from specified IP addresses. You can use this option to restrict access to your server from a specific computer, or group of computers.

By default, access to your FTP Publishing Service is granted to all IP addresses. You can choose to specify the IP addresses of computers you want to deny access to.

You can choose to change the option to deny access to all IP addresses. If you choose this option, you can specify the IP addresses of computers you want to grant access to. There should not be a need to restrict IP addresses in a public, anonymous-access FTP environment.

One example of proper implementation of IP address restriction is if the research and development department of your company has an FTP server, and you wanted to restrict access to only the engineers within the department, you can specify the IP addresses of the engineers.

Limiting Network Bandwidth

If you are running multiple Internet services and have insufficient bandwidth to meet all the needs of your IIS services, you can limit the outbound network bandwidth used by all the Internet Information Server services on your NT Server. This option controls the maximum outbound network bandwidth for your Internet Information Server. If you have limited bandwidth, or are running other Internet services on the NT Server, you may want to enable and set this option to meet your needs.

If you choose to limit the outbound bandwidth used by the Internet Information Server Services, you must have an understanding of the possible implications.

When the actual bandwidth usage remains below the level you set, the read, write, and transfer functions remain enabled. If the actual bandwidth usage approximates the limit you have set, reads are temporarily blocked. If the actual bandwidth exceeds the limit you set, reads are rejected, and file transfers are temporarily blocked. The Internet Information Server returns to normal operation when the bandwidth usage equals or falls below the maximum limit.

Creating Annotation Files

In the FTP Publishing Service, annotation files are sometimes used to summarize the directory description for a specific directory. Each directory within the FTP server can contain an annotation file. Directory descriptions are used to inform FTP users of the contents of a directory on the FTP server. The contents of the annotation file appear automatically to a Web browser when the user views a directory listing.

The name used by the FTP server for annotation files is ~ftpsvc~.ckm. The name annotation file should remain hidden. When the file is hidden, the annotation file is not listed in the directory listing. To change the attribute of an annotation file to hidden, use the Explorer.

To use the annotation file feature of the FTP service, you need to add a key to the Registry. By default, this registry key is not defined in the Registry. To enable directory annotation, you must add an entry to the registry subtree by using the Registry Editor.

To create annotation files, follow these steps:

1. Create a file called ~ftpsvc~.ckm, and place the file into the directory you want to annotate.
2. In the Explorer, select the file. Click the right mouse button within the Attributes option section of the Properties dialog box and check Hidden.
3. Use the Registry Editor to enable annotated directories by adding the value of "1" to the HKEY_LOCAL_MACHINE subtree key called AnnotateDirectories:

The following is the full path to the registry key:

```
HKEY_LOCAL_MACHINE\SYSTEM\CurrentControlSet\Services\MSFTPSVC\Parameters\AnnotateDirectories
Registry subtree key: AnnotateDirectories
Add the value: REG_DWORD
                Range: 0 or 1
                Default = "0" (off)
                set to "1" (on)
```

The preceding value, "0" or "1", defines the behavior of directory annotation. When this value is 1, directory annotation is enabled. When the value is 0, directory annotation is disabled.

If Directory Annotation is enabled on your FTP service, some Web browsers may display error messages when browsing FTP directories. These errors can be eliminated by limiting each annotation file to one line or by disabling directory annotation.

Monitoring FTP Session Connections

The Internet Service Manager can be used to monitor connections to the FTP service. Within the FTP Service property sheet of the Internet Service Manager, a list of users connected to the FTP service appears. You can disconnect an individual user or disconnect all users. This is valuable if you detect an unauthorized user in a secure, nonanonymous FTP environment.

To monitor users currently connected to your FTP site, follow these steps:

1. In the Internet Service Manager, select an FTP server.
2. Double-click on the FTP service to display its property sheets.
3. Click the Service tab.
4. Click Current Sessions.
5. To disconnect a specific user, select the user and then click on Disconnect. To disconnect all user connections, click on Disconnect All.
6. Click Close.
7. Click OK to return to the main menu.

Figure 10.9 shows a sample FTP Service properties sheet.

Figure 10.9
FTP Service properties sheet, FTP User Sessions.

Performance Monitor

The Performance Monitor is a very powerful and useful tool that provides a graphical interface that can be used to view real-time statistics and evaluate the overall operation of the Internet Information Server Services. It can also be used to evaluate and diagnose problems related to the individual Internet Information Server component services, such as the FTP Publishing Service.

With the Performance Monitor, you can view statistics in real time. You can use the Performance Monitor to show how many connections are active on all IIS services, for example, or an individual Internet service.

FTP Server Performance Counters

The Object name used in the Performance Monitor for the FTP Publishing Service is FTP Server. The following is a list of Counters used to monitor the FTP Server object:

Bytes Received/second: Indicates the rate that data bytes are received by the FTP Server.

Bytes Sent/second: Indicates the rate that data bytes are sent by the FTP Server.

Bytes Total/second: Indicates the sum of Bytes Sent/sec and Bytes Received/sec. This is the total rate of bytes transferred by the FTP Server.

Connection Attempts: Indicates the number of connection attempts made to the FTP Server.

Current Anonymous Users: Indicates the number of anonymous users connected to the FTP Server.

Current Connections: Indicates the current number of connections to the FTP Server.

Current Nonanonymous Users: Indicates the number of nonanonymous users connected to the FTP Server.

Files Received: Indicates the total number of files received by the FTP Server.

Files Sent: Indicates the total number of files sent by the FTP Server.

Files Total: Indicates the sum of files sent and received. This is the total number of files transferred by the FTP server.

Logon Attempts: Indicates the number of logon attempts made by the FTP server.

Maximum Anonymous Users: Indicates the maximum number of anonymous users simultaneously connected to the FTP Server.

Maximum Connections: Indicates the maximum number of simultaneous connections to the FTP Server.

Maximum Nonanonymous Users: Indicates the maximum number of nonanonymous users simultaneously connected to the FTP Server.

Total Anonymous Users: Indicates the total number of anonymous users ever connected to the FTP Server.

Total Nonanonymous Users: Indicates the total number of nonanonymous users ever connected to the FTP Server.

IIS Global Performance Counters

The Object name for the Internet Information Server is Internet Information Services Global. The following is a list of Counters used to monitor the Internet Information Services Global object:

Cache Flushes: Indicates the number of times a portion of the memory cache has been expired due to file or directory changes in an Internet Information Services directory tree.

Cache Hits: Indicates the total number of times a file open, directory listing, or service-specific objects request was found in the cache.

Cache Hits %: Indicates the ratio of cache hits to all cache requests.

Cache Misses: Indicates the total number of times a file open, directory listing, or service-specific objects request was not found in the cache.

Cache Size: Indicates the configured maximum size of the shared HTTP, FTP, and Gopher memory cache.

Cache Used: Indicates the total number of bytes currently containing cached data in the shared memory cache. This includes directory listings, file handle tracking, and service-specific objects.

Cached File Handles: Indicates the number of open file handles cached by all the Internet Information Services.

Current Blocked Async I/O Requests: Indicates the current async I/O requests blocked by bandwidth throttler.

Directory Listings: Indicates the number of cached directory listings cached by all the Internet Information Services.

Measured Async I/O Bandwidth Usage: Indicates the measured bandwidth of async I/O averaged over a minute.

Objects: Indicates the number of cached objects cached by all the Internet Information Services. The objects include file handle tracking objects, directory listing objects, and service-specific objects.

Total Allowed Async I/O Requests: Indicates the total async I/O requests allowed by bandwidth throttler.

Total Blocked Async I/O Requests: Indicates the total async I/O requests blocked by bandwidth throttler.

Total Rejected Async I/O Requests: Indicates the total async I/O requests rejected by bandwidth throttler.

Directory Management: Maintaining the FTP Archive

After you have the FTP sever up and running, you need to organize the information and get it up into the archive.

Remember that most browsers used on the Internet enable users to graphically click on and select files for download. The FTP archive gives the user another option for retrieving files. You can provide access to the collection of CAD drawings that an architecture business has, for example, in two ways:

❏ Create an HTML page with a link to the file, in which the URL will instruct the browser to ask the user what to do with the file—including save the file to disk.

❏ Create an FTP archive with a subdirectory full of the drawing files for the user to get and copy to the (current) directory on the user's hard drive.

One big differences here is the port number in use—the FTP service uses port 20 or 21, and the HTTP server uses port 80. As the demands on the Internet HTTP server increase, especially with the use of forms and CGI scripts, the usage of port 80 for file transfer slows the HTTP server down. Thus you can use the FTP service to move larger files between computers on the Internet.

A directory structure needs to be created to enable the organization and storage of files in logical groups. The FTP *manager* can and should delegate the authorities to maintain the subdirectories to the appropriate staff person—if maintaining on a divisional or project basis.

The new owners would be responsible for keeping the files current and organized, creating their own subdirectories, maintaining a README file that outlines the contents of the directory. The README file should contain a listing of the standard file name extensions used, and any nonstandard extensions present in the directory should be identified here.

In the Windows NT environment, use the User Account Editor to set up the rights of ownership for the users.

Why an Archive?

In many cases, information has a shelf-life. At some point in the life cycle of a document, the facts within it may no longer be current. Another version of the document is created, superseding the current version. Expired marketing promotions, for example, are often replaced by newer promotions. Creating an archive of these documents, available on an FTP server, is one way of ensuring that the information will be available if ever it is needed.

Although Caterpillar, the heavy equipment manufacturer, for example, prides itself on being able to meet demand for parts for every machine model ever sold over 96 percent of the time, the engineering drawings of those machines may no longer be required in *today's Internet*. Those older drawings do need to be available for review should someone have the need to do so.

Thus, the FTP server can provide the means for the storage and retrieval of large quantities of information that may be needed infrequently, but needed nonetheless. Many organizations refer to the manager of the FTP archive as the data *librarian* because much of the activity that goes on within the archive is the classification, categorization, and storage of the files. Putting the information into the appropriate locations within the directory structure and providing the necessary links to the documents from within the FTP server is a necessary function.

As mentioned previously in the chapter, the difference in the port numbers where the FTP server and the HTTP server are located are important factors when establishing document retrieval mechanisms. Large files require a longer connection time between the browser and the server when downloading files. By bringing down a 10 MB file through the HTTP server, you are occupying that resource for the length of time of the transfer. If the HTTP server is a busy one, you do not want people *hogging the bandwidth* from your showpiece.

The use of FTP servers (and you may need multiple servers in some cases) within the Internet service provides a means to place a hyperlink on the HTML page of the Internet server pointing at a large file for retrieval. Instead of starting the file transfer process from the HTTP server, however, the link takes you to the FTP server where you select the document and initiate the download. By using the Back button on your browser, you can return to the Internet pages and continue to search the site(s) while the FTP server continues the download in the background. This does not impede the Internet server unless you have the FTP server running on the same physical machine as the HTTP server, the Internet main server.

You should use another computer to run the FTP site from if you are going to have any volume of files, volume of traffic, or large files to transfer.

Troubleshooting

Troubleshooting problems with the FTP service requires you to start at the very beginning, using a somewhat "scientific" approach.

The FTP service requires that users log on to use the service. Once logged on, users can navigate the directories made available to the FTP service. Dedicated FTP clients allow remote users to copy files to the FTP site and issue other FTP commands, including logging off.

Following are steps you can take to determine where the problem has occurred:

1. Log on as the systems administrator and start the Internet Service Manager.
2. Using the Internet Service Manager, check to see that the FTP service has been started and is currently running.
3. Restart the service to ensure that it has been successfully implemented.
4. From a remote workstation, ping the server that the computer is successfully connected to the network and can be found.

5. Attempt to establish a session on the FTP service using the FTP client at the workstation: you must make certain that the workstation can connect to an FTP site, so connect to another FTP site (preferably outside of the company) to determine that the FTP client does work and that the workstation you are using is properly connected to the Internet.

If you are still unable to solve the problem, contact your Microsoft service representative.

Some Alternative FTP Software Choices

Having been through a review of what FTP is all about and having gone through the necessary steps to install the FTP service that comes as part of the Windows NT Server, alternative FTP programs that will run on the Windows NT Server are available. Today, a variety of graphical user interface FTP client programs are available, such as WS_FTP and Cute FTP. These FTP clients have simplified the tasks of logging on, listing, and copying files.

You can use Netscape Navigator and Microsoft's Internet Explorer, as well as other Web browsers, to anonymously log on to the FTP service, browse directories, transfer files from the FTP service, and log off.

Most TCP/IP implementations available on the market, aside from Microsoft, have a set of applications that includes an FTP server and/or an FTP client. Table 10.1 provides a list of several of the vendors and their TCP/IP offerings. These programs are listed here solely to inform you that there are other FTP software programs—you are not forced to rely on or use the Microsoft Windows NT Server implementation of the FTP software. The suitability of these programs for your unique situation cannot be warranted. If you want to explore any of these, or other FTP software, you should run the Windows NT version as a benchmark and then try the other software program(s) to compare the features and functionality of the software.

Table 10.1 TCP/IP Applications for Windows	Vendor	Product
	Frontier Technologies	SuperTCP Pro for Windows
	FTP Software Inc.	Explore OnNet, PC/TCP OnNet; Services OnNet
	Intercon Systems	TCP/Connect II for Windows

continues

Table 10.1 Continued	Vendor	Product
	Netmanage, Inc.	ChameleonNFS
	Novell, Inc.	LAN Workplace
	Spry Inc.	Air NFS
	Sunsoft, Inc.	PC-NFS Pro
	Walker Richer & Quinn	Reflection Network Series
	The Wollongong Group	Pathway Access for Windows

Summary

In this chapter, you learned about the configuration issues for the FTP Publishing Service. Many advanced configuration concepts required to understand the FTP Publishing Service were discussed. You also learned about the importance of maintaining an archive for your organization's purposes—the capability to find and access "old information" can reduce costs in creating what would be a redundant document.

The configuration procedures discussed in this chapter should suffice for the majority of installation situations. The next chapter discusses e-mail and list services, and how they can be used within the context of the Windows NT Internet server.

11

Getting E-Mail and List Services Up and Running

Electronic mail is at the core of electronic communications and the Internet. Long before the World Wide Web existed, e-mail was being used to exchange data electronically around the world. The popularity of e-mail should be no surprise; with the benefits of low cost, and nearly instantaneous delivery, e-mail has become an integral tool for both business and personal communication. Along with e-mail, mailing lists have become another popular tool for communication on the Internet. No Internet server would be complete without offering some sort of e-mail and e-mail lists.

The popularity of e-mail has led to a surge in e-mail solutions, however, ranging from simple systems designed for small business use to very complex solutions designed for large corporations. E-mail also has evolved over the years, enabling users now to send attachments such as graphics and application files. The result is a sea of protocols, each designed to add functionality to e-mail.

Literally dozens of e-mail services are available for Windows NT. They range from free packages available on the Internet to commercial packages such as Microsoft Exchange. Before choosing a mail server, it is important to understand the needs of your organization and to be certain to select the right server for you.

This chapter covers the most prominent protocols used with Internet e-mail and examines Internet mail delivery. A solid understanding of how Internet mail works and the protocols used to implement it will help you make the right decision for your e-mail needs. This chapter also provides some step-by-step configuration information to help get your Windows NT e-mail server up and running. It also gives you some hands-on information regarding list services and how to use them for your company.

The topics covered in this chapter include the following:

❑ E-Mail and list services 101
❑ E-Mail server product options
❑ Installing an e-mail server
❑ NT servers with list support
❑ Establishing list services
❑ Mail server policy issues

E-Mail and List Services 101

Before choosing an e-mail server for Windows NT, you should become familiar with the e-mail needs of your organization. Do you have an internal mail package already in place? If so, compatibility will become a major issue. Migration will be another issue if you plan to make all users change their e-mail packages. Will users be sending only text messages? Or will they be sending graphics or audio files as well? E-mail can be used to exchange messages in the form of plain text, and it can be used to pass along important files such as word processing documents or logos.

This section looks at the following topics:

❑ Definitions of e-mail and list services
❑ Benefits of Internet mail
❑ Mail delivery systems

Definitions of E-Mail and List Services

Electronic mail is analogous to postal mail. With traditional postal mail, you can send a letter, a picture, a record, literally anything. The same holds true for e-mail. You can send whatever you want, provided your mail services have adequate support. Some Internet e-mail systems are quite complex, enabling you to send audio files and images. The e-mail with which you most likely are familiar, however, are the short, text-based messages sent around your office.

An electronic mail list is just a collection of e-mail addresses designed to expedite mass mailings. By collecting the names of e-mail addresses with a common link—for example, all cat lovers—e-mail users can send a message to the list's address, and the mail server forwards the mail on to each member of the list. A mail server that supports list services enables you to establish an e-mail list and then have automated delivery, to archive old messages, and to subscribe and unsubscribe to the list automatically.

Mailing lists have become a very popular form of discussion on the Internet. The lists can be configured in a variety of ways to meet several different needs, such as the following examples:

❏ **Moderated lists.** A moderated list is a list in which one member is appointed the list moderator, who is then responsible for any messages forwarded to the whole list. If a member wants to send a message to the list, he sends it to the moderator, who approves the message and resends it to the list. The moderator may also reject the message.

   Moderated lists can be very useful for helping keep a mailing list on topic. Because mailing lists have a tendency to spawn tangents, a moderator can help keep all messages on track and reduce mail unrelated to the list. Moderated lists might be used for a specific topic discussion group, such as The Model T Mailing List, or perhaps a list used for company announcements.

❏ **Open Lists.** An open mailing list is a list to which anyone on the Internet can subscribe or unsubscribe. Users can send a special message to their mail server that automatically adds them to a specific open list. If your site hosted an open list called Cat Care, for example, anyone could become a member of that list, or leave the list if desired. Open lists are generally used for lists designed to generate discussion on a topic. Open lists can be moderated; a list for professional photographers, for example, might enable anyone interested to join the list, but messages to the list might be moderated to keep the messages relevant.

❏ **Closed Lists.** A closed list is a mail list that requires the permission of the list administrator or moderator in order to join the list. A closed list can also be moderated; by controlling the membership, however, the administrator can usually make certain that the people joining the list are interested in the topic. A company might set up an internal employees list for policy discussions, for example. The list would be closed to prevent just anyone from joining the list, but would not necessarily have to be moderated.

Using subscription control (open, closed) and submission control (moderated), a list can be created to suit most any need. As a supplement to a Web site or newsgroup, mailing lists can also be a great way to communicate with users who have e-mail access but limited access to the Web or news. Mailing lists can also be quite flexible. A digest list or a collection of all messages sent to the list can also be created and sent out periodically for those users who might want to peruse the list content on their own time, without cluttering their personal mailboxes. However you choose to use a mailing list, their simplicity and flexibility often make them a good choice for increasing communications with electronic mail.

Benefits of Internet Mail

Electronic mail can be an internal resource for your server, perhaps being limited to your Local Area Network. Alternatively, it can be a global resource, connecting your users to other people and places through the Internet. If you (or your organization) have been using electronic mail in a local setting, you might be surprised by the gains that you can get by opening up e-mail to the Internet.

First, you open a channel for communication to those outside your organization. With Internet-enabled electronic mail, you can use your e-mail system to contact clients or customers, suppliers or contractors, or even to share information with others in the same industry. In fact, many of the same types of communication that occur over the telephone can be accomplished via e-mail. Written communication, as opposed to oral communication, also offers many benefits.

Second, Internet e-mail systems are now the standards by which other mail clients are developed. Because of the Internet's incredible growth and worldwide usage, the e-mail protocols being developed by software companies are generally designed with the Internet, or Intranet, in mind. This enables you to take advantage of advanced technology that has one of the widest test audiences in the world. Even e-mail products developed for LAN-based mail have been expanding to provide Internet connectivity. The growing popularity of corporate Intranets is a good indicator of how a widely accepted protocol can help increase efficiency and productivity; Internet e-mail is no exception.

Obviously, if you are providing Internet services such as FTP or World Wide Web access, you want to make Internet e-mail accessible as well.

Mail Delivery Systems

E-mail is routed in a number of ways, varying from the simple on local networks to the complex for larger Wide Area Networks. At the heart of e-mail is the transfer of a text file containing information about whom it was sent from and to whom it was sent. This addressing information is used by the various machines on the Internet that relay the message from machine to machine until the message reaches its destination.

An e-mail message can be divided into three basic sections: the header, the body, and attachments.

The e-mail header is the first section of a message that contains the information necessary to deliver the message. The following message header, for example, contains information such as the sender (From:) the recipient (To:) and a Message-ID that serves as a unique identifier for this particular message.

```
Received: from localhost (krawling@localhost) by shooter.bluemarble.net with SMTP id PAA03702
for <dgulbran@bluemarble.net>; Fri, 25 Oct 15:49:45 -0500 (EST)
Date: Fri, 25 Oct 1996 15:49:45 -0500 (EST)
From: Ken Rawlings <krawling@bluemarble.net>
To: Dave Gulbransen <dgulbran@bluemarble.net>
Subject: A Sample Message
Message-ID: <Pine.SUN.3.93.961025154831.3133J-100000@shooter.bluemarble.net>
MIME-Version: 1.0
Content-Type: TEXT/PLAIN; charset=US-ASCII
```

The Message-ID can be used to help track problems with mail or to investigate forged mail. Finally, the header contains information about the content of the message, such as the MIME-version, and the Content-type. The Content-type might be plain ASCII text, or it might be another type of document such as an HTML file attachment.

The body of an e-mail message consists of the actual content of the message. This is usually in the form of plain text, but could be another form of text-based file. The Netscape Mail client, for example, is capable of reading HTML files. Although these are still text files, the header indicates that the text is HTML formatted. Using the information from the header, the Netscape Mail client then displays the message as a formatted HTML page. How your mail messages are handled and displayed is governed by the protocols supported by your mail server and mail client. If your mail client did not support HTML, the file would be displayed as a text file, as opposed to a formatted HTML page.

To send documents of different types, such as word processing documents or images, most mail packages support the use of attachments. Attachments enable you to mail an entire file as a separate document associated with a particular mail message. The attachment can then be viewed separately, or even downloaded to a local machine to be used with a particular application. The text of this chapter was sent as an attachment to the publisher, for example, who then downloaded the chapter for editing and inclusion into this book.

Mail Servers Versus Mail Gateways

Two mechanisms enable establishing Internet mail services: an SMTP (Simple Mail Transfer Protocol) mail server or an SMTP mail gateway. A *mail server* is a software package that acts as both the sending and receiving agent for all e-mail being handled by your server. *Mail protocol* is the syntax language mail servers use to communicate. Many different mail protocols are in use, but the most commonly used protocol for Internet mail is SMTP. If a message needs to be sent out by a user at your site, the mail server takes the message from the user's mail client and delivers it to the remote host across the Internet. The mechanism used to accomplish this is the *Simple Mail Transfer Protocol* (SMTP).

What if a company has been using cc:Mail for several years and has a very large installed user base? Certainly, the company could invest in a new Internet-compatible mail solution, but that might require a considerable investment, not to mention a great deal of planning and effort to ensure users learned and were comfortable with the new system without losing productivity. In cases like this, a number of products known as mail gateways exist to bridge the gap between older e-mail products and the Internet.

A *mail gateway* is an additional server add-on, or sometimes separate server, that can convert proprietary e-mail formats to SMTP and then send the mail on out to the Internet. Mail gateways have the advantage of enabling users to keep using the e-mail package with which they are comfortable. The mail gateways can, however, have significant disadvantages.

Because the e-mail now has to undergo an additional *conversion* step to route it properly out to the Internet, there is one more step in the process to break. Mail gateways are often much slower as well and can frequently end up becoming a bottleneck for e-mail delivery as they struggle to keep up with the demands created by Internet e-mail. Finally, many gateways have incomplete support for Internet innovations—MIME mail, for example, which enables multimedia attachments.

For these reasons, adding a mail gateway can often be more costly than it might first appear. A careful evaluation of your needs should help you determine which solution is right for you. This chapter, however, concentrates on building a new Internet-compatible mail server, not on dealing with mail gateways.

Protocols

An e-mail protocol is a predefined methodology that enables e-mail servers and clients to be compatible for the purpose of sending and receiving mail. The importance of protocol support should not be taken lightly when dealing with Internet e-mail.

The mail server you choose needs to communicate with other servers across the Internet. It also needs to communicate with the mail client that users have chosen to read and compose their mail. If your users have decided that they would like to use a POP mail client, such as Netscape, but your server does not support the POP protocol, you could have a situation where mail does not get through to users.

Four main protocols are commonly used when discussing electronic mail: the Simple Mail Transfer Protocol, the Post Office Protocol, the Internet Mail Access Protocol, and the Multipurpose Internet Mail Extensions. Of course, each of these protocols is referred to by its acronym, and each adds a slight variation to the methods used to transfer e-mail.

SMTP (Simple Mail Transfer Protocol)

The Simple Mail Transfer Protocol is the grandfather of Internet e-mail protocols. It is quite a simple protocol in which each mail server can contact any other mail server and through a series of simple commands transfer an electronic message from one machine to another.

If you are using Internet mail, your e-mail server will be SMTP compatible. Following is what happens when a user decides to send a message:

1. The user composes the message by using his mail client and instructs the client to send the message.
2. The mail program contacts the user's local SMTP server and makes a connection.
3. The client sends the server the FROM address, the TO address, the message body, and any attachments. Then the mail client disconnects from the server.
4. The server scans the header information for the FROM information to determine whether the mail is going to a local user (based on the domain name specified after the @ symbol).

5. If the addressee is a local user, the mail is written to the user's inbox, and the mail is delivered.

6. If the user is at a remote site, the server uses the domain name to contact the remote site's mail server and to establish a connection.

7. After establishing a remote connection, the server relays the message in the same fashion as the client did originally. Then the process of evaluating the FROM information for delivery continues until the message reaches its destination.

The entire process happens quickly. It usually never involves more than a few mail servers, frequently just two. The simplicity of SMTP makes it a very reliable and quite efficient mechanism for delivering mail. That also limits its functionality, however. Because of this, several new protocols have been introduced to the Internet community to add functionality to Internet mail. Keep in mind that most of these protocols still work in conjunction with SMTP rather than replace it.

MIME (Multipurpose Internet Mail Extensions)

The *Multipurpose Internet Mail Extensions* (MIME) were developed to help Internet mail cope with the increased use of graphics images and other media files on the Internet. Rather than limiting e-mail to plain text, MIME-capable readers enable Internet e-mail to contain graphics, sound files, or a number of other multimedia formats, and also provide a mechanism for easily extending the type of documents supported by MIME-compatible mail clients.

The MIME protocol defines a methodology for encoding nontext messages and provides for a content-type header that enables the mail client to determine what the file is. If a user wanted to send a GIF image to another user, for example, he could use a MIME-compatible mail client to attach the image as a MIME attachment. The second user also needs to be using a MIME-compatible mail client to view the attachments after receiving them.

By using a MIME-compatible mail client, the GIF images could be viewed within the mail message or could be viewed by launching an external viewer. The capability to determine the type of attachment, and then to launch an appropriate external viewer, makes MIME very powerful. MIME is not limited to existing file types, but rather new file types can be defined using the content-type header to extend MIME's capabilities. The following is a list of some MIME compatible e-mail clients.

E-Mail Connection

Eudora Lite

Eudora Pro

Pegasus Mail

Netscape Navigator

Microsoft Internet Explorer

POP3 (Post Office Protocol)

So far, all the previously mentioned electronic mail tools would require actually using the same machine to run the Internet mail server and your e-mail client. In most organizations, however, the server is not accessible to users for direct logons. Several ways enable you to work around this, including having users' mailboxes located on the server, so the server can deliver the mail, and then configuring the mail clients to read mail from a network drive. An Internet mail protocol has also been developed specifically to transfer mail from the server to a local machine for mail reading: the Post Office Protocol.

The *Post Office Protocol* (POP) defines a mechanism for POP mail clients to contact the central mail server and then transfer all of the user's mail messages to a local machine. This enables users to have complete control over the e-mail environment and can reduce the burden on your mail server. POP also reduces the connection time necessary to the central server, which can enable offline mail reading and composition.

If your organization has a mobile sales force that needs to travel extensively but still retain e-mail contact, for example, a POP server can help reduce long distance phone calls for e-mail. Traditionally, the remote user would have to dial into the server and remain connected while reading e-mail and composing replies. Even a moderate amount of mail could make that an expensive proposition. With a POP client, the user dials into the server long enough for all the new messages to be downloaded to the local machine and then disconnects. The mail is POPped on to the local machine, and the user can then read the mail and compose replies at leisure. When ready to send replies, the POP client contacts the mail server and sends the messages out from the local machine.

By shifting the burden of mail management from the central mail server to the local machine, the user can gain remarkable flexibility from e-mail. E-mail can be saved and stored in local directories, making it readily available for word processing or printing. The user also has the increased (or decreased if you are not careful) security of having the mail on his personal machine. POP also provides a mechanism for deleting mail from the central server after it has been deleted, to save on central space, or it can be left on the server to provide a backup mechanism.

The majority of mail clients available today for Windows NT support the POP protocol. Netscape, Internet Explorer, Eudora, and Pegasus, for example, are all POP mail clients. The POP protocol does require both a POP mail client and a server that has POP mail support integrated. Without it, the server cannot handle the special requests issued by POP mail clients to download mail messages or handle instructions such as deleting or archiving mail.

IMAP4 (Internet Mail Access Protocol)

The POP protocol has some distinct advantages for users using one machine. The local control of mail can be quite convenient for users, and many users find that POP mail clients are a very user-friendly way to deal with electronic mail.

But what about users who do not have such simplistic needs? What about an executive who uses a laptop on the road and has a PC at home and in the office? For those users who cannot consistently read their mail from a single machine, the limitations of POP mail become quickly apparent. Because POP downloads mail to a single machine, it does not meet the needs of users with multiple machines.

The Internet Mail Access Protocol deals with the issues of more complex mail manipulation that begin where POP mail leaves off. IMAP mail can be used in a similar fashion to POP mail; it can be used to download mail to a single workstation. IMAP, however, also has the capability to use the server as a common remotely accessible mailbox. That is, although POP downloads messages to the local machine, IMAP server support makes more use of the server's resources to manage mail to multiple clients. With an IMAP server, a user can read his mail from a PC at work, and messages on the server are *tagged* as read. Then when the user connects at home, the read messages still appear on the second client at home, but now they are listed as read messages rather than as new. IMAP supports various types of flags for message status and also supports downloading only header information to the remote client. That enables IMAP servers and clients to sync messages between multiple clients, and even enables concurrent multiple mailboxes for maximum flexibility.

Of course, IMAP is a much more complicated protocol than POP, and the software development community has been much slower to adopt it. Now that users are beginning to become much more complex in their e-mail needs, however, IMAP is becoming the standard mail protocol for complex e-mail environments. Already, both Microsoft and Netscape have announced support for IMAP in upcoming versions of their client and server software, and as they lead the way for IMAP support, other developers will surely follow.

E-Mail Server Product Options

The importance of e-mail as an Internet application can be seen in the number of e-mail servers available for the Windows NT platform. More than two dozen e-mail servers and gateways are available for Windows NT, both commercial and shareware. That is certainly more than can be covered in a single chapter. This chapter provides an overview of some of the more popular products and some step-by-step information for some NT Mail Servers. To help find the right server for you, you should look at the features offered by each server and then sign up for a trial of a few of the servers. Running a few on a trial basis can help you see what is involved in configuring and maintaining each particular server, and after you have seen their performance, you can make a better decision about which one will work best for your particular application.

In addition to the servers covered here, you can find a listing of e-mail servers available on the Microsoft Windows NT Server Resource Page (see fig. 11.1).

Figure 11.1

The Microsoft Windows NT Resource Page (`http://www.microsoft.com/ntserver/tools/default.htm`).

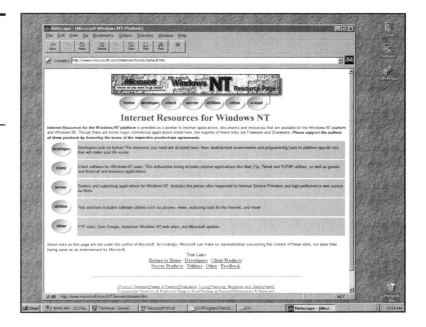

Commercial Products

The most reliable and feature-rich mail servers are commercial servers developed to serve the needs of larger e-mail sites. The servers developed by Microsoft, Netscape, and Digital are all commercial servers designed to deliver enterprisewide e-mail. Each of these servers has some unique features and drawbacks. Also, most of these servers can be evaluated for free before committing to buy. So take a look at them and see which server might suit your needs before you spend your budget.

Microsoft Exchange

The Microsoft Exchange server is the Microsoft answer to e-mail services for networks based on Windows NT. Exchange is designed from the ground up to integrate the functionality of both LAN-based e-mail and Internet e-mail into one package. Exchange is much more than just an e-mail package and can be compared to other groupware products such as Lotus Notes.

Microsoft has a web site devoted to Exchange that can be reached at `http://www.microsoft.com/exchange`. Here you can find information regarding future releases of Exchange and the press releases issued by Microsoft comparing Exchange to other similar products on the market. Certainly, Exchange goes head to head with Lotus Notes and other mail servers, such as the Netscape Mail Server.

Some of MS Exchange's features include the following:

- ❏ Universal mailbox access
- ❏ Remote access with PPP (Point-to-Point Protocol) and RAS (Remote Access Services) dial-in
- ❏ Rules-based filtering and processing of incoming mail
- ❏ Integration of Windows NT security
- ❏ Digital signatures and encryption of messages
- ❏ Group scheduling and calendar functionality
- ❏ SMTP, POP, and MIME support

These features, plus the capability to seamlessly integrate Windows NT applications such as MS Word and MS Excel, make MS Exchange a complete groupware solution, not just an e-mail server.

When you are evaluating e-mail servers for your Windows NT Internet solution, make certain to compare apples to apples. For many sites, the added functionality of Exchange is not necessary and, in fact, causes greater administrative concerns than a plain mail server. There is no doubt that if your site needs the increased functionality, Exchange can deliver, but make certain that the features are useful to you before making a decision.

Netscape Mail Server

The Netscape Mail Server is a full-featured e-mail server that makes up a portion of the Netscape Suite Spot. The server can also be purchased separately. Product information is available at `http://home.netscape.com/comprod/server_central/product/mail/index.html`.

The Netscape Mail Server adopts a similar approach to servers as the rest of the Netscape server product line. The server is quick and easy to install and configure, and is administered through a series of graphical web pages accessible from both the local server and the network (see fig. 11.2). This Administrative Server is one of the Netscape Mail Server's best features.

Figure 11.2

The Netscape Mail Server's administrative console.

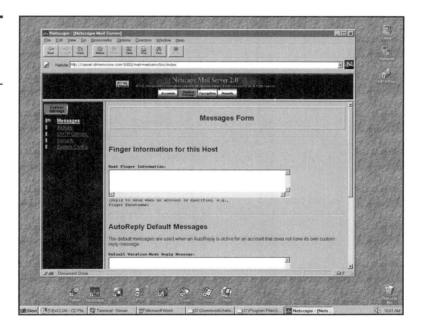

It gives novice administrators a helpful interface that can be configured with verbose explanations of each configuration option. For more seasoned administrators, the help functions can be disabled, and the interface becomes a quick graphical user interface that integrates with the other Netscape Server options. If you are already using a

Netscape server, administering the Mail Server becomes an almost trivial add-on, which for many can be a very attractive feature. Some other features of the Netscape server include the following:

❏ Secure Socket Layer 3.0 support for secure mail connections
❏ S/KEY dynamic single session password support
❏ SMTP, POP, and MIME support
❏ IMAP4 support for remote mailbox management
❏ Autoresponder functionality

These features make the Netscape Mail server a robust and easy to administer Internet mail server. The Netscape server can also be downloaded as a part of the Netscape Server Test Drive program, enabling you to install and use the server for a trial period before committing to purchase the software.

AltaVista Mail

The AltaVista Mail server is the latest server in the AltaVista product line from Digital. The AltaVista Mail server is designed to be a fully functional Internet mail server for the NT platform and is comparable to the Netscape Mail Server. The AltaVista Mail Server homepage is located at `http://www.altavista.software.digital.com/products/mail/nfintro.htm`.

Some of the AltaVista Mail server features include the following:

❏ A graphical administrative interface
❏ SMTP, POP, and MIME support
❏ IMAP4 support for remote mailbox management
❏ Autoresponder functionality
❏ Mailing list support

In terms of features and configurability, the AltaVista server is very similar to the Netscape server. The server features a graphical user interface (see fig. 11.3).

The administration of the AltaVista Mail server is quite simple and can be accomplished by using the standalone server manager, or remotely by using the server manager's web interface. The server also supports mailing lists. Creating a mailing list is quite simple: just follow the format of a Windows Help Wizard. The resulting mailing lists are quite simple, however, and lack the full features, such as moderation and closed lists, that can be found with more advanced mail list products.

Figure 11.3

The AltaVista Mail server administration program.

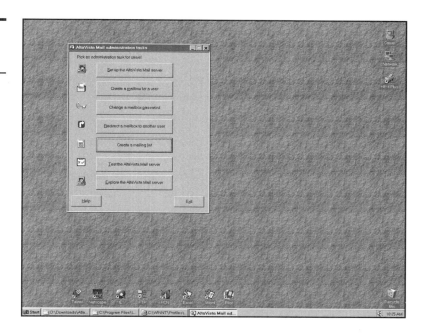

NOTE

Remember: shareware does not mean free. Shareware developers rely on the honor system, enabling you to evaluate a product before buying it. If you keep using the product, register it. Doing so will often get you an update newsletter to help you keep up with product changes and bug fixes. And most important, registering your shareware ensures that developers continue to offer products as shareware, keeping software costs down and promoting innovation outside the influence of large developers.

Shareware Products

In addition to the variety of commercial e-mail servers available, a number of shareware servers are available for Windows NT. These servers can be quite surprising when stacked up against expensive commercial products, often offering similar features at a fraction of the cost.

Despite the cost advantages, be aware that the shareware does not usually have the same offerings in terms of technical support and bug fixes available in commercial software. Good shareware can be every bit as good as commercial software. But a bad shareware application could leave you feeling like you got what you paid for—no bargain. Because the software can be less stable than commercial packages, always make certain to thoroughly test your software before committing to use a shareware package.

Following, this chapter discusses Mdaemon Server and Sendmail for NT—two common shareware programs compatible with Windows NT.

Mdaemon Server

The Mdaemon server is a shareware SMTP server for Windows NT. For the $89 price tag, the server is quite feature rich and is easy to install and use. The complete feature list for Mdaemon can be found at `http://webusers.anet-dfw.com/~arvel/mdaemon.html`.

Some of the Mdaemon mail server features include the following:

❏ SMTP, POP, and MIME support
❏ Alias support for shared inboxes
❏ Autoresponder functionality
❏ Mailing list support

Like the other Windows NT Mail Servers, Mdaemon is administered through a server administrator that has a graphical user interface. The server supports the standard Internet protocols and offers mailing list support. The primary advantage of Mdaemon over some of the commercial packages is that the mailing list support can be configured for moderated or closed lists, and members can manage their own subscriptions with mail messages to the Mdaemon server.

Sendmail for NT

In the Unix world, the default server for Unix mail is Sendmail. Unix Sendmail has quite a nefarious reputation. It can be one of the most confusing and convoluted Unix servers to install and administer. Thankfully, the Windows NT version of Sendmail does not resemble the Unix version in the slightest.

Sendmail for NT was released by MetaInfo, and more information can be found on the NT Sendmail homepage at `http://www.metainfo.com/MetaInfo/Sendmail/Homepage.htp`.

Some of the Mdaemon mail server features include the following:

❏ SMTP, POP, and MIME support
❏ Aliases fully supported
❏ Autoresponder functionality
❏ Forward file mail forwarding
❏ Graphic administrative console

In addition to being a very stable mail server, Sendmail for Windows NT has the advantage of being compatible with Sendmail for Unix. For sites converting from a Unix-based system, or for an administrator familiar with Unix Sendmail, this can be a distinct advantage. NT Sendmail still uses the same cryptic configuration files and strange conventions adopted by Sendmail. The graphical administrative interface, however, makes administration much easier (see fig. 11.4).

Figure 11.4
Sendmail for Windows NT.

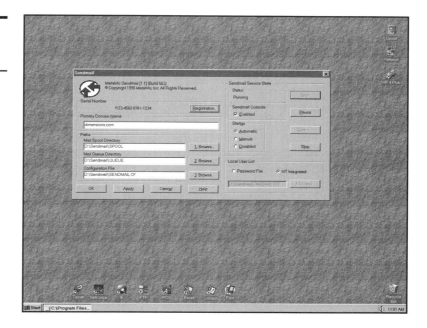

Overall, the stability and prevalence of Sendmail as a mail server makes it a good choice for ensuring compatibility. With a price tag much closer to server offerings from Netscape, however, Sendmail might not be for everyone.

Installing an E-Mail Server

As you prepare to install a server, you should consider several things. This section covers hardware issues such as disk space, and support issues, and then guides you through some actual installations.

Before You Install Your Server

A number of issues need to be addressed when establishing an e-mail server for Windows NT. Because an e-mail server is often the central, mission-critical application of an Internet server, the hardware and software used to establish mail services needs to be robust and reliable. A number of hardware issues need to be addressed before installing your server. A number of support issues also need to be addressed. This section will provide you with the information you need to make the right decision about hardware and support to help get your e-mail server going. Finally, a step-by-step guide to installing the Microsoft Exchange Server should round out the e-mail experience with a practical guide to a production e-mail server.

Hardware Issues

The software that you choose for your mail server is only one half of the equation when it comes to e-mail servers. The hardware that you choose is just as important as the software that runs on it. You certainly you do not want your Web server to crash when users are trying to use it. What happens, however, if your e-mail server goes down? Losing a mission critical application such as e-mail can be devastating to an organization that has come to rely on electronic communications internally and externally. Try walking into any business that has been using e-mail for more than a year and disabling it. The effects can be quite dramatic, with productivity grinding to a halt.

So the hardware you choose to run your Windows NT mail server on should be solid and reliable hardware. You should make certain that the components, such as video card, CD-ROM and, most important, Ethernet cards are all compatible with Windows NT. You can check your Windows NT documentation to ensure that the hardware you are purchasing will work correctly with Windows NT. Obviously, hardware requirements will vary from system to system, but at a minimum, your mail server should have the following:

- ❏ An Ethernet (network) adapter
- ❏ A large hard disk (2 GB or greater)
- ❏ Tape backup (matching your hard drive capacity)
- ❏ A minimum of 32 MB of RAM
- ❏ A uninterruptable power supply (UPS)

You should also make certain to have a solid support contract with your hardware vendor. When evaluating hardware support contracts, you want to pay attention to the details of support. Most vendors offer several levels, each tailored to a different level of response and cost. You should be able to get support ranging from overnight parts to on-site, four-hour service. If the next day is quick enough to get your server back online, there is no need to pay for on-site service. But if you need quick response, on-site service might pay for itself several times over if your mail server crashes.

Again, be certain to read the details of your support contract very carefully before signing. Many vendor's *on-site* service means that they will come to your site only after having shipped you replacement parts to try or only after exhausting all other forms of support. Arguing with the vendor over what *on-site* means while your server sits idle is not an effective support option for most people.

If possible, you should also try to make certain that replacement parts your vendor provides are new parts, not refurbished parts. Many vendors now have a policy of sending out used parts that have been refurbished rather than new replacement parts.

Disk Space

After a mail message is received by your server, the message generally resides in the spool directory until the user reads and deletes the message. Because the spool directory is shared by all the users on your system, if you have a large number of users, the spool can fill up quite rapidly with heavy mail traffic. Keeping an eye on your spool disk space can help you gauge whether the space you have allocated is sufficient. You should also occasionally use a disk utility to check the integrity of the disk that holds the spool directory. Because the spool is read and written to constantly, it often receives more physical wear than other disks on your system. Monitoring the disk space can help you make certain that the spool disk has enough space and is in good enough shape to perform its mail tasks. Just keep in mind that if your spool fills up or the disk crashes, your users will be unable to receive incoming mail. For more information on such issues, see Chapter 15, "Site Management."

Other Hardware Considerations

With a mail server, the hardware issues all come down to reliability. Your support contracts and adequate disk space planning all reflect a desire to make certain that mail is delivered in a timely manner.

Along those same lines, you should consider the reliability of power to your server. Just because the power is out at your site does not mean that power is out all over the world. When dealing with Internet mail, local issues such as power outages will not stop mail from coming into your site. Now, most sites continue to try sending your site mail for a period of several hours to account for unexplained outages. An uninterruptible power supply (UPS) can help keep mail up and reliable.

Chapter 15 deals with some of the specific issues that need to be addressed for regular upkeep and maintenance of your server. You should make yourself familiar with the hardware used in your server and its component parts. That can help you with troubleshooting and diagnostics, and prove an invaluable tool for administrators.

Support Issues

You need to address some support issues with your mail server. Fortunately, most of these issues are straightforward; if monitored regularly, mail servers can be remarkably stable. The following tasks are an important part of administering an Internet mail server:

❏ Monitoring user accounts
❏ Enforcing password policy
❏ Investigating problems reports
❏ Checking the mail queue
❏ Reviewing server logs

Consistent monitoring of these areas can keep your server up and running trouble free for months at a time. Remember that even the most experienced administrators have trouble at times. Even if you follow all these procedures, there still might be unexpected problems with your server. By staying on top of these, however, you can help eliminate smaller problems, or catch big problems while they are still developing, before they rage out of control.

Monitor User Accounts

You should maintain an accurate record of current users and remove old or unused user accounts. Inactive accounts that remain on your system can cause several problems. For one, they can still receive incoming mail, which can consume disk space on your system. They can also provide a target for hackers trying to gain access to your system. If accounts are removed after they are no longer needed, you can get rid of unused files and free up disk space, and remove accounts that could be exploited to gain unauthorized access to your server.

Enforcing Password Policy

The weakest link on any system are user passwords. Each mail user on your system should have a unique password. Using the Windows NT user accounts manager, you establish policies for the users' passwords, including the length of the password and how often the password must be changed.

You should select a password length of at least eight characters and keep a password history that does not allow users to keep using the same password over and over. This can help lock out a hacker who might have discovered an old password.

You should also force users to change passwords regularly. Be careful, however, not to force users to change passwords too often. If users are forced to change passwords more than every few months, they have a tendency to choose easy-to-remember passwords. Usually, an easy-to-remember password is an easy-to-guess password. So although you want to make certain that users are careful about passwords, do not be so overzealous that you create a hostile environment for your users.

Investigating Problems Reports

Most servers provide a mechanism for notification if delivery problems arise. Usually, the server writes an entry in a log file or sends a mail message to the administrator. If you receive notification that there has been a delivery problem, you should investigate it. Normally, you can quickly tell whether the problem was caused by your server or another server on the Internet. After you have determined that it is not your server, you ignore it. But if it reveals a problem with your server, you may have saved yourself from a larger problem down the road. Remember that system notices are your advanced warning system. They can point out a problem and give you information to solve it before it becomes too serious and users start knocking on your door.

Checking the Mail Queue

The mail queue is where outgoing mail is stored if it cannot be immediately delivered. Unless you have configured your server to queue mail first, for scheduled delivery, the queue should generally be empty or have very few entries. Certainly, you cannot control the status of other servers, so do not panic if there are entries in your mail queue. That is normal. After all, that is the point of a queue.

A few entries in the queue might indicate that network traffic is high. Several hundred messages in the queue, however, might indicate that the network is unavailable. If the entries in the queue are all addressed to a common location, this may indicate that the server they are being sent to is unavailable. By looking at how many messages are in your server's queue and where they are going, you can gain all the diagnostic information you need to troubleshoot a problem without compromising your user's privacy.

Reviewing Server Logs

The most important tool at your disposal for any server, including mail servers, are the server's log files. The type and extent of log files kept by your server vary from package to package, but all NT servers support some form of log file. You can also check the Windows NT Event and Services Logs to see whether problems with your server and Windows NT exist.

Taking a few minutes out of each day to glance over log entries can help point you to problems and misconfigurations with your server. But more important, you should keep these logs archived for administrative purposes. The information contained in your server's log files cannot only help you troubleshoot your server, they can also help you track down forged mail or serve as a record that a user sent an illegal message. These logs are the complete record of activity of your server, and as such, they should be maintained regularly. You should rotate logs at least weekly, and if possible daily, to make them easier to search. You should also back up the log files offline. That way you have an offline backup that can be compared to online versions to detect possible tampering with the log files.

Although all this might seem a bit extreme, the server logs are your single best resource for troubleshooting and security. They, therefore, need to be kept in good shape, and you need to be certain that the information contained in the log files is accurate.

Step-by-Step Installation Guide: MERCUR

MERCUR is a robust mail server designed to run under Windows NT as a System Service. The server is easy to install and maintain and has a friendly graphical user interface. MERCUR supports both SMTP and POP3, and also has very functional mailing list support, which makes it a very attractive mail server for Windows NT. The MERCUR server is flexibly priced for small organizations, ranging from $120 to $640 dollars for the complete server package. Because of its full protocol support, inexpensive price tag, and ease of use, the MERCUR server offers a complete NT e-mail solution.

As with many Internet related servers, you can download and try out MERCUR before committing to buy it. Before you need to make a monetary investment, try the server out and make sure it is right for you. In the following sections, you will be given a step-by-step tutorial for the MERCUR server. Before you know it, e-mail will be up and running on your NT Server.

1. Download the ZIP file from the MERCUR Web site that contains the installation program for the MERCUR server. This will be a ZIP file, which should be extracted into a temporary directory for the installation.

2. After you extract the files for the MERCUR server, you can start the installation by clicking on Setup.exe, which launches the MERCUR installation program (see fig. 11.5).

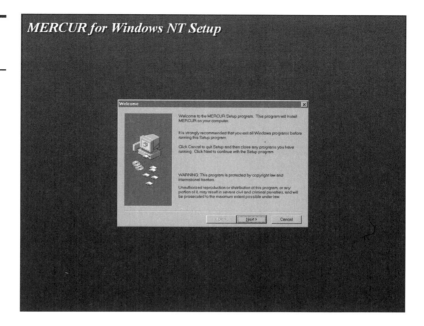

3. First the setup program confirms that you want to install the MERCUR mail server, and waits for your confirmation before proceeding. Next it prompts you to specify the directory where MERCUR is to be installed. You can use the default directory or specify your own directory if you already have a folder where you would like the server installed. After entering the directory where you want MERCUR installed, proceed.

4. Next the installation program asks whether you want to install the complete mail server or just the Administrative tools. Installing the complete mail server installs the server components and the tools to manage the server. If you already had the server running on another machine, you could choose to install only the Administrative tools, which would enable you to administer another MERCUR server remotely. This can be handy for installing the mail server on a central resource while administering the server from your local workstation. The MERCUR server supports remote administration like many servers, including Exchange, Netscape, and AltaVista. Assuming that this is your first installation, choose to install the complete server and proceed.

5. After you choose the package to install, you receive a prompt to Enter the Domain Name of Your Server. This is usually determined for you by checking the NT Configuration; it is then entered in the form of *something.com*. If the default value is correct, you can proceed. Otherwise, double-check with your network administrator and then enter the correct domain name.

6. The installer then prompts you for the machine name, which it should also be able to determine from your Windows NT Configuration. If not, enter the name here.

7. Finally, the installation program asks you to Specify the IP Number for Your Domain's Name Server. The Name Server is the machine used to resolve host names into IP Numbers so that the mail server can find the correct hosts to send mail to remote machines. If this number is not correct, your mail server might not be able to deliver any outgoing mail. The default should be determined from your NT Setup. Be certain, however, to double-check the value with your network administrator; an incorrect number prevents your mail server from functioning properly.

WARNING

The default port numbers chosen for your services are based on standards used in the Internet community. The standard mail port is 25, and the standard POP port is 110. Although these port values can be changed, doing so may cause your server to refuse connections for incoming mail, and users will not be able to use standard POP Clients to connect for their mail. POP Clients can be configured to look for different ports; so if you choose to alter these port assignments in any way, be aware that you need to reconfigure every mail client using your server individually.

Now the installation program completes extracting the necessary files and installing them on your hard drive. The icons for the MERCUR Configuration program are added to your Start menu, and you are now ready to run the MERCUR server.

Configuring the Server

Launching the MERCUR Configuration program reveals a control panel (see fig. 11.6). This control panel enables you to change all the administrative options of your mail server.

From the System panel, you can determine the status of your server to determine which service (SMTP or POP) is currently running. You can also alter the entered values for your server's Domain, Hostname, and Nameserver IP. The Administrator panel enables you to specify which user on the NT Server is to be used as the administrator of the mail server. This user receives bounced messages and error reports.

The Connection control panel enables you to specify the type of connection your server has to the Internet, and enables you to configure the port numbers that clients will use to contact your server.

The *Users* control panel enables the administrator to define a number of user parameters for the MERCUR server (see fig. 11.7).

Figure 11.6

The MERCUR Configuration program.

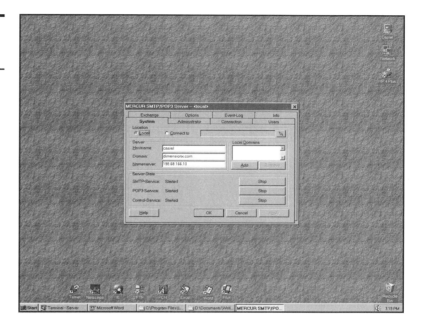

The options shown in figure 11.7 enable you to create new mail user accounts (although the default is to use the NT account manager) to create new mailing lists and to establish Autoresponder addresses. You can also establish remote POP accounts, Server Executables (such as the Password program, used to change users POP passwords), or static routes (which are used to channel mail from one location to another).

The Event Log panel enables the administrator to configure how the server logs errors and notices. Here you can specify the location of log files, view the log files, and set the time limits for how long log entries are kept. As a rule, it is a good idea to keep log entries for several days to one week. For extremely high volume servers, however, the time limit might need to be shortened to free up file space.

The Options control panel enables you to define the protocols used by the mail server to send mail and to specify how it should deal with mail that cannot be delivered. It is always a good idea to have the Mail Server administrators copied on any notices of undeliverable mail so they can make certain that the problem exists with the remote site, not the local server. Usually this type of problem exists because of a bad user name, because the user no longer exists, or because of a typo. If the administrator is aware of the problem though, he can forward the mail to the appropriate user or bounce the message back to the sender, explaining that the user no longer has an account on the system.

Finally, the Exchange control panel enables the configuration of the mail spool and how messages are forwarded (see fig. 11.8).

Figure 11.7
The MERCUR Users Configuration control panel.

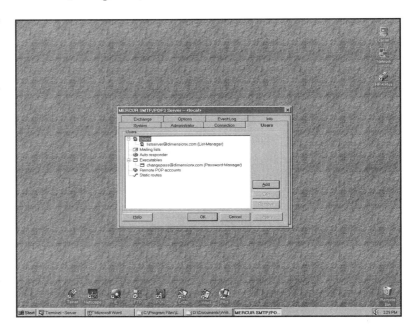

The first option, Forward, determines whether the server will use DNS to look up the forwarding address provided by a user or whether the message will be passed off to a central host designed to route mail at your organization.

The Update Outbasket option enables you to specify when mail messages will be forwarded. If immediately is chosen, mail messages are not held on the server at all. Otherwise, you can specify a time interval so that mail is delivered every x minutes, so the load on your mail server is more balanced.

Finally, the Undeliverable Mail option enables you to set the spool time or the amount of time that must pass before an undeliverable error is generated. Usually, messages are spooled for a few days, during which time the mail server periodically tries to resend the message. If the mail still cannot be delivered after the set amount of time, the message is returned to the sender, and if the option is set, information about the bounce is sent to the mail administrator.

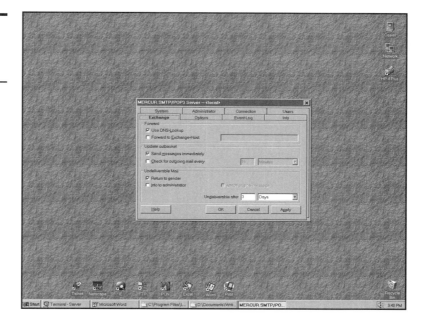

Troubleshooting

The best way to troubleshoot your mail server is to use it. After you have the server configured and everything is ready to go, try sending mail to as many people as possible, including yourself. If you begin to notice that none of the messages are going through, you have a problem.

If a problem does arise, the first place you should look is the error log files. There you can find the details about what is going wrong and try to fix it. The log files are the single best resource for troubleshooting. Also, remember that Windows NT keeps log files for services as well. If you are not finding the answers in your mail server logs, try the NT logs. The problem might be with the mail server as a whole, not just the configuration.

The most important thing to remember is to be patient. Most errors are the result of a typo in the message or in your configuration. It might take you a while to track it down, but in the end you will find it and correct the situation. Be certain to test your server extensively before making it generally available, however. It is much easier to be patient when troubleshooting an experimental server. After the server is in production and users are depending on it for mail, staying patient can be the hardest part of troubleshooting.

After you establish mail services, you will find mail becoming an integral part of your organization. As your mail needs grow, you might find yourself wanting to establish mailing lists for internal or external uses. The next section examines some of the NT Mail Server options available to users with mailing list needs.

NT Servers with List Support

To establish mailing list services with your NT Mail Server, you need to choose a mail server that enables mailing list support. When evaluating servers that claim support for Internet mailing lists, you should be careful to find out which features that means. Some servers do not enable users to subscribe and unsubscribe themselves from lists, meaning that the mail server administrator must do all the work in maintaining the list. Generally, you should go with a mail server that automates the subscription process. If users can add and remove themselves from lists they are interested in, it can cut administrative time dramatically and provide the users with more flexibility for using your list resources as well.

MailSite

The MailSite server for Windows NT (`http://www.rockliffe.com/mailsite.htm`) is a full-featured mail server that offers robust mailing list support. Some of the standard features of the server include the following:

- ❏ Full SMTP and POP3 compatibility
- ❏ Alias support
- ❏ Forwarding and Autoresponder support
- ❏ Full mailing list support
- ❏ Graphical administrative interface

Mail site enables the configuration of mailing lists through a simple administrative console (see fig. 11.9).

Figure 11.9

The MailSite Mailing list configuration interface.

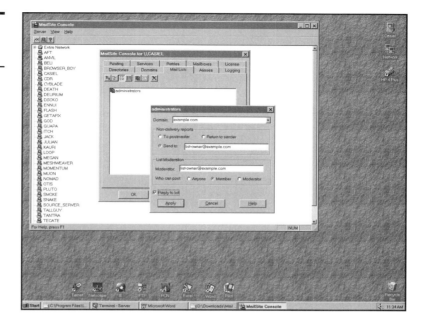

This interface enables you to create a mailing list and to choose a moderator if you want a moderated list. Subscription status is also controlled through this interface, with users being allowed to send *join* and *leave* requests to an address in the form of *listname-request@whatever.com*. Unless the list is moderated, this simplifies user management, enabling members to add or remove themselves from lists of interest. Error reports are also sent to a specified list owner, so that the owner will be notified if the list is not functioning properly, or for access purposes if the list is to be moderated.

These features make all the difference when choosing a mail server that supports mailing lists. Without features such as user subscription requests, mailing list management can grow out of control, eating up valuable administrative time. By incorporating these features, the MailSite server adds a high degree of flexibility to a Windows NT mail server.

MERCUR

The MERCUR Mail Server for Windows NT (http://www.atrium.de/mercur/mcr_eng.htm) is a well-rounded mail solution, providing SMTP and POP support, as well as strong mailing list support. The server features

❏ Full SMTP and POP3 compatibility

❏ Alias support

- Forwarding and Autoresponder support
- Full mailing list support
- Graphical administrative interface

MERCUR can also be extended by server executables. The interface for establishing mailing lists is straightforward (see fig. 11.10).

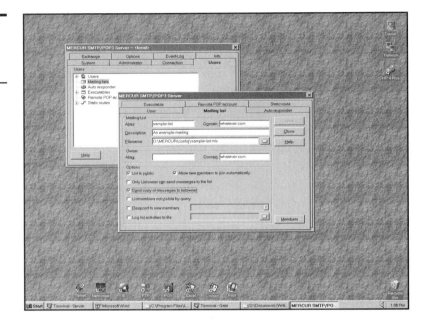

Figure 11.10

The MERCUR Mail Server mailing list configuration interface.

The mailing lists created by MERCUR can be public, enabling members to subscribe and unsubscribe themselves, or private, limiting subscription control to the list owner. Messages sent to the list can also be restricted to the list owner, creating a moderated list. The services supported by MERCUR rival that of other Internet mail list servers such as Majordomo or ListServ, including the capability to have an introductory file mailed out to new list members and a list activity log to keep track of the list's usage.

Overall, the MERCUR server offers a very robust combination of tools and ease of use, which make it a very powerful e-mail tool for Windows NT.

Establishing List Services

Establishing list services is as simple as selecting a mail server that supports mailing lists and then configuring it correctly. All the e-mail servers listed in this chapter feature graphical, easy to configure user interfaces. Setting up a mailing list with these servers is as easy as entering the correct list information.

Now, take a look at the following example of establishing a mailing list by using MERCUR. Some servers out there will not offer all the functionality of the MERCUR server, but this step-by-step guide should help give you an understanding of what each mailing list parameter means; that information is generally applicable across all the mail servers for Windows NT. After you have an understanding of how lists are created and what's involved, switching from one server to another is almost trivial.

Resource Requirements

The resource requirements for mailing lists should not need to be anything above the requirements for your mailing server. Remember that because traffic from the lists is going out to other server, you should not need to worry about excessive disk space usage.

If you are hosting an extremely large list (say 500 or more users), however, the list traffic can be quite considerable. If a majority of those users are local to your server, you might want to add disk space. More important, however, you want to make certain that the traffic generated by the list is not causing a bottleneck at your Internet connection. Transferring large volumes of e-mail can consume bandwidth, and you should monitor network traffic to get an idea of how large mailing lists at your site impact your bandwidth.

Keeping those facts in mind, the normal issues of data and power backups apply the same as they would to any Internet server. The same holds true for administrative access and policy issues. Mailing lists can be a valuable resource to have on your system, and they cost very little in terms of administration.

Configuring Your Mail Servers

As mentioned previously, configuring a mail server for mailing lists is a very straight-forward process. Although it would be impossible to cover the step-by-step configuration of all NT mail servers, here is an example using the MERCUR mail server. The steps followed in configuring the MERCUR server should give you an idea about how the process would proceed using any NT Mail Server. Some slight differences might occur, but overall, the same process is followed for all NT servers.

First, after downloading the MERCUR server from the MERCUR site, you need to run the Setup program. The Setup program for the MERCUR mail server steps you through the initial configuration of the mail server and prompts you for any information needed, such as the Domain Name of your server. After the package is installed, you are ready to configure the Mailing List options by running the MERCUR Configuration program installed in your Start menu.

Launching the MERCUR Configuration program should start the MERCUR server and display an administrative console (see fig. 11.11).

Figure 11.11
The MERCUR mail server administrative console.

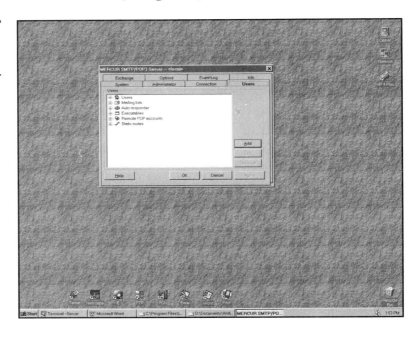

From here, you select the Users tab and then choose Mailing Lists from the displayed options. To configure a new mailing list, click the Add button and then choose Mailing List from the pull-down menu. A new window, containing the mailing list information opens, and you are ready to configure your mailing list.

Next, fill in the following information in the Mailing-List section:

- ❏ **Alias.** The alias is the same as the List Name. If you want to create a mailing list called people@list.com, for example, enter names here.

- ❏ **Domain.** The domain is the domain of your server machine because it will be the host of the list. In this example, it is *list.com*.

- ❏ **Description.** The Description is a description of your list that helps keep track of a list's topic.

- ❏ **Filename.** This is the name of the file where members of the list are stored. It will be automatically entered for you, unless you want to use a file that already contains the membership for your list.

Under the Owner section, you need to select a mail alias for the list's owner. This can be the user name of the list owner—for example, *owner*—if the address is *owner@list.com*. The domain is the domain where the user has mail delivered.

In the Options section, you need to specify the following:

- ❏ **List is Public.** If this option is checked, anyone will be given access to the lists membership and messages upon request to the mail server.

- ❏ **Allow New Members to Join Automatically.** If the list is public and this option is checked, the list has an open subscription policy, enabling members to add and remove themselves from the list.

- ❏ **Only listowner can send messages to list.** If this option is checked, the list is in effect a moderated list. If a member tries to send a message to the list, it is forwarded to the list owner, who then may send it out to the list.

- ❏ **Send copy of messages to listowner.** This option includes the list owner as a member of the mail list.

- ❏ **List members not visible by query.** This prevents members of the list from seeing which other members are subscribed to the list. For moderated lists, this option might be invoked to ensure privacy.

- ❏ **Respond to new members.** This option enables you to specify a Welcome file that will be sent out to any new members of the list, regardless of whether they subscribe themselves or are added by the list owner.

- ❏ **Log list activities to file.** The option enables you to create a log file separate from the normal mail server logs where list activity is logged. Keeping a log file can be a good troubleshooting resource for large lists, but make certain to keep an eye on log files and rotate them on a regular basis.

That's it! After this configuration information has been entered, you can click on Add, and your list will be created. After the list is created, members can start sending messages and enjoying the increased communication that mailing lists can provide.

Managing Lists and Troubleshooting

Before a list is created, you should decide which format you want the list to take. Will it be open or closed? Does the nature of the list require moderation? For most lists, an open subscription policy suffices. Most lists also do not need to be moderated. If the list is geared toward broadcasting information such as a *Notices* list, however, you might consider making the list moderated.

After you first create your list, you can add the founding members of the list by hand. That way, you do not need to have the initial members subscribe. After the list is established, an open list takes care of user management by itself. A closed list needs to be monitored, however. As the owner of the list, you should receive all messages to the list and you should keep an eye out for subscribe or unsubscribe commands. Remember that if your list is closed or moderated, the users of the list are counting on you to keep up with administrative tasks. Because of this, you should keep a close eye on the messages sent to your list and be aware of how users are using the list as a resource. You might find that a closed list needs to be opened to stimulate more interaction, or you might find that an open list needs to be moderated to cut down on junk messages. How each list is configured depends on the list's objectives. Regardless, as the list's administrator, you should keep on top of list management.

Troubleshooting Lists

Most problems with mailing lists are actually problems with the mail server itself. Perhaps the mail server is malfunctioning, for example, and messages are not being forwarded out to list members. Or perhaps a list member's mail is currently down; messages sent to that user from the list bounce back. If your list has a substantial number of members, this type of problem is unavoidable.

The best way to troubleshoot problems with your list is to keep an eye on the list traffic and to watch for error messages sent by the list server to the list owner. If your mail server is having problems with a list or a list member's address, it informs you. From there you can investigate the list logs (if your server supports list logs) or the log files for your e-mail server. Both of these log files should provide you with information regarding errors generated by traffic from your mailing lists. With that information in hand, you can determine the nature of the problem and take corrective action.

Mail Server Policy Issues

Electronic mail raises a whole spectrum of important policy issues that need to be addressed by any individual or organization providing electronic mail services. Electronic communications and e-mail are still new forms of communications, and as such, many issues such as privacy and usage rights have not yet been determined.

If e-mail is offered by a company, it is natural to assume that the e-mail is meant for business use, not personal. Most businesses frown on personal phone calls, for example. Many businesses, however, do not explicitly forbid them. Many companies that do extensive work on the telephone also have policies that say their employees phone calls may be monitored for the sake of quality assurance. So what about e-mail? If e-mail is an integral part of business, how should companies treat e-mail? Undoubtedly, any business that offers e-mail has the right to set any policy for e-mail, including monitoring e-mail. The company owns the server, computer, and network resources used for e-mail, and foots the bill. If surveyed informally, however, most users indicate that they view e-mail similarly to postal mail, and that it is private communications. If a company does establish a policy of monitoring e-mail, therefore, the company does so at the risk of alienating the user community and adversely affecting employee morale.

The most important thing you can do to help address these issues is to have a comprehensive policy regarding e-mail use. With a written policy in place, users should be well aware of what to expect. The best approach to this policy should be to clearly outline the rights of the organization to monitor e-mail and to comply with law enforcement requests for information. This clearly establishes the right to monitor e-mail and to turn messages over to the police in a criminal investigation. It would be wise, however, to have the second part of the document clearly support a policy of user privacy.

Why go on the record to support privacy, creating this seeming contradiction? For two reasons: first, by clearly establishing the right to monitor e-mail, you can avoid confusion and resentment in a unique situation, such as a user violating the law. Second, by showing users that you do respect their right to privacy and will not invoke the policy of monitoring e-mail unless forced to do so by a legal or ethical situation, user morale should not be adversely affected.

The end goal of your policy should be to assure users that their rights will be reasonably protected, but that in an instance where the organization is confronted with an ethical issue or placed in jeopardy by e-mail, the privacy of e-mail might be compromised. This should be a compromise that both an employer and employee should agree looks after the best interests of all involved. Those companies that do not lend some measure of trust to their employees probably have bigger problems than just e-mail abuse, and those employees truly concerned about absolute privacy can purchase a personal e-mail account outside of the company's control.

Keep in mind that users are not the only concern involved with electronic mail. The administrators charged with keeping e-mail in working order are basically entrusted with a very large responsibility. They have the power to view anyone's e-mail (private or business related), including valuable information such as financial data or trade secrets. They have the ability to create mail to and from any user. And in the hands of the wrong person, these almost god-like powers could be seriously abused. For this reason, administrators should also be aware of your policies and held accountable for all of them. Some additional policies might be instituted specifically for administrators, such as forbidding administrative access to user mailboxes without prior written permission, even in the process of troubleshooting. This protects users from rogue administrators and helps protect administrators from false accusations as well. The powers and responsibilities of administrators necessitate some very explicit policies, with very explicit repercussions for policy violations.

Fortunately, administrators tend to be a very professional lot. Most administrators would find the idea of violating user privacy morally reprehensible. If a violation does occur and an administrator is given only a slap on the wrist, the effective message to users is that your organization does not take privacy seriously. Therefore, after guidelines for ethical usage are established, they must be enforced regardless of how extreme they might seem.

Summary

The options available for e-mail and Windows NT are quite staggering. It can seem quite intimidating at first, given the wide range of e-mail servers available for Windows NT. Taking the time to identify your specific e-mail needs, however, can narrow the field considerably. After you have determined your goals, you can find the e-mail server suited to you and not struggle with managing features you do not need or want.

Adding Internet e-mail to your Windows NT Internet server provides you with access to the Internet's most basic service, but also one of its most important. But as you have learned in this chapter, e-mail servers do not have to be complex to administer to add great functionality to your Internet site.

12

Getting News Services Up and Running: NNTP and INS

nternet newsgroups have become a mainstream transport for information exchange. Individuals can participate in discussions and share views with others interested in the same topics. Many companies and organizations have discovered that newsgroups can be used for various applications—communications and technical support, for example.

In the past, Internet news was implemented almost exclusively on Unix systems. Experienced programmers and veteran news administrators considered the daily tasks of news administration and maintenance to be extremely complex. Implementation of the Internet standard, *Network News Transport Protocol* (NNTP), needed to be streamlined. Many NNTP implementations could not host thousands of connections, because too many system resources were required for each client connection. In addition, Internet news traffic loads have substantially increased.

Microsoft saw the need for a more powerful implementation of NNTP. As a result, the *Microsoft Internet News Server* (INS), was developed. INS can handle high traffic loads, host thousands of connections, and share setup, administration, and operation tools with other Microsoft Internet Services.

This chapter guides you through the steps necessary to install and configure the Internet News Service, and to get the service up and running. The following are discussed:

❑ Features of Internet News Server
❑ Installation guidelines
❑ Installing Internet News Service
❑ Understanding the Internet Service Manager
❑ Configuring Internet News Service

Features of Internet News Server

The Internet News Server is a commercial grade NNTP server, which is designed to accommodate high traffic loads, associated with increased Internet news volume. INS enables commercial Web sites and Internet Service Providers (ISPs) to operate public and private newsgroups and distributed bulletin board systems (BBSs). INS provides a scalable distributed replication service for BBSs, which keeps up with over one gigabyte of Usenet news per day, and has the capability to replicate that news to multiple servers.

Internet News Service is a component of the Microsoft Commercial Internet System, formerly code named project Normandy. Microsoft Commercial Internet System is a comprehensive suite of Internet servers that provides an integrated set of services to Internet service providers, companies and organizations integrating external Web sites, and network operators. Trial downloads of individual Microsoft Commercial Internet System components, which are currently under development, are available from the Microsoft Web site. The final release of Microsoft Commercial Internet System is expected to be available in the first quarter of 1997, as individual product members of the Microsoft BackOffice family.

The following servers are included in Microsoft Commercial Internet System:

❑ Commercial Internet Mail Server
❑ Commercial Internet News Server
❑ Conference Server, which includes the Internet Chat Server and Internet Locator Server

- ❏ Merchant Server
- ❏ Information Retrieval Server
- ❏ Content Replication System
- ❏ Personalization System
- ❏ Membership System, which includes the Internet Address Book Server

INS is designed to integrate directly into the Microsoft Internet Information Server (IIS), and is primarily administered through the Internet Service Manager. The Internet Service Manager is a graphical user interface program used for configuration and administration of IIS component services. Operation of the Internet Service Manager is discussed later in this chapter in the section entitled "Understanding the Internet Service Manager" (see fig. 12.1).

Figure 12.1

Internet Service Manager administration tool.

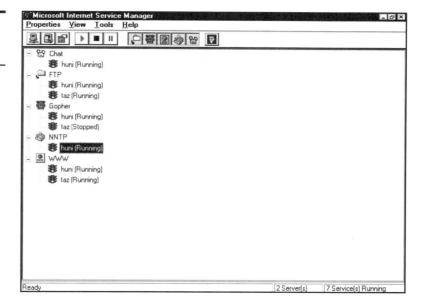

A newly installed INS server can be installed in a relatively short period of time. Configuration and administration can be performed remotely, using the Internet Service Manager.

INS Architecture

INS server installations can be deployed on a small or large scale. A small scale installation involves a single NT Internet server, where incoming and outgoing feeds as well as users all connect to the single server. A large scale implementation incorporates multiple NT Internet servers running the Internet News Service, where the master server is responsible for incoming and outgoing feeds and replication to multiple slave servers. INS can be set up as either a master or slave to any NNTP news server.

A large scale deployment of INS has three major groups of components. The three components are master NNTP news server, slave NNTP news servers, and NNTP clients.

❏ **Master NNTP News Server.** Master servers are used to service incoming and outgoing peer and slave news feeds, as well as to generate message identifiers. Master servers host the news content and propagate the content to slave NNTP News servers.

❏ **Slave NNTP News Servers.** Multiple slave NNTP news servers can be deployed to increase service speed and reliability by enabling client requests to be serviced by any slave server through the use of round-robin Domain Name Service (DNS) resolution.

❏ **NNTP Clients.** Any client for reading and posting news, which supports NNTP or the security-enabled extension of NNTP (NNTPS), can access the slave servers. NNTP clients are widely available for Microsoft Windows 95, Windows NT, Windows 3.x, Macintosh, OS/2, and Unix operating systems. Figure 12.2 shows the Microsoft Internet News client.

Figure 12.2
Microsoft Internet News client.

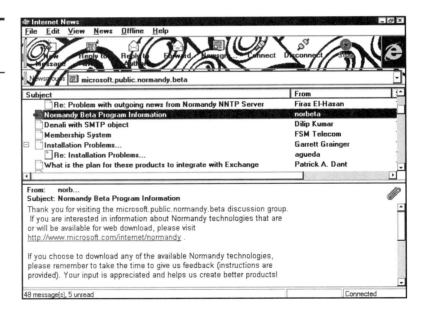

Site Construction

Associated Products

The operation of an INS server requires that IIS be loaded, and that it is running on the Internet server. For added functionality, additional products enhance the operation of an INS server. The following is a list and brief overview of associated products:

❏ **Microsoft IIS.** The Internet Information Server acts as the host for all installed Internet services components. INS is an installable IIS server component, as well as WWW, FTP, and Gopher publishing service. All installed Internet Server component services share a common configuration interface, and are administered by use of the Internet Service Manager.

❏ **NNTP Service.** The NNTP service is the core of an Internet News Server. The NNTP service runs on a Windows NT Internet server, as a component service of IIS.

❏ **Microsoft Commercial Membership System.** The Commercial Membership system is used to expand authentication capabilities. As an option, INS can use the Commercial Membership System to authenticate users connecting to the News server.

❏ **Microsoft Index Server.** The Microsoft Index server can be used to index news articles and support content searches. If you use the Index Server with INS, you need to have the World Wide Web Publishing (WWW) service loaded. Users can connect to the WWW server, and can initiate a search of the newsgroups through a Web page. The Index Server searches the newstree, and displays the results on the browser.

❏ **Microsoft Commercial Content Replication Server.** The Commercial Content Replication Server (CRS) can be used to replicate Windows NT access control lists (ACLs). ACLs are security information attached to directories and files. INS by itself will not replicate this security information between master and slave NNTP servers. In addition to master to slave replication, CRS can be configured to replicate slave to slave.

INS Software Components

INS software components can be divided into five component groups which comprise the service, platform, communications, data, and security aspects of the product. The following is a list describing each component group:

❏ **NNTP Service.** The NNTP service is the Windows NT Internet server component that provides news server and news client functions.

❏ **Internet Information Server.** IIS provides the server platform for the Internet News Server, and handles the connections of the news clients.

- ❏ **Communications Ports.** News clients communicate with the NNTP service through the Windows NT socket, or port 119. If Secured Socket Layer (SSL) encryption is enabled, communication uses port 563.
- ❏ **News Articles and Data Structures.** INS stores individual news articles on an NTFS volume, and also stores descriptive data about articles, newsgroups, and history in a set of six internal data structure files.
- ❏ **Security Components.** INS security can be implemented with multiple authentication protocols, including clear text, anonymous, and Windows NTLM. A Security Support Provider Interface (SSPI) provides the interface between the NNTP service and the NTLM protocol.

Installation Guidelines

The Internet Information Server must be installed prior to installing the Internet News Service. When preparing to install the Internet News Service, you should have an overall understanding of the possible methods of installing the Internet Information Server, as well as the common terms used when discussing the operation and configuration of the Internet Information Server. You must also understand the prerequisites necessary to install the Internet Information Server. For directions on how to do so, please see Chapter 9, "Getting Web Services Up and Running."

Installing the Internet News Service

Installation of the Internet News Service must be performed after the Internet Information Server has been installed. It is recommended that you install the World Wide Web (WWW) Publishing Service at the time IIS is installed. If you install and implement a Web site, for example, Web pages can be a great place to introduce your newsgroups, and to provide links to specific newsgroups.

The WWW Publishing Service is one of three component services that may be selected during the Internet Information Server installation. The other services are the FTP Publishing Service and the Gopher Publishing Service. The Internet Information Server installation Setup program enables you to selectively install the individual component services. To install the WWW Publishing Service, therefore, the general procedure to install the Internet Information Server is followed. Chapter 9 discusses installation of Internet Information Server and the Web publishing service.

INS Installation Prerequisites

To install the INS, you must first be logged on as a user who is a member of the Administrators group. You can verify if you are a member of the Administrators group by looking in the User Manager for Domains, located within the Administrative Tools folder.

In addition, you should confirm the following:

❏ IIS is loaded and functioning properly. The installation procedure used to load IIS is discussed in the section of this chapter entitled "IIS Installation Procedure."

❏ NT Server is installed on an NTFS partition, and your Server is functioning normally. For security reasons, your INS Service must be installed on an NTFS partition.

❏ TCP/IP Protocol is loaded and has been properly configured.

❏ Name Resolution has been set up through the use of either DNS, WINS Server, HOSTS file, or an LMHOSTS file.

❏ Security procedures have been reviewed, and are in order. Do not allow unauthorized access to your NT Server from the Internet. Ensure that all users defined in the User Manager have unique passwords. See Chapter 14, "Security Practices" for detailed security information.

INS Installation Procedure

Installation of the Internet News Service is a relatively simple procedure. The first step toward installation is to obtain a copy of INS. At the time of this writing, INS is in public beta testing, and may be obtained directly from the Microsoft Web site (www.microsoft.com). INS is distributed as a single executable file; upon execution, it starts the setup installation program. After the beta testing phases of the Microsoft Commercial Internet System suite of Internet servers are finished, Microsoft Commercial Internet System will be released as a commercial software product.

The following installation procedure is based on the assumption that you have obtained a copy of the Internet News Service, and are prepared to perform the installation.

To install INS, follow these steps:

1. Run the INS distribution executable file. Locate the file in the Explorer or File Manager, and double-click on the file name. A dialog box appears (see fig. 12.3). Click on Yes to continue.

Figure 12.3

The Proceed dialog box.

2. The Welcome to the Microsoft Internet News Server setup window appears (see fig. 12.4). Click Next to continue.

Figure 12.4

The Welcome to Setup window.

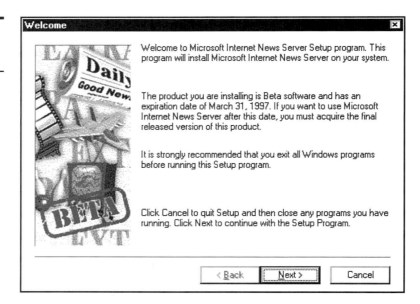

3. The software license agreement screen appears. Read the license agreement, and then click on Yes to accept the terms of the license and continue (see fig. 12.5).

4. You are now asked to enter registration information. Enter your name and company name (see fig. 12.6). Click Next to continue.

5. The Select Components window appears. Check all items on the list to perform a complete installation (see fig. 12.7). Click Next to continue.

Figure 12.5

The License Agreement screen.

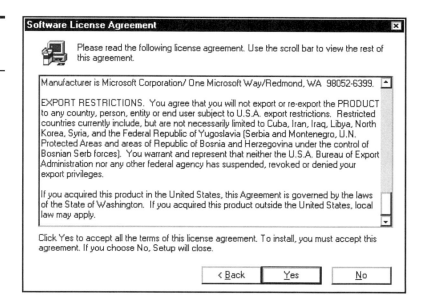

Figure 12.6

The Registration window.

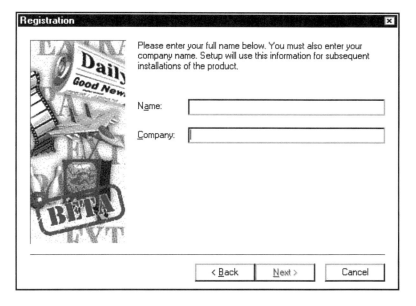

6. If Internet Services are currently running, setup must stop the service before it can continue (see fig. 12.8). Click Yes to stop the running services.

Figure 12.7

The Select Components window.

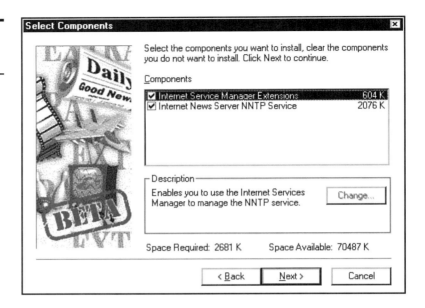

Figure 12.8

The Running Services window.

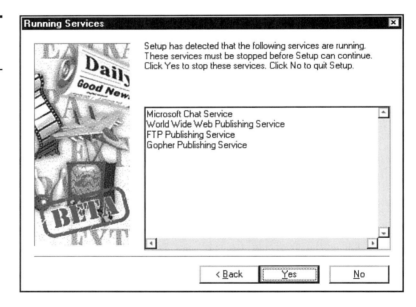

7. You now have the option to choose the NNTP root directory path (see fig. 12.9). Accept the default, or change the directory. If you plan to host large newsgroups, make certain that this directory is on a large disk partition. Click Next to continue.

Figure 12.9

Choose the NNTP Root Directory window.

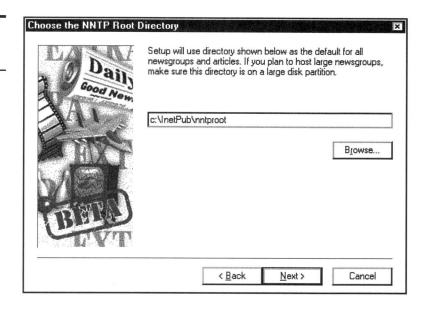

8. You now have the option to choose the location for the NNTP database files (see fig. 12.10). The directory must be different than the NNTP root directory. If you plan to host large newsgroups, make certain that this directory is on a large disk partition. Accept the default, or change the path. Click Next to continue.

Figure 12.10

Choose the NNTP Database Files Directory window.

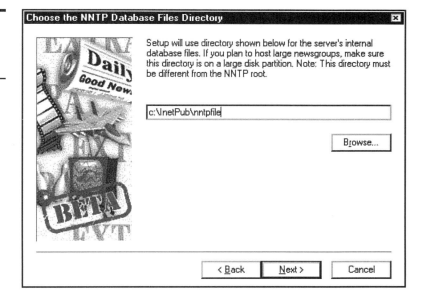

9. You are now asked to select a folder. Choose an existing folder, or enter a new folder name (see fig. 12.11). Click Next to continue.

Figure 12.11
Folder Selection window.

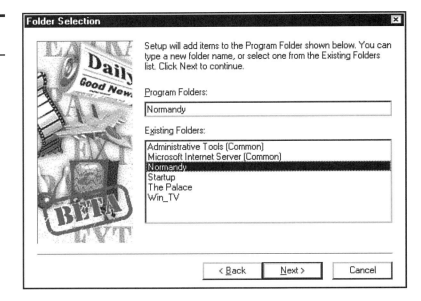

10. The Confirm Setup Information window appears. Setup uses the listed settings to complete the installation. Review the current settings (see fig. 12.12). If they are correct, click Next to continue. If they are incorrect, you have the opportunity to go back to reach the settings you want to change. To go back, click the Back button.

11. Setup is now complete. It is recommended that you read the Readme File (see fig. 12.13). To read the Readme File, check the box. The NNTP service can also be started. To start the NNTP service, check the box. Click Finish to continue.

Upon completion of INS setup, in order to configure INS, you need to understand the Internet Service Manager. The following section discusses the operation of the Internet Service Manager.

Figure 12.12

The Confirm Setup Information window.

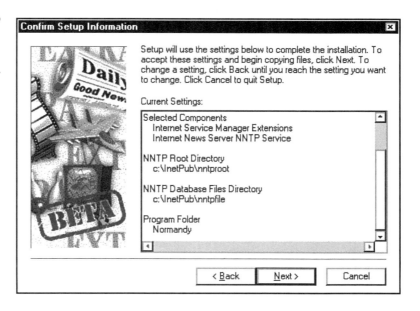

Confirm Setup Information

Setup will use the settings below to complete the installation. To accept these settings and begin copying files, click Next. To change a setting, click Back until you reach the setting you want to change. Click Cancel to quit Setup.

Current Settings:

Selected Components
   Internet Service Manager Extensions
   Internet News Server NNTP Service

NNTP Root Directory
   c:\InetPub\nntproot

NNTP Database Files Directory
   c:\InetPub\nntpfile

Program Folder
   Normandy

< Back   Next >   Cancel

Figure 12.13

The Setup Complete window.

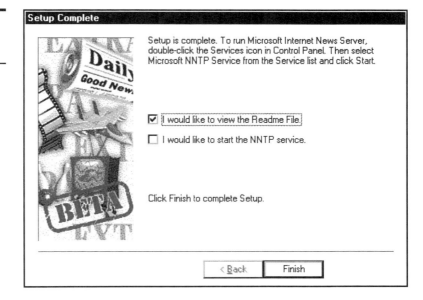

Setup Complete

Setup is complete. To run Microsoft Internet News Server, double-click the Services icon in Control Panel. Then select Microsoft NNTP Service from the Service list and click Start.

☑ I would like to view the Readme File.

☐ I would like to start the NNTP service.

Click Finish to complete Setup.

< Back   Finish

Understanding the Internet Service Manager

In the past, the most common complaints related to managing and maintaining a News server have been the difficulty involved, or the lack of a friendly configuration program. The primary program used to configure the Internet News Service is the Internet Service Manager. This program is very well designed, and is easy to use. After you have completed and tested your installation, you can use the Internet Service Manager and other programs to configure advanced features of the Internet News Service.

Within the Internet Service Manager, you can configure advanced features of the INS Service as well as other Internet services, such as WWW Publishing Service and the FTP Publishing Service. This chapter also discusses configuration of the INS Service. Chapter 9 discusses configuration issues related to the WWW Publishing. Chapter 10, "Getting FTP Services Up and Running," discusses configuration of the FTP Publishing Service.

The following is a partial list of what you can configure within the Internet Service Manager:

- ❏ Default settings
- ❏ Home directories
- ❏ Access permissions
- ❏ Bandwidth usage
- ❏ Logon security
- ❏ Multiple domain virtual servers
- ❏ Encryption requirements
- ❏ Remote Internet Information Server services
- ❏ Comments and Messages
- ❏ Logging

Internet Service Manager Views

When working in the Internet Service Manager, three views are available. You can select a view to display the available Servers and Services, as needed. The views available from the Internet Service Manager are as follows:

❏ Servers view

❏ Services view

❏ Report view

Servers View

The Servers view displays Internet Information Server Services running on NT Servers by server name. You can click on the plus symbol next to a server name to see which services a server has available. You can double-click on a service name to see and configure its property sheets. The Servers view is usually selected when you have multiple computers, and you need to configure or to know the status of whether a service is running or stopped, and the services installed on a specific computer.

Services View

The Services view enables you to list the Internet Information Services on selected NT Servers, grouped by service name (see fig. 12.14). You can click on the plus symbol next to a service name to see which servers are running that service. You can double-click the server name under a service to display and configure its property sheets. The Services view is usually selected when you need to configure or to know which computers are running a specific service.

Report View

The Report view is the default view and is the most common. The Report view lists Internet Information Servers alphabetically, with each available service shown on a separate line (see fig. 12.15). The list can be sorted alphabetically by clicking on the column headings. The Report view is usually selected when you only have one or two servers running Internet Information Server.

Figure 12.14

Services view.

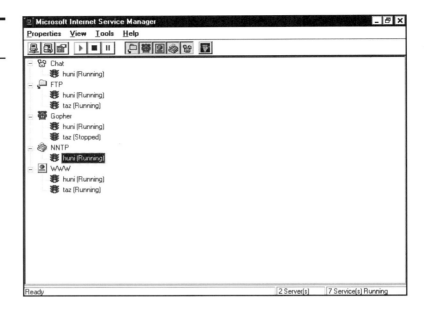

Figure 12.15

Report view.

Connecting to an Internet News Server

To configure a specific INS server after you install it, the Internet Service Manager must connect to an INS server. To do this from the Internet Service Manager, you have two options. You can select a specific server to connect to, or you can have the Internet Service Manager find available servers.

Selecting a Server

To select a specific server to connect to, you need to know the server name, IP address, or the NetBIOS name of the server. To select a specific server to connect to, follow these steps:

1. From the Properties menu in the Internet Service Manager, choose Connect to Server.
2. In the Server Name box, type the server name, IP address, or NetBIOS name.

Finding Available Servers

To find and connect to available Internet Information Servers, follow these steps:

1. From the Properties menu in the Internet Services Manager, choose *Find All Servers*.
2. From the list of servers displayed, double-click on the server that you want to connect to.

Starting, Stopping, and Pausing Services

The Internet Service Manager enables you to start, stop, or pause individual services on a specific server as necessary. When creating a new newsgroup, for example, you need to stop the NNTP service and restart the service after the newsgroup has been created. This enables the NNTP service to access the newsgroup. If you pause a specific service, all users connected to the service are disconnected.

To start, stop, or pause a service, follow these steps:

1. Connect to an Internet Information Server.
2. Select the service you want to start, stop, or pause.
3. From the Properties menu, choose Start Service, Stop Service, or Pause Service.

Configuring Internet News Service

Configuration of the Internet News Service is primarily performed by using the Internet Service Manager. You can use many other programs related to advanced configuration and management. See the section, "Other Configuration Programs and Utilities," found later in this chapter.

INS can be configured as a master or slave news server, or primary and secondary respectively. Slave servers are responsible for receiving replication directives from the master server, and serving news articles to clients. A stand-alone master server can be configured to serve news articles to clients. If needed, additional slave servers can be added to the News server group to accommodate increasing client connections and news traffic.

The following sections describe configuration, and provide an understanding of related configuration programs.

Viewing and Configuring Property Sheets

In the Internet Service Manager, property sheets are used to view and configure the individual Internet Information Server Services. Each Internet Information Server Service has its own set of property sheets.

The Internet News Service has eight main property sheets for viewing and configuration. Many configuration options exist within each property sheet. The property sheets are listed as follows:

- ❏ Service
- ❏ General
- ❏ Feeds
- ❏ Expiration
- ❏ Groups
- ❏ Directories
- ❏ Logging
- ❏ Advanced

To view or configure the property sheets of a selected server, follow these steps:

1. Select a server.
2. Double-click on a service to view or configure.
3. Choose the property sheet to view or configure by clicking on the tab at the top of the property sheet display page.
4. View or configure options as necessary.
5. Click OK to return to the main Internet Service Manager window.

Detailed information about advanced property sheet configuration options can be found in related chapters on security and logging (see Chapter 14, "Security Practices").

Service Property Sheet

The Service property sheet is used to control access rights to the News Service. The account name used for anonymous client requests must be specified (see fig. 12.17). The default user name, in the format *IUSR_computername*, is used for anonymous logons. The default user name is set up during the Internet Information Server installation. All anonymous logons to the service use this user name. If you decide to allow anonymous logons, you should still verify that the security permissions for this user name are correct.

You have the option to specify another user name. You can specify an existing user name, or create a new user account. In either case, you must configure its security permissions relevant to your requirements. It is recommended that the default account name be used. Use the default account name unless you have a specific need relevant to your security requirements.

The password you select is used internally by the NT Server. The password is not presented by another computer during the logon process. See Chapter 14, "Security Practices," for more information.

N O T E

Password authentication options can be selectively enabled or disabled. By default, all password authentication options are checked.

The following is a list of configuration options, found in the Service property sheet:

❑ **Connection Timeout.** This option specifies the amount of time before an inactive connection is closed. The default is 600 seconds.

❑ **Maximum Connections.** Specifies the maximum number of simultaneous connections. The default is the Internet Service Manager (ISM) default.

❏ **Allow Anonymous.** Indicates that the service is to allow anonymous connections. An anonymous connection uses the user's name and password indicated under Anonymous Logon.

❏ **Basic (No Encryption).** Sends the user's name and password in clear text (no encryption) by using the NNTP AuthInfo protocol.

❏ **Windows NT Challenge/Response.** Uses Windows NT log on accounts to authenticate users.

In the Comment option field, you can enter a comment or note, which will be visible in the Internet Service Manager, Report View window (see fig. 12.17). This comment is sometimes used as a reference for the service. For reference purposes, for example, you could enter the IP address or the physical location of the server.

You can use the Internet Service Manager to monitor connections to the NNTP service, and to disconnect users. Within the NNTP Service Property sheet of the Internet Service Manager, you can choose the User Sessions button to display the NNTP User Sessions dialog box (see fig. 12.16). The following section discusses the NNTP User Sessions dialog box.

Figure 12.16
Service property sheet.

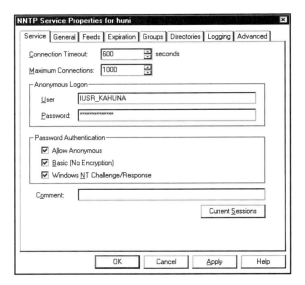

NNTP User Sessions Dialog Box
The NNTP User Sessions dialog box shows the users and feeds connected to the news server. The user's IP address and connection time are also shown.

The following control options are found in the NNTP User Sessions dialog box:

❏ **Disconnect.** Click on this after you select one or more users to disconnect from the news server.

❏ **Disconnect All.** Click on this to disconnect all users from the news server.

❏ **Refresh.** Click on this to update the user list. If any new users have logged on since you opened the dialog box, their names appear in the list.

General Property Sheet

The General property sheet enables you to set general service properties and connection information (see fig. 12.17).

The following list describes configuration options, found in the General Property sheet:

❏ **Allow Client Posting.** Enables clients to post articles with the limits you specify.

❏ **Maximum Post Size.** Shows the maximum size (in kilobytes) of articles that clients can post. NNTP will not post articles larger than this size. If you set this amount to 0, clients can post articles of any size.

❏ **Maximum Connection Size.** Shows the maximum size (in megabytes) of articles that users can post before NNTP disconnects them. If you set this amount to 0, users can post articles of any size.

❏ **Allow Feed Posting.** Allows feeds to post articles with the limits you specify.

❏ **Maximum Post Size.** Shows the maximum size (in kilobytes) of articles that feeds can post. NNTP will not post articles larger than this size. If you set this amount to 0, feeds can post articles of any size.

❏ **Maximum Connection Size.** Shows the maximum size (in megabytes) of articles that feeds can post before NNTP disconnects them. If you set this amount to 0, feeds can post articles of any size.

❏ **Allow Control Messages.** Specifies whether control messages should be automatically processed. Select this box to process control messages automatically and log them in the transaction log. Clear this box to log, but not process, control messages.

❏ **Unique Path ID.** Provides a space to type the unique string that will be placed in the Path header for replication control.

❏ **SMTP Server for Moderated Groups.** Provides a space to type the mail server where all postings to moderated groups will be forwarded.

Figure 12.17
General property sheet.

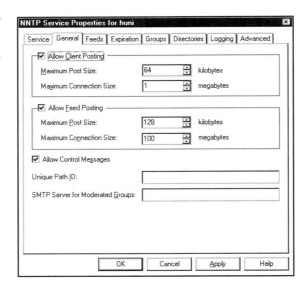

Feeds Property Sheet

The Feeds Property sheet shows a list of all feeds, active and inactive, that the INS server is configured to send or receive (see fig. 12.18).

Figure 12.18
Feeds property sheet.

The following list describes configuration options found in the General Property Sheet:

❏ **Server Feeds.** Displays the Server Name, Feed Type, and ID for all feeds.

❏ **Add button.** Click on this to add a feed to the list by using the Feed Properties dialog box (see fig 12.19).

Figure 12.19
The Feed Properties dialog box.

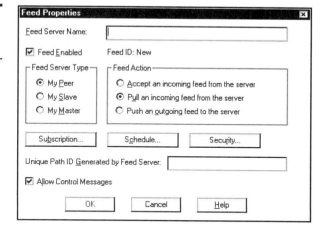

❏ **Edit button.** Click this to edit the feed selected in the Server Feeds list.

❏ **Remove button.** Click this to remove the feed selected in the Server Feeds list.

Feed Properties Dialog Box

The Feed Properties dialog box is used to configure how news is exchanged between the selected server and another specified server (see fig 12.19).

The following list describes configuration options found in the Feed Properties dialog box:

❏ **Feed Server Name.** Provides a space to type the name of the remote server sending or receiving articles.

❏ **Feed Enabled.** Specifies whether a feed will receive articles or not. Select this box to enable the feed. After the feed is enabled, new articles are queued for replication and sent to the specified server according to the Subscription, Security, and Schedule controls. Clear this box to prevent contact with the specified server.

❏ **Feed ID.** Displays the unique ID for this feed.

❏ **Feed Server Type.** Specifies the type of server associated with the feed server.

❏ **My Peer.** Designates the remote server type as a peer. Select this if the remote server does not share article numbers with this server.

❏ **My Slave.** Designates the remote server type as a slave. Select this if the remote server services clients, and forwards all posted articles to the server being configured for replication. The server being configured assigns numbers to all articles, and services all peer feeds.

❏ **My Master.** Designates the remote server type as a master. Select this if the remote server generates all article numbers for the server being configured. The remote server provides all articles and must be the only feed server configured.

❏ **Feed Action.** Specifies the actions associated with the feed server.

❏ **Accept an Incoming Feed from the Server.** Select this option to accept a feed from the server specified in the Feed Server Name box. This option disables the Schedule control.

❏ **Pull an Incoming Feed from the Server.** Select this option to pull incoming newsgroup articles from the feed server by using the newnews NNTP command. Not all servers allow the newnews command. This option is disabled if My Slave or My Master are selected for Feed Server Type.

❏ **Push an Outgoing Feed to the Server.** Select this option to push a feed to the feed server.

❏ **Subscription.** Click this to display the Feed Subscription dialog box, where you specify which newsgroups to replicate from a feed server (see fig. 12.20).

❏ **Schedule.** Click this to display the Feed Schedule dialog box, where you schedule inbound and outbound feeds (see fig. 12.21).

❏ **Security.** Click this to display the Feed Security dialog box, where you can set authentication properties (see fig. 12.22).

❏ **Unique Path ID Generated by Feed Server.** Provides a space to type the unique path ID. This name is inserted in every post by the specified server. This name is usually the DNS name of the feeding server or another unique name determined by the administrator of the remote machine.

❏ **Allow Control Messages.** Specifies whether control messages that are part of this feed should be accepted. Select this option to accept all control messages that are part of this feed, even if control messages are not globally allowed.

Feed Subscription Dialog Box

The Feed Subscription dialog box is used to specify which newsgroups to replicate from a feed server. Newsgroups are specified by expressions. The expressions enable either a full newsgroup name containing alphabetic characters separated with a period ".", or a newsgroup name containing the characters ".*" at the end of the string. The expression comp.* includes all newsgroups that begin with comp.

❏ **Newsgroup.** Provides a space to type the name of the newsgroup or a pattern to match.

❏ **Include.** Click this to add the text that you type in the Newsgroup box to the Subscription List. After you add a newsgroup, it is replicated with the feed server. This button is available only when the Newsgroup box is not empty.

❏ **Exclude.** Click on this to add the text in the edit box to the list of newsgroups to exclude from the feed. This button is only available when an item in the Newsgroup box is selected.

❏ **Subscription List.** Displays a list of newsgroups. The order in which they will be processed by pattern matching can be rearranged.

❏ **Move Up.** Click this to move the selected newsgroup up in the Subscription List. Newsgroups toward the top of the list are processed first by pattern matching.

❏ **Move Down.** Click this to move the selected newsgroup down in the Subscription List. Newsgroups toward the bottom of the list are processed last by pattern matching.

❏ **Remove.** Removes an item from the Subscription List. This button is available only when an item in the Subscription List is selected.

Figure 12.20
The Feed Subscription dialog box.

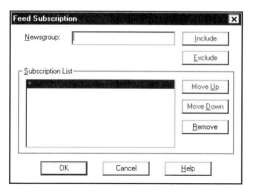

Feed Schedule Dialog Box

You use the Feed Schedule dialog box to schedule incoming or outgoing feeds (see fig. 12.21).

❏ **Run.** Enables you to specify the frequency of connections. The frequency can be weekly, daily, hourly, or a number of minutes that you specify.

❏ **Pull Request Time.** Displays the starting date and time of the feed, using 24-hour time. To change, type or select a new date and time. (The Pull Request Time value can only be changed when setting up a new pull feed.)

❏ **Automatically Disable Feed.** Choose this option, and then type or select the number of unreachable connection attempts made before the feed is disabled.

Figure 12.21

The Feed Schedule dialog box.

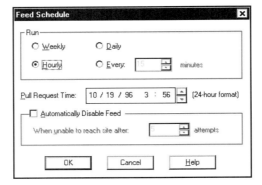

Feed Security Dialog Box

The Feed Security dialog box specifies the security to be used with the selected feed. In the Authentication Scheme area, options indicate which authentication scheme is required for connections with the selected feed server (see fig. 12.22).

Figure 12.22

The Feed Security dialog box.

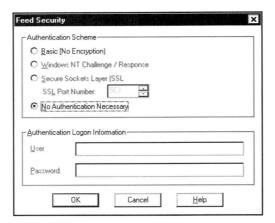

❏ **Basic (No Encryption).** Enables the servers to exchange user's names and passwords over the Internet via clear text. This method provides no security. If you select this option, you can specify authentication log on information.

❏ **Windows NT Challenge/Response.** Enables the servers to exchange authentication via Windows NT Challenge/Response. If you select this option, you can specify authentication log on information.

❏ **Secure Sockets Layer (SSL).** Uses SSL to connect with the feed server. Enter the SSL port number used to make the connection in the SSL Port Number box.

❏ **No Authentication Necessary.** Uses no security or IP-based security for the connection. In the Authentication Logon Information area, if you have selected Clear Text or Windows NT Challenge/Response as discussed previously, you can specify a user's name and password for the connection.

❏ **User.** Provides a space to type a name that enables you to connect to the server.

❏ **Password.** Provides a space to type a password that enables you to connect to the server.

Expiration Property Sheet

The Expiration property sheet displays the criteria for deleting newsgroups. Following are the options:

❏ **Expiration Policies.** Displays newsgroups set up for expiration and the associated expiration information.

❏ **Newsgroups.** Newsgroup names appear in this column.

❏ **Size (MB).** The maximum size that the newsgroup may attain before included articles are expired.

❏ **Time (Hrs).** The maximum age that the newsgroup may attain before it is expired.

❏ **ID.** The ID automatically assigned to an expiration policy after it is added.

❏ **Add.** Click this to display the Expiration Policy Properties dialog box where you add new expiration policies for newsgroups.

❏ **Edit.** Click this to display the Expirations Policy Properties dialog box where you change expiration policies for the selected newsgroup.

❏ **Remove.** Click this to delete the selected newsgroup from the list.

Expiration Policy Properties Dialog Box

The Expiration Policy Properties dialog box appears after you click on the Add button or the Edit button on the Expiration property sheet. You can use this dialog box to set the expiration policy of the newsgroup selected on the Expiration property sheet.

The following list describes configuration options found in the Expiration Policy Properties dialog box:

❏ **Newsgroups Older Than.** Select this option to expire articles after a newsgroup is older than the age specified in the Max___Hours box.

❏ **Newsgroups Bigger Than.** Select this option to expire articles after a newsgroup is greater than the size specified in the Max___Megabytes box.

❏ **Both.** Specifies that articles must be expired when a newsgroup exceeds either the date specified in the Max___Hours box or the size specified in the Max___Megabytes box.

❏ **Newsgroups.** Provides a space to type a newsgroup name. To add the newsgroup to the Expiration property page, click the Add button. You can also remove a selected newsgroup name by clicking the Remove button.

Groups Property Sheet

The Groups property sheet is used to add, edit, and delete newsgroups (see fig 12.23). The following list describes configuration options found in the Groups Property Sheet:

❏ **Newsgroup Name.** Provides a space to type the newsgroup name that you want to look up. After you finish typing the name, click on the Find button. Newsgroups that match the criteria you specify display in the Matching Newsgroups box.

❏ **Limit Results To.** Shows the maximum number of newsgroups that will display in the Matching Newsgroups box.

❏ **Matching Newsgroups.** Displays a list of newsgroups that match the specified criteria.

Figure 12.23
Groups property sheet.

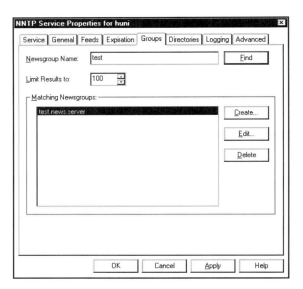

❑ **Create.** Click this to add a new newsgroup (see fig. 12.24).

❑ **Edit**. Click this to edit the newsgroup selected in the Matching Newsgroups box (see fig. 12.24).

❑ **Delete.** Click this to delete the newsgroup selected in the Matching Newsgroups box (see fig. 12.24).

Newsgroup Properties Dialog Box

The Newsgroup Properties dialog box is used specify or change options for a specific newsgroup (see fig. 12.24).

❑ **Newsgroup.** Provides a space to type a name for the newsgroup when adding a newsgroup. If you are editing a newsgroup, this box displays the name of the newsgroup. You can use regular characters, periods (.), or hyphens (-) in newsgroup names.

❑ **Description.** Provides a space to type a description of the newsgroup.

❑ **Read Only.** Select this option to set read-only permissions for the newsgroup specified in the Newsgroup box. After this box is checked, users and feeds cannot post articles to this newsgroup. (You may not want users and feeds to be able to post to newsgroups that publish facts, for example.)

❑ **Moderated.** Select this option to specify that this newsgroup is supervised by a moderator. After articles are posted to a moderated newsgroup, an e-mail message is sent to the moderator. The moderator can review the news articles, and then post with an approved-by header. Posting to moderated groups will fail if SMTP is not configured.

❑ **Moderator.** Provides a space to type the moderator's e-mail name for moderated newsgroups.

Figure 12.24

Newsgroup Properties dialog box.

Directories Property Sheet

The Directories property sheet contains directory configuration information. The default entry in the Directory box is the home directory of C:\InetPub\nntproot (see fig. 12.25). It is assumed that all newsgroups are contained under this directory if no other directories are listed. The user can change the properties associated with the home directory, but cannot remove the home directory. For the NNTP service, the alias is a list of newsgroup specifications similar to the newsgroup specification in the Feed Subscriptions dialog box (refer back to fig. 12.20).

❏ **Directory List.** Lists the directories used by the News service. The directory specifies where to store all the newsgroups specified by the alias.

❏ **Directory.** Displays the path of directories used by the NNTP service.

❏ **Alias.** Displays the path used for virtual directories.

❏ **Address.** Displays the IP address for the virtual server using that directory.

❏ **Error.** Indicates system errors, such as difficulty reading a directory.

❏ **Add.** Click this to display the Directory Properties dialog box, where you add newsgroup directories.

❏ **Remove.** Click this to remove the item selected in the Directory list.

❏ **Edit Properties.** Click this to display the Directory Properties dialog box, where you edit directory information for the item selected in the Directory list.

Figure 12.25

Directories property sheet.

Directory Properties Dialog Box

You can use the Directory Properties dialog box to edit an entry in the Directory list on the Directories property page (see fig. 12.26). The following list describes options found in the Directory Properties dialog box:

❏ **Directory.** Provides a space to enter the name of the directory to use for this set of newsgroups, either by typing it or by clicking on the Browse button and selecting it. This is a required field, and cannot be the same as, or a subdirectory of, any of the directories listed in the Directory list on the Directories property page.

❏ **Home (Default) Directory.** Select this option if the directory is the home directory.

❏ **Newsgroup Subtree.** Indicates that the named directory should be used for a specified subtree only, as specified in the Subtree Root box.

❏ **Subtree Root.** Provides a space to type the subtree root, such as *comp* or *comp.os*.

❏ **Allow Posting.** Select this box when you want clients to be able to post to newsgroups.

❏ **Require Secure SSL Channel.** Select this box when you want clients to connect using secure sockets layer SSL.

❏ **Restrict Newsgroup Visibility.** Select this box when you want only clients with read or post permission to be able to see the newsgroups under the specified directory. Because of the overhead in processing permissions on a per-group basis, this option may cause a loss in performance.

Figure 12.26

Directory Properties dialog box.

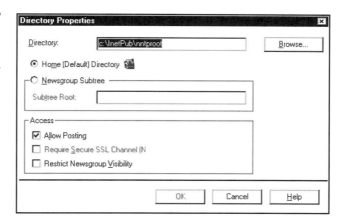

Logging Property Sheet

The Internet Information Server can log the activity of the NNTP Service. Enabling logging is recommended. Logs can provide important information, and can be used for security and statistical review. The logs can tell you how your server is being used.

The IIS log file contains the IP address of the Web browser or news client, date and time of access, service name, host name of service, service IP address, service status codes and bytes sent, and the name of the file accessed.

You can choose to have the log data written to files or to an SQL/ODBC database (see fig. 12.27). If you have multiple Internet Information Servers or Services on your network, you can log all their activity to a single file or database on a specific network computer.

If you would like to have individual log files for specific services, you can choose Log to a file. Individual log files can simplify the task of viewing the statistics for a specific service. If you choose Log to File, you must also specify how often to create new logs and where to log files. Check the box for the frequency of how often you want the Internet Information Server to create new log files, and specify the Log file directory location.

To log the NNTP Service activity to an SQL/ODBC data source, you must specify the ODBC Data Source Name (DSN), table, user name, and password to the database. Logging to an SQL/ODBC database enables you to review the statistics for all your IIS services from a single file.

The following list describes configuration options found in the Logging Property Sheet:

- ❏ **Enable Logging.** Select this box to start or stop logging for the selected information service.
- ❏ **Log To File.** Select this box to log to a text file for the selected information service.
- ❏ **Log Format.** Enables you to choose either Standard format or National Center for Supercomputing Applications (NCSA) format.
- ❏ **Automatically Open New Log.** Select this box to generate new logs at the specified interval. If not selected, the same log file grows indefinitely.
- ❏ **Log File Directory.** Provides a space to enter the directory containing all log files. To change directories, click on the Browse button and select a different directory.

❏ **Log File Filename.** Names the log file. Lowercase letters "yy" are replaced with the year; the letters "mm" are replaced with the month; and the letters "dd" are replaced with the day.

❏ **Log To SQL/ODBC Database.** Select this option to log to any ODBC data source. Set the Data Source name, the table name (not the file name of the table), and specify a user name and password valid for the computer on which the database resides. You must also use the ODBC applet in the Control Panel to create a system data source.

Figure 12.27
Logging property sheet.

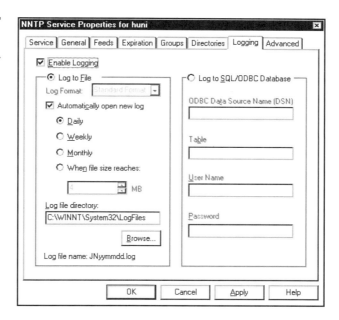

Advanced Property Sheet

The Advanced Property Sheet can be used to configure access restrictions to the Internet News Service, and to limit the total outbound bandwidth of the Internet Information Server Services (see fig. 12.28). You may want to restrict access to your News server for security reasons, or limit outbound bandwidth from your IIS server to satisfy network bandwidth limitations.

The Internet News Service can be configured to have the Internet Information Server grant or deny access from specified IP addresses. You can use this option to restrict access to your server from a specific computer or group of computers. If the content of the Web server was intended for your research and development engineers only, for example, you can restrict access to the Internet Information Server to only the designated IP addresses associated to the engineers computers.

By default, access to your Internet News Service is granted to all IP addresses. You can choose to specify the IP addresses of computers to which you want to deny access.

You can choose to change the option to deny access to all IP addresses (see fig. 12.29). If you choose this option, you can specify the IP addresses of computers you want to grant exclusive access to.

You can limit the outbound network bandwidth used by all the Internet Information Server Services on your NT Server. This option controls the maximum outbound network bandwidth for your Internet Information Server. If you have limited bandwidth, or are running other Internet services on the NT Server, you may want to enable and set this option to meet your needs. See Chapter 15, "Site Management," for more information.

If you choose to limit the outbound bandwidth used by the Internet Information Server Services, you must have an understanding of the possible implications:

❑ When the actual bandwidth usage remains below the level you set, the read, write, and transfer functions remain enabled.

❑ If the actual bandwidth usage approximates the limit you have set, reads are temporarily blocked.

❑ If the actual bandwidth exceeds the limit you set, reads are rejected, and file transfers are temporarily blocked.

The Internet Information Server returns to normal operation when the bandwidth usage equals or falls below the maximum limit.

The following list describes configuration options found in the Advanced Property Sheet:

❑ **Granted Access.** Select this option to grant access to all computers. To then deny access to some computers, click the Add button.

❑ **Denied Access.** Select this option to deny access to all computers. To then grant access to some computers, click the Add button.

❑ **Access list.** If the Granted Access option is selected, it displays computers denied access. If the Denied Access option is selected, it displays computers granted access.

- ❑ **Add.** To add computers to which you want to grant access, select the Granted Access option and click the Add button. To add computers to which you want to deny access, select the Denied Access option and click the Add button.
- ❑ **Edit.** Click this to edit the computer selected in the Access list.
- ❑ **Remove.** Click this to delete the computer selected in the Access list.
- ❑ **Limit Network Use By All Internet Services On This Computer.** You can control your Internet services by limiting the network bandwidth allowed for all the Internet services on the server. Set the maximum kilobytes of outbound traffic permitted on this computer.

Figure 12.28
Advanced property sheet.

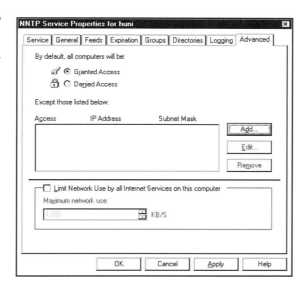

Deny Access On Dialog Box

You use the Deny Access On dialog box to restrict access (see fig. 12.29). The following list describes configuration options found in the Deny Access On dialog box:

- ❑ **Single Computer.** Enables you to grant or deny access to a single computer by identifying its IP address.
- ❑ **Group of Computers.** Enables you to grant or deny access to a group of computers by identifying their IP addresses and subnet mask.
- ❑ **IP Address.** Provides a space to type the IP address for the single computer or group of computers to which you want to deny or grant access. If you don't

know the IP address, click the button to the right of the IP Address box to look up the IP address for a specific computer name.

❏ **Subnet Mask.** Provides a space to type the subnet mask for the group of computers to which you want to deny or grant access.

Figure 12.29
Deny Access On dialog box.

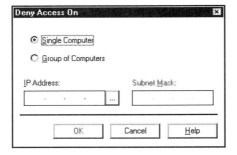

Other Configuration Programs and Utilities

The Internet Service Manager is the primary configuration program used to configure the Internet News Service. You can use other programs and utilities included with NT Server 4 to enhance functionality, perform advanced configuration, and monitor the Internet Information Server Services. This section references other configuration programs and utilities, and explains how they relate to the Internet News Service.

This section references the following topics:

❏ Control Panel configuration options
❏ Explorer
❏ User Manager for Domains
❏ Registry Editor
❏ Performance Monitor
❏ Event Viewer

Control Panel Configuration Options

In the Control Panel, you will find applets related to basic and advanced configuration options of the Internet Information Server. You can configure options related to the Internet Information Server and its Services, in the following applets:

- ❏ Network applet
- ❏ Services applet
- ❏ ODBC applet

The following sections discuss each of these.

Network Applet

The Network applet, located in the Control Panel, can be used to configure your TCP/IP protocol settings and other network services and protocols. The TCP/IP protocol Advanced Configuration property sheet can be used to add additional IP addresses, up to a total of five, for use with multiple domain names within your Web server. When more than five IP addresses need to be added to the TCP/IP protocol configuration, you must use the Registry Editor to manually add additional IP addresses. See Chapter 5, "Understanding the Transport Layer: TCP/IP," for more information on configuring multiple IP addresses.

Services Applet

The Services applet can be used to start, stop, and pause the individual Internet Information Server Services, as well as control startup options.

After you highlight a service name, you can use the Startup button to enable or disable the individual Internet Information Server Services from loading during the NT Server boot process.

You can also configure the Log On As option for the Internet News Service. The Log On As option contains the user name used internally by the Internet Information Server to log on to the service. The default setting for the Log On As option is set during the Internet Information Server installation. You normally only need to change this setting for security reasons. If you change the account user name in the Internet Service Manager Service property sheet for an Internet service, for example, you must also change the Log On As name for the service to the same name.

ODBC Applet

The ODBC applet, found within the Control Panel, is used to configure ODBC connectivity options. The ODBC applet is present if you chose to install ODBC during the IIS installation procedure, or if it was installed as a necessary feature of other software.

Within the ODBC applet, you can add, remove, and configure User Data Source Drivers and System Data Source Drivers. Configuration and selection of ODBC Data Source Drivers is dependent on your specific needs and installed software related to the IIS.

Setting Permissions with the Explorer

By default, security permissions placed on files and directories within the individual IIS services directory tree structure are adequate for most installations. You may have a need to modify the security permission for files or directories within your IIS tree structure for security reasons.

If you find it necessary to change security permissions on files or directories within the News server directory tree structure, you can use the Explorer. If you have a file or directory that contains sensitive or secure data, for example, and you want to restrict access to a specific user or group of users, you can use the Explorer to set or change the security permissions. See Chapter 14, "Security Practices," for more information.

To use the Explorer to set or change directory and file permissions on Windows NTFS drives, follow these steps:

1. Right-click a file or directory name.
2. Click Properties.
3. Click the Security tab.
4. Click the Permissions button.
5. Set the Permissions as needed.

User Manager for Domains

The User Manager for Domains is used to manage security policies, user accounts, and groups for your NT Server. The User Manager for Domains is located in the Administrative Tools folder.

You can use the User Manager for Domains to modify and implement security procedures relevant to the operation of your Internet Information Server.

Registry Editor

The Registry Editor can be used to edit Registry Keys and Values related to the Internet Information Server.

One of the most common uses for the Registry Editor, related to the Internet Information Server, is for adding IP addresses for use with multiple domains. If you are running a multiple domain Web server, and need more than five IP addresses or five domain names linked to your NT Server, you must use the Registry Editor to manually add the additional IP addresses to the Registry.

Performance Monitor

The Performance Monitor is a powerful and useful tool, which provides a graphical interface that can be used to view real-time statistics, and to evaluate the overall operation of the Internet Information Server Services. It can also be used to evaluate and diagnose problems related to the individual Internet Information Server component services, such as the NNTP Service.

With the Performance Monitor, you can view statistics in real time. You can use the Performance Monitor, for example, to show how many connections are active on all IIS services or on an individual Internet service. See Chapter 15, "Site Management," for more information.

NNTP Performance Counters

During the initial installation of the Internet Information Server, Performance Monitor counters are loaded. The Internet News Server installation program loads Windows NT Performance Monitor counters specific to the Internet News Service. The Object names used in the Performance Monitor for the Internet News Service are NNTP Server Svc and NNTP Server Client Requests.

NNTP Server Svc Counters

The following is a list of Counters used to monitor the NNTP Server Svc object:

Bytes Sent/second. The rate that data bytes are sent by the NNTP server.

Bytes Received/second. The rate that data bytes are received by the NNTP server.

Bytes Total/second. The sum of Bytes Sent/second and Bytes Received/second This is the total rate of bytes transferred by the NNTP server.

Total Connections. The number of connections that have been made to the NNTP server.

Total SSL Connections. The number of SSL connections that have been made to the NNTP server.

Current Connections. The current number of connections to the NNTP server.

Maximum Connections. The maximum number of simultaneous connections to the NNTP server.

Current Anonymous Users. The number of anonymous users currently connected to the NNTP server.

Current Nonanonymous Users. The number of nonanonymous users currently connected to the NNTP server.

Total Anonymous Users. The total number of anonymous users who have ever connected to the NNTP server.

Total Nonanonymous Users. The total number of nonanonymous users who have ever connected to the NNTP server.

Maximum Anonymous Users. The maximum number of anonymous users simultaneously connected to the NNTP server.

Maximum Nonanonymous Users. The maximum number of nonanonymous users simultaneously connected to the NNTP server.

Maximum Nonanonymous Users. The maximum number of nonanonymous users simultaneously connected to the NNTP server.

Total Outbound Connections. The number of outbound connections that have been made by the NNTP server.

Total Outbound Connections Failed. The number of unsuccessful outbound connections that have been made by the NNTP server.

Current Outbound Connections. The number of current outbound connections being made by the NNTP server.

Failed Outbound Logons. The number of failed outbound logons made by the NNTP server.

Total Push Feeds. The number of push feeds made by the NNTP server.

Total Pull Feeds. The number of pull feeds made by the NNTP server.

Total Passive Feeds. The number of passive feeds accepted by the NNTP server.

Articles Sent. The total number of files sent by the NNTP server.

Articles Received. The total number of files received by the NNTP server.

Articles Total. The sum of Articles Sent and Articles Received. This is the total number of files transferred by the NNTP server.

Articles Posted. The number of articles posted to the NNTP Server.

Article Map Entries. The entries inserted into the article mapping table of the NNTP server.

History Map Entries. The entries inserted into the history mapping table of the NNTP server.

Xover Entries. The number of Xover entries in the Xover table of the NNTP server.

Control Messages Received. The total number of control messages received by the NNTP server.

Control Messages Failed. The total number of control messages failed or not applied by the NNTP server.

Moderated Postings Sent. The total number of moderated postings the NNTP server attempts to send to an SMTP server.

Moderated Postings Failed. The total number of moderated postings the NNTP server fails to send to an SMTP server.

Sessions Flow Controlled. The number of client sessions currently in a flow-controlled state in the NNTP server.

Articles Expired. The number of articles expired on the NNTP server since it was started.

Articles Sent/Second. The total number of files sent per second by the NNTP server.

Articles Received/Second. The total number of files per second received by the NNTP server.

Articles Posted/Second. The number of articles posted per second to the NNTP server.

Article Map Entries/Second. The entries inserted per second into the article mapping table of the NNTP server.

History Map Entries/Second. The entries inserted per second into the history mapping table of the NNTP server.

Xover Entries/Second. The number of entries inserted per second in the Xover table of the NNTP server.

Articles Expired/Second. The number of articles expired per second on the NNTP server since it was started.

IR Notifications. The number of times the NNTP server has requested that the IR server add a data source.

NNTP Server Client Requests Counters

The following is a list of Counters used to monitor the NNTP Server Client Requests:

Article Commands. The number of ARTICLE commands received by the NNTP server since it was started.

Article Commands/Second. The number of ARTICLE commands per second received by the NNTP Server since it was started.

Group Commands. The number of GROUP commands received by the NNTP Server since it was started.

Group Commands/Second. The number of GROUP commands per second received by the NNTP server since it was started.

Help Commands. The number of HELP commands received by the NNTP server since it was started.

Help Commands/Second. The number of HELP commands per second received by the NNTP server since it was started.

Ihave Commands. The number of IHAVE commands received by the NNTP server since it was started.

Ihave Commands/Second. The number of IHAVE commands per second received by the NNTP server since it was started.

Last Commands. The number of LAST commands received by the NNTP server since it was started.

Last Commands/Second. The number of LAST commands per second received by the NNTP server since it was started.

List Commands. The number of LIST commands received since it was started.

List Commands/Second. The number of LIST commands per second received by the NNTP server since it was started.

Newgroups Commands. The number of NEWGROUPS commands received by the NNTP server since it was started.

Newgroups Commands/Second. The number of NEWGROUPS commands per second received by the NNTP server since it was started.

Newnews Commands. The number of NEWNEWS commands received by the NNTP server since it was started.

Newnews Commands/Second. The number of NEWNEWS commands per second received by the NNTP server since it was started.

Next Commands. The number of NEXT commands received by the NNTP server since it was started.

Next Commands/Second. The number of NEXT commands per second received by the NNTP server since it was started.

Post Commands. The number of POST commands received by the NNTP server since it was started.

Post Commands/Second. The number of POST commands per second received by the NNTP server since it was started.

Quit Commands. The number of QUIT commands received by the NNTP server since it was started.

Quit Commands/Second. The number of QUIT commands per second received by the NNTP Server since it was started.

Stat Commands. The number of STAT commands received by the NNTP server since it was started.

Stat Commands/Second. The number of STAT commands per second received by the NNTP server since it was started.

Logon Attempts. The number of logon attempts that have been made to the NNTP server.

Logon Failures. The number of failed logons.

Reverse Authentication Attempts. The number of reverse AUTHINFOs made by the NNTP server.

Reverse Authentication Failures. The number of failed reverse AUTHINFOs made by the NNTP server.

Logon Attempts/Second. The number of logon attempts per second that have been made to the NNTP server.

Logon Failures/Second. The number of logons per second that failed.

Reverse Authentication Attempts/Second. The number of reverse AUTHINFOs per second made by the NNTP server.

Reverse Authentication Failures/Second. The number of failed reverse AUTHINFOs per second made by the NNTP server.

IIS Global Performance Counters

The Object name for the Internet Information Server is Internet Information Services Global. The following is a list of counters used to monitor the Internet Information Services Global object:

Cache Flushes. The number of times a portion of the memory cache has been expired due to file or directory changes in an Internet Information Services directory tree.

Cache Hits. The total number of times a file open, directory listing, or service-specific objects request was found in the cache.

Cache Hits %. The ratio of cache hits to all cache requests.

Cache Misses. The total number of times a file open, directory listing, or service-specific objects request was not found in the cache.

Cache Size. The configured maximum size of the shared HTTP, FTP, and Gopher memory cache.

Cache Used. The total number of bytes currently containing cached data in the shared memory cache. This includes directory listings, file handle tracking, and service-specific objects.

Cached File Handles. The number of open file handles cached by all the Internet Information Services.

Current Blocked Async I/O Requests. Current Async I/O requests blocked by bandwidth throttler.

Directory Listings. The number of cached directory listings cached by all the Internet Information Services.

Measured Async I/O Bandwidth usage. Measured bandwidth of Async I/O averaged over a minute.

Objects. The number of cached objects cached by all the Internet Information Services. They include file handle tracking objects, directory listing objects, and service-specific objects.

Total Allowed Async I/O Requests. Total Async I/O requests allowed by bandwidth throttler.

Total Blocked Async I/O Requests. Total Async I/O requests blocked by bandwidth throttler.

Total Rejected Async I/O Requests. Total Async I/O requests rejected by bandwidth throttler.

See Chapter 15, "Site Management," for more information.

Event Viewer

The Event Viewer, located in the Administrative Tools folder, is a tool that you can use to monitor system, security, and application events in your system. You can use the Event Viewer to view and manage system, security, and application event logs. The Event Viewer can notify administrators of critical events, such as a stopped or failed service and unauthorized access attempts. It notifies by displaying pop-up messages, or by adding event information to log files. The information enables you to better understand the sequence and types of events that lead to a particular state or situation.

NNTP Scenarios

The following two examples illustrate how Internet News Servers can be deployed:

Example 1: Retail Computer Store

A retail computer store implements INS to provide a customer support newsgroup. Customers post questions on computer hardware and software products that do not require immediate answers. Sales staff answer the questions and respond to all users, and thereby enable more customers to benefit from the information. This newsgroup becomes a forum for everyone to learn from the collective experiences. As more customers become acquainted with the newsgroup, the exchange of product information decreases support costs for the store. Store employees can start new newsgroups for customers—local, special interest user groups, for example.

Example 2: Internet Service Provider

An Internet Service Provider (ISP), Yourcompany Inc., is planning for the perpetual increase of its customer base. This increase will require additional concurrent connections. Running a news service on a single server is undesirable not only from a CPU processing and network bandwidth point of view, but also from a reliability and availability point of view.

Yourcompany Inc. sets up six different machines, one news master, four news slaves, and a news Index server. The Index server will provide the capabilities of full-text searching and indexing. By using round-robin Domain Name Service (DNS), the four slave machines are assigned to the same DNS name. Yourcompany Inc. can load-balance connection requests across the four slave servers. If one machine fails or is offline, the other four machines can still service client requests until the machine that failed can be brought back online. If the primary master fails, one of the slave servers can be promoted to the master.

Summary

In this chapter, you learned about installation and configuration issues for the NNTP Service. The Internet Service Manager was discussed in detail, and other configuration tools were noted.

The installation and configuration procedures discussed in this chapter should suffice for the majority of installation situations.

13

Other Services for Your Users

A t some point, your organization may want to provide users with services other than the most widely used Internet services, such as WWW Servers, e-mail, and UseNET news. Various reasons why your organization would choose to supplement their basic Internet services with additional, less popular services exist. A couple of reasons might be user demand and service growth. For example, users might ask that the organization provide them with remote login capablities using telnet. If the number of an organization's Internet servers is very large, that organization might want to provide DNS services for themselves. It is important to be familiar with some of these additional server options so that when the time comes to implement them, you will already be familiar with what each service entails. This chapter will cover the following additional services:

- DNS Services—Anytime you use a mnemonic rather than numeric address to connect to a given Internet site, you are using the Domain Name System. The DNS, as it is called, is a system which maps mnemonic, human-readable names to numeric IP addresses for organization and ease of use.

- Other Internet Services—Including IRC and Telnet. IRC stands for Internet Relay Chat. IRC is a distributed, worldwide "chat" system that allows realtime, keyboard-based communications. Telnet provides a facility for interactive logins to Internet hosts.

- Microsoft Internet Server Products—Internet server products made by Microsoft, including Internet Information Server (WWW server), Microsoft FrontPage authoring environment, and Microsoft's upcoming Normandy suite of Internet server products.

- Microsoft BackOffice—A suite of network server products for the Windows NT Server platform. These products have been extended by Microsoft for use within the Internet/intranet environment.

DNS Services

The Domain Name System (DNS) is a distributed database providing a hierarchical naming system for identifying hosts on the Internet. DNS was developed to solve the problems that arose when the number of hosts on the Internet grew dramatically in the early 1980s. DNS specifications are defined in RFCs 1034 and 1035. Readers should familiarize themselves with several aspects of DNS. To that end, this section discusses the following topics:

- Introducing the DNS
- Understanding the DNS server service
- Installing the Windows NT 4 DNS server
- Creating and maintaining a simple DNS domain
- Administering a DNS server using DNS manager
- Using the DNS manager for advanced tasks
- Expanding your DNS domains
- Determining whether you should maintain a DNS server

Introducing the DNS

The DNS database is organized in an inverted tree structure called the domain name space. A node in the tree structure is called a domain. Each domain has a name and can contain subdomains. The domain name is used to determine its position in the database in relation to its parent domain. A period (.) separates each part of the names for the network nodes of the DNS domain. The DNS domain name foo.edu, for example, specifies the foo subdomain whose parent is the edu domain; bar.com specifies the bar subdomain whose parent is the com domain.

Top-Level Domains

The Internet Network Information Center, or InterNIC, manages the root and top-level domains (the domains which come directly below the root in the DNS tree) of the DNS database. The top-level domain names are divided into three main categories:

❑ Organizational domains (3-character names)
❑ Geographical domains (2-character country codes)
❑ The IN-ADDR.ARPA. domain (a special domain used for address-to-name mappings)

Organizational domain names were originally used in the United States. As the Internet began to grow internationally, however, it became obvious that an organizational division was inadequate for a global network. Geographical domain names were then introduced. Even though a .us country domain exists, domain names in the United States are still predominantly organizational. As shown in table 13.1, seven organizational domains currently exist.

	DNS domain name abbreviation	Type of organization or institution
Table 13.1 The DNS Organizational Domains	com	Commercial
	edu	Educational
	gov	Government
	org	Noncommercial
	net	Networking
	mil	Military
	int	International

Delegation

The InterNIC delegates responsibility for managing the DNS name space below the top level to other organizations. These organizations further subdivide the name space and delegate responsibility down. This decentralized administrative model enables DNS to be autonomously managed at the levels that make the most sense for each organization involved.

Zones

The administrative unit for DNS is the zone. A zone is a subtree of the DNS database that is administered as a single separate entity. It can consist of a single domain or a domain with subdomains. The lower-level subdomains of a zone can also be split into separate zone(s). The difference between domains and zones can be very subtle. A zone contains the domain names and data that a domain contains, except for domains and data that have been delegated elsewhere.

IN-ADDR.ARPA Zone

The IN-ADDR.ARPA zone is a special zone for address to host name mapping, or reverse lookup. The IN-ADDR.ARPA essentially is an Internet domain that uses addresses as indexes into the database rather than names as indexes into the DNS database, like normal zones.

Names in the IN-ADDR.ARPA domain are written by taking the network portion of an IP address, reversing it, and appending IN-ADDR.ARPA to the end, separated by a period. So, a host with an address of 192.44.25.10 would be in the 25.44.192.IN-ADDR.ARPA zone. It may seem a little strange that zones in the IN-ADDR.ARPA domain are backward, but if you look carefully, you will see why it is done this way.

In a mnemonic Internet address, the right most portion is the least specific, that portion encompasses the greatest number of hosts. A domain address of math.gatech.edu gets more general, for example, as you move toward the right. From left to right it reads: the math department (very specific), at Georgia Institute of Technology (less specific), which is an educational institution (least specific). In the same way, names in the IN-ADDR.ARPA domains get less specific as you move right. Take, for instance, the previous example—25.44.192.IN-ADDR.ARPA. Reading from left to right, you get class C subnet 25 (encompasses up to 255 hosts), class B network 44 (encompasses thousands of hosts), and class A network 192 (encompasses millions of hosts).

Fully Qualified Domain Names

With the exception of the root, each node in the DNS database has a name of up to 63 characters. Each subdomain must have a unique name within its parent domain. This ensures name uniqueness throughout the DNS name space. DNS domain names are formed by following the path from the bottom of the DNS tree to the root. The node names are concatenated, and a period (.) separates each part. Such names are known as fully qualified domain names (FQDN). Here's an example of one:

NOTE

In practice, most DNS host entries appear no lower than the fifth level of the DNS tree, with three or four being more typical.

fubar.foo.bar.com.

DNS uses a client/server model, where the DNS servers (name servers) contain information about a portion of the DNS database (zone), and make this information available to clients (resolvers). A resolver queries a name server for information about the DNS name space. This name server can, in turn, query other name servers as it tries to respond to the query from the resolver.

A DNS zone administrator sets up one or more name servers for the zone. Name servers fall into the following categories:

❏ **A primary master name server.** A primary server contains the master copy of the database files with resource records for all subdomains and hosts in the zone.

❏ **A secondary master name server.** A secondary server receives a replicated copy of the database files from the primary server. When the zone structure changes, the primary master database files are modified and copied to the secondary masters. The secondary master files are never touched.

❏ **A caching-only name server.** Unlike a primary or secondary server, a caching-only server is not associated with any specific DNS zone(s) and contains no database files. A caching-only server starts with no knowledge of the DNS domain structure, and must rely on other name servers for this information. Each time a caching-only server queries a name server and receives an answer, it stores the information in its cache. When additional queries come in for this information, the caching-only server answers them directly from the cache. Over time, the cache grows to include the information most often requested.

Although not required by the DNS software, secondary servers are a good idea for the following reasons:

❏ **Load balance.** Secondary servers ease the load on the primary server. This can be significant in a busy network where name server queries can reach volumes of 20,000 per hour and beyond.

❏ **Fault tolerance.** Secondary servers enable DNS name resolution to continue when the primary server is unavailable.

❏ **Reduced network traffic.** Secondary servers placed in close proximity to client computers reduce Internetwork traffic across routers.

The InterNIC recommends that a site wanting to manage its own zone have at least two secondary name servers. At least one secondary should be located on a network not directly connected to your own. This is to ensure that a name server can still answer queries for your domain, even if the link between yourself and your provider fails.

DNS Records

The DNS database stores information about zones managed by DNS servers in collections of structured resource records. Resource records of 19 types are available to a DNS Server. The most commonly used records are SOA, NS, A, PTR, CNAME, and MX.

The SOA (start of authority) resource record indicates that this DNS name server is the best source of information for the data within this DNS domain. It is the first record in each of the DNS database files.

The NS (name server) resource record identifies the DNS name server(s) for the DNS domain. NS resource records appear in all DNS zones and reverse zones (those in the IN-ADDR.ARPA DNS domain).

The A (address) resource record maps a host (computer or other network device) name to an IP address in a DNS zone. Its counterpart, the PTR resource record, is used to map an IP address to a host (computer or other network device) name in a DNS reverse zone (those in the IN-ADDR.ARPA DNS domain).

The PTR (pointer) resource record maps an IP address to a host (computer or other network device) name in a DNS reverse zone (those in the IN-ADDR.ARPA DNS domain). Its counterpart, the A (address) resource record, is used to map a host (computer or other network device) name to an IP address in a DNS zone.

The CNAME (canonical name) resource record creates an alias (synonymous name) for the specified host (computer or other network device) name. You cannot create a CNAME record with an alias name that matches the DNS name of any existing resource record. You can use CNAME records to hide the implementation details of your network from the clients that connect to it. Ftp.microsoft.com, for example, is an alias (CNAME) for the real name of the computer that runs the FTP Server for Microsoft. Clients connect to ftp.microsoft.com without regard for the real name of the computer. This also enables the FTP Server to be moved to a different computer; only the CNAME record needs to change.

The MX (mail exchanger) resource record specifies a mail exchange server for a DNS domain name. A mail exchange server is a host (computer or other network device) that either processes or forwards mail for the DNS domain name. Processing the mail means either delivering it to the addressee or passing it to a different type of mail transport. Forwarding the mail means sending it to its final destination server, sending it using Simple Message Transfer Protocol (SMTP) to another mail exchange server that is closer to the final destination, or queuing it for a specified amount of time.

For information on the other kinds of DNS resource records, please consult the DNS Manager Help. The DNS Manager is covered later in this chapter.

Understanding the DNS Server Service

Windows NT Server includes an RFC-compliant, DNS name server. You can configure the Windows NT DNS name server to use WINS for host name resolution. This integration enables a form of Dynamic DNS that takes advantage of the best features of both DNS and WINS. DNS resolves the upper layers of the domain name and passes the final resolution to WINS. This final WINS resolution is transparent to the client computer.

Note that the Workstation service is the component responsible for registering a computer's name with WINS. By default, the Workstation service is started automatically when the computer starts. In general, you should leave this setting alone. If you turn it off on a computer, it will no longer be possible for the DNS server to resolve that computer's name with a WINS lookup.

DNS Support in UNC Names

The Windows Uniform Naming Convention (UNC) now supports DNS domain names. UNC names take the form \\server\sharepoint. Previously, the server portion was the NetBIOS computer name of the server on which the sharepoint was located.

You can now use a DNS domain name or IP address in the server portion of the UNC name. \\Tsunami.widgets.com\public, for example, is the name for the public folder on the machine named Tsunami in the Widgets.com DNS domain. If the IP address for Tsunami.widgets.com is 138.57.27.7, then \\138.57.27.7\public and \\Tsunami.widgets.com\public represent the same name.

To enable DNS support in UNC names, you must enable DNS for Windows Resolution.

Installing the Windows NT 4 DNS Server

To install the Microsoft DNS server included with Windows NT 4, follow these steps:

1. Select the Network icon located in the Control Panel.
2. From within the Network Properties dialog box, click the Add button.
3. Choose Microsoft DNS Server from the Network Service list.
4. Type the path to the Windows NT distribution files, and then click Continue.
5. The setup program now installs all the necessary files. To use the DNS server software, restart the computer.
6. After the computer is restarted, you can create and manage domains using the DNS Manager application included in Windows NT 4.

The DNS Manager

The DNS Manager is the administrative tool used to control the Windows NT DNS Server. To use the DNS Manager, click Start, point to Programs, and then to Administrative Tools (Common), and then click DNS Manager (see fig. 13.1). After the DNS Manager is running, you can configure existing DNS zones and servers, and create new zones and servers.

Figure 13.1

Accessing the DNS Manager program.

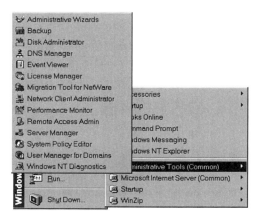

Creating and Managing a Simple DNS Domain

The next sections walk you through creating a simple DNS server containing only a couple of hosts. The sample DNS server is a primary server for a Zone you create. This section walks you through all the necessary steps to set up, including the following:

- ❏ Setting Up a Server
- ❏ Creating a Primary Zone
- ❏ Adding a Primary IN-ADDR.ARPA Zone
- ❏ Adding Host Records
- ❏ Inserting Other DNS Resource Records into a Primary Zone

Setting Up a Server

The first step in creating a domain to manage is to set up a DNS server. Follow these steps to create a new DNS server.

If you are using DNS Manager the for the first time, no servers will be present in the left pane of DNS manager (see fig. 13.2).

Figure 13.2

A fresh copy of DNS Manager.

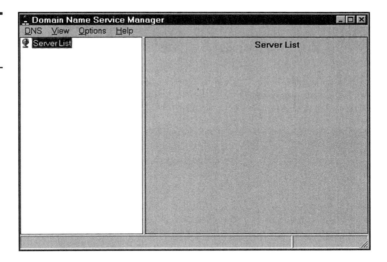

Using the DNS Manager, choose the DNS menu item. Next, click the item labeled New Server. A dialog box similar to that shown in figure 13.3 pops up, prompting you for a name for the server. Enter the host name of the NT Server you are working on. DNS Manager creates a server with the name you entered (see fig. 13.4).

Figure 13.3
The Add DNS Server
dialog box.

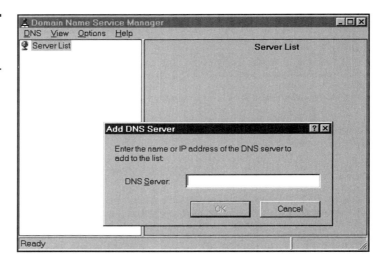

Figure 13.4
A newly created
DNS server.

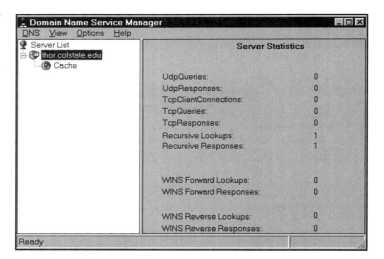

Creating a Primary Zone

The server you created in the previous section will function as the primary server for a zone in the DNS name space. The zone this server will be primary for does not yet exist; you will create it in the following section.

Working from within DNS Manager, click on the server you just created so that it is highlighted. Choose the DNS menu item, and then click on the *New Zone Item*. A

dialog box appears that gives you the choice between creating a primary or a secondary zone. Click *Primary*, and then click *Next*.

A second dialog box appears, prompting you for the name of the zone you want to create. Enter the name **MyDomain.COM**. After you enter the name of the new zone, DNS Manager chooses a default zone file name based on the name of the zone (see fig. 13.5). Accept the file name provided by DNS Manager. Click on Next, and then click on Finish to create the zone.

Figure 13.5

Creating a zone.

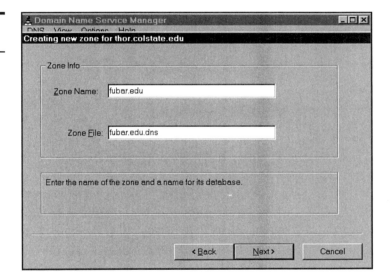

After creating the new zone, check that the automatically created resource records are correct. DNS Manager automatically creates an SOA record containing the primary server DNS name, and Responsible Person Address. The primary server DNS name is created by using the Fully Qualified Domain Name of the computer hosting the DNS server. The Responsible Person Address is the name of the account that created the zone. An NS record is also automatically created. The domain name for the NS record is the name entered during creation of the zone. If the zone name is the same as the target computer's domain name, an A record is created. If the zone name is not the same as the target computer's domain name, an A record must be manually created.

Adding a Primary IN-ADDR.ARPA Zone

Before you can begin adding hosts to your new zone, you should first create a primary IN-ADDR.ARPA zone for each subnet you want to use. The IN-ADDR.ARPA zone will handle address to name mappings in the DNS database.

Creating an IN-ADDR.ARPA zone is exactly like creating a normal forward mapping zone. Click on the server you created previously to highlight it. Click on the DNS menu, and then choose the New Zone item. After the dialog box prompts you, choose Primary, and then click on Next. Enter the network portion of your IP address in reverse order followed by IN-ADDR.ARPA when asked for a zone name. If the IP addresses this server will manage are located on the 192.44.10.0 subnet, for example, 10.44.192.IN-ADDR.ARPA should be entered as the zone name. In this example, use the address 10.5.10.IN-ADDR.ARPA. Click Next, and then click Finish to create the zone using the default data file name. At this point, you should have two zones, the *MyDomain.COM* zone and the *10.5.10.IN-ADDR.ARPA* zone. Figure 13.6 shows what the zones should look like.

NOTE

To enable computers outside your network to reach this zone, you need to register it with its parent domain, in this case In-addr.arpa. For registration information, visit the DNS Resources Directory (`http://www.dns.net/dnsrd/`) on the World Wide Web.

Figure 13.6

Newly created zones.

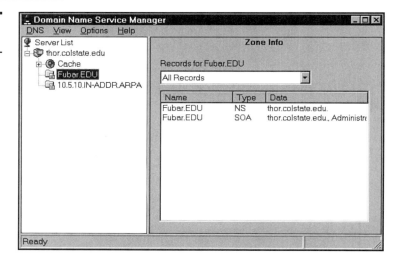

Adding Host Records

Now you are ready to add records for each host you want to appear on the DNS. To add such records, follow these steps:

1. To add a host to the primary zone you created, click the zone icon located in the server list to make it the current selection.

2. Choose the DNS menu item, and then click New Host.

3. A dialog box appears, prompting you for the host name. Enter the single-part computer name, *not* the FQDN. For the purposes of this demonstration, enter `myhost` (see fig. 13.7).

4. In the Host IP Address box, type the following address:

   `10.5.10.5.`

5. Select the Create Associated PTR Record check box. This creates a PTR record for reverse lookup automatically.

The proper IN-ADDR.ARPA zone must exist before the server manager will create PTR records automatically upon adding a host record. That is the reason you created the 10.5.10.IN-ADDR.ARPA zone before attempting to add any host records to the MyDomain.COM zone.

After the preceding procedure is complete, the new host appears as an A record in the Zone Info window of DNS Manager, and a PTR record is added to the appropriate IN-ADDR.ARPA zone (see figs. 13.8 and 13.9).

Figure 13.7

Adding a host to a primary zone.

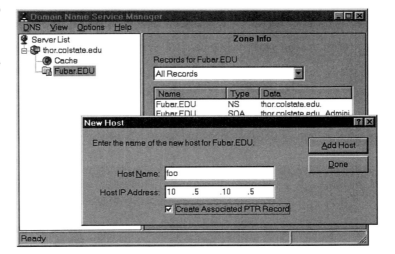

Figure 13.8

Newly created A resource record.

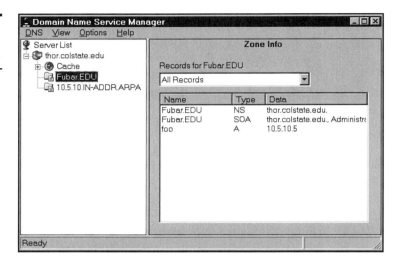

Figure 13.9

Newly created PTR resource record.

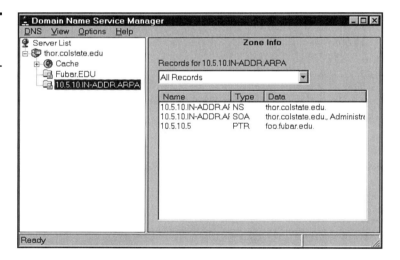

Inserting Other DNS Resource Records into a Primary Zone

The Domain MyDomain.COM is actually now ready to answer DNS queries (if the addresses used were actually valid), although there is only one host in that domain to be resolved. Other DNS resource records can also be added to the domain. Additional resource records are necessary to add new hosts to your domain, or to give a particular host a certain function, such as designating a host to be a mail exchanger for the domain. Two such records, CNAME and MX, will be added to the *MyDomain.COM* domain to round out the domain a bit. An additional A record will also be added to the domain to aid in illustrating the use of CNAME and MX records. Follow these steps to add the necessary records:

1. Add the new A record by following the procedure used to add a host record to a zone. Call the new host *mail*, and use 10.5.10.3 as its IP address. Make certain that DNS manager automatically creates the appropriate PTR record by checking the Create Associated PTR Record check box.

2. Create an MX record by clicking on the *MyDomain.COM* icon to make it the current selection. Select the DNS menu, and then click the New Record item.

3. A dialog box appears containing choices for resource record types to create. Choose MX from the list. Leave the Host Name text field blank, and enter *mail.MyDomain.COM* in the Mail Exchange Server DNS Name text box.

4. Enter *10* in the Preference Number Field (see fig. 13.10).

5. Click OK to create the MX record. DNS Manager creates an MX record making the host mail.MyDomain.COM responsible for handling mail for the MyDomain.COM domain.

6. Create a CNAME record by following the same procedure as given for creating an MX record, except that CNAME is the record type chosen rather than MX.

7. Under Alias Name enter `www` and `myhost.MyDomain.COM` in the For Host DNS Name field (see fig. 13.11). Click OK.

You have now created an alias for myhost.MyDomain.COM named www. Clients can now access myhost as either www or myhost.

Figure 13.10
Adding an MX record.

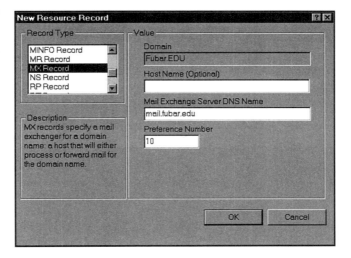

Figure 13.11

Adding a CNAME record.

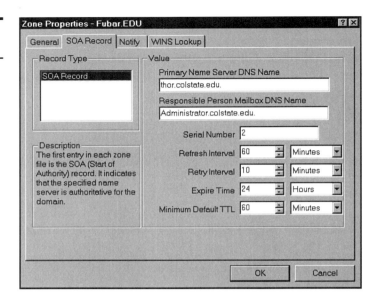

Congratulations! You have now created a two-host domain complete with CNAME, PTR, and MX records (see fig. 13.12). This domain will not work because the addresses used were bogus IP addresses. It is best to practice creating domains and zones two or three times; use bogus addresses to get the hang of things, without having to request addresses to play with and avoiding reusing an address already in use.

Figure 13.12

The completed domain.

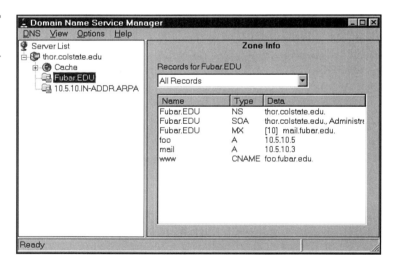

Registering with Your DNS Parent Domain

After you have installed and configured your DNS server or servers, you need to register with the DNS server above you in the hierarchical naming structure of DNS. The parent system needs the name and addresses of your name servers, and will probably want other information such as the date that the domain will be available and the names and addresses of contact people.

If you are registering with a parent below the second level, check with the administrator of that system to find out what information you need to supply and how to submit it.

Administering a DNS Server Using DNS Manager

Creating and registering the domain you have created is only the beginning. There are basic administrative and maintenance tasks that have to be performed on your newly created domain. Tasks such as registering new hosts and deleting hosts are examples of some of the day-to-day administrative tasks involved in running your own DNS server. This section will describe how to accomplish the following administrative tasks:

❏ Starting or Stopping the DNS Service

❏ Pausing a Zone

❏ Modifying an Existing Record in a Primary Zone

❏ Showing Zones Created Automatically by the DNS Manager

❏ Deleting Zones

❏ Forcing a Data File Update on the DNS Server

❏ Having the Primary Notify the Secondaries of Changes

Starting or Stopping the DNS Service

Whenever you perform maintenance on your domain, you need to stop the DNS service, make the changes, and start the service again. This ensures that the server reflects the changes you have made to your domain. To start or stop the DNS server, follow these steps:

1. In the Control Panel, choose Services.
2. In the Service list, click on Microsoft DNS Server, and then click Start, Stop, Pause, or Continue, and then click Close.

Pausing a Zone

When debugging a DNS domain, it often is useful to pause and resume the zone. This will help you determine whether the zone is indeed responding after it has been resumed. To pause a zone, complete the following steps:

1. In the Server List, right-click on the zone icon.
2. Click Pause. The Zone icon changes to indicate that the zone is paused.

You can recognize a paused zone by the | | mark on the icon. Pausing a zone effectively takes it offline. To bring it back online, repeat steps 1 and 2.

Modifying an Existing Record in a Primary Zone

At times, you will need to modify one, or more, of the records in an existing primary zone. This often is done when host information has changed, such as the IP address of a particular host. Your zone information needs to reflect these changes, and that is done as follows:

1. In the Server List, click the Primary Zone icon. The resource records are displayed under Zone Info.
2. To modify a resource record, right-click on it, and then click Properties.

Showing Zones Created Automatically by the DNS Manager

It often is useful to verify that the zones automatically created by the DNS manager contain the correct information. To view these zones perform the following steps:

1. On the Options menu, click Preferences.
2. Select the Show Automatically Created Zones check box.

This displays zones in the zone list that were set up automatically by the DNS manager.

Deleting Zones

If your organization is no longer providing primary or secondary DNS services for a zone, it should be deleted from your server as follows:

1. In the Server List, right-click on the zone icon.
2. Click on Delete Zone.

Forcing a Data File Update on the DNS Server

Changes made to the DNS server data files usually are not written out immediately after they are made. Instead, the changes remain in memory and are written out at certain intervals when the DNS manager or server is shut down. You might want to ensure that the changes you have made are reflected in the data files on disk immediately after making them. This is accomplished by doing the following:

On the DNS menu, click on Update Server Data Files.

This causes DNS to immediately write all changes to the zone data files. Normally these changes are written at predefined intervals and whenever DNS Server or DNS Manager are shut down.

Having the Primary Notify the Secondaries of Changes

Secondary name servers update their data files from the primary at specific intervals. To make the primary server inform the secondaries of changes as soon as they are made, perform the following steps:

1. In the Server List, right-click on the primary zone icon.
2. Click Properties.
3. In Notify List, type the IP addresses of the secondaries.
4. Optionally, to control access to the primary, click on Only Allow Access From Secondaries Included on Notify List.

This setting can be useful for updating secondary services as soon as changes are in the zone.

Using DNS Manager for Advanced Tasks

DNS Manager can be used to configure Name servers running on hosts other than the one on which you are working. You must have administrator privileges on the other servers before you can make modifications to zones on remote name servers.

Adding Remote Servers to the DNS Manager List

1. In the left pane of the DNS Manager window, right-click the Server List.
2. Click New Server.
3. In the DNS Server box, type the name or IP address of a server running the Microsoft DNS Service.

An icon representing the server appears in the Server List.

An icon with a red letter X through it indicates that DNS Manager was unable to connect with the DNS Service on the specified server. For more information about the type of error that occurred, see the Error box at the bottom of the right pane in the DNS Manager window.

By default, the three reverse lookup zones (zones in the IN-ADDR.ARPA domain) associated with each DNS server are 0.IN-ADDR.ARPA, 127.IN-ADDR.ARPA, and 255.IN-ADDR.ARPA. You do not need to do anything with them; they are added for performance reasons.

Removing a Server From the DNS Manager List

To remove a server from your DNS Manager list, follow these steps:

1. In the Server List, right-click the server icon.
2. Click Delete Server.

Deleting a server only removes it from the DNS Manager Server List; it does nothing to the actual DNS Server.

Viewing Server Statistics

To view server statistics, right-click the Server icon in the Server list. The statistics for the selected DNS Server appear in the right pane of the DNS Manager window.

Making DNS Manager Refresh Statistics Automatically

To refresh statistics automatically, follow these steps:

1. On the Options menu, click Preferences.
2. Click Auto Refresh Server Statistics.
3. Optionally, change the value for the Interval.

This automatically updates the server statistics only, which are visible when you click on a server in the Server List.

Expanding Your DNS Domains

As your organization's Internet domains grow in size, it becomes necessary to distribute the load and management burden of providing DNS service to other units within your organization. Your domain can accomplish this distribution of management and load through delegating responsibility for subzones, and by setting up servers acting as secondaries for a zone. For example, you may have many servers located in your R&D department and would like to give them responsibility for their own subzone. Hosts in this zone will have names in the form hostname.Research.MyDomain.COM. This arrangement allows the R&D department to assume responsibility for its own subzone. The following sections briefly cover secondary name servers and subzones.

Creating a Secondary Zone

To create a secondary zone, follow these steps:

1. If possible, add the primary zone's server to DNS Manager's Server List.
2. In the Server List, right-click the server icon.
3. Choose New Zone. Click Secondary, and then click Next.
4. Follow the instructions on-screen. The wizard prompts you for the zone you want to creating the secondary for and the IP address of the primary server for that zone.

You can recognize a secondary zone by the double file-folder icon.

Creating a Domain Within a Primary Zone

To create a Domain within a primary zone, follow these steps:

1. In the Server List, right-click the zone icon.
2. Click New Domain.
3. In the Domain Name box, type the name for the new domain.

This creates a subdomain within the existing zone. Resource records created in the domain will be part of the authoritative data of the existing zone. New records will default to using the time-to-live (TTL) interval specified in the SOA record for the zone, and will be included in any zone transfers.

If a new zone is desired (to enable WINS lookups for hosts in this domain or for some other administrative purpose), create a new zone.

The new subdomain will not work with WINS Lookup. WINS Lookup only resolves names that are direct children of the zone root domain. If you create a domain called subdomain1 within the mycompany.com zone root domain, for example, WINS Lookup will not work for names such as Hostx.subdomain1.mycompany.com because Hostx is not a direct child of the zone root domain mycompany.com.

Under this scenario, you should create and delegate the subdomain. After you delegate the subdomain, it becomes its own zone root domain, and WINS Lookup functions properly within it.

Delegating a New Subzone for a New Domain

Delegating a subzone is a good way to distribute the management and load of DNS services within your organization. You will need a server that will serve as the primary for the new subzone. To delegate a new subzone, follow these steps:

1. In the Server List, add the server that will be authoritative for the new subzone.
2. Click on this server, and create the subzone as a new primary zone.
3. In the Server List, double-click the primary server.
4. If a domain does not exist for the new subzone, right-click the existing zone, and then click New Domain and add a new domain for the subzone.
5. Right-click the new domain, and then click New Record.
6. Under Record Type, click NS Record. For Domain Server DNS Name, type the fully qualified domain name of the DNS server authoritative for the new subzone.
7. Under Record Type, create an A record for the server that will be authoritative for the new subzone, and then click OK.

In step 7, you need only to create an A record if the authoritative server for the new subzone is within the domain of the authoritative zone on the primary server.

If you are authoritative for ms.com and delegating nt.ms.com to bob.ms.com, for example, you need to create an A record. If you are delegating nt.ms.com to bob.otherzone.com, however, there is no need to create the A record.

Determining Whether You Should Maintain a DNS Server

In many cases, you do not need to maintain a DNS server. If you have a small network, or a single network rather than an Internetwork, you will probably find it simpler and more effective to have the DNS client software query a nearby DNS server, such as the one maintained by your Internet service provider. Most providers will maintain your domain information for a fee. If you have your own domain on the Internet, or if you want to access DNS from your LAN, you will want to provide your own DNS server rather than going through your Internet provider.

If you do maintain a DNS server, you probably will want to assign the task to at least two computers: a primary and a secondary name server. Data should be replicated from the primary name server to the secondary name server. This enables the Internet-wide DNS to locate computers on your network, even if one of the name servers is down. How often you schedule replication depends on the frequency with which names in your domain change. Replicate often enough that changes are known to both servers. Excessive replication can tie up your network and servers unnecessarily.

Other Internet Server Possibilities

If your Internet server design includes corporate user interaction, or you simply want to talk to your friends in Australia on your lunch break, several low-cost to free server possibilities exist that you may want to consider. Whether you require conferencing, access to your remote NT Internet server over the Net, or other services, hundreds of third-party, often free, applications on the Net may serve this purpose. Specifically, the remainder of this chapter is broken down into the following subjects:

❏ Microsoft's Internet Server Products
❏ Microsoft BackOffice
❏ Internet Application Development

IRC Chat

IRC has become the de facto standard for Internet real-time chat and conferencing. Although millions of people use IRC for completely unprofessional (and often illegal) purposes, several advances to the IRC design are enabling customizable and innovation conferencing programs for businesses. Many IRC chat programs enable users to display Web page URLs, causing the other viewers' browsers to instantly jump to the designated page. This can enable corporate conferencing and presentations to employees or clients anywhere in the world. Many professional *white board* applications, which provide presentation graphics and often voice chat capabilities, run off of IRC servers. If this could benefit your company, consider an IRC server on your Internet server. Several on the Internet enable easy administration and graphical user interface setup.

Telnet Servers

Windows NT does not ship with a Telnet server, and it is sometimes believed that it does not need one. Most of NT's features can be administered remotely by using graphical client administration tools; most quality Internet servers can be administered remotely over the Web. Instances occur, however, when a Telnet server may be of good use. Windows NT provides command line administration through *Net* commands, enabling an administrator to stop and start services, create or delete users or groups, and administer other services. A Telnet server offers easy access from virtually any Internet host, and provides the same security features built in to Windows NT (with the exception of transmitting passwords over a network). Some text-based Internet services still run via Telnet ports, and many Unix administrators will want Telnet servers on the NT Server just because it has become an Internet server standard.

Microsoft's Internet Server Products

Although Microsoft is certainly not the only contender in the Windows NT Internet server market, its Internet Information Server 2, shipping free with NT Server 4, is a strong candidate for the dominant Windows NT Internet server. Because of its popularity (whether forced or earned), IIS 2 has received enough of Microsoft's attention to merit several add-on specialized servers for Internet and intranet use.

This section outlines the currently available Microsoft server solutions, including those in the BackOffice server suite, that may prove useful to a corporation with intensive data warehousing or online interactive needs. Will you need professional site management software? Access to your corporation's customer database or even IBM mainframes? Microsoft's server solutions, several of them shipping with NT 4, or free for download, may provide an answer. As always, an Internet server administrator should consider all the server options available, including third-party companies.

This section does not seek to push Microsoft's wares; only to inform the reader about obvious Internet/intranet tools from the company that made the operating system. To that end, this section covers the following products:

- ❏ Internet Information Server
- ❏ Microsoft FrontPage
- ❏ Microsoft Index Server
- ❏ Microsoft Proxy Server
- ❏ Other Microsoft Servers

Internet Information Server

Since its release, IIS has become one of the most popular full-featured Internet servers for the NT Server operating system. Several interesting and well-planned reasons account for this. IIS has large performance gains over other NT Internet servers, and has been proven much faster than many popular Unix Web servers. IIS is simple to set up and configure—usually up and running within five minutes. Its graphical administrative tools and easy to use ODBC database access have made it a powerful tool for creating interactive Web sites that tie into a company's information systems. Two more obvious reasons, however, account for why Microsoft Internet Information Server is rapidly becoming a contender for NT's Internet server market share:

- ❏ It's free
- ❏ It ships with NT Server 4

Microsoft knew what it was doing by offering its premier Internet server for free. You won't find an *evaluation* or *demo* copy of IIS, and you won't have to dread the day when you must send in registration fees or stop your usage. Microsoft will continue to offer IIS free of charge for any licensed Windows NT Server users. This has been one of the software giant's most effective marketing plans, and has created a stable base of users. Rest assured that no money is being lost in offering a free Internet server.

Why Consider Internet Information Server?

Why choose Internet Information Server as your Internet server platform? Although IIS may not be the best server solution for you, it is important to know and understand the features and benefits it offers. IIS works only on the NT Server platform, and is optimized as an integrated part of the operating system. Although this limits NT Workstation users to other Internet server solutions, it enables IIS to integrate as a BackOffice server such as Microsoft SQL Server. This also shows the direction Microsoft is taking with its two versions of NT; NT Server will be the recommended and supported Internet server platform.

If you want to maintain a heavy-traffic site, with custom applications for user interaction, IIS has a fully supported API (Application Programming Interface) for creating programs accessible from the World Wide Web. The ISAPI is used to create Dynamic Link Libraries (DLLs) to make your Web site interactive and customizable. IIS also offers database access through ODBC (Open Database Connectivity) drivers that enable viewers to query or update databases from the Web. Online transactions or complex searches can be designed by using any supported database such as Microsoft Access 7 or an SQL Server. Internet Information Server offers more flexibility and administrative benefits, such as:

❏ ISAPI DLLs that run ten times faster than regular CGI scripts.

❏ The Internet Database Connector DLL, which enables access to ODBC data sources and can return customized HTML feedback.

❏ Microsoft SQL Server and ODBC Logging. Administrators can query the entire server's log files.

❏ Greater number of connections per second, compared to all other Windows NT Internet servers.

New Features of Internet Information Server 2

With the release of Windows NT Server 4 comes the second incarnation of the Internet Information Server, version 2. There have been major upgrades and improvements to IIS in this new release in areas of speed, security, and ease of administration. IIS 2 now ships with Windows NT Server 4, making it the de facto Internet server for the NT Server 4 system. If your company is using, or plans to use, NT Server 4, you should strongly consider IIS 2 for your Internet server needs. The new features, as heralded by Microsoft, include the following:

❏ Integration with NT Server 4

❏ Point-to-Point Tunneling Protocol. A secure protocol for establishing private networks over the Internet. This is built into Windows NT 4.

❏ New Web Page Administration. Like Netscape's Commerce Server, IIS 2 now offers HTML administration pages for administrators to configure IIS 2 across the Internet.

❏ ODBC Connection Pooling. This delivers up to three times the performance of database access compared to IIS 1.0.

❏ Microsoft Index Server integration. Query all HTML or other files (such as Microsoft Office documents) specified for keyword searches, and so on.

❏ Designed for intranets. IIS 2 and its support products are designed to propel Microsoft's commitment to intranets using Microsoft's products and services.

- ❏ NCSA and CERN imagemap file support. This makes it easier to port imagemap files from Unix systems.
- ❏ Web Server Administration. IIS 2 enables administration of all Web servers on a network with the Internet Server Manager.

Microsoft FrontPage

FrontPage is a Web site creation and management tool with built-in security for group management. FrontPage includes a powerful Web page editor with several templated Web pages a company or individual will find useful. The editor enables custom *bots*, or preconfigured Web tools that enable interaction with dynamic Web pages. FrontPage also includes Web extensions that enable compatibility with several other Web servers for both NT and Unix. FrontPage is not contingent on Internet Information Server, although it comes with IIS 2 extensions for easy integration. FrontPage also features its own personal Web server for developing and testing Internet and intranet sites. Three tools comprise FrontPage:

NOTE

For a closer look at FrontPage, see *Designing Web Pages with FrontPage*, by Ken Milburn and Jessica Burdman (New Riders, 1996).

- ❏ The FrontPage Editor, for creating dynamic Web pages.
- ❏ The FrontPage Explorer, for traversing and administrating the custom *Webs* created with FrontPage.
- ❏ The FrontPage Administrator, for installing extensions, new versions of the product, and administering site information.

The following sections detail what FrontPage's tools offer, and demonstrate some of the capabilities of the software.

The FrontPage Explorer

The FrontPage Explorer is the tool that helps you create your own intranet *web* by using Microsoft's *wizards* to design and layout entire Web sites for corporate or personal use. Some of the standard Web wizards included in FrontPage are:

- ❏ Customer Support
- ❏ Corporate Presence
- ❏ Personal Page
- ❏ Project

After you are through filling out the wizards and determining the needs of your Web site, FrontPage Explorer compiles the information into a graphical representation of your Web site. This conceptual view enables point-and-click access to different pages, stages of development, and a To Do List that enables delegation of tasks among multiple designers. Explorer creates the Web site directly on the Web server specified—either your existing server, or on the FrontPage personal server. Figure 13.13 shows FrontPage Explorer's conceptual model of a simple corporate presence Web site.

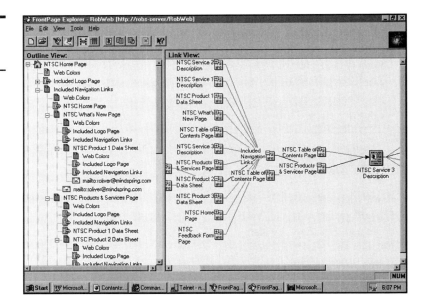

Figure 13.13
Microsoft FrontPage Explorer.

FrontPage can create feedback and interactive forms, releasing the administrator of the burden of CGI scripts or DLLs for the Internet server. Using FrontPage Explorer, administrators can not only create the Web site, but can also manage it easily. Feedback answer pages, generated when someone fills out a form and sends the request, are listed in the site information for each Web. Just open the Web you want to administer, and all pages, links, and information retrieval pages are listed in a tree format as seen in the illustration above. Some of FrontPage Explorer's most useful features include the following:

❏ Create clickable imagemap images
❏ Link verification, to ensure that your links are valid, whether on your own site or on the Internet

- ❏ Enforce security on pages and Webs, to limit the access of your content designers
- ❏ Rename any file on your Web, and have it automatically renamed in any links that call it
- ❏ Several designers can work on the same page, remotely over an intranet or the Internet

The FrontPage Editor

After creating a custom Web with FrontPage Explorer, the designer uses the FrontPage Editor to customize and extend the capabilities of the Web pages. FrontPage provides comments and other information on the template pages, making it easier for the beginner to develop interactive and visually pleasing pages. The Editor also features the To Do List, which keeps track of tasks for all designers, and can take a designer directly to the task to be completed with a click of the mouse (see fig. 13.14).

Figure 13.14
FrontPage To Do List.

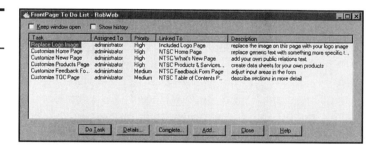

The FrontPage Editor has some attractive features, though experienced HTML designers may opt to develop their pages the old fashioned way (see fig. 13.15). (Some of the best Web pages are created in Notepad!) What the editor provides that regular HTML authoring tools do not is the capability to add WebBots, the automatically configured interactive tools that replace the need for many CGI scripts. A click on the inserted WebBot fields enable the designer to add extended features and parameters to the bot's functionality. FrontPage Editor can also add standard design and interactive Web page features, such as the following:

- ❏ Forms fields
- ❏ Push buttons
- ❏ Check boxes and radio buttons
- ❏ Tables

Figure 13.15

Microsoft FrontPage Editor.

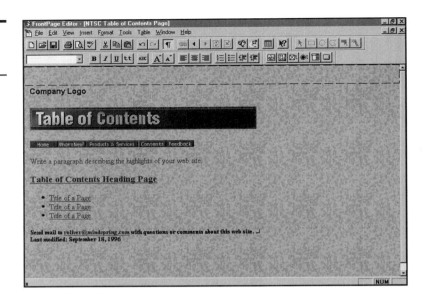

One typical complaint about Web page editors, especially a large package like FrontPage that could become a company's main Web development platform, is the extensibility and support of the most current HTML standards. Although any Web page can be enhanced with the most recent HTML features, an HTML editor will eventually fall behind. It is expected that, because of its huge shift toward Internet and intranet development, Microsoft will continually offer upgrades to FrontPage's HTML capabilities and server extensions.

FrontPage Server Administrator

FrontPage offers server extensions to enable many of today's popular NT and Unix Web servers to use its features. These are installed and configured with the FrontPage Server Administrator. The Server Administrator, pictured in figure 13.16, offers other features such as site security and authoring. A Web administrator can choose to allow other designers to author pages that are secured by user account and IP address restriction. New extensions can be installed, uninstalled, or upgraded.

FrontPage Server Extensions

Currently, FrontPage server extensions are available for most of the popular cross-platform, World Wide Web servers. These extensions mean development of Web sites on a Windows NT machine is possible, even if the actual Internet server is running on another operating system. Some of the Web servers supported are:

- ❏ Microsoft Internet Information Server (Windows NT)
- ❏ Netscape Commerce Server
- ❏ Netscape Communications Server
- ❏ O'Reilly and Associates WebSite
- ❏ NCSA, CERN, and Apache Web servers for Sun Microsystems, Silicon Graphics, and Hewlett-Packard systems.

Figure 13.16
Microsoft FrontPage Server Administrator.

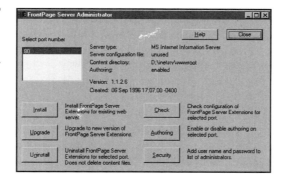

Microsoft Index Server

Would giving your users the ability to search your entire Internet site and document contents for a string or parameters prove beneficial? What if you are running an intranet in your company, and want to be able to query documents, databases, spreadsheets, text files, and other data files for information on a company or project? Microsoft's Index Server is a document search server that can be used from Web pages to search through a multitude of file and document types for information. Index Server is an add-on server product for Microsoft Internet Information Server (or Microsoft Peer Web Services), and is suited for Internet sites, intranet servers, and simple NT file or print servers if needed. Index server provides several advanced querying features, indexing capabilities, and multiple language support.

Index Server Querying and Indexing

Index Server enables queries to access all the matching documents on a site, and return a result set of all documents matching the query and any restrictions established. Queries can be limited and restricted on their result sets by using several methods. Index Server queries can be specified with parameters such as:

❏ Word and phrase search

❏ Boolean properties, AND, OR, and NOT

❏ Wild cards such as * and ?

The search features of Index Server can be compared to the text search capabilities of the Unix *grep* utility, in that many of the same search options, such as finding words close to a matching phrase, can be used. Index Server can also rank the hits in order of quality of matching, and can be returned using filters and preset specifications for the HTML pages. A sample index query site is included with the installation of Index Server, and can be used to query document and file information (see fig. 13.17).

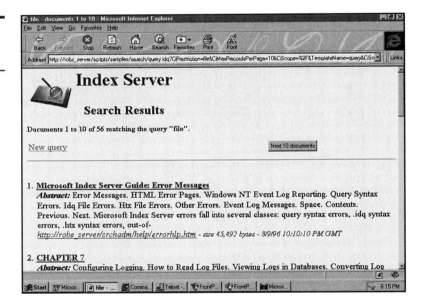

Figure 13.17
Microsoft Index Server sample querying pages.

Index Server creates indexes on a server, which can be used frequently in searches, saving time on future searches. Index server requires hard disk space of approximately 40 percent of the size of all documents and sources available for querying. The administration of Index Server can be fairly complex, and several indexing concepts should be understood before jumping into indexing services on your server. If you are interested in powerful indexing and querying services on your Internet server or intranet site, however, Index Server is a free solution that integrates quickly and easily with Internet Information Server 2.

Microsoft Proxy Server

Would your organization benefit from Internet access across the entire LAN, without installing and managing TCP/IP protocols and services? Do you need to bring Web browsers, multimedia access, or conferencing services to your non-TCP/IP compatible desktops? Microsoft's Proxy Server, or *Catapult Server* as it has been code named, is a full-featured proxy server that enables networked computers to access the Internet, or intranet based resources. Proxy Server boasts security features that leverage NT's high security, and provides other network oriented security services. Proxy Server runs on Windows NT Server 4, with Internet Information Server 2.

Proxy Server Internet Support

Microsoft Proxy Server supports a multitude of standard Internet protocols, bringing multimedia and interactive capabilities to any desktop. Proxy Server currently supports all Internet standards and protocols, including the following:

- ❏ HTTP (World Wide Web)
- ❏ FTP file transfer
- ❏ POP3 and SMTP (e-mail)
- ❏ NNTP (News protocols for newsreaders)
- ❏ RealAudio
- ❏ VDOLive streaming video
- ❏ IRC chat

Proxy Server Security

Site security with a proxy server is a major consideration; Microsoft Proxy Server has received several impressive reviews of its security features. Integrating with the Windows NT operating system Internet IIS, Proxy Server offers higher-speed access, security, and ease of administration. Administrators can easily deny or grant access based on several criteria: user, IP address, port, or even service. Site access can also be blocked to prevent access of unsuitable resources, Web pages, or privileged intranet site information.

Microsoft Proxy Server exists in beta version at the time of this writing. As a beta, it is offered free for download on the Microsoft Web and ftp site at http://www.microsoft.com.

Microsoft Commercial Internet System Servers

Microsoft has launched an extensive campaign to detail the advantages and uses of this new Internet server family. The Commerical Internet System (CIS) servers run on the Windows NT and Internet information Server platform, and provide several professional Internet server solutions.

The CIS servers are primarily targeted to corporations that would benefit from online technical support, real-time chat, news and mail capabilities, and other services that require customizable and personal design. Internet Service Providers and Web content managers also are suggested users of the servers because Normandy includes an entire family of Internet servers.

The concept behind CIS is the creation of Internet *communities*, and thus is driving the goal for a more personalized and user friendly Internet environment. By using ActiveX technology and other Internet standards, CIS attempts to achieve a better user experience and a more secure and scalable Internet server architecture.

See Appendix A, "Overview of the Microsoft Commercial Internet System Servers" for a complete description of this new suite of products.

Microsoft BackOffice

BackOffice is Microsoft's suite of network server products for the Windows NT Server platform. Although BackOffice is primarily a LAN and WAN networking suite, Microsoft has expanded many of the server products for use with intranets and the Internet. Table 13.1 explains the current components of BackOffice.

Table 13.1 Uses for Server Software	Server Software	Usage
	Windows NT Server	The operating system BackOffice runs on
	Internet Information Server	Suggested Internet and intranet server for integration with other BackOffice servers
	Exchange Server	Messaging and mail (including e-mail) server
	SQL Server	Relational database management server, accessible through a multitude of clients

Server Software	Usage
Systems Management Server	Complete network and management server tool for administering remote computers and software installation
SNA Server	Supports access to IBM mainframes
Mail Server Proxy Server	Microsoft Mail server services Internet access to non-TCP/IP networks (explained previously)

Internet Information Server and Microsoft Proxy Server have already been discussed in this chapter. Two other important BackOffice servers that might interest an Internet server administrator are Microsoft Exchange Server and Microsoft SQL Server.

Microsoft Exchange Server

Exchange Server is an enterprise-wide messaging and scheduling server that coordinates internal office mail, as well as Internet e-mail. Coupled with an Internet server, Exchange Server can help complete your total Internet presence, enabling e-mail for each employee in your company. Exchange also offers group scheduling administration and rich content transfer such as multimedia files over network mail.

Microsoft SQL Server

Most Windows NT Server-based Web and ftp servers can use SQL Server to log files and to provide database access to your Web users. SQL Server is a database management system that can scale to large corporations or small businesses. It is accessible over TCP/IP sockets, multiple protocols, and acts as a client/server back end to information systems. SQL Server has rich development support because of its use of SQL (Structured Query Language), ODBC connectivity, and constantly updated APIs for custom application development.

NOTE

For complete information about Microsoft's BackOffice suite of products, visit the Microsoft BackOffice Web site at http://www.microsoft.com/backoffice.

As a large scale database management system, SQL Server could offer access to information from multitudes of databases in your company. Your Internet

Information Server's ease of use with SQL Server could mean quick access to any crucial data, with security enhancements from not only Windows NT, but also from IIS and SQL Server.

Internet Application Development

Many sites require custom applications for Internet and intranet usage—applications such as Java applets or ActiveX controls, two of the current buzzwords of the Internet application industry. Some Internet Web sites need more complicated and specific applications than simple CGI scripts and data transfer; intranets are benefiting from browser-embedded fully functional Windows-like programs distributed to each desktop at a per-need basis from a central application server or Internet server. Although Web development is not within the scope of this book, knowledge of the software design tools used to create professional Web applications is an important part of administering and planning dynamic Internet sites. Custom software is a substantial part of interactive data access on a Web site, and has even been used to control remote resources such as scientific and measurement equipment.

If you are going to be using Microsoft products to build your Internet server, you want to be familiar with all the innovations out there. Two important factors in choosing Internet tools for both site management and user benefits are Internet applications and the development of those applications. Microsoft's latest Web browser, Internet Explorer 3, is the software leader's latest Internet client platform. Competing with Netscape's Navigator (still the leading Web browser, with a strong user base and cross-platform dominance), Internet Explorer 3 is quickly becoming a Web browser platform for Internet and intranet application usage. From Java applets to ActiveX controls, IE 3 supports software developments that can leverage existing development skills. ActiveX controls are essentially the same software component as an OCX (OLE control), which can be written in, and accessed with, several popular Microsoft languages such as Visual C++ and Visual Basic. Java, a C++ like language used for Web development, is supported on almost all popular Web browsers on all platforms.

The rest of this chapter covers some of the major Internet software development strategies, tools, and Microsoft innovations. Some of these tools will be specific to Microsoft's Internet Explorer 3 Web browser; others will be generic and platform independent. The designer of a Web site's custom software should be aware of both third-party and generic tools, as well as those provided by Microsoft.

ActiveX

Microsoft's ActiveX component software design standard for the Web has enabled software developers to create OCX controls for use in the Internet Explorer 3 Web browser. ActiveX controls download and installs automatically, embedding seamlessly in a Web page for a more native and natural interface. It also succeeds in replacing bulky plug-ins, and leveraging software development knowledge. ActiveX controls not only enable a wider variety of development options, but also bring the advantage of real Windows-like software components to a Web page.

ActiveX has been criticized as a *Microsoft only* technology, which exists only on the Internet Explorer 3 platform. Although Microsoft intends to create cross-platform versions of Internet Explorer, it should be understood that ActiveX is currently a technology for use on Windows NT 4 and Windows 95 platforms. As an intranet software solution, ActiveX is a feasible choice if your desktops are running mostly Windows 95 or NT Workstation. The overall look and feel of ActiveX controls, along with the sleek interface of IE 3, provide a more user-friendly and professional look to Internet applications than many standard Java-based applications.

The ActiveX SDK (Software Development Kit) is available for free download on Microsoft's Web and ftp site. The SDK includes documentation, samples, and all necessary files for writing ActiveX controls, Internet capable applications, and VBScript—the Visual Basic scripting language supported by Internet Explorer 3. The documentation for the ActiveX SDK has been traditionally rather cryptic and unclear; it is, however, being improved. ActiveX development is also being made easier by new tools and samples. For more information, see *VBScript with ActiveX* (New Riders Publishing, 1997).

Java and Microsoft J++

Java is the C++-like language developed by Sun Microsystems for creating interactive and powerful programs for the Web. Java is a cross-platform language that compiles into Java byte code, and has been used in a subset form as a scripting language: JavaScript. Web designers have used Java applets to create professional-quality interfaces for graphics-intensive Web pages, small applications for use with conferencing programs, database access, and simpler functions that used to lie specifically in the domain of CGI scripts. Java is a relatively easy language to learn, being similar to C++ (though many argue the merits of the two languages when compared) in implementation.

Sun Microsystems offers two tools for developing Java applications. Both can be downloaded from the Sun Web site for free or trial use.

❏ Java Developers Kit (JDK) is the basic Java development environment for creating applets conforming to the Java API. For cross-platform Java development, a free compiler and language is hard to beat.

❏ Java WorkShop is a professional Java development environment for the more advanced developer. This suite of tools and applications is actually a collection of Java applets contained in a Web browser front-end. This not only makes the entire environment Web-aware, but also enables it to be easily cross-platformed. Project management, debugging, and application testing are also supported.

NOTE

Sun Microsystem's Java development World Wide Web site can be accessed at http://www.sun.com.

Microsoft's own version of the Java language, J++, is offered with the same professional development environment as its widely popular Visual C++ language: Microsoft Developer's Studio (see fig. 13.18). Visual J++ provides the same environment, including a Class Viewer, which makes navigation within your source code simple. Online books and support for the Microsoft Developer's Network CD also make the Visual J++ Developer Studio an attractive tool for learning or advancing in the Java language. Currently, Visual J++ is in its beta stages, and is offered free for download on Microsoft's Web site. Visual J++ also builds Java ActiveX controls, which make the ActiveX architecture more accessible and justifiable.

Internet Information Server API (ISAPI)

Microsoft Internet Information Server provides its own API (Application Programming Interface) for developing programs for use on the Web. The ISAPI enables software developers to create professional applications in C or C++ that outperform regular CGI (common gateway interface) scripts by approximately ten times. ISAPI programs compile into DLLs (Dynamic Link Libraries), a Windows standard for dynamically loaded code sections of an executable. Because of the user of DLLs, the ISAPI program is loaded into the same memory address space as Internet Information Server. Such a loading makes it run more securely, robustly, and efficiently. Many ISAPI programs extend database connectivity and provide filters for incoming and outgoing HTML information. If you are using Internet Information Server, and require high-speed custom programs rather than slower CGI scripts, consider developing ISAPI DLLs. Microsoft's Visual C++ 4.2 development environment includes templates for creating these DLLs, making the process much easier and the learning curve less steep. Other Web servers, such as Netscape's Commerce Server, also provide their own native server APIs for custom software development. If you are

Figure 13.18
Visual J++ Developer's Studio.

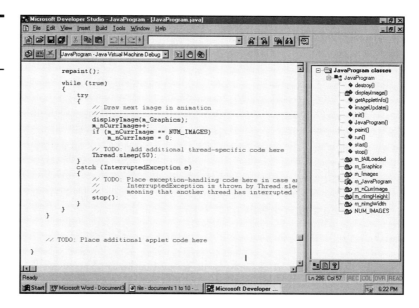

interested in speed and getting the most out of your server, consider developing programs with close integration with your Web server.

Summary

This chapter discussed additional user services you might want to take advantage of, including DNS services, IRC Chat and Telnet, and Microsoft Internet server products. It also included information about Microsoft BackOffice suite and Internet application development with ActiveX, VBScript, Java, and J++.

IV

System Administration

14

Security Practices

Security of your server and network data is of capital importance when introduced to the Internet community. Even if your existing network requires only minimal security, your Internet server should benefit from ample security and access precautions.

The first half of this chapter discusses basic policy practices, covering such tactics as firewalls, and the second half of this chapter covers the Windows NT security model. You also learn about TCP/IP security.

Network Security Policies

Although one of the most common forms of internet security is firewalls, it is not enough to have a firewall protecting your network from attack. A dedicated hacker can still break into your network. Firewalls were used during two highly publicized break-ins recently. One occurred in the private network of security expert Tsutomu Shimomura, and the other took place at Los Alamos National Laboratories.

To make certain that your network is protected, perform the following steps:

1. Establish and enforce a uniform security policy throughout your organization.
2. Take a census of your network's weak points.
3. Consider using a commercial security testing firm or employing a commercial security tool.
4. Create a report of known weaknesses.

The following sections cover these concepts in more depth.

Establishing and Enforcing a Uniform Security Policy

The first thing to do when creating a network security policy is to define which information, computer resources, and assets are sensitive. Defining what is sensitive enables you to decide what needs to be protected and from whom. Next, it is necessary to develop a policy regarding user passwords. Train users in basic rules of password protection. Deploy methods that enable you to control user passwords, such as password expiration and disallowing of password reuse.

In addition to creating a network security policy, it is important to enforce it. Do not allow users to scribble passwords on Post-It notes that might then be left lying around. Enforce password creation rules by requiring users to choose passwords that are not easy to guess and forbidding users from reusing old passwords. If the security policy is not enforced throughout the organization, it does not serve its intended purpose.

Taking Census of Your Network's Weak Points

Find out the security holes in each platform deployed on your network. You can accomplish this by looking at vendor-provided security advisories or advisories put out by agencies such as CERT (Computer Emergency Response Team;—see http://www.cert.org). Check each node on the network for human programming errors, looking for misconfigured network client and server software. Seek out places where information may cross paths such as dialin modem pools, intranet Web servers, and e-mail gateways. You essentially are looking for any place on your network where an intruder may gain access from the outside and perhaps even from the inside. At this point, you are trying to gather as much data as possible about your network's current security status. You will use this data later to formulate solutions to any problems that may have been found.

Using Commercial Network Security Consultants or Tools

Periodically using security consultants to probe and test your network security can go a long way toward determining which areas of your network have weak security. Many firms specialize in probing networks for weaknesses. Many of these firms also offer software that scans your network for many known security holes. A number of these companies have Web sites whose addresses can be found via the Yahoo! list at http://www.yahoo.com/Business_and_Economy/Companies/Computers/Security/Consulting/. One such company is Internet Security Systems (http://iss.net/), whose security analysis tool, Internet Scanner, looks for 130 known security holes on firewalls, routers, Unix, Windows and Windows NT, and any other devices accessible over TCP/IP. A list of other software companies who make security software is available at http://www.yahoo.com/Business_and_Economy/Companies/Computers/Software/Systems_and_Utilities/Security/.

Creating a Report of Known Weaknesses

By the time the previously mentioned steps are taken toward improving your organization's security, you will have a good idea of the security weaknesses present in your organization. The data gathered enables you to determine how best to secure access and monitor the bidirectional flow of data, whom to give access to, how up to date your security mechanisms are, how much the security system will cost, and how much the data you are trying to protect is worth in relation to the cost you will incur protecting it. Your organization should perform audits and update security policies annually or when major changes take place in the network.

Of course, besides preparing your organization on a conceptual level, some specific measures can be taken to improve security, such as implementing firewalls.

Firewall Basics

A firewall is a system or group of systems that enforces an access control policy between two networks. The actual means by which this is accomplished vary widely. In principle, the firewall can be thought of as a pair of mechanisms: one that exists to block traffic, and the other that exists to permit traffic. Probably the most important thing to recognize about a firewall is that it implements an access control policy. If you do not have a good idea regarding the kind of access you want to permit or deny, or you simply permit someone or some product to configure a firewall based on what that person or product thinks it should do, that outsider is making policy for your organization as a whole.

Reasons for Deploying a Firewall

The Internet, like any other society, is plagued with the kind of people who enjoy the electronic equivalent of writing on other people's walls with spray paint, tearing their mailboxes off, or just sitting in the street blowing their car horns. Some people try to get real work done over the Internet, and others have sensitive or proprietary data they must protect. Usually, a firewall's purpose is to keep the intruders out of your network yet still enable you to get your job done.

Many traditional-style corporations and data centers have computing security policies and practices that must be adhered to. In a case where a company's policies dictate how data must be protected, a firewall is important because it is the embodiment of the corporate policy. Frequently, the hardest part of hooking to the Internet, if you are a large company, is not justifying the expense or effort, but convincing management that it is safe to do so. A firewall provides not only real security—it often plays an important role as a security blanket for management.

Lastly, a firewall can act as your organization's ambassador to the Internet. Many organizations use their firewall systems as a place to store public information about products and services, files to download, bug fixes, and so on. Several of these systems have become important parts of the Internet service structure (for example, `UUnet.uu.net`, `whitehouse.gov`, `gatekeeper.dec.com`) and have reflected well on their organizational sponsors.

Types of Firewalls

Firewalls exist on two levels:

❏ Network level

❏ Application level

Network level and application level firewalls do not differ as greatly as you might think. The latest technologies are blurring the distinction to the point at which it is no longer clear if one is better or worse than the other. As always, you need to be careful to pick the type that meets your needs.

Network Level Firewalls

Network level firewalls generally make their decisions based on the source, destination addresses, and ports in individual IP packets. A simple router is the traditional network level firewall; it is unable to make particularly sophisticated decisions about what a packet is actually talking to or where it actually came from. Modern network level firewalls have become increasingly sophisticated and now maintain internal information about the state of connections passing through them, the contents of some of the data streams, and so on. An important distinction about many network level firewalls is that they route traffic directly though them; to use one you usually need to have a validly assigned IP address block. Network level firewalls tend to be very fast and to be very transparent to users. One problem with network level firewalls is that they are vulnerable to IP spoofing attacks.

NOTE

IP spoofing is an attack whereby a system attempts to illicitly impersonate another system by using its IP network address.

You can choose from the following three types of network level firewalls:

❏ Screened host gateways

❏ Screened subnets

❏ Hybrid gateways

Each has its own strengths, and implementation of a certain type depends on the security needs of your organization. They are described in more detail in the following sections.

Screened Host Gateways

Generally, the screened host gateway is secure, yet it remains fairly easy to implement. Typically, a bastion host is configured on the private network, with a screening router between the Internet and the private network, which only permits Internet access to the bastion host. Because the bastion host is on the private network, connectivity for local users is good, and problems presented by exotic routing configurations do not present themselves. If the private network is, as many are, a virtual extended local area network (no subnets or routing), the screened host gateway works without requiring any changes to the local network, as long as the local network is using a legitimately assigned set of network addresses. The zone of risk of a screened host gateway is restricted to the bastion host and the screening router. The security stance of the screened host gateway is determined by the software running on that system. If an attacker gains login access to the bastion host, a fairly wide range of options exist for attacking the rest of the private network. In many ways, this approach is similar to the dual-homed gateway, sharing similar failure modes and design considerations with respect to the software running on the bastion host.

Screened Subnets

A screened subnet is usually configured with a bastion host as the sole point of access on the subnet. The zone of risk is small, consisting of that bastion host(s) and any screening routers that make up the connections between the screened subnet, the Internet, and the private network. The ease of use and the basic stance of the screened subnet will vary. Generally, however, a screened subnet is appealing only for firewalls that are taking advantage of routing to reinforce the existing screening. This approach forces all services through the firewall to be provided by application gateways and places the stance strongly in the *That which is not expressly permitted is prohibited* category.

If a screened subnet-based firewall with internetwork routing blocked is attacked with an intent to destroy it, the attacker must reconfigure the routing on three networks, without disconnecting or locking himself out, and without the routing changes being noticed. No doubt this is possible, but it can be made difficult by disabling network access to the screening routers or by configuring the screening routers to permit access only from specific hosts on the private network. In this case, an attacker would need to break into the bastion host, and then into one of the hosts on the private network, and then back out to the screening router—without setting off any alarms.

Another advantage of screened subnets is that they can be put in place in such a way that they hide any accidents of history that may linger on the private network. Many sites that would like to connect to the Internet are daunted by the prospect of readdressing and resubnetting existing networks. With a screened subnet with blocked internetwork routing, a private network can be connected to the Internet and changed gradually to new subnet and network addresses. In fact, this approach has been observed to significantly accelerate the adoption of new network addresses on loosely controlled private networks. Users will be more receptive to changing host addresses if they can realize the benefits of Internet connectivity because hosts not correctly addressed cannot use the firewall properly. In most other respects, the screened subnet is very much dependent on the suite of software running on the bastion host. Screening a whole subnet provides functionality similar to the dual-homed gateway or screened host gateway; it differs primarily in the extra level of complexity in routing and configuration of the screening routers.

Hybrid Gateways

Security through obscurity is not sufficient in and of itself, but there is no question that an unusual configuration (or one difficult to understand) is likely to give an attacker pause, or to make the attacker more likely to reveal himself in the process of trying to figure out what he is facing. On the other hand, an easy to understand security configuration has its advantages, including being easier to evaluate and maintain.

Imagine a hybrid gateway that consists of a box sitting on the Internet, which is capable of routing traffic, but also maintains a complete notion of the state of every TCP connection, how much data has gone across it, where it originated, and its destination. Presumably, connections can be filtered based on arbitrarily precise rules, such as: permit traffic between host A on the private network and all hosts on network B on the Internet via the Telnet service if the connection originated from host A between the hours of 9:00 a.m. and 5:00 p.m. and log the traffic. This sounds terrific, providing arbitrary control with great ease of use, but some problems refuse to go away. Consider that someone wanting to circumvent the firewall, who broke into the private network via an unguarded modem, might very easily set up a service engine that was piggybacked over the Telnet port. This is a fairly easy firewall to destroy.

Another hybrid gateway might take advantage of various forms of protocol tunneling. Suppose that the requirement is to connect to the Internet with very tight restrictions, but that a high degree of connectivity is required between the private network and an external network that is somewhat trusted (for example, a corporate R&D department needs to be able to run remote GUI applications on a supercomputer at another facility). The usual archetypal gateways discussed here could provide general purpose e-mail connectivity, but for secure point-to-point communications, an encrypted point-to-point virtual TCP/IP connection might be set up with the remote system after users authenticated themselves with a cryptographic smart card. This would be extremely secure and might be made fairly easy to use, but it has the disadvantage that the protocol driver needs to be added to every system that wants to share communication. It is hard to make any guesses about the failure mode of such a system, but the zone of risk is neatly limited to all the hosts that are running the tunneling protocol driver and to which the individual user has smart card access. Some of this might be implemented in hardware or in the routers. In the future, the rapid growth of the Internet will most likely fuel more development in this area, and various hybrid gateway schemes will appear on the market. The basic issues surrounding configuring a firewall will probably remain the same as the ones discussed here.

Figure 14.1 shows a network level firewall. In this example, a network level firewall called a screened host firewall is represented. In a *screened host firewall*, access to and from a single host is controlled by means of a router operating at a network level. The single host is a *bastion host*—a highly defended and secured strong-point that should be able to resist attack.

Figure 14.1
A screened host firewall.

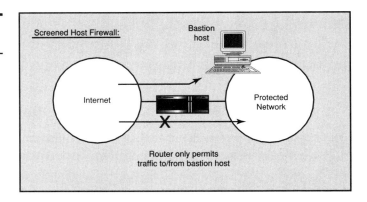

Figure 14.2 shows another network level firewall. In this example, a network level firewall called a screened subnet firewall is represented. In a *screened subnet firewall*, access to and from a network is controlled by means of a router operating at a network level. It is similar to a screened host, except that it is, effectively, a network of screened hosts.

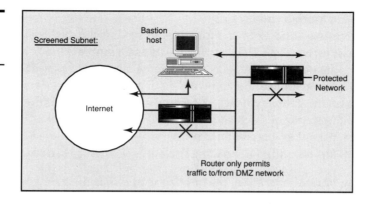

Figure 14.2

A screened subnet firewall.

Screened Subnet:

Bastion host

Internet

Protected Network

Router only permits traffic to/from DMZ network

Application Level Firewalls

Application level firewalls are generally hosts running proxy servers, which permit no traffic directly between networks and which perform elaborate logging and auditing of traffic passing through them. Because the proxy applications are software components running on the firewall, it is a good place to do a lot of logging and access control. Application level firewalls can be used as network address translators because traffic goes in one side and out the other after having passed through an application that effectively masks the origin of the initiating connection. In some cases, having an application in the way may impact performance and may make the firewall less transparent. Early application level firewalls, such as those built using the TIS firewall toolkit, are not particularly transparent to end users and may require training. Modern application level firewalls are often fully transparent.

Application level firewalls tend to provide more detailed audit reports and tend to enforce more conservative security models than network level firewalls.

Proxy Servers

A *proxy* server (sometimes referred to as an *application gateway* or *forwarder*) is an application that mediates traffic between a protected network and the Internet. Proxies often are used instead of router-based traffic controls to prevent traffic from passing directly between networks. Many proxies contain extra logging or support for user authentication. Because proxies must understand the application protocol being used, they also can implement protocol-specific security—an FTP proxy might be configurable to permit incoming FTP and block outgoing FTP, for example.

Proxy servers are application-specific. To support a new protocol via a proxy, a proxy must be developed for it. One popular set of proxy servers is the TIS Internet Firewall Toolkit (FWTK) that includes proxies for Telnet, rlogin, FTP, X-Window, HTTP/Web, and NNTP/UseNET news.

Dual-Homed Gateways

An often-used and easy to implement firewall is the *dual-homed gateway*. Because it does not forward TCP/IP traffic, it acts as a complete block between the Internet and the private network. The way the systems manager chooses to set up access—either by providing application gateways such as Telnet forwarders or by giving users logins on the gateway host—determines its ease of use. If the former approach is taken, the stance of the firewall is clearly *That which is not expressly permitted is prohibited*; users can only access Internet services for which there is an application gateway. If users are permitted logins, the firewall's security is seriously weakened.

During normal operation, the only zone of risk is the gateway host itself because it is the only host reachable from the Internet. If user logins are on the gateway host, and one of the users chooses a weak password or has his account otherwise compromised, the zone of risk expands to encompass the entire private network.

From a standpoint of damage control, the administrator may be able to track the progress of an intruder based on the access patterns of the compromised login, but a skillful vandal can make this quite difficult. If a dual-homed gateway is configured without direct user access, damage control can be somewhat easier because someone logging in to the gateway host becomes a noteworthy security event.

Dual-homed gateways have an advantage over screening routers because their system software is often easier to adapt to maintain system logs, hard copy logs, or remote logs. This can make a post-mortem easier for the gateway host itself, but may or may not help the network administrator identify which other hosts on the private network may have been compromised in an island-hopping attack.

Attacking a dual-homed gateway leaves the attacker a fairly large array of options. Because the attacker has what amounts to local network access if a login can be obtained, all the usual attacks that can be made over a local network are available. Shared file systems, automatic software distribution systems, network backup programs, and administrative scripts may all provide a toehold on systems on the internal network. After a toehold is secured, it then provides a base from which to launch attacks back at the gateway itself. The weakest aspect of the dual-homed gateway is its failure mode. If the firewall is destroyed, it is possible that a skillful attacker might re-enable routing and throw the entire private network open to attack.

Figure 14.3 shows an application level firewall. In this example, an application level firewall called a dual-homed gateway is represented. A dual-homed gateway is a highly secured host that runs proxy software. It has two network interfaces, one on each network, and blocks all traffic passing through it.

Figure 14.3

A dual homed gateway firewall.

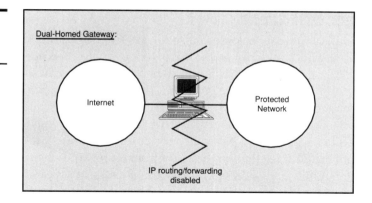

Firewall Design Decisions

In configuring a firewall, the major design decisions with respect to security are often already dictated by corporate or organizational policy; specifically, a decision must be made as to whether security is more important than ease-of-use, or vice versa. Two basic approaches summarize the conflict:

❏ That which is not expressly permitted is prohibited.

❏ That which is not expressly prohibited is permitted.

The importance of this distinction cannot be overemphasized. In the former case, the firewall must be designed to block everything, and services must be enabled only on a case-by-case basis after a careful assessment of need and risk. This tends to impact users directly, and they may see the firewall as a hindrance. In the second case, the systems administrator is placed in a reactive mode, having to predict which kinds of actions the user population might take that would weaken the security of the firewall, and preparing defenses against those actions. This essentially pits the firewall administrator against the users in an endless arms race that can become quite fierce. Users can generally compromise the security of their logins if they try or are not aware of reasonable security precautions. If the user has an open access login on the firewall system itself, a serious security breach can result. The presence of user logins on the firewall system tends to magnify the problem of maintaining the system's integrity.

A second important statement of policy is implicit in the *That which is not expressly permitted is prohibited* stance. This stance is more fail safe because it accepts that the administrator is ignorant of which TCP ports are safe or which holes may exist in the manufacturer's kernel or applications. Because many vendors are slow to publicize security holes, this is clearly a more conservative approach. It is an admission of the fact that what you don't know can hurt you.

Levels of Threat

A firewall can fail or be compromised in several ways. Although none of them are good, some are decidedly worse than others. Because the purpose of many firewalls is to block access, it's a clear failure if someone finds a loophole that permits them to probe systems in the private network. An even more severe situation results if someone manages to break into the firewall and reconfigures it such that the entire private network is reachable by anyone. For the sake of terminology, this type of attack is referred to as *destroying* a firewall, as opposed to *breaking-in*. It is extremely difficult to quantify the damage that might result from a firewall's destruction. An important measure of how well a firewall resists threat is the information it gathers to help determine the course of an attack. The absolute worst thing that could happen is for a firewall to be completely compromised without any trace of how the attack took place. The best thing that can happen is for a firewall to detect an attack and to inform the administrator politely that it is undergoing attack but that the attack is going to fail.

One way to view the result of a firewall being compromised is to look at things in terms of what can be roughly termed as *zones of risk*. In the case of a network directly connected to the Internet without any firewall, the entire network is subject to attack. This does not imply that the network is vulnerable to attack, but in a situation where an entire network is within reach of an untrusted network, it is necessary to ensure the security of every host on that network. Practical experience shows that this is difficult because tools such as rlogin permit user-customizable access control and are often exploited by intruders to gain access to multiple hosts in a form of *island hopping* attack. In the case of a typical firewall, the zone of risk is often reduced to the firewall itself or a selected subset of hosts on the network, significantly reducing the network manager's concerns with respect to direct attack. If a firewall is broken into, the zone of risk often expands again to include the entire protected network. An intruder gaining access to a login on the firewall can begin an island hopping attack into the private network by using the firewall as a base. In this situation, hope remains because the vandal may leave traces on the firewall and may be detected. If the firewall is completely destroyed, the private network can undergo attack from any external system; reconstructing the course of an attack becomes nearly impossible.

Firewalls can be viewed in terms of reducing the zone of risk to a single point of failure. In a sense, this seems like a bad idea because it amounts to putting all one's eggs in a single basket, but practical experience implies that at any given time, for a network of non-trivial size, at least a few hosts are vulnerable to break-in by even an unskilled attacker. Many corporations have formal host security policies designed to address these weaknesses, but it is sheer foolishness to assume that publishing policies will suffice. A firewall enhances host security by funneling attackers through a narrow gap where a chance exists to catch or detect them first.

Attacks a Firewall Can Protect Against

Generally, firewalls are configured to protect against unauthenticated interactive logins from the outside world. This, more than anything, helps prevent intruders from logging in to machines on your network. More elaborate firewalls block traffic from the outside to the inside, but permit users on the inside to communicate freely with the outside. The only way to protect your network against any type of network-borne attack is to disconnect it from the Internet.

Some firewalls permit only e-mail traffic through them, and thereby protect the network against any attacks other than attacks against the e-mail service. Other firewalls provide less strict protections and block services known to cause problems.

Firewalls are also important because they can provide a single choke point where security and audit can be imposed. Unlike in a situation in which a computer system is being attacked by someone dialing in with a modem, the firewall can act as an effective phone tap and tracing tool. Firewalls provide an important logging and auditing function; often they provide summaries to the administrator about which kinds and amount of traffic passed through it, how many attempts there were to break into it, and so on.

Attacks a Firewall Cannot Protect Against

Firewalls cannot protect against attacks that do not go through the firewall. Security breaches that do not use the network, such as physical access to sensitive documents through an unlocked door in a building, are examples of attacks that are not able to be prevented using a firewall. Many corporations that connect to the Internet are very concerned about proprietary data leaking out of the company through that route. Unfortunately for those concerned, a floppy disk can be used just as effectively to export data. Many organizations terrified (at a management level) of Internet connections have no coherent policy about how dial-in access via modems should be protected. It is foolish to build a 6-foot thick steel door when you live in a wooden house, but a lot of organizations are buying expensive firewalls and neglecting the numerous other back doors into their network. For a firewall to work, it must be part of a consistent overall organizational security architecture. Firewall policies must be realistic and reflect the level of security desired in the entire network. A site with top secret or classified data, for example, does not need a firewall at all; that site should not be hooking up to the Internet in the first place. Likewise, the systems with the truly secret data should be isolated from the rest of the corporate network.

Another thing a firewall cannot really protect against is traitors or careless users inside your network. Although an industrial spy might export information through your firewall, he's just as likely to export it through a telephone, fax machine, or floppy disk. Floppy disks are a far more likely means for information to leak from your organization than is a firewall! Firewalls also cannot protect you against carelessness. Users who reveal sensitive information over the telephone are good targets for social engineering; an attacker may be able to break into your network by completely bypassing your firewall if he can find a *helpful* employee inside who can be fooled into giving access to a modem pool.

Other Things Firewalls Cannot Protect Against

Firewalls cannot protect very well against things such as viruses. Too many ways of encoding binary files for transfer over networks exist—and too many different architectures and viruses to try to search for them all. A firewall cannot replace security-consciousness on the part of your users. In general, a firewall cannot protect against a *data-driven attack*—attacks in which something is mailed or copied to an internal host where it is then executed.

Organizations deeply concerned about viruses should implement organization-wide virus control measures. Rather than trying to screen viruses out at the firewall, make certain that every vulnerable desktop has virus scanning software run when the machine is rebooted. Blanketing your network with virus scanning software protects against viruses that come in via floppy disks, modems, and the Internet. Trying to block viruses at the firewall only protects against viruses from the Internet. Remember that the vast majority of viruses are spread via floppy disks.

Source-Routed Traffic

Normally, the route a packet takes from its source to its destination is determined by the routers between the source and destination. The packet itself only says where it wants to go (the destination address) and nothing about how it expects to get there.

There is an optional way for the sender of a packet (the source) to include information in the packet that tells which route the packet should use to get to its destination (thus the name *source routing*). For a firewall, source routing is something to consider because an attacker can generate traffic claiming to be from a system inside the firewall. In general, such traffic would not route through the firewall properly, but with the source routing option, all the routers between the attacker's machine and the target will return traffic along the reverse path of the source route. Implementing such an attack is quite easy; firewall designers should not dismiss it as unlikely to happen.

In practice, source routing is not used very often. The main legitimate use of source routing is in debugging network problems or routing traffic over specific links for congestion control for specialized situations. When building a firewall, source routing should be blocked at some point. Most commercial routers incorporate the capability to block source routing specifically, and many versions of operating systems that might be used to build firewall bastion hosts have the capability to disable or ignore source-routed traffic.

ICMP Redirects

An ICMP Redirect tells the recipient system to override something in its routing table. Routers use this legitimately to tell hosts that the host is using a nonoptimal or defunct route to a particular destination (that is, the host is sending it to the wrong router). The wrong router sends the host an ICMP Redirect packet that tells the host what the correct route should be. If you can forge ICMP Redirect packets and if your target host pays attention to them, you can alter the routing tables on the host and possibly subvert the security of the host by causing traffic to flow via a path the network manager did not intend. ICMP Redirects also may be employed for denial of service attacks, in which a host is sent a route that loses it connectivity or is sent an ICMP Network Unreachable packet telling it that it can no longer access a particular network.

Many firewall builders screen ICMP traffic from their network. This limits the ability of outsiders to ping hosts or to modify their routing tables.

Denial of Service Attacks

Denial of service is when someone decides to make your network or firewall useless by disrupting it, crashing it, jamming it, or flooding it. The problem with denial of service on the Internet is that it is impossible to prevent. The reason has to do with the distributed nature of the network: Every network node is connected via other networks that in turn connect to other networks, and so on. A firewall administrator or ISP has control of only a few of the local elements within reach. An attacker can always disrupt a connection upstream from where the victim controls it. If someone wants to take a network off the air, he can do it by either taking the network off the air, or by taking the networks it connects to off the air. Many ways exist for someone to deny service, ranging from the complex to the brute-force. If you are considering using Internet for a service that is absolutely time or mission critical, you should consider having a fall-back position in case the network is down or damaged.

Issues in Implementing a Firewall

A number of basic issues should be addressed by the person who has been tasked with the responsibility of designing, specifying, and implementing or overseeing the installation of a firewall.

The first and most important reflects the policy of how your company or organization wants to operate the system: Is the firewall in place to explicitly deny all services except those critical to the mission of connecting to the Net? Or, is the firewall in place to provide a metered and audited method of *queuing* access in a nonthreatening manner? Degrees of paranoia range between these positions; the final stance of your firewall may be more the result of a political decision than an engineering decision.

The second issue is the level of monitoring, redundancy, and control that you want. Having established the acceptable risk level (how paranoid you are) by resolving the first issue, you can form a checklist of what should be monitored, permitted, and denied.

You start by figuring out your overall objectives and then combine a needs analysis with a risk assessment and sort the almost always conflicting requirements into a list that specifies what you plan to implement.

The third issue is financial. This issue cannot be addressed here in anything but general terms, but it is important to try to quantify any proposed solutions in terms of how much it will cost either to buy or to implement. A complete firewall product may cost between $100,000 at the high end and nothing at the low end. The free option, of doing some fancy configuring on a Cisco or similar router, costs nothing but staff time and cups of coffee. Implementing a high-end firewall from scratch might cost several man-months, which may equate to $30,000 worth of staff salary and benefits. The systems management overhead is also an important consideration. Building a home-brew is fine, but it is important to build it so that it does not require constant and expensive maintenance. It is important to evaluate firewalls not only in terms of what they cost now; continuing costs such as support must also be considered.

On the technical side, a couple of decisions must be made based on the fact that for all practical purposes what is being discussed is a static traffic routing service placed between the network service provider's router and your internal network. The traffic routing service may be implemented at an IP level via something like screening rules in a router, or at an application level via proxy gateways and services.

The decision must be made whether to place an exposed stripped-down machine on the outside network to run proxy services for Telnet, FTP, news, and so on, or whether to set up a screening router as a filter, permitting communication with one or more internal machines. Advantages and disadvantages correspond to both approaches, with the proxy machine providing a greater level of audit and potential security in return for increased cost in configuration and a decrease in the level of service that may be provided (because a proxy needs to be developed for each desired service). The old trade-off between ease-of-use and security now becomes more apparent. It is also possible to combine the proxy approach and the filter approach. You can only allow traffic from certain addresses into your internal network by using the screening router, and you can limit which applications you will allow to be accessed from the filtered addresses by using the proxy machine.

The Future of Firewalls

The future of firewalls lies somewhere between network level firewalls and application level firewalls. Network level firewalls will most likely become increasingly aware of the information going through them, and application level firewalls will become increasingly low level and transparent. The end result will be a fast packet-screening system that logs and audits data as it passes through. Increasingly, firewalls (network and application layer) incorporate encryption so that they may protect traffic passing between them over the Internet. Firewalls with end-to-end encryption can be used by organizations with multiple points of Internet connectivity to use the Internet as a *private backbone* without worrying about data or passwords being sniffed.

Although firewalls can be used to implement a layer of protection between your internal network and the Internet, the issue of securing the individual servers in your internal network remains. Windows NT provides its own security model that you can use to implement security for the servers in your internal network. The following sections discuss the Windows NT security model in more detail.

General Windows NT Security Practices

Windows NT has been designed and tested as a highly secure network and stand-alone operating system, but security administration and planing are in the hands of the administrator. A majority of the NT security weaknesses and loopholes often discussed on the Internet are, in actuality, the errors of sloppy administration. The principle Windows NT security concerns and solutions are briefly mentioned here.

The Administrator Account

The Windows NT Administrator account, created during NT setup and installation, is often a primary target for hacking attempts and other network mischief. It is recommended that the Administrator acount be renamed to a more cryptic name, barring hackers from attempting password cracks on an administrative account. If the administrators of the server normally only use account or server administration privileges, consider creating your administrative accounts as members of the Server Operator or Account Operator group. This ensures that the number of full Administrators Group accounts remains low.

Other considerations concerning the Administrator account are timeouts and password uniqueness. Windows NT can restrict the number of logon attempts (explained earlier) so that a set number of multiple bad logon attempts will restrict other attempts under that account for a specified amount of time. A server's account policy, for example, could restrict a user from trying to log on for 30 minutes after three failed logon attempts. This means that any hacker using a dictionary password cracker program cannot cycle through hundreds of passwords a minute. The danger that does exist, however, is in the Administrator account, which cannot be locked out with this security protection. (You would never want your highest level account to be locked out!) Although this means a hacker or mischievous user can't lock out your Administrator account, it does mean that it is constantly susceptible to open password attack. By renaming the Administrator account and providing a unique password that cannot be found in a dictionary, an administrator can tremendously reduce one of the largest security loopholes on a Windows NT Server.

Passwords

One of the largest and most menacing security problems is the hacking or discovery of passwords. Although keeping passwords secure and resistant to hacking or guessing is not a particularly difficult task in theory, it is rather difficult to enforce on users and even administrators. Several password-cracking programs use a dictionary file that enables the program to iterate through an entire dictionary, using each entry as a password attempt. Though bad logon attempt lockouts can restrict barrages of password-cracking attempts, this is no excuse to be lax in password uniqueness. A few rules about passwords follow:

❑ Don't make them simple, short, or easy to guess by those who know you. Try to use nonstandard words, upper and lowercase letters, numbers, or any other character string that can't be cracked with a dictionary password cracker.

❑ Enforce adequate password length. Don't use short passwords; they are much easier to crack and easier to notice when typed. A five character minimum password policy is adequate. For tighter security, eight characters is a good practice.

❑ Never make hard copies of passwords. Do not write down passwords unless absolute necessary (mailing users account information, for example).

The Windows NT Security Model

Windows NT offers impressive access control to secured resources. With its object-based operating system design, built-in security features, and discretionary access via security levels, NT offers a very stable and secure platform for networking and creating Internet servers. The Windows NT security model illustrates just how NT security works within the operating system and how each user accesses (whether successfully or unsuccessfully) resources. The example starts from the perspective of a logon attempt and then progresses through the Windows NT Security subsystem and access of file resources on an NTFS partition.

The Windows NT operating system is comprised of several subsystems; one each for Win32, OS/2, POSIX, networking, and security. The Security Subsystem interacts with the Win32 Subsystem because that is the subsystem that controls all user interface options and, thus, security access attempts. The information presented in this section pertains to the Security Subsystem and related Win32 Subsystem functions.

The Logon Process

Windows NT requires users to log on either locally or over the network, using an already established user account. The logon process involves a constantly active process waiting for an attempt by a user to log on the system. Typically (and unless a custom logon has been developed for the particular NT system), the logon process involves typing a user name and password. This logon process passes along the user information to the Security Subsystem, which checks the credentials against the Security Accounts Manager's security database. If the security database confirms that the account is acceptable for logon, an Access Token is attached to the user's process, which is then passed back to the logon process and finally given over to the Win32 Subsystem, logging the user on to the system. The Win32 Subsystem creates a process for the user and attaches the Access Token to the process for the duration of the session. If the Security Subsystem cannot validate the user, the user is rejected; the process goes no further.

The standard local WinLogon procedure is the Ctrl+Alt+Del keypress to activate the Windows NT logon dialog box. This key combination is a protected kernel mode process that ensures no other process can run at the same time. Trojan horse programs, such as password sniffers and other threat programs that can compromise security, cannot access the WinLogon process and steal keystrokes or other information.

Access Tokens

An Access Token, generated by the Security Subsystem after an account has been verified, contains information on the user and all security access allowed that user. The Access Token contains the following information about the logged-on user:

❏ **SecurityID.** A unique identification used by the operating system to identify the user.

❏ **GroupID.** Identification of all groups in which the user belongs. This ID, along with the user SecurityID, is used to determine security access to system resource objects.

❏ **Privileges.** Any user privileges granted to the user.

❏ **Default Owner.** The initial owner of the file or resource object when created.

❏ **Primary Group.** The main group assigned permissions to the resource object.

❏ **Default ACL.** Access Control List, which contains security access information to be used by resource objects (discussed in the next section).

Access Control Lists and Access Control Entries

The Security Subsystem uses an Access Token to help determine whether the user is allowed access to a resource, and if so, the limitations on the access privilege. Windows NT is an object-based operating system; all resources are treated as objects with individual attributes and functions. When created, each resource object requiring security (such as files, processes, tokens, and so on) is assigned a security descriptor that contains a list of security access information, an Access Control List (ACL). Each ACL is comprised of Access Control Entries (ACEs) that include user Security ID and the user's access rights. When a user attempts to access a resource, the user's Access Token is used during a check against the resource's ACL. If the user's Security ID matches one of those in an ACE, the user may access the resource according to the rights specified.

In figure 14.4, a user attempts to access a file object. Notice that the user's Access Token is used in a query of the file's ACL. The user has been provided with Read and Write permissions to the specific file. The ACEs are iterated through, first to last, and when an ACE matching the requested user access is found, a handle is returned to the user, enabling access. If the user attempts to access an object in a prohibited manner (such as trying to delete a file marked only for Read permissions), the object will not return a handle, and the user will be denied access.

Figure 14.4

Access a secure resource.

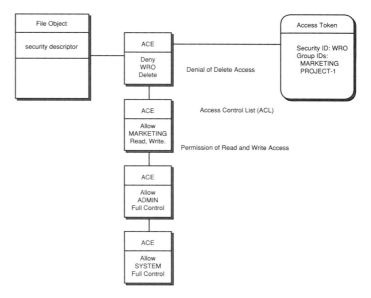

Windows NT Account Security

Windows NT requires individual user accounts for access to either the local system or to a network server. Through accounts, security and auditing can be increased with individualized or group attention to resource access. Just as in Unix, files and directories can be owned by a user and can have access rights assigned by a per-user basis. Windows NT has several built-in groups for ease of administration, each with its own unique privileges. Windows NT Server and Workstation provide slightly different built-in accounts; NT Server running as a domain controller offers domain-wide system accounts and global groups for the entire network. This section outlines the Windows NT built-in accounts, security considerations, and the various policies governing account security. Before learning about the various groups and their security issues, the concepts of global and local groups should be clear (see fig. 14.5). Although a Web or FTP server requires less account administration than a LAN server, integration into an existing WAN or intranet may require some substantial understanding of user groups.

Figure 14.5
Distinctions between Windows NT global and local groups.

Local Group

•Accounts from the local computer
•Domain global groups
*Domain accounts

Global Group

•Users within the domain
•Only available when a domain exists.

Windows NT Built-In Groups

Because Windows NT Server is the primary choice for an NT-based Internet server, the account information that follows will be more specific to Server. Most of the information is also valid for Workstation, however; the security model works identically on both versions.

Both Windows NT Workstation and Windows NT Server provide the following built-in groups for use with administration and general system access:

❏ **Administrators.** It's not hard to guess that this is the full-privileged administrative group. During installation, NT creates the generic administrative account *Administrator* and includes it in this group. Administrators have full control over file access, security, accounts, and system settings.

❏ **Users.** The default group for any new user. This low access group is usually given generic privileges to files and resources of lower security. The Users group is usually given permission explicitly or through the Everyone file permission.

❏ **Guests.** The Guests group is another general purpose account with low security access, usually assigned to temporary users or generic services. The Guest account is automatically created during Windows NT Setup. Many Internet Web and FTP servers use the Guest group for accessing resources because of the limited access typically enforced on the account.

❏ **Backup Operators.** This group enables a user special administrative capabilities to back up and restore files and directories without sacrificing critical administrative control or security. Members of the Backup Operators group can log on to a server locally and shut down the server. This is obviously a useful administrative group for use with an Internet server.

❏ **Replicator.** This special administrative group is used with the Windows NT Directory Replication services to replicate data from the local system to another system for file protection purposes.

❏ **Power Users.** The Power Users group is an extended user group with greater access to the system and its resources. Windows NT Server provides this group for regular server installations only and not with Primary or Backup domain controller installations. Windows NT Workstation always includes this group.

A Windows NT Server installed as a domain controller (primary or backup) includes global groups for NT domain-wide administration. The following groups are global equivalents to their local group counterparts:

❏ Domain Admins

❏ Domain Users

❏ Domain Guests

By using the built-in user groups, an Internet server administrator can control security access to the local system by customizing accounts, and can also restrict access to resources for remote users. Custom user groups can also be created and assigned privileges to the local system. Domain and account administration is beyond the scope of this book, but should be well understood before attempting to establish any NT server in an existing LAN environment. Internet servers are often separate from the LAN (either physically or by isolating the TCP/IP protocol to the Internet server only) and require less local administration.

Other Groups and Security Considerations

Setting NTFS file and directory permissions are discussed later in the chapter, but one important issue concerning file security is the existence of other built-in groups in Windows NT. These are the special groups:

❏ **Everyone.** This group (not surprisingly) includes all users. Pay special attention to this group in file permission settings; it enables any logged on user of the system to access the file or resource.

❏ **NETWORK.** This enables access to a file or object over the network, as opposed to local logons.

❏ **INTERACTIVE.** This enables local access to a file or object, as opposed to network logons.

❏ **CREATOR OWNER.** The creator (and thus owner) of the file or object.

Often it is desirable to remove the Everyone group from any listing of directory permissions. When an NTFS partition is first formatted, the Everyone group has Change access to the entire drive. This should be changed immediately to preserve file security, especially on an Internet server which will likely offer public anonymous access to Web or FTP services.

Windows NT Account Policies

Individual account security is not always a primary consideration for Internet servers that will primarily run Web and FTP servers, but access to the local system should be monitored and secure. With this in mind, an understanding of the user account policies on a Windows NT Server are well justified.

To administer NT's user policies, use the User Manager tool in the Administrative Tools program group to view the user accounts and groups on the server. The Policies menu contains choices for each of Windows NT's user policies. The policies are discussed in more detail in the following sections.

Account Policy

The Account Policy dialog box enables administrative control over the system policy for all accounts. Password restrictions and account lockout are maintained with this utility. Figure 14.6 shows the Account Policy dialog box.

Figure 14.6

*The Windows NT
Account Policy
dialog box.*

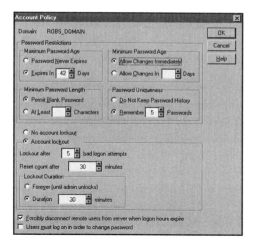

The Account Policy dialog box enables the administrator to perform the following actions on the overall system accounts policy:

❑ Set minimum and maximum password age. This requires users to change their password at regular intervals, ensuring better security against attempts to crack or learn passwords.

❑ Set minimum password length. Password length increases uniqueness of passwords, which means better security of accounts.

❑ Set password uniqueness. This prohibits users from using the same password for a set number of password changes.

❑ Account lockout. Locking out a user after bad logon attempts is useful in preventing hacking of accounts. NT enables an administrator to set the number of bad logon attempts before the system locks out the user. Lockout duration and account reset can also be regulated for increased security.

❑ Forcibly disconnect users after logon hours expire. Windows NT user accounts can be given time restrictions for accessing the network server. This option determines whether Windows NT forces the user's session to be terminated (when checked), or (when cleared) whether the user may remain online, but without making any more network connections.

❑ User must log on to change password. If checked, a user will not be able to change his password after it expires, and the administrator must be contacted.

Otherwise, a user will be able to change his password upon expiration, immediately upon network logon to the NT Server.

Obviously, certain restrictions could have adverse effects with an Internet server. If your server must allow individualized personal accounts, will your users be able to change their passwords? Will they be required to change their passwords at regular intervals? These considerations are important when developing a secure account policy for your Internet server; few administrators want to change each user's password every 30 days!

User Rights Policy

The User Rights Policy dialog box is used mainly to assign individual user rights to accounts for access to the local system. Because most of these user rights are preset and are not typically of interest to a dedicated Internet server, this section covers only general use and security considerations.

The User Rights Policy dialog box enables some important security rights to be assigned—several basic and advanced rights that may prove useful for administrators to either assign or restrict. Figure 14.7 shows the User Rights Policy dialog box. Following are some of the user rights of particular importance to Internet server security:

❏ **Access this computer from network.** Obviously, this is quite important for network connections; it applies to accessing the server over a Windows NT network only, however, either within the domain or over the network to an NT Workstation. Even if you have no groups listed in this space, your Internet server will enable connections.

❏ **Back up files and directories.** To assign the individual user right instead of including a user in the Backup Operators group, this can be used. If your Internet server security requires that administrative assistants have only limited access (that is, non-administrator accounts) with backup capability, consider this option. Use it sparingly for tighter security!

❏ **Manage audit and security log.** Windows NT audit and security logs (discussed in detail later) are another way to enforce security and access monitoring. This option is important in assigning rights to view, manage, and use these logs.

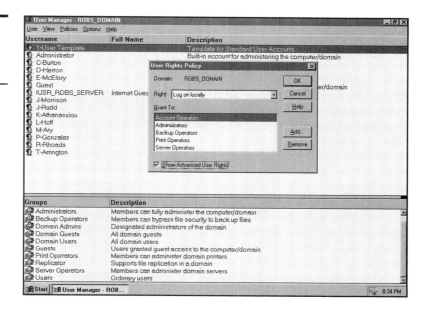

Figure 14.7

The Windows NT Server User Rights Policy dialog box.

The Audit Policy

Windows NT provides auditing of several system security resources through the Audit Policy. Using this dialog box (see fig. 14.8), the administrator can select which security access events are to be logged in the Windows NT security logs. Audits can be generated for both successful and failed attempts and should be selected carefully because they can not only slow the system down, but also take up room in the security logs. The following list shows the different access rights that can be audited:

❏ Logon and Logoff

❏ File and Object Access

❏ Use of User Rights

❏ User and Group Management

❏ Security Policy Changes

❏ Restart, Shutdown, and System

❏ Process Tracking

Internet server administrators can use the Windows NT auditing capabilities for a number of security purposes; monitoring of local system security in a corporate environment can be just as important to your Internet server as monitoring Internet security problems. Logon and logoff access can be monitored from the security logs, ensuring a reliable report of how Windows NT handled access attempts. File and object access attempts are another important consideration for an Internet server. For increased security, Windows NT offers individual file and directory auditing, tailored to report attempts based on user, group, and success or failure of each type of access (see fig. 14.9). File auditing is discussed in the next section.

Figure 14.8
Windows NT Audit Policy dialog box.

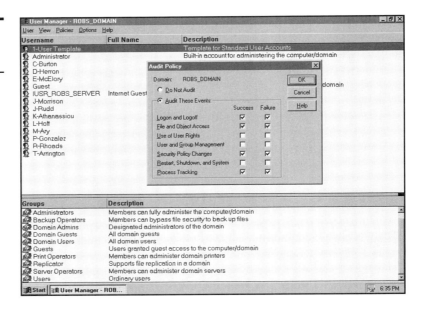

Figure 14.9
The Windows NT Event Viewer: security logs.

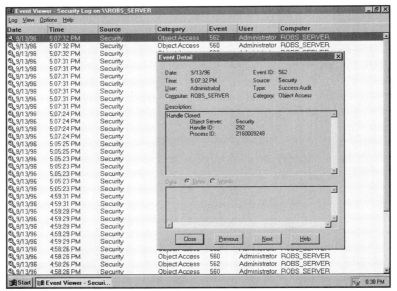

Windows NT File Security

The Windows NT operating system provides a highly secure transaction-based file system, NTFS, which enforces security down to the individual file level. This security can impose limitations on type of access, access by specific users, or entire groups of users. Windows NT account security can be enforced through file security settings, as well as through assignment of groups (such as Administrator or Backup Operator) and security policies. This section details the concepts of Windows NT accounts and NT file security by covering the following topics:

❏ An Overview of NTFS
❏ Windows NT File and Directory Auditing

An Overview of NTFS

Windows NT's native file system, NTFS, has been designed as a high performance file system with several increased security capabilities. Ownership, access privileges, and auditing are typical advantages to NTFS. Windows NT treats files as objects of the operating system; thus, NTFS files and directories can be secured with the native operating system security model. Not only is NTFS secured within the Windows NT operating system, but an NTFS partition is inaccessible by any operating system besides Windows NT. The exception to this are the new developed file system access utilities now available on the Internet. These utilities enable any DOS, Windows, or Windows 95 computer to access a local NTFS partition. A version of this software for the Linux operating system also exists, and possibly more will be developed as user interest increases.

All directory and file security access is accomplished with the Windows NT 4 File Explorer (the NT 4 counterpart to the old Windows File Manager, which

NOTE

The existence of free NTFS access utilities may unnerve some NT network or Internet server administrators; it should. Physical access to a file server, however, will always pose security problems. The capability for someone to boot up your Internet server with a DOS boot floppy and use an NTFS reader is obviously more of a problem of a secure room than a secure file system!

is still available in NT 4). By right-clicking on the directory or file and choosing the Properties menu, and then the Security tab (see fig. 14.10), an administrator can choose to set ownership, permission, or auditing security features.

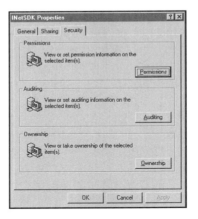

Figure 14.10
The Windows NT File Explorer Security tab.

Securing NTFS Files and Directories with Permissions

Windows NT file access is controlled by assigning permissions to directories and files on an NTFS partition. Using the NT Explorer to assign permissions is a simple task, but should be well understood before any attempt on an Internet server, where file permissions on public directories may have adverse affects on system security. File and Directory permissions are set by right-clicking on that particular file or directory, choosing the Security tab from the Properties menu, and then choosing the Permissions button. Figure 14.11 shows the Windows NT Explorer dialog box for Directory Permissions.

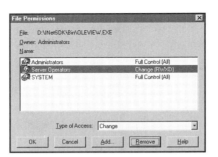

Figure 14.11
Windows NT File Explorer File Permissions dialog box.

The File Permissions dialog box lists all groups assigned permissions to the individual files and enables new groups or individual users to be added or removed. The file permissions are followed in parentheses by their access rights at the file level. An example of this is Change(RWXD), which designates Read, Write, eXecute, and Delete access to the file.

Most security concerns can be taken care of easily with standard permissions. If you don't want users to have access to a directory and its contents, remove those users from the list, or give them more restrictive access. Some security requirements demand more specialized access. The following list explains the six types of file access rights with the NTFS file system, categorized by the letters that represent them in the Directory/File Permissions dialog boxes.

- ❏ **RRead.** Display file's data and information about the file such as date and time created, file size, and so on.
- ❏ **XExecute.** Execute the file.
- ❏ **WWrite.** Capability to change the file or its file attributes, but not the capability to delete it.
- ❏ **DDelete.** Delete the file.
- ❏ **PChange Permissions.** This enables the user to change permissions on the file or directory.
- ❏ **OTake Ownership.** Enables a user to become the owner of the directory and its contents, enabling permission setting and some administrative capability. Ownership will be discussed in more detail later in this section.

The following table lists the NTFS file permissions and their use for securing files. The access right letters mentioned in the preceding list are used to represent their privileges.

Table 14.1 Windows NT NTFS File Permissions	Permissions	R	X	W	D	P	O
	No Access	no	no	no	no	no	no
	Read	yes	yes	no	no	no	no
	Chan	yes	yes	yes	yes	no	no
	Full Control	yes	yes	yes	yes	yes	yes
	Special Access*	yes	yes	yes	yes	yes	yes

Special Access is an undefined access type that enables any combination of access rights to be set. Although each right is marked with a yes in the table, it should be understood that this only signifies the possibility of the privilege. Use Special Access when the other four standard built-in permissions do not fit your security requirements.

The Directory Permissions offer a few extra permission settings along with subdirectory control. Figure 14.12 shows the Directory Permissions dialog box, accessed for a directory as you would a file. Notice that the Directory Permissions dialog box shows two sets of file access rights in the parentheses after each permission. These two sets of rights apply to directory permissions and file permissions respectively. Also notice the following two check box choices for file and directory control:

❏ Replace Permissions on Subdirectories
❏ Replace Permissions on Existing Files

Figure 14.12
The Windows NT Directory Permissions dialog box.

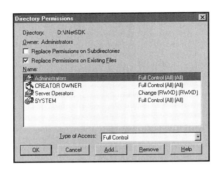

Table 14.2 for directory permissions is similar to the one for file permissions, with the exception of a few extra permissions.

Table 14.2
Windows NT NTFS Directory Permissions

Permissions	R	X	W	D	P	O
No Access	no	no	no	no	no	no
List	yes	yes	no	no	no	no
Read	yes	yes	no	no	no	no
Add	no	yes	yes	no	no	no
Add & Read	yes	yes	yes	no	no	no
Change	yes	yes	yes	yes	no	no
Full Control	yes	yes	yes	yes	yes	yes
Special Access	yes	yes	yes	yes	yes	yes

Two permissions of note are List and Add. Although List may seem identical to the Read permission, look at the access rights list after the List permission: List (RX) (Not specified). Although directory permissions enable read and execute access, no permissions are specified for files. Add enables execution and writing, but no reading. Consider this privilege if you are custom tailoring a directory for use with executing a script or DLL to write to a file—possibly securing Web server access to a directory on your Internet server.

Windows NT File and Directory Auditing

Auditing is a powerful method of maintaining security information on any file and directory resource prone to unauthorized access attempts. Windows NT can generate audit logs on any NTFS partition for file and directory access attributes, whether successful or unsuccessful. To start directory or file auditing, remember to establish File and Object Access auditing in the Windows NT Audit Policy (located in the NT User Manager, discussed earlier). The Directory Auditing dialog box shows the events that can be audited on an existing directory or file (see fig. 14.13).

Figure 14.13
Directory Auditing dialog box.

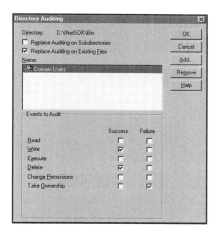

The Directory Auditing dialog box has options for creating audit logs for the following successful and unsuccessful access attempts:

- ❏ Read
- ❏ Write
- ❏ Execute
- ❏ Delete
- ❏ Change Permissions
- ❏ Take Ownership

Windows NT and C2 Security

The United States National Security Agency developed the C2 security rating to evaluate a secure computer system according to rigorous software and hardware specifications. The C2 evaluation for a stand-alone system, known as the *Orange Book*, was developed by the Department of Defense's National Computer Security Center (NCSC). Both Windows NT Server and NT Workstation have passed Orange Book evaluation for a stand-alone, C2-secured system. The requirements for a C2-secured system are explained in this section, along with details on how Windows NT meets these requirements. Although a C2-secured network is only guaranteed by the security skills of the network administrator, a tool exists for evaluating the C2 security compliance of a stand-alone NT Workstation or NT Server. The C2 Configuration tool is also explained later.

Requirements for a C2-Certified System

Although the requirements listed here are not the complete specifications for the NCSC's C2-certification evaluation, they are the more important and NT-specific prerequisites. The full Orange Book and Red Book (the networking equivalent of C2 security) documentation on C2 security can be obtained from the NCSC.

❏ Orange Book—Trusted Computer System Evaluation Criteria
❏ Red Book—Trusted Network Interpretation of the Trusted Computer System Evaluation Criteria

Microsoft's *Windows NT 3.5 Guidelines for Security, Audit, and Control* details the Windows NT specifications for establishing a secure networking environment using Windows NT. If mission-critical high security is among your networking needs, this book is a must-have. Following are the key requirements of a C2 certified system:

❏ Discretionary Access Control
❏ Object Reuse
❏ Identification and Authentication
❏ Auditing

Discretionary Access Control

Discretionary Access Control means that the owner of a file or other resource must be able to control this resource. Windows NT users automatically have full control over any file or resource they create. The capability to take ownership, assign permissions, and administer that resource is granted each time a user creates a new resource.

Object Reuse

Windows NT is an object-based operating system—resources, subsystems, users, security access, processes, and threads—everything is arranged as an object with attributes. Object reuse must be carefully controlled by the operating system so that memory or other system resources are not randomly reused by other processes. After a resource is freed (has no objects with handles to it), it should not be able to be used by another process until a handle is properly established. This ensures that other processes cannot trick the system into giving up secured resources and also maintains stability by keeping unwanted memory demands out of protected space. NT also enforces similar restrictions on hardware such as drives and input/output devices.

Identification and Authentication

Each user of the system must have a unique method of identification (such as a name and password) to distinguish himself from other users of the system. Windows NT provides secure accounts with both user name and password, but can also support custom methods of user logon. For very high security needs, some organizations develop their own NT logon sequences including everything from swipe-card access to retinal scans. NT uses each individual account's list of access rights to check against a resources Access Control List (ACL) to determine whether the user is given access.

Auditing

The methods of auditing Windows NT files, directories, and other security access have been discussed already in this chapter. C2 security requires a system to be capable of auditing both security-related events and the actions of individual users.

The Windows NT C2 Configuration Manager

Included in the Windows NT Resource Kit (available from Microsoft) is a tool called the C2 Configuration Manager. This simple to use point-and-click tool helps administrators evaluate the security level of their NT Workstation or Server and makes

changes in the operating system when requested. Some of the security considerations addressed with the C2 Security Configuration Manager are discussed in the following list. This is by no means a tutorial on how to bring your system up to C2 compliance (indeed, if you address every concern in the Configuration Manager, you won't have networking protocols to *run* an Internet serve with!), but to explain some of the security requirements you may want to consider.

❏ **File Systems.** For C2 security on a Windows NT computer, the only acceptable file system is NTFS. Any FAT or HPFS file system must be converted.

❏ **Operating Systems.** Only Windows NT should exist on the system. Any other OS should be deleted, and the BOOT.INI file system startup timer should be set to 0.

❏ **OS/2 and POSIX Subsystems.** Because the OS/2 and POSIX environments are not C2 secure, they must be deleted to establish a C2 secure Windows NT environment.

❏ **Security Log.** The security log must not overwrite events after a preset time. The administrator should save and restart security logs manually so that no security information is lost.

❏ **Blank Passwords.** C2 security requires that blank passwords never be permitted.

❏ **Guest Account.** The Guest account must be disabled for a C2-secured system.

❏ **Networking.** C2 requires that no networking components be installed on the system. This is certainly not recommended if you are going to be running an Internet server!

❏ **Hardware Options.** The C2 Configuration Manager lists the hardware practices that should be implemented after the system is C2-software compliant.

❏ **Other C2 Security Concerns.** The C2 Configuration Manager automatically brings registry settings up to C2 specifications, as well as the file systems if they are both running NTFS. User rights must also be configured properly, although this is outlined in the *Windows NT C2 Security System Administrator's Guide*, which is, unfortunately, not included in the Resource Kit.

Windows NT's C2-security capabilities make it a powerful tool in high security, mission-critical operations such as banking or government projects. NT not only meets the C2-security requirements for a stand-alone operating system, but exceeds several of the requirements and adds more real-world security and administration features.

Implementing Windows NT TCP/IP Security

The nature of Windows networking over TCP/IP makes securing an NT network from attack pretty easy. Windows networking does not use TCP/IP for native networking tasks; instead, TCP/IP is used for *tunneling*. Tunneling means that one protocol is encapsulated within another, enabling the traffic of one protocol to travel over a network not running that protocol. Windows networking encapsulates NetBIOS over TCP/IP to overcome some of the deficiencies of Window's native protocol NetBEUI. NetBEUI is not routable and does not scale well, so Microsoft developed NBT (NetBIOS over TCP/IP) to enable windows networks to take advantage of IP routing and TCP reliable delivery. All NBT traffic travels over two TCP/IP ports, 138 for UDP connections and 139 for TCP connections. The use of only two TCP/IP ports for communications greatly simplifies the task of securing a Windows network using TCP/IP. All that is needed to protect Windows hosts is to block traffic on ports 138 and 139. Enabling your router's packet filter and disabling traffic on ports 138 and 139 is the easiest way to secure NBT communications. Note that just blocking the two ports NBT uses does not guarantee that your Windows NT host is protected from attack. This is especially true if your NT servers provide other TCP/IP services such as NFS, FTP, and Telnet. These other TCP/IP services should be secured on the individual machines that provide those services. Also, basic NT security practices are not to be abandoned just because an NBT is being filtered at the router. The filtering setup is meant to complement traditional NT security methods.

Summary

Security is a capital demand among most network administrators, and an even more important necessity when Internet servers are involved. Because an Internet server is open to the millions of users of the Internet, certain security precautions should be considered. Firewalls are an effective method of controlling network access; both incoming and outgoing network traffic can be regulated, enabling a tight and standard security practice. Network security and Internet security should be augmented if an Internet server will provide certain users access to privileged data or critical systems. Windows NT-specific security covers network considerations, local system policies, and account management. By understanding the internals of how Windows NT's object-based security model works, the administrator gains a better understanding of the C2-compliant features of Windows NT's security system. The combined knowledge of Internet, networking, and system security provide a strong background in security planning and troubleshooting for both the Internet server and the corporation's security policy.

15

Site Management

Section two, "Requirements and Planning," dealt with the issues of software and hardware planning that went into establishing Internet services on your Windows NT Server. If you have thoroughly planned your server before you launch your Internet services, then your administrative tasks will go smoothly. There is no substitute for adequate planning when establishing Internet services, and the same holds true for maintaining your servers once they are up and running.

There are a number of issues regarding server maintenance, and, surprisingly, many are not technical issues. Of course software upgrades and hardware repairs will be needed, but there also will be issues such as backup scheduling and planning downtime. These types of issues affect the end user of your servers as much as or more than adding memory to improve performance. When you plan for your site, it is much easier to make changes before users come to rely on your Internet services for information. When users enter the picture, support and maintenance become complex issues.

In this chapter, you are given an overview of what typical server maintenance requires. From this overview, or template, you can begin to customize your maintenance regime to fit the services you offer and the demands of your users. Keep in mind that entire books are written on server maintenance—look to this chapter as a place to get started and then begin to investigate other sources on your own. Now that you have an Internet server up and running, get the Net to work for you.

This chapter helps you do that by covering the following issues:

❑ Software maintenance
❑ Hardware maintenance
❑ Log File management
❑ Backups
❑ Content management
❑ Performance tuning
❑ User management issues

General Management and Administration

Now that your server is up and running, you can turn your attention to the daily tasks required to keep your server in good condition and running smoothly. Keep an eye on software maintenance, hardware maintenance, and administrative tasks. In addition to the expected technical maintenance of your server, you also need to be aware of other issues.

Technical problems are not the only potential stumbling blocks to your server. There are the issues of content management and user policies. When you offer services that are scrutinized by the whole Internet community, content issues are very important. For example, if you decide to update the content of your site, and you accidentally erase your legal disclaimer page, having a means of recovering lost content might come in handy. Revision control and backups can be very important parts of administration.

Software Maintenance

One of the main aspects of software maintenance is upgrades. If you are happy with the software you are currently using, why should you bother with software upgrades? In the world of Internet software, where updates are released weekly, this is a good question. There are several reasons why software upgrades can be important to your server:

❑ **Compatibility.** When providing Internet services, you might be forced into a server upgrade by the user community. For example, if your server's users all want to use a mail client that utilizes the IMAP protocol, you need to make sure your mail server supports it. This is a common reason for server-software upgrades. As new standards and services are developed, software is adapted, and you will need to upgrade your server to stay current with your users' client or browser software.

❑ **Security.** With Internet services, the most compelling reason for upgrading is security. Because offering Internet services opens your machine and network to attacks from around the globe, make sure you are adequately protected. As software companies scramble to make their Internet software as secure as possible, hackers scramble to find new bugs they can exploit to break into your servers. Software upgrades can fix these bugs before hackers get a chance to cause widespread mayhem. However, if you fail to upgrade to a new security release, you leave your site vulnerable to a well-known attack, and you compromise security for all of your users as well.

❑ **Features.** This may not be a factor for your server. If you want your server to remain on the cutting edge and take advantage of the latest technologies, then you should perform software upgrades to keep up with the latest innovations. For example, you might want to use new encryption techniques or a new server revision-control feature that was not available previously. The key to these kinds of features is a software upgrade.

So, although it might seem as though software companies are hyping upgrades more than is actually needed, there are some compelling reasons to keep your software current. The best course of action is to carefully evaluate any new software update to be sure that you want the new features it has to offer and that it is compatible with your current configuration and goals.

The two types of common updates to software are incremental upgrades and major releases. An incremental upgrade might be an upgrade from version 1.4 to version 1.5. These upgrades usually are the result of a bug fix or a security fix. They generally do not result in major changes to a server's functionality, but it is usually a good idea to install them because of the improvements in stability.

Major releases need to be treated with more caution. Major releases often involve entirely new sets of features or major product revisions. For example, the difference between version 1.1 and version 2.0 of the Internet Information Server is a major upgrade.

Whenever you make a major software upgrade, you should sure you address the following:

1. Back up your previous installation. A backup of your currently installed software gives you something to fall back on if the upgrade fails. Otherwise, you might be installing the software again from scratch.

2. Become aware of all product changes. Although upgrades are designed to fix bugs and incompatibilities, they sometimes introduce new ones. Making yourself aware of what changes are contained in the upgrade will help you identify possible conflicts before the new software is installed on your system.

3. Adequately prepare users for any changes they will encounter when the new software is operational. Because it is not always possible to know how users are utilizing a software package, make them aware of the changes before they happen so they can prepare, and possibly warn you in advance of possible conflicts.

Keeping Current

After you enter the world of the Internet, there is no turning back. Software is updated at a breakneck pace, and new security flaws are being discovered and fixed daily. In such a chaotic environment, the best step you can take toward administering your server software is to stay current. Keep an eye on trends in server software and read the periodic updates you might receive from your server's vendor. If you decide to use the Microsoft Internet Information Server, then you should frequent the Microsoft Web site (http://www.microsoft.com) to watch for new releases and product reports. Likewise, if you are installing a Netscape Server Product (http://www.netscape.com), you should visit the Netscape site to keep up on developments of your server software.

Some other Web sites, such as the Manufacturers Information Net (`http://mfginfo.com/htm/website.htm`), also provide information about Windows NT and Internet services. A number of UseNET news groups also deal with Windows NT and related software issues as well, such as the following:

- ❏ comp.os.ms-windows.nt.admin.misc
- ❏ comp.os.ms-windows.nt.software.backoffice
- ❏ comp.os.ms-windows.nt.software.services

These groups offer a way for you to pose questions to other Windows NT users who might be able to give you some insight to your problem.

Additionally, many vendors have specific resources for software help. Sites such as Netscape's technical-support site (`http://help.netscape.com`) offers bug reports. Netscape Newsgroups and documentation can be excellent resources for server administrators. Check with your server's vendor to see what types of support sites might be of help.

Installing Software Upgrades

If you decide that a software upgrade for your server is in order, you should work out a few details before installing the upgrade. Remember, just because a vendor promises a smooth, easy update does not mean you will get one.

First, you should always have a copy of the original software and any license numbers or keys needed for the installation. If something does go wrong and you need to reinstall a previous version of the software, you will have everything you need, and you won't be stuck trying to dig up old disks.

Second, you should always have a fresh backup of your server before beginning a new installation. You should perform this backup, in addition to your regularly scheduled backups, right before you update the software. This gives you a safety net to fall back on should something go catastrophically wrong.

It is not all that likely that any trouble will result from a routine software update. Most of the time, the software will update with no problems, and you will not need to do anything special to the server. Occasionally, a new feature might not work as promised, or a new bug might be introduced. So why all the caveats about upgrade procedures? If the one time you have a malfunction is the time you neglected to perform a backup, that's a question you won't ever ask again.

If possible, you may first want to install the new software on a backup system in order to familiarize yourself with the installation procedure and program differences. This can help you work through problems at your leisure before you install the new server as your organization's primary server. After you have prepared for the upgrade installation, backed up your system, and notified users of changes, you can upgrade the server software. Keep in mind that you should monitor the software version periodically to make sure everything is working properly once it is in place as a production server.

Also remember to inform any users or content developers of the changes you make to the server software. New features might affect service in some way you aren't aware, or users might be confused by a change in features or user interface. Although this rarely results in a server tragedy, common courtesy prevails.

Hardware Maintenance

The services you choose to run are only as stable as the hardware you run them on. Even if you have installed your IIS server perfectly, bad RAM or a bad hard drive can still bring your server to a halt. Therefore, it is important that you consider hardware maintenances as well as software.

Granted, not everyone can afford to keep a spare server lying around waiting for the day the primary server fails. But you can take some precautions to make sure that, if disaster does strike, you are prepared.

Know Your Hardware

You should keep a running list of the hardware that makes up your Internet server. Be aware of the following:

❏ The size, type, and speed of your RAM

❏ The type and manufacturer of your video card

❏ The type and manufacturer of your network card

❏ The size, type, and manufacturer of your hard drive

You should also make a note of any other unique hardware that might be installed on your system, such as SCSI device controllers. If any of these devices fail, you would have at your fingertips the information you need to replace them. You should also be aware of the warranty period on your system and components. Having this information in a convenient place can help you save time in the event of an emergency and get your machine back into working order quickly.

Knowing the details about your hardware also can help you keep up with software maintenance. By keeping up-to-date with the manufacturers of your hardware, you can count on the current drivers and support software as well.

Backup-Parts Inventory

Even if you have all the specifics of your hardware ready to go, a hardware failure can still result in serious downtime. The most reliable manufactures can run short of replacement parts, and it will always take some time to get the part from your dealer. For this reason, it is suggested you keep some sort of a backup-parts inventory.

Following are the components most subject to failure:

- ❏ RAM—SIMMs and DIMMs (of same size and type)
- ❏ Hard drive (with pre-installed system)
- ❏ Power supply

TIP

Mechanical devices, especially hard drives, are more prone to failure than electronic components. If your budget provides for only one piece of backup hardware, make it a hard drive.

The decision to keep a spare-parts inventory will be a factor of your budget and your application. If you are running a personal server that can be down for a day or two while parts are ordered, there will be no problem. But if you are running a small business server that clients rely on for data, you are faced with a quandary.

There is no quicker way to solve a hardware failure than with a backup-parts inventory. By having the replacement parts you need on hand, a failure might only interrupt your service for a matter of minutes while you replace the part. For example, if your hard drive fails and you have a spare drive on hand, you can replace the drive and restore your site from backup tapes. This might take a few hours, but if you have to find a new drive, or service the old one, you might be down more than a few hours, possibly several days.

Even for the most conscientiously structured site, not all parts need backups. For example, processor failure is so rare, and processors are so costly, that it makes little sense to keep a spare processor lying around. If you are truly concerned about the failure of processors or motherboards (both of which do fail, albeit rarely) then you should consider a complete backup system.

With spares on hand, if a failure does occur, you can replace the part and get your server back up with a minimum delay. That allows you more leisure in servicing the broken part. Keep in mind, though, that once you have used a spare, it needs to be replaced with the serviced part or a new one.

Preventative Medicine

It pays to be prepared for hardware failure, but you can take precautions to help avoid a disaster before it happens. These precautions include defragmenting your hard drives, monitoring log files, and using Scandisk. These steps can often provide you with information that will help you spot trouble before it occurs.

Defragmenting Hard Drives

Defragmenting your hard drives can improve the overall performance of your machine, and it can help reduce the wear and tear on your drive. Because hard drives use a mechanical device to retrieve data from various areas on a disk, a badly fragmented drive can lead to mechanical failure or seized drive heads. Take the time occasionally to check your disk's fragmentation—if it exceeds 12 to 15 percent, defragment the drive.

Monitor Log Files

The log files maintained by the Windows NT operating system can provide you with valuable information about the status of your server. By using the Event Viewer (see fig. 15.1), you can view the system logs and security logs for your NT Server.

This information can prove quite valuable if you are trying to track down an obscure hardware problem, such as a memory or interrupt conflict. By simply clicking on a logged event, you can get detailed information about the event. Although it is certainly not necessary to view these logs constantly, an occasional glance at the event log, and especially the security log, can help you stay on top of what your server is doing.

Scandisk

Scandisk provides you with an excellent way to check the integrity of your hard drive, so it should be used and logged. Many NT users, from the novice to the expert, view Scandisk as a utility to run if there is a problem. However, after a problem has occurred, it often is too late to use Scandisk; it should be used as prevention and not an after-the-fact method. Running Scandisk affects the performance of your machine, so you might want to limit runs to once a month or so. Watch for increases in bad sectors on your hard drive. If you start to notice a dramatic increase in bad blocks, then you should institute frequent and complete backup procedures and prepare to replace the drive.

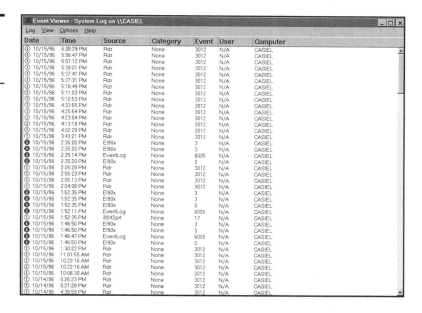

Figure 15.1

The Event Viewer enables you to view Windows NT System notices.

Unfortunately, most diagnostics are limited to hard drives, so they do little to predict an impending memory failure. However, because hard drives are often the most likely component to fail, these tools can help you spot a problem before a catastrophic failure takes place.

Scheduling Maintenance Times

Maintenance takes time. It does not matter if you are performing a routine software upgrade or replacing a bad hard drive. These activities take both time and system resources. It might also be necessary to shut down or reboot your server before upgrades take effect. To perform maintenance, you need the full run of your server—that is why you should budget some time to make any repairs that might be necessary.

Establishing a regular time to perform routine maintenance will provide you the following benefits:

❏ Serve as a reminder for you to perform rote and sometimes boring tasks

❏ Provides users with an advance notice of outages

❏ Keeps your systems and software up to date

You should schedule your maintenance for a time of day when the system is utilized the least, usually sometime in the early hours of the morning, such as 3 a.m. However, appropriate maintenance times will vary from organization to organization, so watch your log files to determine what day and time would work best.

You also should get in the habit of taking the server offline during the maintenance time regardless of what is scheduled. This will help get users accustomed to services being unavailable during the maintenance window, and they will work it into their schedules.

Uninterruptible Power Supplies

One of the most overlooked pieces of server hardware for Internet servers is the uninterruptible power supply (UPS). Because your server provides services to users around the world, power outages at your site can affect a user anywhere. In addition to keeping your services available on the Internet, a UPS can help save your hardware from unpleasant crashes. Power outages, brownouts, spikes, and surges can all cause damage to your server hardware, leaving you out of commission, even if the power is restored to your site. An adequate UPS can help provide some protection from the hazards of the electric company and keep your server running during an outage.

Power outages and surges can do more than shut down your server. Because Windows NT needs to properly clean up swap space and temporary files before a shutdown, a power outage can actually damage your NT file system, causing a hard-disk failure. An uninterruptible power supply provides battery power, which enables you to properly shut down your system in the event of a power outage. In fact, many UPSes have a serial interface that enables your server OS to monitor the status of the UPS. With software from the UPS manufacturer, your server can then be configured to shut itself down when it receives a signal from the UPS that a power outage has occurred. UPSes also can offer a degree of protection from power spikes, surges, and brownouts that might occur on the electrical line. This helps keep the supply of electricity to your server steady and reliable under all conditions.

You need to choose a UPS that provides adequate power for your server and peripherals to operate, and that provides at least enough power to complete a system shutdown. UPS units are rated by the power they provide (in volts AC). You can determine the amount of power your server and peripherals draw by referring to your hardware manuals, each device should list its power requirements in a specification chart. After you determine how much power you need, you should select a UPS that provides the required power, or more, and has an adequate number of outlets with which to plug your components directly into the unit.

In the event of a power outage, an adequate UPS enables you at least to shut down your server properly to preserve user data. If the UPS is powerful enough, or the outage short enough, the UPS can even provide operating power. In any event, you should plan a procedure for dealing with power outages, including the installation of a UPS.

A number of manufacturers supply UPSes that work with Windows NT servers. When you are selecting a UPS, you should always choose a UPS that is UL Listed, as with any electrical component. APC and Triplyte are among some of the well-known vendors supplying mid- to high-end power supplies. Both vendors offer models that are easy to set up and configure. Installing a UPS is as simple as plugging it into the wall and plugging in your server. If you choose a model that can shut down your server in a power failure, the unit will simply connect to one of the server's serial ports and should come with its own monitoring software for Windows NT.

Log File Management

Another essential part of general administration is maintenance of your Internet services log files. In addition to the log files kept by the Windows NT operating system, all Internet services for Windows NT keep some type of logging information to help you track the server's usage and to provide information for security reasons.

The Microsoft Internet Information Server, for example, enables you to alter its logging features through the Internet Services Manager, as shown in figure 15.2.

With Internet Services Manager, you can choose to use a standard (or common) log-file format, or you can use the NCSA Style logging. The type of log file you choose might be influenced by any analysis software you intend to run. Some Web site analysis packages, for example, require an NCSA Style log file. You also can specify where you want the log files stored and how often new log files should be created. Keep in mind that if your server is busy, log files can grow very large very quickly. For busy sites, it is quite reasonable to rotate the log files daily. That can help your analysis go faster, and if you need to search the log files for a particular incident, it can make wading through all of the information mush easier.

Figure 15.2
The Internet Services Manager Log dialog box.

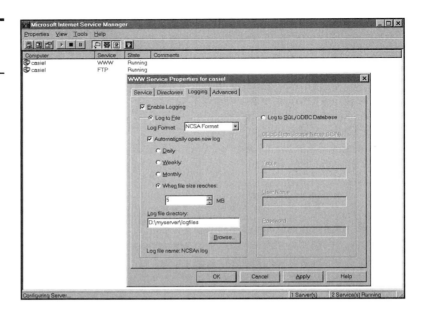

Because log files can become quite large, you also should rotate old log files off your server when they become out of date. You can coordinate the removal of old log files with your server backup so that the log files no longer consume valuable disk space but a copy is still accessible from the tape archive.

One of the most critical duties you will perform as an administrator is the routine backup. Having adequate backups of your file system, configuration files, and content can be essential for disaster recovery. There is nothing special about performing backups. A number of backup utilities are available for Windows NT, including the Backup utility provided with the operating system.

Backups

A solid backup policy can offer a level of protection for every aspect of your server. A backup can provide protection for the server content, user files, and any installed software and associated configuration files. But to be effective, backups need to be performed often and on a regular schedule. An out-of-date or incomplete backup can often be less valuable than nothing.

When developing a backup policy, you need to address two primary issues: file selection and frequency.

File Selection

What you back up is as important as how often you back it up. Although it might seem obvious that you want to back up everything, many administrators neglect to back up important configuration files. Others might worry only about the operating system files and ignore important user files that make up the content of your server. Selecting which files or file systems you want to back up is the first step to a successful backup program. You can perform three basic types of backups for your server: full, selective, and incremental backups.

A *full* backup backs up all files on the server. This includes every storage volume, system files, and user files. A full backup provides the most comprehensive level of backup protection, allowing any file on the server to be recovered. Full backups are costly, however. Because file systems can contain several gigabytes of information, a full backup might require multiple backup tapes, and sometimes it cannot be performed unattended. Full backups also require that the server be taken offline in order to prevent file-system modifications during the backup procedure, modifications that might corrupt the backup. A full backup also takes a great deal of time; gigabytes of information do not back up instantly. It increases the time during which your server is unavailable.

Selective backups are just that—selective. You can choose to archive single files or complete file systems, such as the volume where your users store files. A selective backup enables you to back up a section of your server, allowing a shorter backup time than a full backup and the ability to perform unattended backups.

Incremental backups enable you to back up only files that have changed since the last backup. This can be very helpful to backup files that change frequently, such as user files. These backups can be performed as quick, unattended backups.

Each of these types of backups has an important role in a complete backup plan. By manipulating how each type of backup procedure is used in a schedule, you can maximize the benefits of your backups while minimizing the hassle.

Frequency

How often you back up files is just as important as when you back them up. If you wait too long between backups, you run the risk of your backups being out of date and providing inadequate recovery of your files in the event of an emergency.

Full backups take a considerable amount of time and attention. Because they involve backing up all of the server files, including system-level files that do not change frequently, full backups should be performed with limited frequency, perhaps once a month.

Selective backups are designed to provide more immediate protection of your data; they should be performed more often than full backups to help keep the stored data current. For example, if the content of your server changes frequently, a selective backup of the content directories provides you protection for your content, without spending time backing up unchanged files. From there, perhaps directories containing mission-critical data can be added to the schedule as needed.

Incremental backups should be performed daily. This enables you to have maximum protection of your user data and files that have been updated. In an incremental backup, you back up only those files that have changed since the last backup was performed. This helps ensure that you back up only the most recent work you have performed. If an incremental backup is performed daily, you will never lose more than one day's work.

The file systems you choose to back up incrementally should be the directories that contain the most important information on your server. This could include server content or user files (if your users provide content). You should be aware of all of the file systems on your server, what types of files are stored there, and their relative importance to your server. Knowing what does and does not need to be backed up is essential to developing a solid backup schedule.

Scheduling and Performing Backups

Taking the time to develop an adequate backup schedule can save you many hours of tedious work performing unnecessary backups. Establishing a schedule and sticking to it will keep you from forgetting to perform a backup and jeopardizing your data.

Keeping the frequency of backups and file choice in mind, when should you perform your backups? Well, that answer depends on your needs. Table 15.1 shows an example of a backup schedule that provides adequate protection of data without being intrusive into users' schedules.

	Day of Month	Time of Day	Type of Backup
Table 15.1 Sample Backup Schedule	First Saturday	2 a.m.–4 a.m.	Full backup of all server file systems, OS, and content
	15th and 30th	2 a.m.–4 a.m.	Backup of content directories
	Daily	3 a.m.–4 a.m.	Incremental backup of modified files

In this schedule, a full backup is performed once a month, and each new set of tapes can be archived to an off-site location. Selective backups are performed twice a month, and incremental backups are performed daily to provide full backup coverage. You might alter this schedule to fit your needs; for example, performing a selective backup only once a month, coinciding with the regular updating of your site's content.

How you schedule the backups for your site varies, based on your needs. What should never vary is your adherence to the schedule. Performing the backups, even if they seem unnecessary, is the only way to establish good backup procedures and ensure the integrity of your data.

A number of different backup-software packages are available for Windows NT. Unfortunately, the backup software bundled with the operating system is not very flexible; however, it will allow for full and selective backups. The NT Backup Utility does not allow for remote backup of user machines and is quite lacking in the restore options available for recovering files. However, many packages, such as ARCServe from Cheyenne Software, offer an incredible amount of flexibility, including scheduled, full, selective, and incremental backups, and even the ability to back up open files. Before you select your backup software, it pays to look at the features offered by each software package and choose the software that fits your needs.

There are some steps you can follow to help ensure that your backup program balances your time and your reliability concerns. Some of the things you should consider when developing your own backup schedule include:

❏ Keep a backup log
❏ Keep backup archives
❏ Perform multiple full backups
❏ Maintain physical backup security

Keep a Backup Log

Whenever you perform a backup, you should record an entry in a log book. This enables you to keep track of the fact that backups have been performed and provides information about who performed the backup. It also enables the backup operator to enter any error information that might be generated by the backup software to help preserve the integrity of your backups.

Keep Backup Archives

Although it is not necessary to keep all your server backups (doing so might cost a small fortune!), it might be a good idea to keep an archive copy of your full backups. This can enable you to go back and retrieve log files from a specific period and can help you analyze problems with new server implementations and security issues. If your full backup can fit on a few DAT tapes, the tape costs amount to only a few dozen tapes a year, which is a small price to pay for such a large safety net.

Perform Multiple Full Backups

The protection offered by backups is limited to the quality of the backup itself. In addition to problems that can arise in performing the backup, magnetic tapes are not the most reliable storage media. Although we often rely on tapes and disks as if they were foolproof, tapes are still a magnetic medium and have a fairly high failure rate. Improper storage or handling can introduce errors into your backups, rendering them useless. So when performing full, and perhaps even selective, backups, it is a good idea to make multiple copies of the backups to guard against failure.

Physical Backup Security

Your backups are only as safe as the place they are stored. You would not think about keeping your backup tapes in the trunk of your car, right? So where are your backup tapes stored on site? They should be kept in a safe, cool, dry place. You might want to keep them in a fire safe, or a safe designed specifically for computer backup tapes. Keep in mind that if your server contains sensitive data, that data also is contained on the backup tapes. Because it is much easier to walk out of an office with a small DAT in your pocket than to steal a whole machine, backup tapes should be guarded with the same level of security applied to your server and its data.

A secure, off-site copy of your backup tapes should be a part of your backup routine as well. A location such as a bank safe-deposit box or other secure location off-site can protect your data in the event of a natural disaster or fire. If your organization is destroyed by a earthquake, and your only set of backups are stored on-site, they are not much good for rebuilding your information systems.

Content Management

Another issue that fits well with backup schedules is content management. Because the Internet is a rapidly developing and ever-changing environment, your server should be, too. Most statistics gathered about people's Web-surfing habits show that users are less likely to return to a site if the information provided is more than a month old.

So what does that mean to you? It means that to keep your Internet server popular, and to keep users coming back, you need to update the features and content of your site often. However, each time you change the content or a service feature, such as a new CGI script, you run the risk of introducing errors to your server.

Some advanced servers, such as those provided with the Netscape Suite Spot, offer an advanced system of revision control for site documents and server configurations. This enables you to use the software to keep track of older site configurations and revert to an older configuration at the click of a button, if necessary. Basically acting as an *online* backup. However, other servers, such as the Internet Information Server from Microsoft, do not have a Revision Control Mechanism.

If your Web server does not have integrated Revision Control, the best way to prevent serious mishaps is to perform a backup immediately before changing your site's elements. Then, in the event of a major catastrophe, you can at least restore your data from the backup tapes, and you are back to your previous configuration. Even if your server does have a revision control mechanism, nothing beats a physical backup for keeping your data secure and ensuring that you will have a previous version of a file to fall back on in case of an emergency.

Performance Tuning

Although there is no substitute for planning your server ahead of time, it can often be difficult to predict exactly how your server is going to be utilized once you open it to the world. You might have predicted the demand for your services accurately, and you don't need to worry about your server performance at all. Or you might find that your service has become extremely popular, and you are faced with an underpowered server.

Regardless of the application, be it Web serving, news serving, or electronic mail, you want your server to operate to its maximum potential.

Monitoring Performance

Windows NT has a number of built-in features that enable you to keep track of how your server is performing and how your system's resources are being allocated. The Disk Administrator, Task Manager, and Performance Monitor are tools bundled with the operating system and can provide you with excellent feedback about your server's performance. By using these tools, you can determine how much your Internet Service is taxing the server's processor, how much RAM is being used, and how much disk space is being consumed for content.

The Disk Administrator

The Windows NT Disk Administrator, shown in figure 15.3, is a quick and easy tool to see how your server's disk space is being utilized.

Figure 15.3
The Windows NT Disk Administrator.

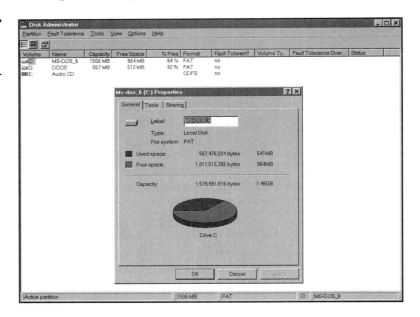

The Disk Administrator displays all the disk partitions mounted by your server and enables you to view the amount of used and free space on each volume.

You can find the Disk Administrator in the Start Menu, in the Programs section under Administrative Tools. Upon launch, the Disk Administrator initializes itself with the information about your systems disks and displays the disk information in a browser format. It lists information about the total capacity, the amount of free space, and the percentage of the disk used. You also can use the tools provided to format drives and assign drive letters to partitions.

The Task Manager

The Windows NT Task Manager, shown in figure 15.4, can provide you with information about the programs and processes running on your NT Server. You can activate the task manager by right-clicking on the Taskbar and selecting Task Manager from the pop-up menu.

Figure 15.4

The Windows Task Manager.

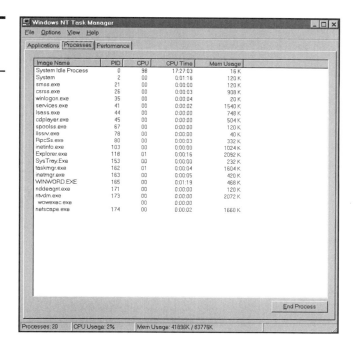

You then can use the Task Manager to display various pieces of information about the processes running on your NT Server. You can view the status of currently running applications. You also can view the CPU time and memory used by each of the currently running processes. This information can help you evaluate memory needs and determine which applications or servers are most resource-intensive.

You can access Task Manager by right-clicking on the Task Bar and choosing Task Manager from the pop-up menu. From there, the Task Manager enables you to monitor the status of Applications, which consists of the following:

❏ Open programs that are not servers or NT services

❏ Processes, which include any servers, NT services, and the application executables

❏ Performance, which enables you to track CPU usage and memory performance

Administrators can "view switch" between any of the views using the labeled tabs at the top of the Window.

Although useful for looking at CPU and memory performance, the best use for the Task Manager is to check on the status of applications and processes that may seem to have locked. If the status is listed as Not Responding, an administrator can choose End Process to kill a process that is out of control.

Performance Monitor

The most comprehensive tool provided by Windows NT for monitoring system resources is the Performance Monitor (see fig. 15.5). The Performance Monitor keeps track of performance statistics in real time and displays them for you in a graphical format to aid interpretation.

In addition to its real-time aspect, another advantage of the Performance Monitor is its flexibility. You can choose to track a variety of performance variables, such as memory usage, CPU usage, and even specific types of HTTP requests, all of which enable you to see which actions are using most of your server's resources.

You can access the Performance Monitor from the Start Menu, in the Programs section under Administrative Tools. After you launch Performance Monitor, you can configure it to monitor performance, using the following:

❏ **Chart.** This tool enables administrators to construct a real-time graph of various performance benchmarks. Choose Chart from the View menu, and different parameters can be specified by choosing Add to Chart from the Edit menu. The chart will reflect in real time whatever performance features are specified.

❏ **Alert.** If an administrator wants to be notified when a benchmark hits a certain level, the Alert feature enables you to set a level for performance traits at which an Alert will be recorded. For example, you could select Alert from the View menu and add Processor to the Alerts using the Add to Alert option. If you specify 20 percent for the processor level, then an Alert generates whenever the processor hits 20 percent or higher. Alert can be a great way to set performance limits so that you are notified when your server resources are strained.

❏ **Log.** The Log feature enables you to specify performance parameters similar to the Chart and Alert features but the data gathered is written to a log file. Keep in mind that writing the information to a log file also consumes system resources. For noninteractive performance monitoring, however, the Log feature can come in handy.

❏ **Report.** The Report feature is similar to the Chart feature in that it logs performance in real time at scheduled intervals. Rather than graphing performance, however, the Report option lists the performance statistics in a text summary format. You can easily cut and paste this information into a word processor or spreadsheet.

With the information from these tools, you should be able to paint a fairly accurate picture of what your server is doing, and how hard it is working to do it. This information is invaluable when it comes to performance-tuning your server and for determining the optimal levels of CPU power and RAM needed for your Internet services.

Figure 15.5
The Windows NT Performance Monitor.

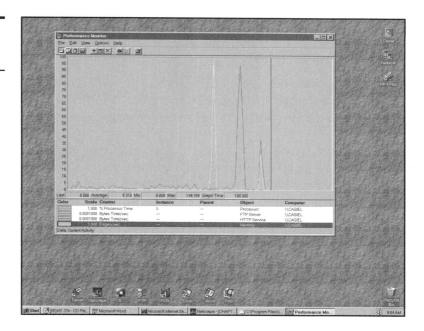

Optimizing Your Server

As an administrator, you can do a number of things to ensure that your server is running and will continue to run the best it can. Most of these performance issues can be resolved through hardware upgrades to your server, although some elements are closely related to software as well. The best way to gauge the performance of your server is to use it. If you don't establish contact with your server as an end user, you cannot get a good feel for the server's performance. Although the numbers might tell you everything is all right, if you cannot use the server, there obviously is a problem.

After you use the tools provided by NT to see where your trouble spots are, you can do a few things to optimize the server's performance, including increasing disk storage space, adding RAM, processing power, and even increasing your network bandwidth.

Hard-Disk Storage Space

Adding more disk space to an existing system is one of the easiest performance upgrades to consider and to perform. Because the disk space on your server is consumed mostly by user files and content files, you can keep a close eye on disk consumption and take corrective action before a problem becomes evident.

Hard-drive space also is used by Windows NT for virtual memory and system swap space; so if your disk drives become too full, your server might suffer performance problems ranging from file errors to slow response times.

Keep an eye on the amount of disk space being used on your system. For example, if you notice that your file space is 75 percent full, it might be time to start planning to add hard-drive space to your system. If you do not have the budget to add hard-drive space at this time, ask users to perform housekeeping tasks, such as deleting unused files, or you may have to begin enforcing user quotas. The solution depends on your needs. As long as you plan ahead, however, you can avoid space problems. The key is to react *before* your hard drive is full. You should establish a level at which you will start enforcing quotas, or at which you will add more disk space to your system. Many systems begin to suffer from performance problems when disk space is more than 90 percent full, so you might want to monitor disk usage and watch for 90- or even 80-percent capacity to give yourself a comfortable buffer to install more disk space.

If you are operating a UseNET news server on your Windows NT machine, you should pay very close attention to disk space. News is transmitted by copying a large number of small files to your local hard drive, and from there the "articles" are sent to users' news readers. The problem is the sheer volume of traffic generated by news. A full newsfeed can consume anywhere from 10 to 16 gigabytes of hard-drive space very quickly. And because that space is consumed with hundreds and thousands of small files, news spool disks can become seriously fragmented very quickly.

If you are operating a news server, you should monitor your disk space daily, if not more. You can adjust the number of newgroups your server provides to ease up on disk-space usage. You also can shorten article-expire time to reduce the overall disk usage without scaling back groups offered. Usually one or a combination of these approaches will lessen your disk-space burden. Careful monitoring of your disk-space consumption and performing routine hard-drive maintenance (such as defragmenting) once a month can help you manage your disk space and get the most effective use without adding more hardware. If you find that you are using high levels of disk space, and you do not want to scale back services, then adding more physical disk space is your only option.

Backup Capacity

It is easy to overlook adequate backup capacity when upgrading disk space; however, backup capacity can seriously impact server administration. For example, if you have a server with 4 GB of disk space and a 4-mm DAT backup drive that can archive 8 GB to one tape for a backup, you don't have problem. But what happens if you add another 12 GB of disk space to the server? Now you can no longer fit the entire backup to one tape. This could be a problem, not because the backup needs two tapes, but because the tape must be switched in the middle of a backup. If your organization previously ran an unattended backup overnight, you now need an operator to be present to switch the disks in the middle of the backup. This may or may not be an issue for your organization, but it is something to think about. If the alternative is to add a graveyard-shift operator to perform attended backups, the cost of upgrading to a larger capacity storage solution might make better sense.

RAM

Unlike with disk space, it is more difficult to determine when it is necessary to upgrade the RAM installed on your server hardware. Obviously, you should begin operating your server with at least the minimum amount of RAM recommended for the servers you have chosen to install. You should also increase the RAM accordingly if you are running multiple servers, such as both a Web server and an FTP server, on the same machine.

You can use the Task Manager to give you an idea of how much RAM all your services require when they are initially launched. After you add up the total amount of RAM required to run the services, you should budget at least 16 MB (if not more) of additional RAM to cope with incoming requests. You then can use Performance Monitor to get an idea of how the RAM is being used as users contact your site. If you begin to see a steady pattern of heavy memory usage, you might want to consider upgrading your RAM.

Processing Power

Determining when to add processing power to your machine is the most difficult performance upgrade to ascertain. The biggest indicator will probably be how performance "feels" on your machine, which is not a very scientific performance benchmark.

However, if you have performance problems with adequate disk space and RAM, perhaps your processor is not up to the load you are placing on it. The Task Manager can give you an idea about how much of your CPU power is being used, and Performance Monitor can track CPU usage in real time. You will find that most Internet servers do not use a large amount of CPU power. If your site hosts integrated search features or links to a locally hosted database, and if your server is popular, however, then you might see a sustained strain on your CPU. Anytime your CPU is operating at more that 75 percent for an extended period of time, you should consider upgrading the CPU. Do not worry about spikes that shoot the CPU usage up to 100 percent; those types of spikes are normal for starting complex tasks. The key to monitoring all resource usage is the sustained level.

Network Interfaces

Network interfaces are a frequently overlooked area of server performance. Most machines have a built-in interface to the local area network or an added network card that performs the same function. Just as an outside line to the Internet can become congested with traffic, so can a network interface card on a server. If you are having performance problems that can be traced back to heavy network use (through routing, hub, or switch logs), you also might want to configure your machine for multiple network interfaces. Using multiple network interfaces has the same effect as ordering a bigger line to the Internet. With more than one outlet for network traffic, your server can handle more traffic and, therefore, serve more users.

The Windows NT Diagnostics Tool can provide you with valuable network traffic information, in addition to information similar to that of the Task Manager or Performance Monitor (see fig. 15.6).

You can use the Network feature of this diagnostic tool to get a rough idea of how your server is handling network functions. You might also need to determine whether the problem is related to your general local area network traffic, or through your line to the Internet. LAN Analysis software can help you get an idea of traffic patterns on your LAN, and your Internet service provider should be able to provide you with statistics about how your connection to the Internet is being utilized. Just as with hard drives, if your connection to the Internet is operating at more than 80 percent of its capacity (sustained, not burst) then you should consider adding an additional line.

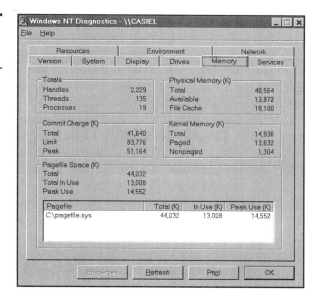

Figure 15.6

The Windows NT Diagnostics tool.

User Management Issues

If you are going to enable users to access your server system, it is essential that you have a well-established set of user guidelines for access and usage of your system. Putting these policies in writing can help you avoid uncomfortable situations in the long run and can help you make sure the server is used properly in conjunction with your goals.

User management can be a complex task. Because users range from very experienced to complete novice, your user policies need to be as comprehensive as possible, and they should be flexible enough to change with the needs of your company and incorporate new technologies if necessary.

Acceptable Use

The first item that needs to be addressed is acceptable use. What is your server going to be used for? If it is a personal server, then this issue becomes much clearer. But what about a server for your small business? Or a workgroup server in a larger corporate setting? Setting a usage policy for your server that reflects the goals of your environment is essential to avoiding problems down the road.

Keep in mind that server resources are valuable. You might want to extend certain personal user privileges, such as e-mail use, to enable users a chance to become more comfortable with the Internet and new technologies. At the same time, you should be clear about the uses that are and are not permitted. For example, if you allow employees to use personal e-mail and read personal news groups, you should specify if adult-oriented groups are permitted. Many organizations have found it necessary to restrict access to certain resources in order to provide a non-offensive working environment to all employees, regardless of age, sex, race, religion, or sexual orientation.

Although it might seem obvious to you that viewing or reading certain materials is inappropriate at the office, not all users will see eye to eye on these issues, and the only way to prevent abuse is to provide well-written, clear guidelines for acceptable use. You can back these policies up by restricting access to unacceptable resources, but a written policy is your best protection against abuse.

Account Rights

Establishing account rights and membership of groups is an essential part of user management. If you are allowing personal resources on your server, then you should provide a level of privacy for those resources as well. In addition, if the server is to be used by a group, you need to make sure members of the same group have access to similar resources. Therefore, properly assigning user rights is an important part of establishing user accounts.

Account Termination

You also should have a policy regarding account termination in the event that someone is no longer with your organization or no longer needs access to your server. Although it is certainly an unnecessary, and possibly a very bad idea, to allow someone to retain access after leaving, it might be courteous to provide mail forwarding, or some means of notifying other users that the user is no longer available at your server's address. Doing so is strictly a professional courtesy and might not be necessary, but in certain circumstances it can prove quite valuable to someone finding a new home on the Net.

Access Policy

Determining which users have access to your server can be an essential part of maintaining security and integrity of your Internet server. Access issues involve both remote and console access and are a central part of security for any server.

Because remote shell logins are not possible with Windows NT, users must be given access to the server console, server access through a network, or ftp access. What type of access you provide will vary depending on the Internet service you intend to offer and the security level of your server. If you are running a business Web site, you might not want to offer ftp access so that you keep your site more secure. In that case you would need to provide other users of your server access to the server through a local area network.

Keep in mind that NT provides very flexible user rights, and you should review each user's account rights with User Manager before allowing access to accounts. Also keep in mind the rights that you assign to any shared volumes. Allowing users to read and write each other's files might seem like a great way to share data but can quickly lead to ownership and access problems.

Ethical Issues

When dealing with files, such as user accounts and e-mail, that might contain sensitive or personal information, you should address certain administrative issues. Just as users should be aware of usage policies, administrators also should be held accountable to a high level of professional and ethical standards.

You should clearly outline a policy that deals with several issues faced by administrators and guidelines for dealing with those situations. Some issues include the following:

- ❏ Dealing with user violations of system policies
- ❏ Dealing with law-enforcement requests for information
- ❏ Assisting other systems administrators with tracking violations
- ❏ Harassment
- ❏ Privacy issues

All these issues are dealt with routinely by system administrators, and you should have clear guidelines for each of these issues, as well as a clear set of consequences for an administrative violation of policy.

Take the issue of user privacy, for example. The nature of administrative tasks gives administrators the capability to read anyone's e-mail files. Most users, however, consider e-mail to be private communication, and if your policy provides for e-mail privacy, an administrator reading another user's e-mail is a serious ethical violation.

As another example, consider a case at a large corporation in which an administrator had recently broken off a romantic relationship with a fellow employee. Policies about staff relationships aside, the administrator began reading the former partner's e-mail to see if that person was seeing anyone else. This was a serious violation of the user's privacy. The administrator was fired as a result of this ethical breech and was fortunate not to be prosecuted for harassment as well.

Recently, a California Internet service provider had a similar situation arise when an administrator decided that it would be funny to send forged e-mail to a user as a practical joke. Unfortunately, the user did not find the joke funny and complained to the ISP management. The administrator should have been aware that forged e-mail was a violation of company policy, but she felt that her status as an administrator somehow put her above those usage policies. Nothing could be further from the truth. Because of the power held by administrators, they must adhere to the most professional and ethical standards. Although the ISP was a small business with a very informal management structure, the administrator still had to be fired. Although this action might seem extreme in some cases, a failure to do so could undermine user confidence, not to mention lead to serious system problems such as complaints from outside systems.

By outlining these ethical issues in a policy for administrators, you reinforce the idea that administrators will be held to professional ethical standards. Most administrators take their positions seriously and would not consider violating these policies, but having the policies in writing provides you with a solid method for reprimanding violators.

Summary

This chapter covered a wide variety of administrative topics and gave you an idea of what is involved with managing your Windows NT Internet server. The task of administering an Internet server can be quite formidable; however, with the proper planning and foresight, it also can be quite enjoyable. Keep in mind that there is no substitute for practical administrative experience. Because your server will be unique to your needs, your management style and procedures need to be tailored to your server as well. The topics outlined in this chapter should serve as a starting point to help you make sure not to miss any major administrative points. You then can take these tasks to heart and customize administration for your very own Internet server.

V

Appendices

Overview of the Microsoft Commercial Internet System Servers

M icrosoft's new suite of Internet servers, the Microsoft Commercial Internet System servers, (formerly code-named Normandy) is the software company's attempt at creating a complete, high-volume Internet server solution for both service providers and major commercial networks. Commercial Internet System servers are created for the Windows NT and Internet Information Server platform, and will be offered as extended members of the Microsoft BackOffice server suite.

The technology has been developed and field-tested through Microsoft Network (MSN), and soon will be in use by the online service CompuServe. Although the Commercial

Internet System servers are in their second run of beta testing at the time of this writing, they promise to be a heavy-duty solution for companies desiring a large, personalized Internet service that uses Microsoft technology, running on standards-based protocols and procedures. This chapter is an outline of basic Internet Server design and business advantages, with a brief overview of each server in the Internet server suite. Although this information is not acutely technical, it should provide a good understanding of the emerging technology and server products that are making the Commercial Internet System such an attractive prospect.

This section covers the overall concept of the Microsoft Commercial Internet System; explaining the target market, and the corporate and engineering advantages to the products. The following are important items on which to concentrate:

❏ The Microsoft Commercial Internet servers
❏ Internet Server design and standards
❏ Who should consider using Microsoft Commercial Internet System servers?

The Microsoft Commercial Internet System Servers

The Microsoft Commercial Internet System server is the inclusive name for the current eight specialized Internet servers from Microsoft. Each server will be able to run separately, integrated into Microsoft's Internet Information Server. This tight integration with IIS means simple configuration and setup, and a one-stop management utility for all Internet servers. Because the Commercial Internet servers use the IIS platform, which is included with Windows NT Server 4, the following servers are already included with Windows NT Server 4:

❏ Web Server
❏ FTP Server
❏ Gopher Server

Microsoft Commercial Internet servers were designed with the idea of a community oriented existence on the Internet; services such as chatting, posting ideas, and personalizing each user's Internet environment, are all heavy factors involved in both creating and using the Commercial Internet System server system. The following are the current servers that are now under development:

- ❑ **Conference Server.** An IRC chat server that enables both public and private conferences and chat sessions to be held. It can be accessed by using standard IRC clients, or by using ActiveX controls embedded in a Web page.
- ❑ **Internet News Server.** NNTP newsgroup services for information and idea exchange.
- ❑ **Internet Mail Server.** A standard electronic mail server that uses SMTP and POP3 standard protocols.
- ❑ **Information Retrieval Server.** Indexing and search capabilities (similar to a Web search engine) for searching both HTML Web pages and Microsoft Office files.
- ❑ **Personalization Server.** Enables personalized Internet browsing for each user and utilizes Microsoft's ActiveX technology.
- ❑ **Membership Server.** A secure method of maintaining membership records and rights, which features interfaces to other billing systems, enabling it to fit easily into an existing service. Also includes the White Pages Server, which is a membership directory that enables users to list personal information, interests, and other information for use with member searches.
- ❑ **Content Replication Server.** Distributes content data among several Web servers for logical retrieval.
- ❑ **Merchant Server.** Online transactions and commerce; enabling users to securely purchase products or information over the Internet.

Internet Server Design and Standards

Microsoft is designing its Internet servers around several advantageous principles. Its open-ended standards-based environment enables integration with other platforms that are running on other operating systems. Its personalization capabilities reflect the growing trend toward providing Internet users with highly individualistic content. The Commercial Internet System server suite's most notable design goals center around its standards-based, scaleable engineering, and the concept of a personalized Internet "community" experience for the end user. The following are the major design considerations discussed in this appendix:

- ❑ Standards-Based Design
- ❑ Scalability
- ❑ Personalization
- ❑ An "Internet Community"

Standards-Based Design

The Microsoft Commercial Internet System servers adheres to published Internet standards and protocols, enabling end users to access services like most Internet service providers—from any operating system platform, using any client software that supports Internet standards. An example of this is using a mail client on a Macintosh system to check e-mail (via the POP3 standard Internet mail protocol). This standards-based approach not only enables Commercial Internet System servers to provide Internet services to all users on any platform, but it also means easy integration with other server solutions. Legacy systems, non-Windows NT platforms, and third-party products that support regular Internet standards, can all be easily integrated in a site. This capability to work alongside other servers and platforms lends itself to another major design goal—scalability.

Scalability

Scalability, the capability to ascend to larger networking hardware designs or demands is a crucial factor in deciding on Internet servers for a large online service. If the user-base climbs into the hundreds of thousands, or even the millions, the server software and hardware must be able to easily scale with this momentum. Scalability is not only measured by the capacity for growth and whether or not it can handle a large number of users, but also by the ease of this expansion and its administrative overhead.

The Microsoft Commercial Internet System servers offer scalability benefits in several ways. Because the Commercial Internet System servers operate on the Windows NT platform, it uses multi-threaded design to scale to multiple processors. This means the Internet servers can make the most of asymmetrical multiprocessing on Windows NT, ensuring high-speed content and services. Commercial Internet System servers are also geared to support up to millions of users, and has been field-tested in its precursor form, the Microsoft Network, with over one million users.

Personalization

The Microsoft Commercial Internet System server aims to provide a highly-personalized environment to the Internet service user. Most of the interactive content on the Internet today is viewed with Web browsers. With the Personalization Server, information about the user is gathered each time he or she visits a designated Web page, and more personalized information based on learned interests, region, and other data, can be offered dynamically. Aside from Web-based interaction, the Commercial Internet Server system provides the Membership Server for not only administrating subscription information on commercial sites, but also for offering informational profiles set by each user. Current users of online services, such as America Online or CompuServe, are familiar with such personal profiles. To find members with similar interests or certain keywords in their descriptions, users of the online service can query these profiles.

An Internet "Community"

Microsoft is designing the Commercial Internet System server with several user-friendly, "community"-oriented goals in mind. Microsoft's Conference Server, Internet Mail Server, and Internet News Server are all common Internet servers that support communication among members of the online service and the Internet. With personalization of services and the addition of online purchasing, however, the idea of an online community starts to expand into something more identifiable. The Merchant Server provides for secure transactions for true Internet commerce by using security encryption standards and protocols. These server solutions, along with the Membership Server, all fit together to create the possibility for a large virtual community of members.

The Microsoft Commercial Internet System Server Family

This section details each member of the Microsoft Commercial Internet System server family, and briefly discusses the corporate benefits, protocol standards, and general uses of each server.

Commercial Internet Mail Server

Providing Internet e-mail is a necessity for Internet service providers; any large online service will require individual e-mail accounts for each user. Commercial Internet Mail Server can host millions of e-mail accounts, and features robust architecture for efficient mail transfer. E-mail servers also can be used in conjunction with other regional servers to provide the most efficient e-mail capabilities throughout the country. Large online services benefit from this by providing a consistent set of e-mail addressing schemes while distributing servers in different cities or states. Like all other Commercial Internet System servers and services that run on Internet Information Server, Internet Mail Server is easy to administrate from remote locations.

The Standards Used

Internet Mail Server uses the Internet standards for mail and document transfer over TCP/IP networks. The following are the three standard mail protocols used:

- ❏ **SMTP**. Simple Mail Transport Protocol, used to send e-mail across the Internet.
- ❏ **POP3**. Post Office Protocol 3, used to retrieve user mail from the server. This is the protocol that enables users to check their mail.
- ❏ **MIME**. Multipurpose Internet Mail Extensions, a protocol used to attach documents and files to e-mail messages.

Commercial Internet News Server

News servers provide newsgroup forums for users to exchange similar interests, technical information, and any other useful interchange. Commercial Internet News Server provides a platform for offering newsgroups, with a detailed but easy to use configuration manager. Companies benefit from newsgroup offerings because newsgroups provide a common method of idea exchange, in which all forums are public over the online service or the Internet. The following are some of the increasingly popular uses of newsgroup technology in business today.

- ❏ Providing a technical bulletin board for discussion of problems and solutions pertaining to a company's products, or primary technologies.
- ❏ Keeping in constant contact with beta users of new software, select users of pre-release products, and so on to maintain a careful focus on the direction of production and marketing.
- ❏ Offering online technical support discussion, enabling users to view past posts to the newsgroup and discover solutions to their problems offered by other users or company technical representatives.

The Standards Used

Commercial Internet News Server uses the Internet standard for news server protocols, NNTP (Network News Transport Protocol). Because of its NNTP compliance, News Server enables a service's users to use any NNTP compliant news reader of their choice. The use of NNTP also means improved security that uses security extensions; this is an important feature for any service that requires users to log in to a news server by using a password. News Server integrates easily with other NNTP news servers, providing scalability and flexibility.

Administration

Commercial Internet News Server administration is one of its most attractive features. An administrator can install News Server and have newsgroups available to the public in only a few minutes. Learning proper news server administration is not so instant, but Commercial Internet News Server is still easily configurable. Newsgroups can be configured to enable local postings, remote postings such as from users over the Internet, and moderated postings that require the approval of a designated newsgroup moderator. Public and private newsgroups are also easy to create and maintain. This ease of administration and total control over the news server and newsgroups enables both expert site administrators and relative beginners to maintain an online information exchange service.

Conference Server

Chat servers were once thought of merely as entertainment, or places where software pirates traded the latest cracked software. Today, however, Internet Relay Chat (IRC) servers are becoming useful tools for providing technical support and conferencing to companies all over the world. Chat Server is an implementation of the IRC chat protocol, and provides a robust and expandable way to communicate with others, by using anything from popular IRC clients to ActiveX controls embedded in Web pages. Another important addition to Conference Server is the Locator Server, which enables users to locate other users online, specifically for connecting to those users with conferencing applications, such as Microsoft NetMeeting, or one of the many Internet phone applications that enables real-time voice conferencing.

Companies are realizing tremendous benefits to running chat servers, both publicly and privately. Many of today's top meeting and conferencing applications, such as Microsoft's NetMeeting and other popular "whiteboard" applications, use IRC chat servers to establish chat connections. This means that a company with a chat server could run its own system of online meetings, exchanging documents, viewing Web pages, and collaborating on drawing diagrams and outlines. Customer support also is a key issue when deciding on a chat server; will the company benefit by offering online real-time customer support over the Internet?

The Standards Used

The standard protocol Chat Server uses the IRC. This is a well-tested, popular form of Internet communication, with millions of experienced users. Because of its use of the IRC standard, Chat Server enables any IRC client to connect, including the increasingly popular conferencing programs and whiteboards that use IRC servers. ActiveX controls, mentioned earlier, are being developed to access IRC servers, which means a site can now offer embedded chatting in Web pages, all by using the standard protocols.

The Information Retrieval Server

NOTE

The Information Retrieval Server can integrate with the Personalization Server to provide users with even more user-specific information, based on whatever user attributes are pertinent. Imagine a search for nationwide store outlets returning an index with the nearest stores first.

The Information Retrieval Server (IR) provides lookup and indexing for a vast array of document types on a server. Although standard Web-based search engines can provide a huge amount of data per request lookup, much of this data often is extraneous, and is gathered only because of simple text matches. The IR Server searches for requested matches for information, and indexes the databases to provide much faster searches. Companies realize benefits in this by providing end-users with a complete searchable content site—specialized information in several file formats across multiple servers can be retrieved and viewed. Users will benefit from rapid and complete information retrieval of business data, pricing information, company information, and any other publicly available content can be offered effortlessly.

The Personalization Server

The Personalization Server is one of the emerging new technologies appearing on interactive, dynamic Web sites around the Internet. By using this new server, a site can maintain highly-personalized Web page offerings to each separate user of the online service. Popular examples of this are the personalized pages offered by the Microsoft Network, which uses the Personalization Server to provide user-definable "start pages."

By using personalized content technology, a site can deliver the most pertinent advertisements to a user based on region, interests, and even income. Personalization Server's use with Web pages means limitless ideas for including new Web content to make each user's Web surfing more enjoyable and memorable than standard viewing.

The Membership Server

The online service, whether it be a unique commercial service, or a standard Internet service provider, needs reliable and secure billing and membership information.

Membership Server offers security, flexibility, and support for millions of users. Services often require time-based billing options, and billing for extra services, often reached through third-party locations. Membership Server benefits a company by providing tight control over user account security, and offers database access to the entire user-base. The following are the three main components to the Membership Server, all discussed in this appendix:

❏ Membership Server Security Services
❏ White Pages Server
❏ Network Tools

Membership Server Security

Security is a major design issue with Membership Server, and is offered in various methods throughout its architecture and use. The following are some of the key security advantages to Membership Server.

❏ **Windows NT File System security.** Using the NTFS file system for secure information is always an immediately effective security enhancement because the security is enforced from the file level.
❏ **Distributed Security Solution.** Maintains control of the security while enabling access to third-party sites and resources.
❏ **Standards-Based Security.** Internet standard security protocols such as Secure Socket Layer (SSL), and soon Public Key encryption, will be integrated into Membership Server.

White Pages Server

White Pages are listings of public information that users offer about themselves. The White Pages Server provides a large database of user attributes and interests to enable other users to search for common interests, occupations, and so on. This approach can benefit an online service by creating user interest in both the online community and the service provider itself. With easy access via both Web pages and client software conforming to the LDAP (Lightweight Directory Access Protocol), users can search through over five million users on each server.

Network Tools

Because service providers need to offer telephone dial-up access to customers, keeping up-to-date listings of access numbers, ensuring that these numbers are operational, and authenticating logons from these numbers, are of major importance. The

Network Tools offered with Membership Server provide for securely enabling users the capability to log onto online services from the nearest local access line.

Content Replication Server

Large Internet sites requiring time-sensitive updates of information, statistics, and results often run into the problem of needing content replication. Content Replication Server provides a means to distribute the network load of content servers, and increase accurate and simultaneous data for a site. By using multiple servers with Content Replication Server, the total network load is distributed out, while still ensuring accurate and timely updates are provided for the entire network. The following are examples of this:

❑ Constantly updating stock reports on a network that enables access to multiple servers. Each server providing the stock results information must correlate exactly with all other servers or the information is not up to date.

❑ A consistently-updated database of online statistics might need to be kept for users to view the latest results in polls, decisions, or data. Content Replication server could easily distribute the content update to all servers, providing users in every location with the same accurate time-sensitive data.

❑ An Internet service with servers in several areas of the country or world might want to create a mirror site, with identical content, to evenly distribute the network load on a server.

Key Features

Content Replication Server is a reliable, secure method of providing content replication and distribution. It is designed to handle large amounts of data for commercial quality networks, and thus is optimized for data integrity, speed, and ease of use. Some of the more important features are:

❑ Data inconsistency checking.

❑ Reconnection and re-authentication after a disconnection.

❑ Parallel replication to multiple servers.

❑ Regular replication schedules, as well as automatic replication of directories, useful in mirror sites.

Merchant Server

Online transactions have become a standard for online services, and are quickly becoming popular over the Internet. Although security is always an issue when transferring credit card or bank account numbers over a network, there have been significant improvements in security that have made the process very reliable and safe. Microsoft Merchant Server is an online transaction service for use with major large-scale services. Merchant Server is a completely scalable and flexible solution that offers database connectivity, third-party billing integration, as well as a host of promotional and network tools to help in developing a professional point of sale site. Accessible over HTML Web pages and with custom ActiveX applications, Merchant Server sales sites are ideal for an online transaction standard. The following are some of the major design and administrative advantages.

❏ ODBC database connectivity enables use of any ODBC-compliant relational database, such as Microsoft SQL Server, or Oracle SQL Server.

❏ HTML templates and dynamic page generation for queries and user interaction, to reduce administrative and authoring overhead.

❏ Analysis of results for promotional advantages, tracking user trends, and so on.

N O T E

Information on the Microsoft Commercial Internet System servers, and any current beta software can be located on the World Wide Web at `http://www.ms-normandy.com`. Information on Microsoft's BackOffice suite of servers can be found at `http://www.microsoft.com/backoffice`.

At the time of this writing, Microsoft's Commercial Internet System servers were just introduced into the BackOffice platform. Due to Microsoft's constantly changing Internet (and marketing) strategies, the Commercial Internet Servers might exist in a somewhat altered form by the time this book is published. Pricing, availability, and servers might change.

Summary

The Microsoft Commercial Internet Servers are not for every Internet provider or company. The entire server suite as a whole is targeted toward the large-scale Internet service provider or specialty online service. The servers offer high-quality, extremely scalable server solutions that can integrate with other platforms in a heterogeneous networking environment, while running on the Windows NT and Internet Information Server platform. All Commercial Internet System servers are standards-based; that is, easily configurable platforms that enable cross-platform interaction with any standards-based client software. The following are the fundamental principles Microsoft claims for its servers.

❏ Scalability
❏ Personalization
❏ Large-scale commercial use

❏ Flexibility

❏ Programmability with published APIs

The concept of the Commercial Internet System servers centers around commercial quality and high bandwidth needs. The suite of servers consisting of Internet Mail, Internet News, and Conferencing, however, might be all a service provider needs. The Conferencing, Mail, and News servers can provide a complete, standards-based Internet solution with the help of IIS, and the Web, ftp, and Gopher servers included in IIS.

Windows NT Server Command Reference

A lthough the majority of Windows NT functions can be executed using graphics utilities, there are several reasons for using NET commands at the command prompt. In some cases, entering a command at the command prompt is faster than starting a graphics utility and stepping through menus. Of greater significance is that NET commands can be put into batch files, which are useful for building logon scripts, executing commands at schedule times, or performing functions when events are triggered. The UPS command, for example, can be configured to execute a batch file before shutting down Windows NT. Although the NET commands are described in online help displays, they are summarized here for your convenience.

The following conventions are used to indicate command syntax:

- ❏ **Bold** letters are used for words that must be typed as shown.
- ❏ *lowercase italic* letters are used for items that vary, such as file names.

- ❏ The [and] characters surround optional items that can be supplied with the command.
- ❏ The { and } characters surround lists of items. You may select one of the items in the list.
- ❏ The ¦ character separates items in a list. Only one of the items can be included with the command.

  For example, in the following syntax, you must type **NET COMMAND** and either **OPTION1** or **OPTION2**. Supplying a name is optional.

  `NET COMMAND [name] {OPTION1 ¦ OPTION2}`

- ❏ The [...] characters mean you can repeat the previous item, separating items with spaces.
- ❏ The [,...] characters mean you can repeat the previous item, separating items with commas or semicolons, not spaces.
- ❏ When service names consist of two or more words, enclose the service name in quotation marks. For example, NET PAUSE "FTP SERVER" pauses the FTP server service.

To view a listing of syntax conventions for the online help, type the command **net help syntax**.

NET ACCOUNTS

NET ACCOUNTS is used to maintain the user account database. It can modify password and logon requirements for all user accounts. When entered without options, NET ACCOUNTS displays current settings for the password, logon limitations, and domain information for the logged-on account.

Syntax

```
NET ACCOUNTS    [/FORCELOGOFF:{minutes ¦ NO}]
                [/MINPWLEN:length]
                [/MAXPWAGE:{days ¦ UNLIMITED}]
                [/MINPWAGE:days]
                [/UNIQUEPW:number]
                [/DOMAIN]
NET ACCOUNTS [/SYNC] [/DOMAIN]
```

Options

/FORCELOGOFF:{*minutes* | NO}

Minutes specifies the number of minutes a user has before being automatically logged off when an account expires or logon hours expire. NO is the default value that specifies that forced logoff will not occur.

/MINPWLEN:length

Length specifies the minimum number of characters required for a password. The range is 0-14 characters. The default is 6 characters.

/MAXPWAGE:{*days* | UNLIMITED}

Days specifies the maximum number of days a password is valid. The UNLIMITED option specifies that no limit is imposed. /MAXPWAGE cannot be less than /MINPWAGE. The range is 1-49,710 and the default is 90 days.

/MINPWAGE:*days*

Days specifies the minimum number of days that must pass before a user can change his or her password. A value of 0 specifies no minimum time. The range is 0-49,710; the default is 0 days. /MINPWAGE cannot be greater than /MAXPWAGE.

/UNIQUEPW:number

Specifies that the user's passwords must be unique for the number of changes specified by *number*. The maximum value is 8.

/SYNC

Synchronizes the account database.

/DOMAIN

Include this option to perform the specified action on the entire domain controller instead of the current computer. This option is effective only when executed on Windows NT computers that are members of a domain.

Examples

NET ACCOUNTS can be used to make global changes to all user accounts. To change the minimum password length for all user accounts to five days, enter the following command:

```
NET ACCOUNTS /MINPWAGE:5
```

Figure B.1 shows an example of using the NET ACCOUNTS command without options.

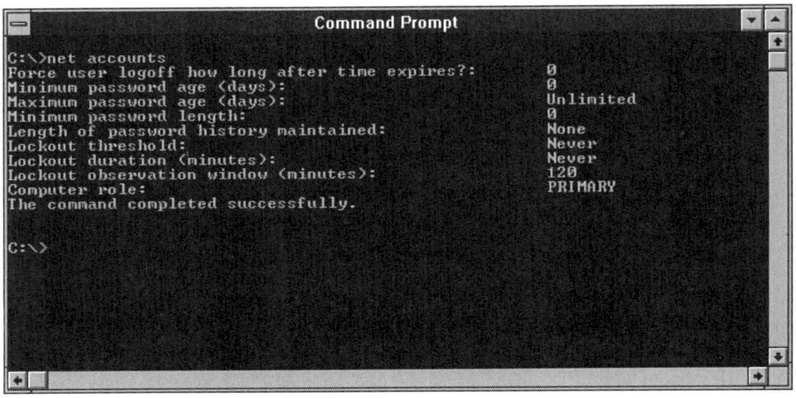

Figure B.1

Displaying account information with the NET ACCOUNTS command.

```
                          Command Prompt
C:\>net accounts
Force user logoff how long after time expires?:        0
Minimum password age (days):                           0
Maximum password age (days):                           Unlimited
Minimum password length:                               0
Length of password history maintained:                None
Lockout threshold:                                     Never
Lockout duration (minutes):                            Never
Lockout observation window (minutes):                  120
Computer role:                                         PRIMARY
The command completed successfully.


C:\>
```

Notes

Before options used with NET ACCOUNTS will take effect, the following conditions must be true:

❑ User accounts must have been set up by the User Manager or the NET USER command.

❑ The Net Logon service must be running on all domain controllers.

NET COMPUTER

Use this command to add or delete computers from the domain database.

Syntax

```
NET COMPUTER \\computername {/ADD | /DEL}
```

Options

computername	The name of the computer to be added or deleted.
/ADD	Adds the computer to the domain.
/DEL	Deletes the computer from the domain.

Example

To add a computer named GEORGE to the domain, enter this command:

```
NET COMPUTER \\GEORGE /ADD
```

Notes

This command is available only with Windows NT Server.

NET CONFIG SERVER

Use this command to display or change settings for the server service. This command affects only the server on which it is executed.

You must be logged on as a member of the Administrators group to configure the server.

Syntax

```
NET CONFIG SERVER    [/AUTODISCONCONNECT:time]

                     [/SRVCOMMENT:"text"]

                     [/HIDDEN:{YES|NO}]
```

Options

/AUTODISCONNECT:*time*	*Time* specifies the number of minutes an account can be inactive before it is disconnected. Specify -1 to never disconnect. The range is 1-65,535 minutes. The default is 15.
/SRVCOMMENT:"*text*"	The message in "*text*" specifies a message that is displayed with the server in many Windows NT screens. The message can consist of up to 48 characters and must be enclosed in quotation marks.

| /HIDDEN:{YES ¦ NO} | Determines whether a computer name is advertised in listings of servers. YES hides the server. NO includes the server name in lists. |

Example

To display the current configuration for the Server service, type **NET CONFIG SERVER** without parameters. An example NET CONFIG SERVER display is shown in Figure B.2.

Figure B.2
Example NET CONFIG SERVER display.

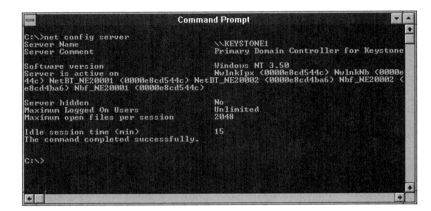

NET CONFIG WORKSTATION

This command displays and changes settings for the Workstation service.

Syntax

NET CONFIG WORKSTATION   [/CHARCOUNT:*bytes*]

[/CHARTIME:*msec*]

[/CHARWAIT:*sec*]

Options

| /CHARCOUNT:*bytes* | Specifies the *bytes* of data that are collected before data is sent to a communication device. If /CHARTIME is set, Windows NT relies on the value that is satisfied first. The range is 0-65,535 bytes. The default is 16 bytes. |

/CHARTIME:*msec*	*msec* specifies the number of milliseconds that Windows NT collects data before sending it to a communication device. If /CHARCOUNT is set, Windows NT relies on the value that is satisfied first. The range is 0-65,535,000 milliseconds. The default is 250 milliseconds.
/CHARWAIT:*sec*	Specifies the number of seconds Windows NT waits for a communication device to become available. The range is 0-65,535 seconds. The default is 3,600 seconds.

Notes

To display the current configuration for the Workstation service, type **NET CONFIG WORKSTATION** without parameters.

NET CONTINUE

NET CONTINUE reactivates a Windows NT service that has been suspended by NET PAUSE.

Syntax

```
NET CONTINUE service
```

Options

service   Is any of the following paused services:

❑ FILE SERVER FOR MACINTOSH

❑ FTP SERVER

❑ LPDSVC

❑ NET LOGON

❑ NETWORK DDE

❑ NETWORK DDE DSDM

❑ NT LM SECURITY SUPPORT PROVIDER

❑ REMOTEBOOT

❑ REMOTE ACCESS SERVER

❏ SCHEDULE
❏ SERVER
❏ SIMPLE TCP/IP SERVICES
❏ WORKSTATION

NET FILE

Use this command to list ID numbers of files, to close a shared file, and to remove file locks. When used without options, NET FILE lists the open files on a server along with their IDs, path names, user names, and number of locks.

Syntax

```
NET FILE [id [/CLOSE]]
```

Options

`id`   The identification number of the file.

`/CLOSE`   Include this option to close an open file and remove file locks. This command must be typed from the server where the file is shared.

Notes

This command works only on computers running the Server service.

NET GROUP

This command adds, displays, or modifies global groups on servers. Enter the **NET GROUP** command without parameters to display the group names on the server.

Syntax

```
NET GROUP [groupname [/COMMENT:"text"]] [/DOMAIN]
NET GROUP groupname {/ADD [/COMMENT:"text"] ¦ /DELETE} [/DOMAIN]
NET GROUP groupname username [...] {/ADD ¦ /DELETE} [/DOMAIN]
```

Options

groupname	This parameter specifies the name of the group to add, expand, or delete. This parameter is also included when user names are to be added to or deleted from a group. Supply the group name alone to see a list of users in a group.
/COMMENT:"*text*"	This switch adds a comment of up to 48 characters, as specified by *text*. Enclose the text in quotation marks.
/DOMAIN	Include this switch to perform the operation on the primary domain controller of the current domain. Without the /DOMAIN switch the operation affects only the local computer.
username[...]	Specifies one or more user names to be added to or removed from a group. Multiple user name entries must be separated with a space.
/ADD	Adds a group to a domain or adds a user name to a group.
/DELETE	Removes a group from a domain or removes a user name from a group.

Examples

To view membership of the local group Server Operators, enter this command:

NET GROUP "SERVER OPERATORS"

To add a group named Blivet Engineers, you would use the following command:

NET GROUP "Blivet Engineers" /ADD

NET HELP

Use this command to display a help listing of the options available for any NET command.

Syntax

```
NET HELP command
```

or

```
NET command /HELP
```

Options

Help information is available for the following commands:

NET ACCOUNTS	NET HELP	NET SHARE
NET COMPUTER	NET HELPMSG	NET START
NET CONFIG	NET LOCALGROUP	NET STATISTICS
NET CONFIG SERVER	NET NAME	NET STOP
NET CONFIG WORKSTATION	NET PAUSE	NET TIME
NET CONTINUE	NET PRINT	NET USE
NET FILE	NET SEND	NET USER
NET GROUP	NET SESSION	NET VIEW

Notes

`NET HELP command ¦ MORE` displays Help one screen at a time.

`NET HELP SERVICES` lists the network services you can start.

`NET HELP SYNTAX` explains how to read NET HELP syntax lines.

NET HELPMSG

The NET HELPMSG command displays explanations of Windows NT network messages, including errors, warnings, and alerts. Type **NET HELPMSG** and the 4-digit number of the Windows NT error. Although network error messages include the word NET (for example, NET1234), you do not need to include NET in the message# parameter.

Syntax

```
NET HELPMSG message#
```

Options

message#   Is the 4-digit number of the Windows NT message you need help with.

Example

Figure B.3 shows an example of using the NET HELPMSG command.

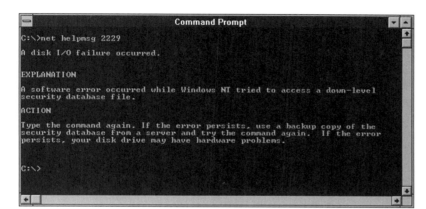

Figure B.3
*An example of a
NET HELPMSG
command.*

NET LOCALGROUP

Use this command to modify local groups on computers. Enter the NET
LOCALGROUP command without parameters to list the local groups on the
computer.

Syntax

```
NET LOCALGROUP [groupname [/COMMENT:"text"]] [/DOMAIN]
NET LOCALGROUP groupname {/ADD [/COMMENT:"text"] ¦ /DELETE} [/DOMAIN]
NET LOCALGROUP groupname name [...] {/ADD ¦ /DELETE} [/DOMAIN]
```

Options

groupname   *groupname* specifies the name of the local group to add,
                             expand, or delete. Supply a group name without parameters
                             to list users or global groups in the local group. If the group
                             name includes spaces, enclose the name in quotation marks.

/COMMENT:"*text*"	This switch adds a comment of up to 48 characters, as specified by *text*. Enclose the text in quotation marks.
/DOMAIN	Include this switch to perform the operation on the primary domain controller of the current domain. Otherwise, the operation is performed on the local computer. By default, Windows NT Server computers perform operations on the domain. This option is effective only when executed on a computer that is a member of a domain.
name [...]	Specifies one or more user names or group names to be added to or removed from the local group. Multiple entries must be separated with a space. Include the domain name if the user is from another domain (Example: WIDGETS\CHARLES).
/ADD	Adds the specified group name or user name to a local group. User and group names to be added must have been created previously.
/DELETE	Removes a group name or user name from a local group.

Examples

To display the membership of the local group "Domain Admins," enter the following command:

NET LOCALGROUP "DOMAIN ADMINS"

To add the user Harold to the local group Widgets, enter the command:

NET LOCALGROUP WIDGETS HAROLD

NET NAME

The NET NAME command adds or deletes a messaging name at a computer. A messaging name is a name to which messages are sent. Use the NET NAME command without options to display names accepting messages at this computer.

A computer's list of names comes from three places:

❏ Message names, which are added with NET NAME.

❏ Computer names, which cannot be deleted. The computer name is added as a name when the Workstation service is started.

❏ User names, which cannot be deleted. Unless the name is already in use on another computer, the user name is added as a name when you log on.

Syntax

```
NET NAME [name [/ADD | /DELETE]]
```

Options

name   The name of the user account that is to be added to the names that will receive messages. The name can have as many as 15 characters.

/ADD   Adds a name to a computer. /ADD is optional and typing **NET NAME** *name* works the same way as typing **NET NAME** *name* /**ADD**.

/DELETE   Removes a name from a computer.

NET PAUSE

Use the NET PAUSE command to suspend a Windows NT service or resource. Pausing a service puts it on hold. Use the NET CONTINUE command to resume the service.

Syntax

```
NET PAUSE service
```

Options

service   The service to be paused. Please see the NET CONTINUE command for a list of services that can be paused.

Notes

If the Server service is paused, only users who are members of the Administrators or Server Operators groups will be permitted to log on to the network.

NET PRINT

Use this command to list print jobs and shared queues. For each queue, the command lists jobs, showing the size and status of each job, and the queue status.

Syntax

```
NET PRINT \\computername\sharename
```

```
[\\computername] job# [/HOLD ¦ /RELEASE ¦ /DELETE]
```

Options

\\computername	Specifies the name of the computer sharing the printer queue(s).
sharename	Specifies the share name of the printer queue.
job#	Specifies the identification number assigned to a print job. Each job executed on a computer is assigned a unique number.
/HOLD	Assigns a "hold" status to a job so that it will not print. The job remains in the queue until it is released or deleted.
/RELEASE	Removes the "hold" status on a job so that it can be printed.
/DELETE	Removes a job from a queue.

Examples

To display active print jobs on a computer named Blivets, enter the following command:

```
NET PRINT \\BLIVETS
```

To hold job number 234 on the computer Blivets, for example, the command is

```
NET PRINT \\BLIVETS 234 /HOLD
```

NET SEND

This command sends messages to other users, computers, or messaging names on the network.

Syntax

```
NET SEND {name ¦ * ¦ /DOMAIN[:domainname] ¦ /USERS} message
```

Options

name	Specifies the user name, computer name, or messaging name to which the message is sent. If the name contains blank characters, enclose the name in quotation marks.
*	An *, when substituted for *name*, sends the message to all the names in your group.
/DOMAIN[:*domainname*]	Specifies that the message should be sent to all users in the domain. If *domainname* is specified, the message is sent to all the names in the specified domain or workgroup.
/USERS	Sends the message to all users connected to the server.
message	The text to be sent as a message.

Examples

To send a message to everyone in a domain, type a command like the following:

```
NET SEND /DOMAIN:WIDGETS A message for everyone in Widgets
```

You can also specify a user, in this case, Mabel:

```
NET SEND MABEL A message for Mabel
```

Notes

The Messenger service must be running on the receiving computer to receive messages.

You can send a message only to a name that is active on the network.

NET SESSION

The NET SESSION command lists or disconnects sessions between the computer and other computers on the network. When used without options, NET SESSION displays information about all sessions running on the computer that currently has the focus.

Syntax

```
NET SESSION [\\computername] [/DELETE]
```

Options

\\computername	Lists the session information for the named computer.
/DELETE	Ends the session between the local computer and computername. All open files on the computer are closed. If computername is omitted, all sessions are ended.

Notes

This command works only when executed on servers.

NET SHARE

The NET SHARE command is used to share a server's resources with network users. Use the command without options to list information about all resources being shared on the computer. For each shared resource, Windows NT reports the device name(s) or path name(s) for the share along with any descriptive comment that has been associated with the share.

Syntax

```
NET SHARE    sharename
NET SHARE    sharename=drive:path
             [/USERS:number ¦ /UNLIMITED]
             [/REMARK:"text"]
NET SHARE    sharename [/USERS:number ¦ /UNLIMITED] [/REMARK:"text"]
NET SHARE    {sharename ¦ devicename ¦ drive:path} /DELETE
```

Options

sharename	Specifies the network name of the shared resource. Typing NET SHARE with a share name only displays information about that share.
devicename	Specifies one or more printers (LPT1 through LPT9) shared by *sharename*. Use this option when a printer share is being established.
drive:path	Specifies the absolute path of a directory to be shared. Use this option when a directory share is being established.
/USERS:*number*	Specifies the maximum number of users that will be permitted to simultaneously access the shared resource.
/UNLIMITED	Specifies that no limit will be placed on the number of users that will be permitted to simultaneously access the shared resource.
/REMARK:"*text*"	Associates a descriptive comment about the resource with the share definition. Enclose the text in quotation marks.
/DELETE	Stops sharing the resource.

Examples

To share the directory C:\APPLICATIONS with the share name APPS, enter the command:

```
NET SHARE APPS=C:\APPLICATIONS
```

You can limit the number of users who can access a share by using the /USERS options. The following example limits users to 10:

```
NET SHARE APPS=C:\APPLICATIONS /USERS:10
```

To stop sharing the printer on LPT3, enter the following command:

```
NET SHARE LPT3: /DELETE
```

Notes

Printers must be shared with Print Manager. NET SHARE can be used to stop sharing printers.

NET START

Use the NET START command to start services that have not been started or have been stopped by the NET STOP command. Enter the command **NET START** without options to list running services.

Syntax

```
NET START [service]
```

Options

service   One of the following services to be stopped:

- ❏   ALERTER
- ❏   CLIENT SERVICE FOR NETWARE
- ❏   CLIPBOOK SERVER
- ❏   COMPUTER BROWSER
- ❏   DHCP CLIENT
- ❏   DIRECTORY REPLICATOR
- ❏   EVENTLOG
- ❏   FTP SERVER
- ❏   LPDSVC
- ❏   MESSENGER
- ❏   NET LOGON
- ❏   NETWORK DDE
- ❏   NETWORK DDE DSDM
- ❏   NETWORK MONITORING AGENT
- ❏   NT LM SECURITY SUPPORT PROVIDER
- ❏   OLE
- ❏   REMOTE ACCESS CONNECTION MANAGER

- REMOTE ACCESS ISNSAP SERVICE
- REMOTE ACCESS SERVER
- REMOTE PROCEDURE CALL (RPC) LOCATOR
- REMOTE PROCEDURE CALL (RPC) SERVICE
- SCHEDULE
- SERVER
- SIMPLE TCP/IP SERVICES
- SNMP
- SPOOLER
- TCPIP NETBIOS HELPER
- UPS
- WORKSTATION

These services are available only on Windows NT Server:

- FILE SERVER FOR MACINTOSH
- GATEWAY SERVICE FOR NETWARE
- MICROSOFT DHCP SERVER
- PRINT SERVER FOR MACINTOSH
- REMOTEBOOT
- WINDOWS INTERNET NAME SERVICE

Notes

To get more help concerning a specific service, see the online Command Reference (NTCMDS.HLP).

When typed at the command prompt, service names of two words or more must be enclosed in quotation marks. For example, NET START "COMPUTER BROWSER" starts the computer browser service.

NET START can also start network services not provided with Windows NT.

NET STATISTICS

NET STATISTICS displays the statistics log for the local Workstation or Server service. Used without parameters, NET STATISTICS displays the services for which statistics are available.

Syntax

```
NET STATISTICS [WORKSTATION ¦ SERVER]
```

Options

SERVER   Displays the Server service statistics.

WORKSTATION   Displays the Workstation service statistics.

NET STOP

NET STOP stops Windows NT services.

Syntax

```
NET STOP service
```

Options

service   Is a Windows NT service that can be stopped. *See the NET START command for a list of eligible services.*

Notes

NET STOP can also stop network services not provided with Windows NT.

Stopping a service cancels any network connections the service is using. Because some services are dependent on others, stopping one service can stop others.

You must have administrative rights to stop the Server service.

The Eventlog service cannot be stopped.

NET TIME

Use the NET TIME command to synchronize the computer's clock with that of another computer or domain. NET TIME can also be used to display the time for a computer or domain. When used without options or a Windows NT Server domain, it displays the current date and time at the computer designated as the time server for the domain.

Syntax

```
NET TIME [\\computername ¦ /DOMAIN[:domainname]] [/SET]
```

Options

`\\computername`	Specifies the name of the computer you want to check or synchronize with.
`/DOMAIN[:domainname]`	Specifies the domain with which to synchronize time.
`/SET`	Synchronizes the computer's time with the time on the specified computer or domain.

NET USE

This command connects a computer to a shared resource or disconnects a computer from a shared resource. NET USE without options lists the computer's connections.

Syntax

```
NET USE [devicename ¦ *]
        [\\computername\sharename[\volume] [password ¦ *]]
        [/USER:[domainname\]username]
        [[/DELETE] ¦ [/PERSISTENT:{YES ¦ NO}]]
NET USE [devicename ¦ *] [password ¦ *]] [/HOME]
NET USE [/PERSISTENT:{YES ¦ NO}]
```

Options

devicename

Specifies a name to assign to the connected resource or specifies the device to be disconnected. Device names can consist of the following:

❑ disk drives (D through Z)
❑ printers (LPT1 through LPT3)

Type an asterisk instead of a specific device name to assign the next available device name.

\\computername

Specifies the name of the computer controlling the shared resource. If the computer name contains blank characters, enclose the double backslash (\ \) and the computer name in quotation marks. The computer name may be from 1 to 15 characters long.

\sharename

Specifies the network name of the shared resource.

\volume

Specifies the name of a volume on a NetWare server. You must have Client Services for NetWare (Windows NT Workstations) or Gateway Service for NetWare (Windows NT Server) installed and running to connect to NetWare servers.

password

Is the password needed to access the shared resource.

*

Produces a prompt for the password. The password is not displayed when you type it at the password prompt.

/USER

Specifies a different user name with which the connection is made.

domainname

Specifies another domain. If *domainname* is omitted, the current logged on domain is used.

username

Specifies the user name with which to log on.

/HOME

Connects a user to his or her home directory.

/DELETE

Cancels a network connection and removes the connection from the list of persistent connections.

/PERSISTENT{YES ¦ NO}	YES saves connections as they are made, and restores them at next logon. NO does not save the connection being made or subsequent connections; existing connections will be restored at next logon. The default is the setting used last.

Use the /DELETE switch to remove persistent connections.

Examples

To connect drive M to a directory with the share name APPS on the server BLIVETS, which has the password LETMEIN, you would type the following:

```
NET USE M: \\BLIVETS\APPS LETMEIN
```

If you do not want the password displayed on the screen, include an * in the password position as follows, so that you will be prompted to enter one:

```
NET USE M: \\BLIVETS\APPS *
```

You can access a share that is secured to another user account if you have a valid password. To access the share using Mabel's account, enter this command:

```
NET USE M: \\BLIVETS\APPS * /USER:MABEL
```

NET USER

NET USER creates and modifies user accounts on computers. When used without switches, it lists the user accounts for the computer. The user account information is stored in the user accounts database.

Syntax

```
NET USER [username [password ¦ *] [options]] [/DOMAIN]
NET USER username {password ¦ *} /ADD [options] [/DOMAIN]
NET USER username [/DELETE] [/DOMAIN]
```

Options

username	Specifies the name of the user account to add, delete, modify, or view. The name of the user account can consist of up to 20 characters.

password	Assigns or changes a password for the user account. A password must meet the minimum length requirement set with the / MINPWLEN option of the NET ACCOUNTS command. The password can consist of up to 14 characters.
*	Displays a prompt for the password, which is not displayed when typed.
/DOMAIN	Specifies that the action should be performed on the primary domain controller of the current domain.
	This parameter is effective only with Windows NT Workstation computers that are members of a Windows NT Server domain. By default, Windows NT Server computers perform operations on the primary domain controller.
/ADD	Adds a user account to the user accounts database.
/DELETE	Removes a user account from the user accounts database.
options	The available options are shown in table B.1:

Table B.1
Available Options

Option	Description
/ACTIVE:{YES ¦ NO}	Activates or deactivates the account. When the account is deactivated, the user cannot access the server. The default is YES.
/COMMENT:"*text*"	Adds a comment consisting of up to 48 characters, as specified by *text*. Enclose the text in quotation marks.
/COUNTRYCODE:*nnn*	*nnn* is the numeric operating system country code that specifies the language files to be used for a user's help and error messages. A value of 0 signifies the default country code.
/EXPIRES:{*date* ¦ NEVER}	Specifies a date when the account will expire in the form *mm,dd,yy* or *dd,mm,yy* as determined by the country code. NEVER sets no time limit on the account. The months can be a number, spelled out, or

Option	Description
	abbreviated with three letters. The year can be two or four numbers. Use commas or slashes(/) to separate parts of the date. No spaces can appear.
/FULLNAME:"name"	Specifies a user's full name (rather than a user name). Enclose the name in quotation marks.
/HOMEDIR:pathname	Specifies the path for the user's home directory. The path must have been previously created.
/HOMEDIRREQ:{YES ¦ NO}	Specifies whether a home directory is required. If a home directory is required, use the /HOMEDIR option to specify the directory.
/PASSWORDCHG:{YES ¦ NO}	Specifies whether users can change their own password. The default is YES.
/PASSWORDREQ:{YES ¦ NO}	Specifies whether a user account must have a password. The default is YES.
/PROFILEPATH[:path]	Specifies a *path* for the user's logon profile.
/SCRIPTPATH:pathname	*pathname* is the location of the user's logon script.
/TIMES:{times ¦ ALL}	*times* specifies the hours a user account may be logged on. *times* is expressed as day[-day][,day[-day]],time[-time][,time [-time]], limited to 1-hour increments. Days can be spelled out or abbreviated. Hours can be specified using 12- or 24-hour notation. With 12-hour notation, include am, pm, a.m., or p.m. ALL means a user can always log on. A blank value means a user can never log on. Separate day and time entries with a comma, and separate multiple day and time entries with a semicolon.

continues

Table B.1 Continued	Option	Description
	/USERCOMMENT:"*text*"	Specifies a comment for the account.
	/WORKSTATIONS: {computername[,...]	*}	Lists as many as eight computers from which a user can log on to the network. If /WORKSTATIONS has no list or if the list is *, the user can log on from any computer.

Examples

To display information about a user named Charles, type the following:

```
NET USER CHARLES
```

To create an account for a user named Harold, while prompting for a password to be assigned, enter the following command:

```
NET USER Harold * /ADD
```

Notes

This command works only on servers.

If you have large numbers of users to add, consider creating a batch file with the appropriate NET USER command. Following is a simple example of a file:

```
NET USER %1 NEWUSER /ADD /HOMEDIR:C:\USERS\%1 /PASSWORDREQ:YES
```

Of course, you would include other options as required. This file makes use of a batch file parameter %1 to pass a command argument to the batch file commands. %1 will pass a user name that you specify to the NET USER command where it is used to name the user account and the user's home directory.

If the file is named ADDUSER.BAT, you could add the user Mabel by typing this:

```
ADDUSER Mabel
```

NET VIEW

The NET VIEW command lists resources being shared on a computer. NET VIEW without options displays a list of computers in the current domain or network.

Syntax

```
NET VIEW [\\computername ¦ /DOMAIN[:domainname]]
NET VIEW /NETWORK:NW [\\computername]
```

Options

\\computername	Specifies a computer with shared resources you want to view.
/DOMAIN:domainname	Specifies the domain with computers whose shared resources you want to view. If domainname is omitted, NET VIEW displays all domains in the local area network.
/NETWORK:NW	Displays all available servers on a NetWare network. If a computer name is specified, the resources available on that NetWare computer are displayed.

Examples

To list the resources shared by the computer Widgets1, enter the following command:

```
NET VIEW \\WIDGETS1
```

If Widgets1 is in another domain, include the domain name with the /DOMAIN option:

```
NET VIEW \\WIDGETS1 /DOMAIN:WIDGETS
```

To list all available domains, omit the *computername* parameter:

```
NET VIEW /DOMAIN
```

Security
Resources

Organizations exist that specialize in Internet security, providing users with bulletins, Web sites, FTP archives, and advice. In addition to the vendors, government-sponsored groups such as national CERTs, and university organizations, such as COAST, can help you in protecting your systems or dealing with intrusions. The following provides a review of the major sites of interest that readers may find useful.

CIAC

The U.S. Department of Energy's Computer Incident Advisory Capability group, the CIAC, was created in 1989 in response to the Internet Worm. It primarily serves the DOE from its Lawrence Livermore National Laboratory site, but it also provides e-mail advisories and an ftp/Web site for anyone on the Internet. The Web site is one of the best security pages, offering advisories, security documents, and

FTP links to many significant programs.

- ❏ The FTP address is `ftp://ciac.llnl.gov/pub/ciac`.
- ❏ The Web address is `http://ciac.llnl.gov`.
- ❏ The e-mail address is `ciac@llnl.gov`. (E-mail information is available by sending help to `ciac-listproc@llnl.gov`.)

COAST

Founded by Eugene Spafford, the Purdue University COAST project (Computer Operations, Audit, and Security Technology) is dedicated to improving network security. COAST has an impressive Web site, featuring links to large numbers of security sites. Offering a comprehensive FTP archive, COAST features one of the largest collections of papers and tools on the topic of network security. COAST also issues a newsletter. COAST works closely with major companies and government agencies and has created a number of useful tools and informative studies of network security.

- ❏ The FTP address is `ftp://coast.cs.purdue.edu`.
- ❏ The Web site is `http://www.cs.purdue.edu/coast/coast.html`.
- ❏ The e-mail address is `coast-request@cs.purdue.edu`.

CERT

The U.S. CERT (Computer Emergency Response Team) was founded in 1989, by the U.S. Department of Defense to protect the infrastructure of the Internet. Situated at Carnegie-Mellon University, in Pittsburgh, Pennsylvania, CERT consists of about a dozen employees who respond to reports from Internet users regarding network security, issuing bulletins, notifying vendors, characterizing the state of the Internet from a security standpoint, working with the mass media to publicize and address concerns, and researching solutions to Internet security problems. CERT is frequently mentioned in media reports from the *New York Times* to *Scientific American*.

Some criticize CERT for delaying the release of bulletins; this criticism, however, is unjustified to a certain degree because CERT attempts to ensure that vendors are able to address the vulnerabilities before they announce the hole.

CERT has one of the largest mailing lists for security advisories, with more than 100,000 subscribers. It permits anyone to subscribe. The CERT FTP archive contains a wide range of security programs, as well as every advisory and bulletin that CERT has issued.

The CERT group recommends that you encrypt security information before e-mailing; they support DES, PGP, and PEM. They have a 24-hour hotline at 1-412-268-7090. CERT advisories are posted on `comp.security.announce`.

❏ The FTP address is `ftp://info.cert.org`.

❏ The e-mail address is `cert@cert.org`. (You can subscribe by sending a request to `cert-advisory-request@cert.org`.)

Many other countries have also formed CERTs, notably Germany (DFN-CERT) and Australia (AUS-CERT). Visit the FIRST Web site for contact information on these and other CERT groups.

FIRST

The Forum of Incident and Response Security Teams, or FIRST, is a non-profit corporation of representatives from the vendors, universities, national and international government agencies, and large private corporate computer users. A complete list of members (currently 45 groups), along with contact information, is available. CERT redirects requests regarding security problems to the appropriate FIRST member, so that they can address the issue and provide resolution information back to CERT for the CERT advisory or bulletin.

FIRST provides a forum for security response teams to share security information, tools, and practices. FIRST sponsors a yearly week-long meeting of representatives, a mailing list for discussions among members, and a point of contact for Internet users with security concerns.

❏ The FTP address is `ftp://csrc.ncsl.nist.gov/pub/first`.

❏ The e-mail address is `first-sec@first.org`.

❏ The http address is `http://www.first.org/`.

❏ Contact the list at `http://csrc.ncsl.nist.gov/first/team-info/`.

Vendors

Most vendors have Web pages and security response teams that can provide assistance in dealing with network vulnerabilities. The FIRST Web page provides contact information, but most vendors typically respond to security-alert@<vendor-domain> (for example, `security-alert@hp.com`).

Vendors typically offer free security bulletins to anyone who signs up on the appropriate mailing list, along with a Web/ftp archive of previous bulletins. Contact your vendor for details on subscribing.

Security product vendors usually offer useful Web sites.

❑ Cygnus offers information on Kerberos at `http://www.cygnus.com/data/cns`.

❑ TIS offers information on firewalls at `http://www.tis.com`.

❑ RSA offers information on cryptography at `http://www.rsa.com`.

Others

There are individuals who have created Web sites with links to many security pages. These Web sites are frequently posted to `comp.security.unix` and can be quite helpful in locating new FTP archives, tools, or papers. These come and go, but one interesting site is `http://www.iesd.auc.dk/~johnson/secure.html`.

Internet Security References

Table C.1 contains a list of the ftp sites and Web sites that contain Internet security-related programs and files. Table C.2 contains a list of UseNET groups regarding security information.

	Program	Site
Table C.1 Web/FTP sites	Argus	`ftp://ftp.sei.cmu.edu/pub/argus-1.5`
	AT&T Web Sites	`http://www.research.att.com/ftp://` ➥`Research.att.com/dist/` ➥`internet_security`
	Bind (DNS)	`ftp://gatekeeper.dec.com/pub/misc/vixie`
	CERN WWW	`http://www.w3.org/pub/www/Consortium`
	CERT FTP Archive	`ftp://ftp.cert.org`
	CIAC	`ftp://ciac.llnl.gov/pub/ciachttp://` ➥`ciac.llnl.gov`
	Ckpasswd	`ftp://gatekeeper.dec.com/pub/usenet/` `comp.sources.unix/volume28/ckpasswd`
	COAST Project	`http://www.cs.purdue.edu/coast/` ➥`coast.html(Purdue University) ftp://` ➥`coast.cs.purdue.edu/pub`
	Computer Systems	`http://www.spy.org/Consulting`
	COPS	`ftp://ftp.cert.org/pub/tools/cops`
	Courtney	`ftp://ciac.llnl.gov/pub/ciac` `http://ciac.llnl.gov`
	Crack	`ftp://ftp.cert.org/pub/tools/crack`
	Cygnus Kerberos Information	`http://www.cygnus.com/data/cns`

	Cypherpunks	`ftp://ftp.csua.berkeley.edu/pub/`
		➥`cypherpunks`
		`http://www.csua.berkeley.edu/`
		➥`cypherpunks`

	DDN Security Bulletins	`ftp://nic.ddn.mil/scc FTP Archive`
	Firewall Web Page	`http://www.access.digex.net/~bdboyle/` ➥`firewall.vendor.html`

	FIRST	`ftp://csrc.ncsl.nist.gov/pub/`
		`http://www.first.org/`
		`http://csrc.ncsl.nist.gov/`

	Fremont	`ftp://ftp.cs.colorado.edu/` ➥`pub/cs/distribs/fremont`
	Gabriel	`http://www.lat.com/gabe.htm`

continues

	Program	Site
Table C.1 Continued	Greatcircle FTP	`ftp://ftp.greatcircle.com/pub` `➡Archive—Firewall information`
	httpd	`http://www.ncsa.uiuc.edu`
	ISS	`http://iss.com/`
	Kerberos Information	`ftp://athena-dist.mit.edu/pub/` `➡ATHENA`

	NEC Security tools—	`ftp://ftp.inoc.dl.nec.com/pub/`
		`socks, sudo, cops`
		`➡security`

	Netscape	`http://www.netscape.com`

	NIST (U.S. National	`http://cscr.ncsl.nist.gov/`
		`http://`
		`Institute of Standards`
		`➡www.nist.gov/`
		`and Technology)`

	PGP and IDEA Archives	`ftp://ftp.informatik.uni-`
		`hamburg.de`
		`➡/pub/virus/crypt/disk`
		`http://web.mit.edu/network/pgp-`
		`➡form.html`

	PGP Documentation	`http://www.pegasus.esprit.` `➡ec.org/people/arne/pgp.html`
	PGP elm	`ftp://ftp.viewlogic.com/pub/`
	PGP Public Key Server	`http://www-swiss.ai.mit.edu/` `~bal/pks-Âtoplev.html`
	RFCs	`ftp://ietf.cnri.reston.va.us`
	RSA Data Security, Inc.	`http://www.rsa.com/`
	Secure Telnet	`ftp://ftp.adfa.oz.au/` `➡pub/security/adfa-telnet`
	sendmail	`ftp://ftp.cs.berkeley.edu`
	SGI Security Information	`ftp://sgigate.sgi.com/security/`

	SNMP FTP Archives	`ftp://ftp.denet.dk/pub/snmp/`
		`cmu-➡snmp`
		`ftp://lancaster.andrew.cmu.edu/`
		`pub/Âsnmp-dist/`

	socks	`ftp://ftp.nec.com/pub/security/`
		`➡socks.cstc`
		`http://www.socks.nec.com`
		`ftp://ftp.cup.hp.com/dist/socks`

Program	Site
SRI Computer Science Lab	http://www.csl.sri.com/ http://www.sri.com/ftp:// ftp.csl.sri.com
ssh (Secure Shell)	ftp://ftp.cs.hut.fi:/pub/ssh/ http://www.cs.hut.fi/ssh
SSLeay Source	http://www.psy.uq.oz.au/~ftp/ ➥Crypto/
tcpdump, libpcap	http://ciac.llnl.gov
Texas A&M University Security Archives	ftp://ftp.tamu.edu ftp://Net.Tamu.edu/pub/ ➥security/TAMU
VeriSign	http://www.verisign.com
ViaCrypt	http://www.viacrypt.com
Wietse Venema FTP Archive	ftp://ftp.win.tue.nl:/pub/ security
wu-ftpd	ftp://wuarchive.wustl.edu
xinetd	ftp://ftp.ieunet.ie/pub/ security/

The newsgroups shown in table C.2 are an excellent day-to-day source of information for security-minded people of all walks, both novice and expert alike. Investigate them all to start, and stay with the ones you find most useful.

Table C.2 UseNET Newsgroups	Newsgroup	Description
	comp.security.misc	A good newsgroup for security
	alt.security	Also a good resource, though increasing amounts of noise
	sci.crypt	A lot of theory on cryptography
	comp.security.firewalls	Discussion of firewalls
	comp.security.announce	CERT advisories
	alt.security.pgp	Discussion of PGP
	alt.security.ripem	Discussion of PEM, little traffic
	comp.protocols.kerberos	Discussion of Kerberos
	talk.politics.crypto	Interesting discussions on cryptography

What is on the CD-ROM

Adobe Acrobat Reader

Version: Version 2.1
Company: Adobe Systems Incorporated
World Wide Web: www.adobe.com
Address: 1585 Charleston Road, P.O. Box 7900, Mountain View, CA 94039

Location on CD-ROM: \Acroread

Adobe Acrobat software gives you instant access to documents in their original form, independent of computer platform. With the Acrobat Reader, you can view, navigate, print and present any Portable Document Format (PDF) file.

HTML Links to NT Resources on the Internet

The program group for this book contains an icon entitled HTML Links. To open this HTML document, you should have a Web browser, such as Internet Explorer installed on your computer. To use this file, open the program group for this book and double-click the HTML Links icon.

Internet Explorer

Company: Microsoft Corporation
Address: One Microsoft Way, Redmond, WA 98052-6399
Electronic Mail: sales@microsoft.com
Telephone: 1-800-426-9400
Fax: 1-206-936-7329
World Wide Web: www.microsoft.com
Location on CD-ROM: \Iexplore

This CD-ROM contains versions of Microsoft Internet Explorer for Windows 95, Windows NT, and Windows 3.1. For additional information and installation click on the link below, which applies to your computer.

Internet Explorer for Windows 3.1

Version: 2.1
Company: Microsoft Corporation
Address: One Microsoft Way, Redmond, WA 98052-6399
Electronic Mail: sales@microsoft.com
Telephone: 1-800-426-9400
Fax: 1-206-936-7329
World Wide Web: www.microsoft.com
Location on CD-ROM: \Iexplore\Win31

Internet Explorer 2.1 for Windows 3.1, the Web browser that puts Windows 3.1 users a step ahead on the Internet! Now with unique HTML and dialer support, Internet Explorer provides the best browsing experience for end users, organizations and content developers who are using the Windows 3.1 platform.

Internet Explorer for Windows 95 and NT

Version: 3.0
Company: Microsoft Corporation

Address:	One Microsoft Way, Redmond, WA 98052-6399
Electronic Mail:	sales@microsoft.com
Telephone:	1-800-426-9400
Fax:	1-206-936-7329
World Wide Web:	www.microsoft.com
Location on CD-ROM:	\Iexplore\Win95_nt

Internet Explorer 3, the Web browser that puts you a step ahead on the Internet! Now with unique HTML, ActiveX, Java, and Plug-in support, IE3 provides the best browsing experience and the most technically advanced development platform for end users, organizations, and content developers. And with innovative Internet conferencing, collaboration, and browser customization, IE3 provides the richest feature set of any browser while still offering an easy to use and personalized Internet experience.

Microsoft Internet Assistant for Microsoft Excel

Company:	Microsoft Corporation
World Wide Web:	http://www.microsoft.com/msoffice/msexcel/internet/ia/
Address:	One Microsoft Way, Redmond, WA 98052-6399
Location on CD:	\netassnt\excel

Microsoft Excel Internet Assistant makes it easy to leverage existing Microsoft Excel spreadsheet data to create, edit, and convert information for publishing on an intranet, or the Internet. With Internet Assistant for Microsoft Excel, it takes only a few steps to have your data ready to put on the WWW or an intranet, or to combine with another HTML document for posting. Click Internet Assistant Wizard on the Tools menu in Microsoft Excel, follow the instructions on your screen, and your spreadsheet data is ready to go.

The Internet Assistant for Microsoft Excel add-in file, HTML.XLA, should be saved in the Microsoft Excel Library directory. The path to this directory is different depending on which version of Microsoft Excel you are running.

For stand-alone Excel 5.0, you will find the Library directory directly under the EXCEL directory (for example, C:\EXCEL\LIBRARY on a Microsoft Windows system and My Computer:Microsoft Office:Microsoft Excel:Macro Library on an Apple Macintosh system).

For MS Office and Excel 7.0, you will find the Library directory under the MSOFFICE and EXCEL directories (for example, C:\MSOFFICE\EXCEL\LIBRARY).

Microsoft Internet Assistant for Microsoft Word

Company: Microsoft Corporation
World Wide Web: http://www.microsoft.com/msword/internet/ia/
Address: One Microsoft Way, Redmond, WA 98052-6399
Location on CD: \netassnt\word

Internet Assistant for Microsoft Word makes it easy to create and edit great-looking documents for the Internet and intranets from within Microsoft Word. If you know how to use Microsoft Word, you already have most of the skills you need to create great-looking Internet documents. That's because Internet Assistant adds functionality to Microsoft Word so that you can use the tools you already understand to create Web pages. There is no need to learn complicated HTML tags…just save your Word documents as HTML and Internet Assistant automatically applies the correct HTML tags to them.

New Riders' NT Server Simulator

Company: New Riders Publishing
Address: 201 W. 103rd Street, Indianapolis, IN 46290
FAX: 1-317-817-7448
Support: support@mcp.com
CompuServe: GO NEWRIDERS
World Wide Web: http://www.mcp.com/newriders
Location on CD: \NTSIM

New Riders' Windows NT Server Simulator walks you through common NT Server procedures by presenting a series of annotated screen shots and on-screen instructions. The Simulator covers the following topics:

- ❏ Explorer
- ❏ Event Viewer
- ❏ Performance Monitor
- ❏ Diagnostics
- ❏ Control Panel
- ❏ User Manager for Domains

- ❏ Network Monitor
- ❏ Task Manager
- ❏ Server Manager

To run the simulator, you do not need to have NT Server running. Two versions of the simulator are provided. The 32-bit version runs under Windows 95 and Windows NT. If you are running Windows 3.*x*, you should run the 16-bit version.

About Shareware

If you use any shareware items beyond an initial trial period, you are obligated to follow the guidelines set forth by the vendor or developer; this is usually in the form of a reasonable shareware payment set forth by the developer. Your purchase of this book and accompanying CD-ROM does not release you from this obligation. Refer to the "read me" and other information files, which accompany each of the programs, for additional information.

Sunbelt Software's Windows NT Utilities

Company:	Sunbelt Software
Address:	101 North Garden Avenue, Suite 230, Clearwater, FL 34615
Telephone:	1-800-688-8404
FAX:	1-813-562-5199
Sales:	ntsales@ntsoftdist.com
Support:	daved@pssi.com
Internet:	http://www.ntsoftdist.com
Location on CD:	\SUNBELT

Sunbelt Software has graciously mirrored their Web site on this CD-ROM. To explore SunBelt's Web pages, you need a Web browser, such as Netscape Navigator or Microsoft Internet Explorer. On these Web pages, you will find information about Sunbelt products, which provide "Mainframe power for Windows NT." Evaluation software is easily "downloaded" from these pages.

- ❏ Quota Manager for Windows NT (Intel & Alpha)
- ❏ Octopus—Fault Tolerance for Windows NT
- ❏ Diskeeper for WinNT- FREE 4.0 DEFRAGGER HERE...
- ❏ FREE Diskeeper File Fragmentation Analysis Utility (fat & ntfs)

- ❏ Sentry—Event Log Alert Management System
- ❏ Batch Job Server v2.0 Full Release
- ❏ Blues For Windows - IBM Mainframe Link
- ❏ Purveyor NT Web Server Software with Encryption
- ❏ SuperDisk-NT—First NT RAM DISK—Now Released for Intel & Alpha!!
- ❏ Remotely Possible32-NT:Remote Control for NT 4.0!
- ❏ Kane Security Analyst for Win NT!
- ❏ Norton NT Tools
- ❏ Trusted Enterprise Mgr. - Powerful Distributed User Management
- ❏ GoldFax—Faxing for Win NT! (Now For 4.0)
- ❏ WhatsUp—NT Network Sanity Check
- ❏ Express License Metering!
- ❏ PerfMan—NT Performance Management!
- ❏ Fortress-NT—Log-off Idle Users!

Unlocking Microsoft Internet Information Server

Company:	New Riders Publishing
ISBN:	1-56205-605-0
Address:	201 W. 103rd Street, Indianapolis, IN 46290
FAX:	1-317-817-7448
Support:	support@mcp.com
CompuServe:	GO NEWRIDERS
World Wide Web:	http://www.mcp.com/newriders
Location on CD:	\IISERVER

Internet Information Server is Microsoft's answer to the challenging environment of Internet server administration. After teaching the basics of Windows NT Server 4 configuration, this task-oriented reference tool will take you on a step-by-step tour through implementing IIS. You'll also receive expert advice on configuring IIS's key components to conquer the needs of multi-purposed Internet sites. Because putting information up for public access exposes your site to possible security breaches, this book will also demonstrate the core security techniques and utilities used by experienced site administrators. Detailed converage of multi-homing, CGI scripting, and ISAPI form processing ensures that you are conversant in advanced administration tasks that help you create dynamic, secure, well-constructed Internet sites.

WebBase v4.2 30-Day Evaluation

Company: Expertelligence, Inc.
Address: 203 Chapala Street, Santa Barbara, CA 93101 USA
Telephone: 1-805-962-2558
FAX: 1-805-962-5188
Sales: Sales@expertelligence.com
Support: Support@expertelligence.com
Orders: http://www.webbase.com/WbOrderW.htf
Examples: http://www.webbase.com/Samples.htm
Product Information: http://www.webbase.com/default.htm
Web Site: http://www.Webbase.com
License Number: http://www.webbase.com/webbase/wbtrial.htf
Loation on CD-ROM: \webbascd

WebBase is a Web Database Server that enables you to easily and powerfully include existing databases on your Web site. It works stand-alone or in cooperation with any Web server. WebBase enables any browser to hypersearch a database as easily as hypertext is used in a document. If it is contained in a database, you can display it on a Web page. WebBase works with over 50 database formats. This trial version of WebBase stops working after a trial period of 30 days.

To try WebBase, run the installation program. The first time you run WebBase, you will be prompted to enter a license number. To obtain a license number, direct your Web browser to `http://www.webbase.com/webbase/wbtrial.htf`.

To run the samples, you must have a Web browser, such as Netscape Navigator, and ODBC drivers installed. WebBase may be purchased from major resellers and distributors. You can also purchase WebBase by directing your browser to `http://www.webbase.com`.

Webmaster's Professional Reference

Company: New Riders Publishing
ISBN: 1-56205-473-2
Address: 201 W. 103rd Street, Indianapolis, IN 46290
FAX: 1-317-817-7448
Support: support@mcp.com

CompuServe:	GO NEWRIDERS
World Wide Web:	http://www.mcp.com/newriders
Location on CD:	\WEBMASTR

Webmaster's Professional Reference provides site administrators, consultants, and developers with an all-in-one resource for Internet connectivity options, hardware and software alternatives, and detailed instructions on setting up and troubleshooting multiple types of Internet servers. Cutting-edge topics such as VRML, MBone, and Internet agents are also covered in detail—keeping you up to date and informed. Other topics covered include Perl and Oracle CGI scripting, firewalls, SATAN, and digital cash transactions.

❏ Learn how to keep your Internet server secure

❏ Evaluate your connectivity, hardware, and software options

❏ Discover the possibilities of doing business on the Internet

❏ Understand Perl and Oracle CGI scripting

❏ Get hands-on practice building the most common types of Internet servers used today

❏ Learn tips from the experts for setting up and maintaining an Internet server

This comprehensive book acts both as a thorough tutorial on the Internet and a complete reference that you will turn to time and time again. Put the power of the Internet at your command with *Webmaster's Professional Reference*.

WinSite Information

Company:	WeMake CDs, Inc.
Address:	5344 N. Tacoma Avenue, Indianapolis, IN 46220
Telephone:	1-317-465-0009
E-Mail:	wemake@indy.net
Web Site:	Web Site: http://www.a1.com/wemake/

The WinSite directory of the CD-ROM contains a collection of more then 250 32-bit shareware, freeware, and public domain programs, compiled by WeMake CDs, Incorporated. WeMake CDs, Inc. developed this collection in association with WinSite, one of the largest and most popular Windows archives on the Internet. If you've ever wanted a definitive collection of 32-bit programs for Windows NT, this is it. WeMake CDs offers other excellent shareware collections, in addition to this one. For more information, contact WeMake CDs at the address listed above.

To explore "The Best of WinSite for Windows NT," open the program group for this book and double-click the "Best of WinSite for Windows NT" icon. This starts a front-end interface program to the collection, enabling you to choose programs by category, and to display a brief description of each program. The files you select are automatically unzipped to the destination directory of your choice, making installation easier. Please note that the winsite.exe interface program is a 32-bit executable. It is designed to run under Windows NT or Windows 95, and will not run under Windows 3.*x*. Likewise, the programs in this collection are 32-bit only, and are not designed to run under Windows 3.1.

Many of the computer programs require payment if they are used after a defined trial period or used commercially. If you use a shareware program beyond its initial trial period, you are obligated to follow the guidelines set forth by the vendor or developer of the program; in most cases a reasonable shareware payment is requested by the developer. Your purchase of this book and accompanying CD-ROM does not release you from the obligation to pay shareware fees; the publisher has not paid any registration fees for you. Refer to each product's "read me" files for information concerning registration, length of trial period, and other restrictions.

SUPPORT

New Riders Publishing can not provide technical support for this collection beyond the replacement of physically damaged CD-ROMs. If you have questions or problems with a software program, please contact the developer of that application. Contact information is usually provided in the "read me" files, which accompany each program.

DISCLAIMER

This software is sold AS IS without warranty of any kind, either expressed or implied, including, but not limited to, the implied warranties of merchantability and fitness for a particular purpose. No liability is assumed by New Riders Publishing, its dealers, distributors, WeMake CDs, Inc., WinSite, or InterAct, for any alleged or actual damages arising from the use of the programs in this product. (Some states do not allow the exclusion of implied warranties, so this exclusion may not apply to you.)

administration

establishing business presence on the Internet,
17-21

Ethernet networks, 93

evaluating business needs on the Internet,
16-17

Event Viewer, administering IIS, 288

Everyone group, 464

Excel (Internet Assistant), 559

Exchange Server, 25, 433

Excite Web site, 51

expanding domains in DNS services, 419-420

expansion buses, 175-177

Expiration Policy Properties dialog box, 379

Expiration property sheet (INS), 379-380

Explorer, setting IIS service permissions, 284

F

FAT (File Allocation Table) file system, 66, 236
data sharing, 239
file size support, 238
partitions, converting to NTFS partitions, 238

fault tolerance
NT Server, 65, 71-72
NT Workstation capabiltities, 71-72

Feed Properties dialog box, 375

Feed Schedule dialog box, 377

Feed Security dialog box, 378

Feed Subscription dialog box, 376

Feeds property sheet (INS), 374-379

File Allocation Table, *see* FAT file system

File and Folder Access wizard (NT Server), 188

file security (NT Server), 469-473

file systems
data sharing, 239
FAT, 236
file compression support, 239
file size support, 238
NT Server, setup, 237-239
NTFS, 64, 236, 469-473
operating system compatibility, 238
security, 238

File Transfer Protocol, *see* FTP

file-level security (NT Server), 61, 66

files
administration, 528
auditing, 473
compression, 239
securing with permissions, 470-473

filters, 192, 263

FIND/SVP Web site, 49

finding IIS services, 267

finger, 139

firewalls, 444
application level, 449-450
attack prevention, 453
break ins, 452
compromising, 452
denial of service attacks, 455-456
design decisions, 451-452
destroying, 452
future developments, 457
ICMP Redirect packets, 455
implementing, 456-457
limitations, 453-454
network level, 445-448
source routing, 454-455
threat levels, 452
TIS Firewall Toolkit Web site, 552
validating a need for, 444
virus protection, 454

**FIRST (Forum of Incident and Response
Security Teams), 551**

**floating point errors, troubleshooting during
NT Server setup, 243**

**FPM RAM (Fast Page Mode RAM)
memory, 166**

FRADs (frame relay access devices), 119

frame relay connectivity, 99-102
advantages, 102
committed information rate, 101-102
configuration, 122
frame switching, 101
speed, 99
working architecture, 100

establishing business presence on the Internet

int domains (DNS services), 401

integrating business partners via Internet, 38-39

Intel x86 architectures, 151-153

INTERACTIVE group, 464

interfaces

    hard disks, 171-175

        IDE, 172

        SCSI, 172-173

    network interfaces, monitoring performance, 502

    NT Server, 79

Internet, 261

    access hardware, 117-120

    advertising potential, 45

    applications, development, 434-437

    as global marketplace, 29-30

    as information system, 11

    businesses

        audience targeting, 50-52

        case studies, 12-13

        competitiveness, 21

        customer service, 39

        growth potential, 20

        information distribution, 36-38

        information value, 50-52

        internal services, 48-49

        long distance contracting, 20-21

        marketing benefits, 18

        marketing indexes (online), 52

        needs, evaluating, 16-17

        partner integration, 38-39

        presence, establishing, 17-21

        research benefits, 20

        updating, 50-52

        users, 39-45

    caveats, 12

    commerce, 11

    connectivity, 95-96

        ADSL, 107

        cable modems, 109-110, 123

        DSL, 104-109, 123

        frame relay, 99-102, 122

        HDSL, 106

        ISDN, 102-104, 122

        leased line, 97-99, 121

        LMDS, 110-112, 124

        required components, 96

        SDSL, 106

        VDSL, 108

    corporate sites

        business advantages, 34-39

        customer communication, 18

        customer services, 46-48

    defined, 4

    developmental history, 7-9

        ARPAnet, 7-8

        Because It's There Network (BITNET), 8

        Computer Science Network (CSNET), 8

    e-mail capabilities, 6

    e-mail overview, 44

    electronic commerce

        evolution, 39-50

        overview, 34-39

    employee communication in businesses, 17-18

    FTP usage, 40

    future development, 14

    Gopher usage, 40-42

    multimedia content, 10-11

    potential audience, 31-34

    protocols, 6

    regulation/standards, 13-14

    search engines, 51-52

    servers

        commercial applications, 15-16

        NT Workstation, 76

    software compatibility

        NT Server, 77-78

        NT Workstation, 77-78

    software distribution, 11-12

    Telnet usage, 44

    usage, 4-6

    UseNET newsgroups, 6, 42

    user demographics, 31-34

    WAIS usage, 42

    Web sites, customer base, 35-36

J–K–L

NET PRINT command

S

scalability (NT Server), 24, 61

Scandisk, 486

scheduling

    newsgroup feeds, 377

    NT Server backups, 492-494

    NT Server maintenance, 487-488

screened host gateways (network level firewalls), 446

screened subnets (network level firewalls), 446-447

SCSI (Small Computer Systems Interface) hard disk interfaces, 172-173

SDRAM (Synchronous Dynamic RAM), 166-167

SDSL (Single Line Digital Subscriber Line) connectivity, 106

search engines, 51

searching Web sites, 429-430

secondary servers, 403

secondary zones (DNS services), creating, 419

sector sparing (NT Server support), 66

securing directories/files with permissions, 470-473

security

    C2 security, 474-477

    Dept. of Defense, 24

    e-mail servers, 336

    file systems, 238

    FTP sites related to, 553

    Network Monitor, 192-193

    networks, 442-444

        checking for weak points, 443

        commercial utilities, 443

        consultants, 443

        reports, 443-444

    newsgroup feeds, 378

    newsgroups discussing, 555

    NT Server, 24, 61, 72

        accounts, 462-468

        backups, 494

        C2 security, 61

        file security, 469-473

        file-level, 61, 66

        model, 459-461

        network-level, 80

        practices, 458-459

        TCP/IP security, 477

    NT Workstation, 72

    online resources, 549-555

    packets, 192-193

    policies, establishing for networks, 442

    vendors, 552

    WWW sites related to, 553

    see also firewalls

selective backups, 491-492

sending messages to network accounts, 535

Sendmail for NT, 332-333

servers

    BDC, 242

    caching-only server, 403

    commercial applications, 15-16

    Commercial Internet System servers, 509-520

    Content Replication Server, 518

    customer communication, 18

    database servers, 11, 25

    deleting from DNS Manager, 418

    DNS, 219-220

        administration, 415-417

        maintenance, determining, 420-421

        setup, 407

        statistic displays, 418

    e-mail, 322-323

        administration, 336-338

        AltaVista Mail Server, 330

        configuring for mailing lists, 347-350

        Exchange Server, 25

        hardware requirements, 334-336

        installation, 333

        log files, 337

        mailing list support, 344-346

        MailSite, 344-345

        Mdaemon Server, 332

REGISTRATION CARD

Building a Windows NT 4 Internet Server

Name _____ Title _____

Company_____ Type of business _____

Address _____

City/State/ZIP _____

Have you used these types of books before?　☐ yes　　☐ no

If yes, which ones? _____

_____

How many computer books do you purchase each year?　☐ 1–5　　☐ 6 or more

How did you learn about this book? _____

Where did you purchase this book? _____

Which applications do you currently use? _____

_____

Which computer magazines do you subscribe to? _____

_____

What trade shows do you attend? _____

_____

Comments: _____

_____

_____

Would you like to be placed on our preferred mailing list?　☐ yes　　☐ no

☐ **I would like to see my name in print!** You may use my name and quote me in future New Riders products and promotions. My daytime phone number is: _____

New Riders Publishing　　201 West 103rd Street　◆　Indianapolis, Indiana 46290　USA

Fax to **317-817-7448**

Fold Here

||||

NO POSTAGE
NECESSARY
IF MAILED
IN THE
UNITED STATES

BUSINESS REPLY MAIL
FIRST-CLASS MAIL PERMIT NO. 9918 INDIANAPOLIS IN

POSTAGE WILL BE PAID BY THE ADDRESSEE

**NEW RIDERS PUBLISHING
201 W 103RD ST
INDIANAPOLIS IN 46290-9058**